Hexham 1854-1939

Local Government in a Market Town

David Jennings

**Hexham Local History Society
Occasional Publication No. 6**

Hexham Local History Society

2005

Published in 2005 by Hexham Local History Society
c/o Liz Sobell,
Turf House, Steel,
Hexham NE46 0HP

ISBN 0 9527615 6 4

Printed by Robson Print Ltd.,
Haugh Lane Industrial Estate
Hexham NE46 3PU

Contents

Preface

Hexham is a small market town with a mostly medieval street plan. However, the exterior of a good number of its buildings have been given the veneer of the 18th and 19th centuries, while many of the buildings are 18th and particularly 19th and early 20th century replacements. These latter two periods saw the start and the completion of Beaumont Street, which enhanced further the Victorian and Edwardian feeling about much of the town. In spite of the imprint of these periods on Hexham, hardly anything of substance has been written about the history of Hexham in the 19th and 20th centuries and the material that is in print is often misleading and inaccurate. This book aims to contribute to correcting that lack.

This book has, as its theme, Local Government in Hexham during the period 1854 to 1939. The choice of the first date was obvious, since it was when modern local government made its appearance. The second seems a more arbitrary choice, particularly as the Urban District Council was functioning up to 1974 much as it did 1894, when it came into being. Yet the onset of war can be seen to be the end of an era not only in social terms but also in historical terms. Thus, while there are persons still around who have vivid memories of what Hexham was like in the 1930s, because these persons were in their youth at the time, we are unable to obtain first-hand information about how those in charge of running the town were operating. Thus, right up to 1939, one is forced rely very much on the archives.

There is much detail in this book, though Volume 3 of the *History of Northumberland* (Hinds, 1896) concerned with Hexham matches the amount, being a splendid source of information through the extensive quotation from original documents, that are, for the most part, pre-1800. Though the quotations here are much less extensive, the considerable factual content, with associated citations, means this book is also a source of information, providing what one hopes are helpful signposts to the archives. The reader will realise that the text is peppered with reference citations. That is partly due to my scientific background; but there is a more positive reason, namely that, since the majority of references are the dates of newspaper issues and Local Government minutes, the reader can keep track of dates of particular events.

The greater portion of the text deals with a range of administrative topics and policy matters. While the chapters that deal with them have been located within a particular period, the reader will quickly realise that the contents of some of these chapters spread chronologically outside that period. Narrative history is confined to Part II, where the problems of achieving a satisfactory water supply and those relating to the acquisition of open spaces for the recreation of townspeople are best dealt with as an unfolding story. This has allowed not only a discussion of the issues involved but given an opportunity to describe the role of various individuals in the decision-making processes.

The reader will realise that a number of topics have not been covered in this book, e.g. the relationship of the Local Authority with the Gas Company, the fire brigade and the increasing problem of refuse disposal. The fact that these topics are essentially self-contained, hardly impinging on other aspects of local government in Hexham suggested to me that, in the context of the book, that what was being presented in it would not derive benefit from the inclusion of these topics. Indeed, the book would be lengthened without very much benefit. Also, various characters flit in and out of the book, depending on their involvement in the topic under consideration. Those readers who wish to know a little more about many of the persons under consideration are referred to the book *Hexham Cemetery* (Jennings & Jennings, 2003), which contains a number of relevant short biographies. For some idea of the other events taking place during the period 1800-1939, the reader should turn to *The Heart of All England* (Jennings *et al.,* 2005).

The great majority of the figures have been chosen to illustrate specific points made in the text. However, I have included some figures as an Appendix. These include a chart showing the changes in how Hexham was administered from earliest times, together with maps of the boundaries of the Hexham Local Board of Health and the Urban District Council and the census areas. These and other Appendix figures are listed with the other figures on pages v-vii. I am extremely grateful to Maureen Lazzari for drawing the great majority of the maps and plans; she has added a great deal to the book as a result of her skilled draughtsmanship.

I greatly appreciate the help of my wife, Ruth Jennings, for her extensive knowledge and understanding of the historical period covered this book. She read through the text and offered valuable advice about improvements, which in almost every instance I was very pleased to take. Brian Jenkins also read the text and much improved what I had written. I am also grateful to Colin Dallison, who was of most helpful in getting me started on the research, while Philip Clark was a mine of information about Hexham prior to 1939 and in the early years following the War.

As the reader will realise this book is heavily dependent on both the information contained in the back issues of the *Hexham Courant* and also the wealth of archival material in the Northumberland Record Office. My very considerable thanks go to both organisations for their help at all times. That said, I must highlight the patience of the staff of the Record Office, both at Melton Park, Gosforth and at Morpeth, in dealing with my many requests for help and their assiduousness in bringing to the surface such a wonderful range of material for my use.

I am most grateful to John Vinton of Robson Print for his invaluable help in the production of this book.

David Jennings

Illustrations

In the Text

As an Appendix

Between pages 233 & 234

CHAPTER 1

Hexham before the establishment of the Local Board of Health

Introduction

This book is about history of how local government functioned in Hexham in the period 1854-1939. The initial date is that for the start of the form of local government from which our present system has evolved. Here, what was present before 1854 is described.

Hexham is a small market town in Northumberland, almost mid-way between Newcastle and Carlisle in the Tyne valley. The town owes its origins to the foundation in c671 by Wilfrid, Bishop of York, of the Abbey on the glacial terrace above the Tyne on its south side. Wilfrid had been able to sustain a monastic church through land in the surrounding area given to him by Queen Ethelrreda of Northumbria. Subsequently, in the 9th century, the monastic church fell into decline and decay. However, the monastic community was revived as a priory in the 12th century. It is probably the presence of this community that led to the firmer establishment of the town as we know it from more recent times. The Priory remained until 1537, when it was dissolved, as part of Henry VIII's assault on the monasteries. The Priory church without its nave became the Parish church that dominates the market place. The land given to Wilfrid formed the basis of the Hexhamshire, an administrative area under the control of the archbishops of York. In this way, the area remained outside the jurisdiction of the sheriff of Northumberland and the conventional mechanisms of royal government. The archbishops controlled Hexhamshire through their bailiffs. Hexham, as the seat of power of the bailiffs, saw the establishment of a hall, for which the Moot Hall was built as a gatehouse, and eventually the Archbishop's Gaol, part of the machinery for maintaining law and order.

In 1572, Hexhamshire was assimilated into Northumberland. In time, Hexham established itself not only as a place where the Manor Court functioned under lay control but as a centre within the county where Petty and Quarter Sessions could be held. In parallel, the town developed as a centre for the surrounding area for trade, the hiring of labour and provision of services. Hexham's importance as an administrative centre was enhanced in 1836, when the Hexham Union of parishes, centred upon the town, was established to administer the Poor Law Amendment Act of 1834. The Workhouse was the physical presence of the Hexham Union and its functioning, under the control of the Guardians of the Poor is described in Chapter 5.

The Poor Law Amendment Act took the administration of relief away from the parishes, which had been adopted by the Elizabethan Law as the appropriate administrative units, with the duty the duty of caring for the poor being attached to the office of churchwarden. In addition special overseers of the poor were appointed and, to cover the cost of maintaining the poor, a local tax, the poor rate, was instituted. From earliest times the inhabitants belong to the church met in the parish assembly elected parishioners as churchwardens and transacted business through the churchwardens and the parson. As time progressed, the assembly no longer met in the church but in the vestry and, in consequence, the parish meeting took its name from the at place. With the Poor Law Amendment Act, the vestry no longer had any role in taking care of the poor. However, by the eighteenth century, vestries had often accreted other functions, so that they became important as political and administrative systems (Eastwood, 1997). Hexham was no exception and as will be seen below, the Hexham Vestry played an important role in the running of the town in the early 1800s.

Hexham seems to have made no attempt to achieve formal borough status (Rossiter, 1996). There appears to be no record of a charter of incorporation. Webb & Webb (1908, p.89) state that Hexham was one of a very small number of towns in which government was shared between the still functioning manor court and one or more of the trade guilds, these being, in Hexham, Skinners and Glovers; Tanners and Shoemakers; Weavers; and Hatters. Rossiter has described how such a system operated in Hexham in the 17th and 18th centuries.

Continuing with the focus on Hexham, the administrative forces shaping the town were the Vestry and the Manor Court. Since this is so, it is necessary to say a little as to how they operated in the town. Also, because of his influence on the functioning of Hexham, through wealth and ownership of land in Hexham and the surrounding area, I have provided some details about the Lord of the Manor.

The Vestry and Borough Court

The vestry seems to have come into prominence as a deliberating body towards the start of the 19th century. The first extant minute book of the Hexham Vestry that deals first strictly with the affairs of the Abbey and more gradually with more general Parish affairs commences in 1810 (NRO/EP/184/171). There is no indication as to whether there had been previous minute books dealing with similar matters, though there is a Vestry minute book dealing essentially with Poor Law matters over the period 1785-18. However, this latter book only very occasionally strays, and then for good reason, into more general matters of public policy:

> 4 January 1813 – Resolved that the Bailiff of the Regality be desired to require the constables to attend to the Lodging Houses in this Town that no improper persons be harboured there and that the Overseers cause Boards to be put up at all the Principal Entrances into the Town giving Notice to vagrants and other disorderly persons that they will be dealt with according to the law (NRO/EP/184/168).

Be that as it may, the generation of purposeful business recorded after 1810 may be a symptom of the feeling within the country around that time that vestries ought be more democratic and out-going (Keith-Lucas, 1952). In any case, the Vestries Act of 1818 (58 Geo. III, c. 69) required that 'Minutes of the Proceedings and Resolutions of every Vestry shall be fairly and distinctly entered in a Book......' By the 1830s, one has the impression from the minutes of the Vestry that it was filling a vacuum generated by the lack of any other policy-making body in the town. Indeed, the only major capital project financed with what can be called 'public money', before Hexham Local Board of Health financed new water works in 1860s, was the new building erected on the Seal in 1856 for the Subscription School. As will be described in Chapter 17, the money came to the Parish Vestry from the building of the railway across the common land of Tyne Green.

Together with the decision that the railway money should go towards a new building for the Subscription School the Vestry made two other decisions that were key to the development of Hexham. First, on 14 October 1833, it agreed that

> the provisions and regulations of the Act of 3rd and 4th years of the reign of William the 4th c: 90 [for the lighting and watching of parishes in England and Wales......] be and it is hereby adopted by the said Township of Hexham so as regards the lighting of the Town only.

At the same meeting, seven men were appointed Inspectors for carrying out the provisions of the Act. The Hexham Gas Company was established on 28 November 1833. I have not been able to establish a direct link between the two events but it seems unlikely that they are not in some way connected. Whatever the case, the installation of gas lighting made a great improvement to life in Hexham (Robb, 1882). Prior to the use of gas, the town had been lit for about twelve years with fish or whale oil lamps that often went out before their time and the glass was always begrimed by sooty and greasy smoke (*HC* 17.9.1881).

The other important decision of the Vestry was that made on 29 July 1857 to initiate the establishment of a new Cemetery (Jennings & Jennings, 2002). Thereafter, almost certainly because of the establishment of the Local Board of Health in 1854, the Vestry dealt almost entirely with more routine matters such as the election of overseers and churchwardens. Though the duties of the overseers in respect to the administration of poor relief were in 1834 transferred to the Guardians, the most important duty remaining being to make and levy the poor-rate.

Finally, in this consideration of local government prior to 1854, there is a need to say something about the Borough Court. In the 17th and 18th centuries, as well described by Rossiter (1996), it played an important part in the running of the town. Jasper Gibson gave to Robert Rawlinson (1853) details, of what he called in his report 'the ancient government of the town'. He found the powers described (in what was the minutes of the meeting 21 April 1852 of the Court quoted in full by Rawlinson) as being 'nearly useless'. Thus, by 1853, it seems that the Borough Court was a spent force. However, not entirely, for at the just mentioned meeting it was minuted that William Robb (interestingly, because of being a man of known integrity) was fined 2s.6d for contempt of court while two others, Robert Headley and William Hunter were fined for separately taking soil from Tyne Green.

The Lord of the Manor

I have earlier referred to the Lord of the Manor, Wentworth Blackett Beaumont. The Beaumonts had, for over a century, been a power in the district, their wealth coming initially from the W.B. lead mines in Allendale, that were developed in the early 18th century. At one time the amount of lead produced by the Beaumont mines in Allendale and Weardale was equal to one-seventh of total lead production in the U.K. By 1853, lead production was on the decline. Nevertheless, as has been indicated, Beaumont's wealth was still considerable. Not only was he able to build Beaumont Street but also he paid for the restoration of the east end of the Abbey in 1860. Not only did he own considerable tracts of land in the lead-mining areas referred to but also he owned the estates at Bywell, Dilston and Bretton Park, near Wakefield in Yorkshire. He was Liberal M.P. for South

Division of Northumberland from 1852 to 1885 and the Tyneside Division from 1886 until 1892, when he retired. He was elevated to the peerage in 1906, taking the title of Lord Allendale. He died in 1907 and was succeeded to the title by his son, Wentworth Canning Blackett Beaumont, who had become M.P. for Hexham in 1895 and who died in 1923. Though in 1924 the 3rd Lord Allendale was consulted over the provision of tennis courts and a bowling club on the Seal (see Chapter 19), by that date the influence of the Lord of the Manor had considerably waned. Thus it is W. B. Beaumont and his son who figure largely in this history.

W. B. Beaumont owned considerable tracts of land in Hexham (*see* Fig. H), such as the Seal, the Abbey Grounds, land around the station, Fairfield, where the police station is now located and the land between Shaftoe Leazes and the Cockshaw Burn, which he developed for housing in 1893 (HLBH 14.11.1892). He also owned the market tolls. An idea of the extent of these tolls is given in the resolution of owners and ratepayers, by which they consented on to the purchase of the tolls by the Local Board of Health from W. B. Beaumont for £200:

> [purchase] of all and singular, the tolls and stallages arising, due or payable at markets, fairs and hirings, held in and upon the streets and Market Place of the town of Hexham, and of all the estate and interest of the said Wentworth Blackett Beaumont in the land and buildings in the said Market place, called the Shambles, upon terms contained in the draft identiture (HLBH 4.1.1896).

This meeting was almost the final stage of three years of negotiations, culminating in the Board taking ownership in March of 1896 (HLBH 29.3.1896). The details of the resolution show that the Lord of the Manor essentially controlled a wide range of activities in the streets of Hexham and did in fact have ownership of the Market Place and the Shambles. On the other hand, except for a roadway that ran through the centre of the Market Place, he was responsible for its upkeep and that of the Shambles (Rawlinson, 1853).

Finance

In this book, I will show that availability of finance was an important factor controlling the development of Hexham. In particular there was a continuing concern about the burden of local taxation. So, it is instructive here to examine the financial claims on the wealthier citizens made through rates and taxes (Table 1).

In Table 1, I have included the details of taxes raised to indicate the total financial burden on those who were rated and taxed. Apart from the poor and church rates, which were set by the vestry, it is not clear which bodies either determined or collected the rates listed. Other than the highways and lighting, no rate was levied for maintaining the fabric of the town and other costs. Further, the requirement to service the considerable financial needs of the Workhouse and related activities meant the poor rate dominated the other two rates. Taxes and other charges that were raised were 75% of the total raised by rates. It is not difficult to see that those who were major contributors to the rates and taxes were none too keen to have these financial burdens increased. There were 770 properties with rateable values of £15 or less, giving a total rateable value of £6990 (this is an overestimate because I have treated all rates lumped together at 'below £5', as being at £5). In contrast, there were 202 with higher values, giving almost the same total rateable value of £6840. Of these 202, there were 24 with values between £50 and £500 (one property) giving a total rateable value of £1940. One suspects that it from the ranks of the owners of the 202 properties came those who were most vocal in complaining of severe rating and taxation burdens.

TABLE 1. *Details of rates and taxes levied in Hexham in 1852 (Rawlinson, 1853).*

Type of rate or tax	Amount levied in 1852	Further details
Rates		
Poor-rate	£1880.7s.4d	
Lamp and watch rate	£248.14s.6½d	
Highway rate	£156.13s.2d	Town only; 'fell' portion rated separately
Church rate	£66.7s.5¼d	Collected along with the poor rate
Taxes, etc.		
Property and income tax	£679.7s.1d	
House tax and assessed taxes	£430.10s.3d	
Land tax	£54.5s.7d	
Tithe rent charge	£550.0s.0d	
Lord's rents	£21.18s.7d	

Thus, the Hexham Poor Law Union took the lion's share of money raised through the rates. Rawlinson thought the Hexham's poor rates were excessive. Even so, little if any of these rates came back to the ordinary citizens of the town. Thus there was no proper system of sewerage. What sewers there were, were paid for out of the highway rates. As far as one can establish, there was no body with any financial resources to bring improvements to the town. Those improvements that came about were the result of private initiatives. The most striking such initiative was that which led to the removal of buildings in front of the east end of the Abbey. The initiative got under way in 1841, fuelled by private subscriptions (Jennings, 2003). Even then, the money raised was not sufficient and, by 1850, the project could only be finished with money from the Lord of the Manor, W. B. Beaumont, who owned a number of the buildings on the south side of the Abbey and abutting onto the Market Place. He pulled these down and, in 1866, as a commercial venture, built the street that now bears his name. When it was known that the street was to be built the Hexham Corn Exchange Company was formed, that through share capital, was able to build what is now the Queen's Hall, also completed in 1866.

Hexham as a place to live

The census of 1851 (an analysis of which is given in Jennings, 2000) put the population of the township of Hexham at 5231. A large proportion were living in the town itself, the remainder in scattered dwellings in the area around it, as far as Craneshaugh, Dukes House and Oakerlands to the east; to Dipton, West Petral Field and Black Hill to the south; to East Nubbock and Kingshaw Green to the west. The bulk of the population (60.8%) was under 30 years of age, 27.2% being ten or under. Only 2.8% reached over 70. It was an essentially youthful population.

In 1851, the major industries revolved round leather – tanning, glove and shoe making (Table 2). The seeming significant number of persons involved in these industries disguises their decline that had been going on since at least 1826 when glovers had their wages reduced because of cheaper gloves produced elsewhere (*HC* 17.1.1931). At one time, about 1000 women and girls (employed in sewing) and 120 men and boys were involved in making gloves (the so-called 'Hexham Tans') (Parson & White, 1827). There was a vigorous export of gloves, large numbers going to the United States. Indeed, the import duty imposed by that country was another contributory factor to the decline of glove manufacture in Hexham (*HC* 10.3.1888). Though we have no direct evidence that shoes were also exported from Hexham, the number of shoemakers in employment can only be explained that there was a market for their products much further afield than Hexham (Higgins & Jennings, 2004).

TABLE 2. *The major occupations in Hexham as determined by the 1851 census (Jennings, 2000)*

Occupation	Number	% total workforce
Domestic servants	242	11.6
Labourers	159	7.6
Glovers	125	6.0
Farm workers	115	5.5
Tanners, etc.	102	4.9
Shoemakers	97	4.6
Dressmakers	85	4.1
Gardeners	75	3.6
Building trades	67	3.2
Shopworkers	52	2.5
Total in above occupations	1119	53.5
Total workforce	2092	

A greater proportion of the gardeners were probably involved in the commercial gardening, mostly between Haugh Lane and the Tyne, producing for the most part vegetables mostly for sale in towns to the east of Hexham. All the other occupations making or producing items for sale were small-scale (Table 3). The remaining just under a thousand persons in employment can be said to be in essentially service occupations, such as accountants, auctioneers, butchers, cattle dealers, drapers, hairdressers, lodging house keepers, ministers of religion and teachers. Heading the list of service occupations, indeed heading the list of all occupations, were domestic servants (Table 2).

Domestic service was an almost entirely all-female occupation, there being only twelve men similarly employed, though this excluded grooms and coachmen who were classified as horse workers. Domestic servants did not always live-in; many lived at home. Three-quarters of the glovers and half the hatters and half the teachers were women.

One feature that the 1851 markedly points up is the heterogeneous pattern of occupancy within the town in that the working and middle classes lived cheek by jowl. Also, there were six lodging houses within the town – two in Battle Hill (one holding 15 lodgers and the other 11), Broadgates

(8), and three in Gilesgate (12, 12 &13). Significantly, in these six lodging houses there were 30 persons originating from Ireland; five families contribute to the group. Such persons are likely to have been driven out of Ireland as the result of the Great Famine. There were a considerable number of other lodgers (roughly someone paying rent for accommodation) in the town, sometimes as many as three or four, in what can otherwise be described as ordinary households. Also, there were boarders (someone treated as part of the household), very often 'scholars', an informal arrangement allowing a child who lived at a distance to come to school in Hexham.

TABLE 3. *Details of those involved in productive trades in Hexham at the time of the 1851 census (Jennings, 2000).*

Occupation	No. employed	Comment
Baker	12	
Basket maker	3	
Blacksmith	19	
Brewer and brewery worker	4	Armstrong's brewery in Priestpopple
Broom maker	9	
Cabinet maker	10	
Coach builder	13	
Gunsmith	3	Most significant being E. Dixon in Priestpopple, later Fore Street
Hatter	29	16 master hatters in 1823 (Wright, 1823)
Metal worker	24	Iron foundry functioning; taken over by Davison family in 1855
Miller	11	
Miner	41	Working at Acomb and Stublick?
Paper maker	14	Some working at Fourstones paper mill that was established in 1763 (Mandl, 1985)?
Pipe maker	12	
Rope maker	8	Two functioning rope walks – one located on west side of Hallstile Bank; the other north of Co-op car park (building still standing) (OS map 1860)
Tile maker	5	
Saddler	14	
Watch & clock maker	16	
Weaver	15	38 looms in operation in 1823 (Wright, 1823)

The principal market day, as now, was on Tuesday (Parson & White, 1927). There was what has been describes as an inferior market on Saturdays. A cattle market was held, from October to Christmas, on alternate Tuesdays in Priestpopple, while there were fairs for horses and cattle 6 August and 9 November on Tyne Green and for the sale of stock in the Market Place on 25 March.

A wool fair was held on the 2 July. Hirings (of farm labourers and servants) were held each year – on the first Tuesday in March for hinds (male farm labourers) and the last Tuesdays after the 12 May and 12 November for male and female servants.

The state of the fabric of the town comes clear in the following chapters, which also describe the extent to which improvements to it were by made the Local Board of Health and its successor authority, Hexham Urban District Council. The efforts of these two bodies to bring about the improvements form a central theme of this book. As we shall see, the efforts did not always lead to a totally satisfactory outcome. There were often reasons for this, finance being the dominant one.

But it was not only the fabric of the town that needed to be improved. All the early accounts of the town make little reference to recreation in the modern sense of the word. The outstanding institution catering for the leisure hours of men was the Hexham Mechanics', Literary and Scientific Institution (Jenkins, 2002). As the 19th century drew to a close, many local authorities felt the need to enhance the recreational facilities in their district. Here too, financial reasons seem to have been a major reason for the local authority in Hexham seeming to be less able to do the same.

CHAPTER 2

The establishment of the Local Board of Health

In 1848 the first Public Health Act (11 & 12 Vict., c. 63) was passed. It is the foundation stone of national sanitary legislation. Though it did not apply to London, it was intended mainly for cities and towns. A General Board of Health was established with members appointed by the Crown and the Board was empowered to appoint inspectors to help bring about sanitary improvement within the terms of the Act. The Board also had power to create Local Boards of Health through the machinery of an Order in Council. In most cases the Board could act only on a petition from the ratepayers; exceptionally where the death rate was unusually high it could act on its own motion.

The machinery for the establishment of a Local Board in Hexham was set in motion on 31 January 1851 with a letter to the Local Government Board from James Kirsopp of the Spital (now the club house for Hexham Golf Club) (NA MH/13/91). In that letter he complained about the horrible nature of 'the stench' coming from the manufacture, in what is now the Tyne Green Road area, of what he termed 'guana' (fertiliser) by Ralph Ridley, who 'procures dead horses pours vitriol on them steams the refuse produced the boiling is carried out in metal Pots and the steam escaping is allowed to escape into the air'. The reply from the Board indicated that it had no power to deal with the matter but could respond to a petition to it, as directed by Section 8 of the Public Health Act of 1848 for an inquiry into the sanitary circumstances of the locality. After being assured that any inquiry will not be a charge upon the locality, a petition from 152 of the rated inhabitants of the town ('more than one sixth of the whole') was forthcoming on 30 August 1851.

Eventually, in September 1852, the petition was followed by an inspection into the sanitary conditions of the town by a Superintending Inspector of the Board, Robert Rawlinson. Essentially the inspection consisted of a meeting with the leading citizens in the Board of Guardians room followed, presumably the next day, by a tour of the town itself, when Rawlinson was accompanied by some of the leading citizens who had been at the meeting.

Rawlinson's presence in the town in 1852 quickly stimulated those, opposed to the Public Health Act and to having it applied, forcibly to make their presence felt. Specifically, they submitted a petition against the adoption of the Public Health Act in Hexham, signed by at least 215 persons (Rawlinson, 1853). Essentially it claimed that there was an ample supply of water for the town, that it was one of 'the most healthy towns in the kingdom' and that the any nuisances from 'time to time recurring' and lack of sanitary regulations were amply provided for by the powers vested in the Board of Guardians. Significantly, it was made clear that the town was not in a position to pay any further taxation, the poor rate being obtained with great difficulty. Amongst those against enforcing the Public Health on Hexham were two surgeons, Thomas Jefferson and Robert Stokoe. Such medical opposition to sanitary reform was new to Rawlinson, who said that 'the Senior Surgeons of Hexham will not believe in sanitary improvement'. Jefferson was contemptuous of those wanting improvement. In a letter to the General Board of Health he wrote

The project was first hatched in an overruling society of tradesmen who are teetotalley preachery – Men wise in the ways of Mammon the leader of this band is a man of good capacity and determined resolution they have had the Mechanics Institute very much in their own hands – they are the saints of the place – strong in family ties, determined of purpose, novel and changeable in their religious notiory (?) – at one time calling themselves New Lights earnest Proselytizery (sic) – I think you can now guess the source of the application to the Board...... they found encouragement with my Bro. in Law Jas. Gibson the Bailiff of the Manor, our curate Mr Hudson, three young medical practitioners viz Mr Stainthorpe Mr Pearson and Mr Nicholson – and very few others (NRO/ZBK/1/B/3/9/108).

In March 1853 Rawlinson submitted his printed Report (Rawlinson, 1853) to the General Board of Health. It was based on his own findings and documentary, historical statistical and other evidence provided by various groups in Hexham. The Report makes fascinating reading. For not only is it a report on the sanitary conditions of the town but, as I have indicated, it provides a wealth of information about the town and the way it functioned in 1853. Here we focus on what the report says about the sanitary conditions.

Rawlinson was blunt about what he found

I have examined into the sanitary state of many of the towns in England from Plymouth to Berwick-upon-Tweed, from Sunderland to Liverpool, and in no town of a parallel population have I found more filth, overcrowding, and general neglect, than in Hexham......
It is ever painful to witness the concurrence of so many conditions favourable to the generation of disease, but it is more painful to find this state of things defended; and in Hexham this is the case; even medical men, who are usually the most active promoters of sanitary reform, have in Hexham, come prominently forward, and, by their evidence, attempt to perpetuate this state of things.

The Report details, what then, was the incredible state of the town. Several quotations from the report are given in Jennings *et al.* (2004). The following chapters concerned with particular sanitary problems, detail the nature and extent of the squalor that the citizens were exposed to. Nevertheless, as Rawlinson makes clear, there were many in Hexham who did not want the Public Health Act of 1848 applied to Hexham. A petition against the Act, signed by 250 persons, and a memorial against the Inquiry, signed by 302, testify to the opposition. However, in 1853, there was an outbreak of cholera in Hexham, which led to 23 deaths and 1,200 cases of diarrhoea (Jennings, 2002). The outbreak stimulated the supporters of the application of the Act to Hexham to send a memorial to the General Board of Health emphasising the need for application of the Act. The Board sent Dr William Lewis, one of the Board's Medical Officers and William Lee, a Superintendent Inspector to Hexham to obtain a first-hand view of the situation. Not only was Lewis critical of the way the local medical men were handling the outbreak but also he was also extremely disparaging about the sanitary state of the town. However, he also communicated some heartening news. He said that 'whereas 'there had been great division and opposition in the Town' to the Public Health Act, 'a great majority now wish for it'. Indeed, they were 'extremely anxious' that the Privy Council issue an order to that effect 'at once'. Nevertheless, there was still a vociferous group fighting for the *status quo,* sending at the end of October 1853 yet another petition, signed by 612 ratepayers (this was a significant number, given that the figure of 770 for the number of rateable properties given in Chapter 1 relates closely to the number of ratepayers) expressing its opposition to the implementation of the Act.

With all the evidence of the unsatisfactory sanitary state of the town, it is not surprising that the General Board of Health, admittedly going against the majority of ratepayers in the town, applied the Public Health Act of 1848 'throughout the township of Hexham' *(The London Gazette,* 1853). An elected Local Board of Health was established to consist of nine members, the first election to be held on 15 December 1853. The first meeting of the new Board took place on the 9 January 1854.

Before describing the activities of the Hexham Local Board of Health, and the successor authority Hexham Urban District Council, there follow three chapters devoted to what might be loosely called administration. The first details operation of the two bodies – their strong similarities means that they can be considered together – and the second provides information as to how they were financed. The third chapter describes the Workhouse, a public institution functioning throughout the period 1854-1939 and governed by the Hexham Union of Parishes until 1929, thereafter by Northumberland County Council.

FIG. 1 Balmoral Hotel, as it used to be called, in Priestpopple, which was the offices of the Hexham Local Board of Health then the Urban District Council from 1890-1930. The building now houses the solicitors Nicholson Portnell. The archway on the left leads into a yard where there were stables and where the fire engine and other equipment were kept.

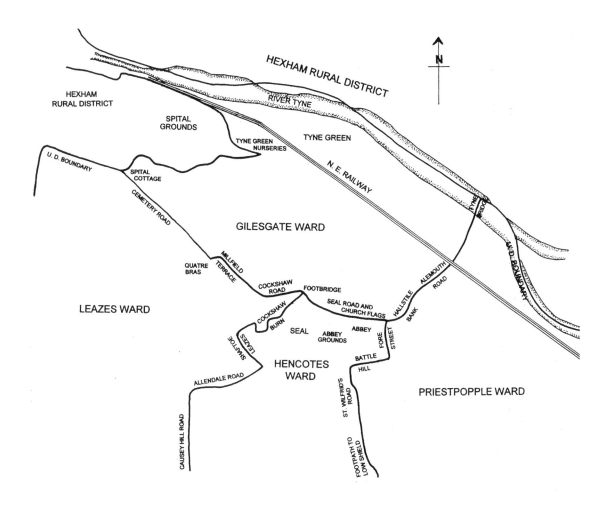

FIG. 2 Hexham Urban District, as it was divided in 1909 into wards for Council elections. The names of the wards and their boundaries remained very much the same until recently. Redrawn from the original sketch plan (*HC* 13.11.1909).

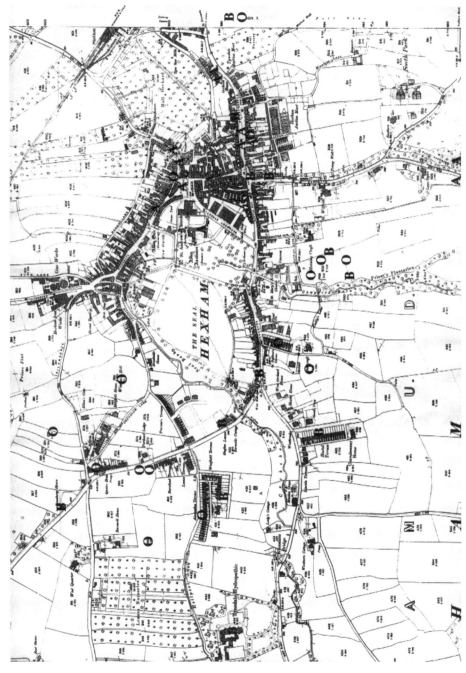

FIG. 3 The 1895 Ordnance Survey of Hexham showing the location of residences of members of the Local Board of Health and Urban District Councillors during three periods during the years 1854-1939. Only in one or two instances are the locations precise, since the information as to the location of the others does not contain house numbers. **A**, refers to the period 1854-68, **B**, to 1898-1908 and **O**, to 1919-39. For the last period it is the place of work not the residence of two Councillors that is located in the centre of Hexham. Letters on the periphery of the map indicate only the direction off the map but not the location of residences.

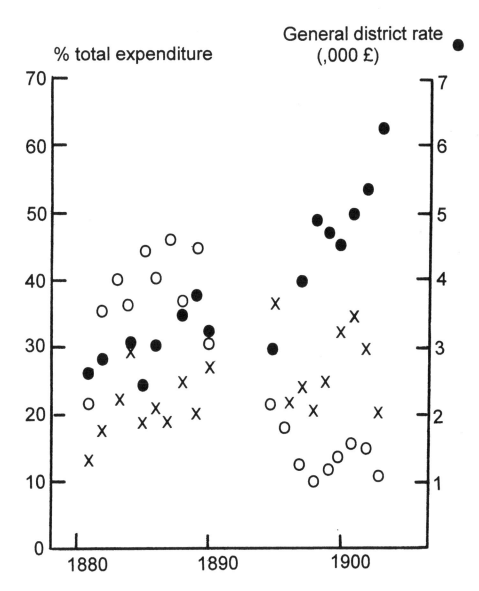

FIG. 4 A graph showing the annual general district rate for Hexham during the period 1881-93 and the expenditure on roads and the repayment of loans, as a percentage of the total expenditure of the Urban District Council. Please refer to the text for further details.

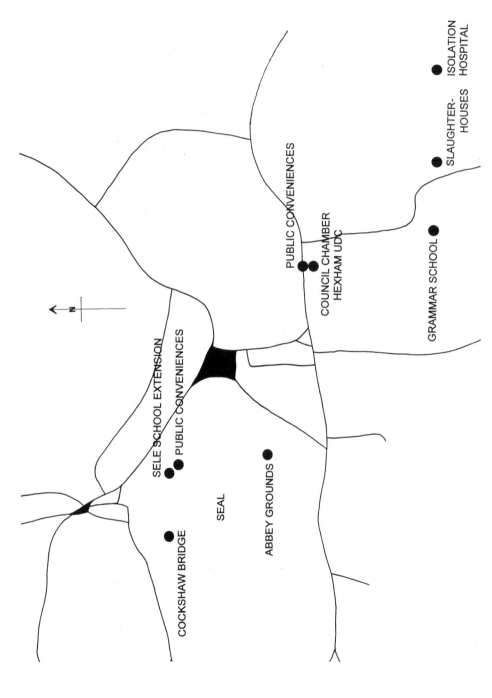

FIG. 5 A map of Hexham with the roads, together with the Market Place in black, showing the buildings and structures built with public money in the period 1894-1914. One building is missing, namely the small mortuary c100 metres to the east of the Isolation Hospital. The Abbey Grounds is on the map, since it represents a similar kind of capital outlay to the building projects. The Sele School extension was built by the School Board, while much of the money for the new Grammar School came from the County Council (Jennings, 1999). Everything else was built by the Urban District Council.

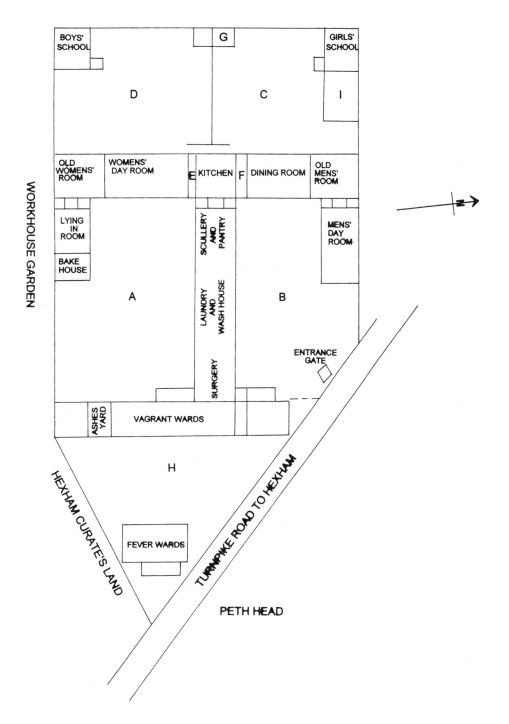

FIG. 6 The earliest known plan (1841) of Hexham Workhouse. The Turnpike Road is now Dean Street. Redrawn from Cadman (1976).

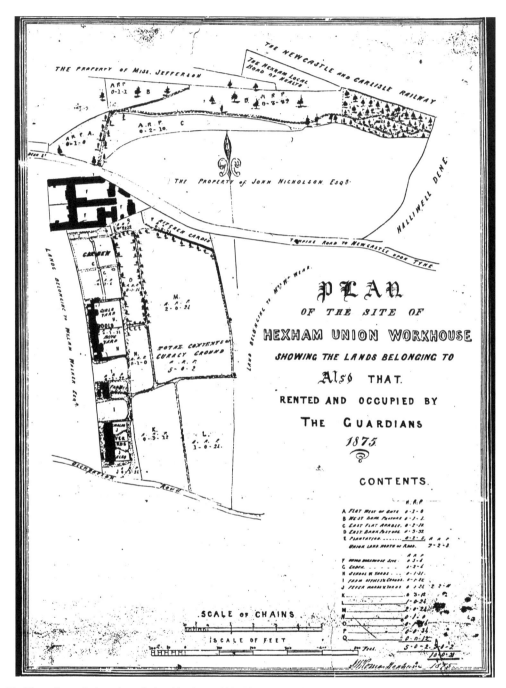

FIG. 7 The plan of the site of the Hexham Workhouse in 1875. As can be seen, on the two acres of land to the south of the main buildings purchased in 1843 were eventually located (in order, moving south) the school, a farm building and fever wards. Reproduced with the permission of Hexham Library.

FIG. 8 The Master's house of Hexham Workhouse erected in 1883, along with other buildings (see text for details)

CHAPTER 3

The mechanics of local government

Introduction

For one hundred and twenty years, from 1854, Hexham was governed by the Local Board of Health (from 1854-94) and the Urban District Council, which superseded the Board following the passing of the Local Government Act of 1894 (56 & 57 Vict., c. 73) from 1894-1974. These two bodies are treated together because, except for certain, what might be called peripheral, functions, the rules of operation of the two bodies were essentially similar and changed little over the whole period. Nevertheless, throughout the 120 years local government in England and Wales evolved to meet the changes brought about by government legislation, other external pressures and the requirements of the electorate. As we will see, the same was true for Hexham. It should be noted that following the Public Health Act of 1872 (35 & 36 Vict., c. 69) Hexham Local Board of Health was also the Hexham Urban Sanitary Authority. Essentially this was just another title; the more significant change following the Act was that it gave the responsibility for running the newly established Hexham Rural Sanitary Authority to the Guardians.

On Tuesday, 4 October 1853, *The London Gazette* published the order in Council. It noted that there appeared to be

> no Act of Parliament in force within the said township for paving, lighting (otherwise than for the profit of proprietors or shareholders [refers to the Gas Company]), cleansing, watching, regulating, supplying with water, or improving such township, or any part of thereof, or anywise relating to the purposes of the said Public Health Act [of 1848].

The Order then said that the Public Health Act and every part, except section 50, should be applied throughout the township of Hexham. The Local Board was to consist of nine persons, with first election on December 15 1853, to be overseen by Jasper Gibson, who had been named as Returning Officer by the Government, through its General Board of Health, probably on the advice of Rawlinson. One third of the Board should go out of office on March 31 each year. Every member was to have a personal estate of not less than £1,000 and the electorate was to be owners of property and ratepayers.

It needs to be stressed that the Local Board of Health was not an independent entity. It had to operate within the limits prescribed by the Public Health Act of 1848. Thus in a number of matters it had to defer to the authority of the General Board of Health in London. That body was central to the 1848 Act and was composed of a President and two other persons appointed by the Crown. The Board was empowered to appoint inspectors (such as Robert Rawlinson), etc., to see that the provisions of the Act were carried out. As we have seen, the General Board was empowered to create a Local Board. Once such a Local Board, such as Hexham, was operating it had to apply to the General Board for approval with respect to a number of matters. The most important one to note here is the confirmation of bye-laws. The General Board was not popular but, in modified form, it continued to operate until 1858, when its duties and powers fell to the Home Secretary and Privy Council. This must be considered as a backward step in terms of sanitary progress. A Royal Sanitary Commission appointed in 1868 issued a report that 'set out with utmost clearness the incompleteness, imperfections, and unworkability of the present system' (Redlich & Hirst, 1958, p.115). The report spelt out what needed to be done and why:

> There should be one recognised and sufficiently powerful minister, not to centralise administration, but, on the contrary, to set local life in motion – a real motive power, and an authority to be referred to for guidance and assistance by all sanitary authorities for Local government throughout the country.

The Local Government Act of 1871 (34 & 35 Vict., c. 70) carrying into effect the recommendations of the Royal Commission, resulted in the establishment of the Local Government Board. This not only replaced the General Board of Health but also took on new functions. It became the central department of State with general supervision of local government matters. Thus it took all the powers and duties of the Poor-Law Board; all the powers and duties of the Privy Council relating to vaccination and prevention of disease; all the powers and duties of the Home Office in relation to public health, drainage and sanitary matters, baths and washhouses, public and town improvements, artisans' and labourers' dwellings, local government, local returns and local taxation.

The 1871 Act was followed by another Public Health Act in 1872. As far as this story is concerned, the significance of this latter Act lies in the establishment of sanitary authorities throughout England Wales. For the urban districts, it meant only a change in name. However, in rural areas, prior to 1872, the vestries had been the sewer authorities and, as such, had other sanitary powers conferred on them. The new Act transferred all these powers to the Guardians. In urban districts, vestries had for some years lost such powers. Initially, it became customary to speak of the Hexham Urban Sanitary Authority. However it was not very long before there was reversion to Hexham Local Board of Health

Officers

When the Local Board of Health was established 1854, four officers were soon appointed – the Clerk, the Collector, Inspector of Nuisances and Treasurer.

Clerk – The post was, and continued to be, a part-time position. The first holder of the post was John Stokoe, who had headed the poll in the first election but resigned from the Board at its second meeting in order to be Clerk. Stokoe, like all subsequent holders of the post was a solicitor and, as such, the legal advisor to the local authority. He was to be paid a salary of £30 per annum. He was also Clerk to the Board of Guardians. Holding more than one post in this manner was frequent. An outstanding example was Isaac Baty. He succeeded his father in 1888 as Clerk to the Local Board and Clerk to the Burial Board, being already (since the age of 23) Clerk to the Guardians that carried with it the duties of the clerk of the Union Rural Sanitary Authority, clerk of the Assessment Committee, and clerk to the School Attendance Committee. He was also Clerk to the Bellingham Highway Board, local manager of the North-Eastern Banking Co., solicitor to the

Hexham Permanent Building Society, auditor to the Tindale Ward Savings Bank, solicitor to the Gas Co. and, from 1889, Superintendent Registrar of Births Marriages and Deaths. He was also a keen farmer and involved in a wide range of local sporting clubs. He died from diphtheria in 1894 (HC 22.9.1894).

Collector – This was a very important post, because the person concerned was responsible for collecting the rates. William Wilson was the first collector. As with all posts entailing the handling of money on behalf of the Local Board, the collector before entering the post had to provide a sum of money for the faithful execution of his financial duties. The minutes of the Local Board give no information as to what surety Wilson provided. We do know that in 1858, he collected £414.13s.0d in rates. He was succeeded in 1863 by William Charlton, who when he was also appointed 'Inspector of Nuisances and Sanitary Inspector', used William Stainthorpe, auctioneer and Charlton's predecessor, William Wilson, Ironmonger, as sureties (13.7.1863). It is only after the fourth collector, Thomas Wilthew, was appointed that we find that the two sureties had to total £500. We also learn that he was to be paid four pence on each pound collected (HLBH 2.7.1866). The use of collectors was not a very effective method of gathering in the money. Ratepayers could unavailable when the collector called and, even if they were in they could browbeat a collector into agreeing to payments being delayed. This was concern to the auditor of the Board's accounts:

> There seems in Hexham, however, to be a systematic postponement of rate payment, which is anything but creditable. The collecting officer has not a 'fair chance' and more rate has to be laid on to make up for the deficiencies you have been under should cause these matters to be looked seriously in the face and a rigorous push be made to overcome them. A new appointment of joint collectors is a good measure (HLBH 11.6.1877).

The only way the Board of Health could recover the arrears of rates was to have recourse to the Justices. In 1872, this procedure seems to have been remarkable effective. A number of people were summoned before the Magistrates but every case, except two, were settled previous to the day of the hearing.

The reference to the there being two collectors was a consequence of the Collector, Thomas Forrester, who appointed on 11 July 1870, being found to be not up to the job (HLBH 28.5.1877). After considering the situation, the Board allowed Forrester to be helped by his son, William. But, even the two of them together were not very efficient; in consequence of which on 2 March 1879, they were made to resign. Edward Turnbull who succeeded them seems to have brought order into the job. He was to remain in post until 5 January 1892 to emigrate to Australia. The post of Collector continued in the 1920s and 30s, with rents replacing rates as the major part of the operation

Inspector of Nuisances – William Wilson was also the first such inspector at a weekly salary of 10/-. His duties were not defined at the time of his appointment, since the minute appointing him also ordered the Clerk to write to the clerks of Alnwick, Morpeth and Penrith asking for their bye-laws and, to the same effect, to the General Board of Health (23.1.1854). Eventually, on 15 May 1854, bye-laws were produced based for the most part on those of Penrith. The job of the Inspector of Nuisances was to ascertain what nuisances exist that call for abatement under the powers of the

Public Health Act of 1848, according to the bye-laws established by the Board. The Act itself indicates what was required of the Inspector:

> Houses, &c. – The Local Board are also required to see the houses are properly furnished with the necessaries (privies) and they are kept in order, for the decency and comfort of the inhabitants.
> Nuisances &c. – Full powers are given for the removal of all kinds of nuisances, and also for prohibiting the establishment of noxious trades, &c.

It is worthwhile at this point to give a small example of what could be considered as nuisances. Thus at the meeting of the Board on 27 April 1863, it was

> Ordered that Mr Storey [who was then Inspector] wait upon the owners or occupiers of the undermentioned premises and request that the respective Nuisances set forth be removed or abated viz:– to have the Privy in Grapes Inn Yard put into better order and suggest that the Ash Pit be reduced in its dimensions – the Slaughter Houses in Half Moon Yard to be Whitewashed and otherwise cleaned – To caution the parties who throw Potato pealings etc. into Grate near Charlton's Eating House to desist – The Pigs to be removed from three Pigstyes in John Robinson's Yard Gilligate [Gilesgate] Bank placed against Shields House in Haugh Lane – No one to be permitted to leave Carts standing in Old Burn Lane – the Ashpits and Privies behind House on Gilligate Bank belonging to Mr Charlton, Battle Hill to have Soil mixed with the refuse for the purpose of being deodorized – The same with Privy and Ashpit behind John Aydon's House in Holy Island – The same with Privy behind Jameson's Coopery on Bull Bank.

Not surprisingly, whoever was appointed Inspector faced problems in getting people to keep to the sanitary regulations. Indeed, almost from the very beginning, there are indications that the person first appointed to the post, William Wilson, had difficulty in getting nuisances abated. In 1857, the Local Board resolved that the Head Police Officer should succeed him. However, Major Browne, High Constable, declined to permit County constables to act as inspectors of nuisances (HLBH 20.7.1857). It is worth noting that, at the same time, the Police within the County became authorised to inspect the common lodging houses, which had to be registered with the Board. This indicates that the police were moving towards a more social role in the community. At any rate, Major Browne clearly had a change of heart, because on 30 December 1861, the Board resolved 'that Superintendent George Stephenson, Sergeant Andrew Pike and Police Constable Henry Robinson...... be appointed Inspectors of Nuisances......'

Treasurer – It was the duty of the person holding this little-mentioned but important post to receive and make all payments on behalf of the Local Board. Several persons were approached before the first treasurer was appointed. In no case is it clear why the invitation to serve was turned down. Possibly, the required surety of £1,000 was too high a sum to put forward. However, on 12 June 1854, Mr J. D. Bell, who was a banker, was appointed Treasurer. A year and a half later, Bell seems to have resigned – there are indications that there was some sort of altercation between him and the Board as to what was owed to him as remuneration and what he owed the Board (HLBH 8.12.1856). At any rate, he was succeeded by Matthew Ord, a watchmaker and jeweller in Fore Street (1851 census). After he died in February 1862, Miss Margaret Ord succeeded him. She was almost certainly Matthew's sister, having joined her brother in Fore Street by the 1861 Census. It is striking that she was the only woman ever to be associated with the running of the town until well into the 20th century (HLBH 7.4.1862). After she resigned from the post in 1864, the post of Treasurer was held by a banker or a bank.

Though not amongst the initial Officers of the Board of Health, there were two important posts that need to be referred to here:

Surveyor – This post was not established until 1865, when the Board decided to advertise in the *Builder, The Engineer, Hexham Courant* and the *Newcastle Courant* 'for a suitable person as Surveyor.' One imagines the Board must have been convinced of the need for such a person after having undertaken the difficult task of building its new water supply, without the in-house expertise that would have helped the Board to keep more effective control of the project. Even so, initial holders of the post had a difficult time, owing to their lack of expertise and the tendency of Board members to feel that they knew more than their employee. There is no doubt that some Board members were quite knowledgeable about sanitary matters but they expected the Surveyor to be subservient to them and take instruction without question. Towards the end of the 19th century, surveyors with considerable ability began to be appointed and who, without difficulty, held the respect of the elected representatives. Interestingly, the 1848 Public Health Act required that government approval was required for an appointment to be made to the post, though the establishment of the post was not obligatory.

TABLE 4. *Schedule of established posts of the Urban District Council as of 2 May 1938. Numbers in brackets indicates the number of persons in a particular post.*

Officers
Clerk to the Council (part-time)
Medical Officer of Health
Surveyor
Accountant
Collector
Rent Collector and Housing
Supervisor
Rate Clerk
Nurse
Sanitary Inspector
Typist

Servants
Cook
Foreman
Tip attendant
Storekeeper
Sewerman

Pleasure Grounds Attendants (4)
Watermen (3)
Slaughterhouse Attendant
Cemetery Attendant
Joiner
Caretaker
Convenience Attendant
Cartmen (2)
Dustmen (5)
Scavenger (7)
Roadmen (4)
Motor Drivers (2)
Grave Diggers (2)
Under-Foreman
Pleasure Grounds Attendant*
Labourers (3)
Mason
* It is not clear how this post differs from the four above

Medical Officer of Health – Section 10 of the Public Health Act of 1872 made it the duty of every urban and rural sanitary authority in England and Wales to appoint a properly qualified medical officer of health. His duties were defined by an order of 11.November 1872. Importantly, in terms of the story that unfolds later, he was not only to report from time to time to the Urban District Council but also to the Local Government Board in London. The first holder of the post was Dr. Daniel Jackson, who was appointed in April 1873 at an annual salary of £20 (HLBH 28.4.1873).

As time passed and the complexity of the local authority operation increased, more and different kinds of staff were appointed. Some idea of the change in size of Hexham's local Authority administration is given in Table 4. In 1938, there was a distinction between Officers and the now intriguing title of Servants

Offices

The first meeting of the Local Board of Health on 9 January 1854 was in the office of Mr Matthew Smith (first Chairman of the Board) in Back Street (St Mary's Chare). At the second meeting it was resolved that

> Miss [Sarah] Walton's Room in Back Street be taken for the use of the Local Board as a Board Room until May next the Rent to be paid for the same after the rate of Five Pounds per annum (HLBH 9.1.1854).

On 5 November 1854, the Board decided that Sarah Walton's remuneration for attendance, coals and candles be two shillings per Board meeting. Seemingly, Sarah Watson was a dress-maker and rented a shop (from Matthew Smith; NRO/PHU/A4). Regretably, we do not know where in Back Street Matthew Smith had his office, or where Sarah Walton had her shop.

The Local Board of Health continued to use Sarah Walton's room until 1866, when in October the Board rented two rooms and an ante-room on the south side of the 'new Town Hall' from the Corn Market Company for an annual rent of £20 plus rates and gas. Eventually, the space available became far too small for the needs of the Board and it was decided to look for more spacious accommodation (HLBH 18.4.1889). A committee set up to look at suitable properties reported to the 4 November meeting that the two most suitable properties were the Balmoral Hotel, also known as Priestpopple House (Fig. 1), owned by William Henry Harrison, a Newcastle Merchant (Dallison, 2000) and Mr Wylam Walker's premises, the location of which is not identified in the minutes. The former was thought to be 'very much more suitable'. The asking price was £1150. Ten years later, it was purchased for £1175 (HLBH 18.11.1899). The Board took possession the following year. Offices were made for the Surveyor, the Clerk and the Collector, and one large room at the back of the first floor became the Board Room. The yard adjoining the building was used for workshops and stables

The offices of the Local Board of Health and the successor authority, the Urban District Council, remained in Priestpopple for forty years. In 1926, Mr J. E. Tulley offered Hexham House and grounds to the Urban District Council for £3,500.The offer at what was then thought to be an attractive price was accompanied by a gift of £500 from four of its leading citizens. On this basis, the Council felt there was a case for purchasing the property for 'general Public Health purposes', though this really meant that the Council did not have a clear idea as to what to do with the building (HUDC 4.1.1926). Use as a library or museum had been suggested. In the end, the Council decided that the best policy was to sell its offices in Priestpopple, using Hexham House instead. The Council moved into the building on 1930; Hexham House has been use as local authority offices ever since. The bowling green, behind Hexham House, was opened by Mr Tulley in 1929, after what had been several decades of public pressure for such an amenity (*see* Chapter 19). After the move to Hexham House, the Priestpopple offices were sold to the solicitors John Harbottle Nicholson and his son Geoffrey.

Election of Board members and Councillors

In the period 1854-1909, the Local Board of Health or the Urban District Council consisted of nine elected representatives, three coming up for re-election each year after the initial election in 1854 electing the whole nine. After 1909, the District was divided up into wards, with four coming up for re-election each year after the initial election in 1910 electing all twelve. Elections took place in the first week of April. Throughout the whole period under consideration, the electorate was the ratepayers – either owners or occupiers.

1854-1894

Up to 1894, owners had one to six votes according to rating qualification from £50 (one vote) up to £250 and above (six votes), the intermediate number of votes being associated with £50 increments; occupiers had a similar number of votes for the same rating qualification. Thus a person who was both an owner and occupier had a possible maximum twelve votes. For Local Board of Health elections, voting papers were left by appointees of the Board at houses and collected after three days. Thus, for the election of 1879, Nicholas Rewcastle, Thomas Walton, George Pattinson, Matthew Ritson, John Smith and John Coxon were appointed to deliver the voting papers and to be paid 7/6 a day for each day engaged (HLBH 17.2.1879). The votes of anyone who had not paid their rates or whose names had not been long enough on the rate books were discounted. There is evidence that the system was open to abuse as this exchange on the day of the poll shows:

> Returning Officer: Your name is Marty Weldon?
> Mrs W: Yes
> Question: Was there a voting paper left at your house?
> Answer: Yes
> Q: Who filled up for you?
> A: Peter the Glazier
> Q: Did he ask you who you were going to vote for?
> A: I met him in the street, and he asked me if I had got a voting paper. I said 'Yes' and he asked would I let him fill it up for me? He said he wanted to put two men in. I sad 'Yes.' He said 'Who do you want to put in,' and I said 'Matthew Smith for one.' He said 'There is only another woman forebye you in the town would have him in.' I said Mr Smith had never done me any harm.
> The Returning Officer: Did you expect he put Smith in for one
> A: Yes

Q: Who did he say he wanted in?
A: Ridley and Davison.
Q: Can you read? Did you try to read the names?
A: I cannot read. He told me to put the paper away and let no one look at it.
The Returning Officer: You are down for Ridley and Davison (HC 5.4.1873).

As far as qualification for office was concerned, those standing for election to the Board had to have at least £500 in personal property or have property of £15 rateable value. Had Hexham had a population over 20,000, the figures would have been £1,000 and £30.

Little information is to hand, except in a very general way, as to the factors governing the outcome of an election. As is demonstrated in the chapter concerned with the establishment of the water supply, expenditure on a large public project could raise passions either for or against it, such that a majority of candidates from one or other of the two camps could be elected, depending on who had the greater ability to sway the voters to their cause. But, when more mundane issues were uppermost, it is not easy to establish what might lead a member of the electorate to vote in a particular manner.

We are fortunate that for the 1888 election an analysis of the individual votes was published in the *Courant* (14.4.1888). There were five candidates and the result is shown in Tables 5 & 6. Stainthorpe, Robb and Lisle were elected; indeed they were returned as Board members, since, prior to the election they had come to the end of their three-year terms. If we look at Stainthorpes's votes in Table 6, it is clear that he was not only popular with the supporters of Robb and Lisle but also with those of Bulman. It was the votes from Bulman's supporters that enabled Stainthorpe to acquire the greatest share of the total votes. On the other hand, most of Robb's votes came from Lisle supporters (79.8%); likewise most of Lisle's votes came from Robb supporters (85.2%).

TABLE 5. *The result of the Hexham Local Board of Health election of 1888, giving both the votes cast and the distribution of votes as a percentage of the total.*

Candidate	Occupation	Place of Abode	Total vote (% total)
Robert Stainthorpe	Parliamentary Registration Agent	Shaftoe Leazes	1064 (28.3)
James T. Robb	Draper	Abbey View	821 (21.8)
John Lisle	Provision Merchant	Lane Dykes	769 (20.4)
Thomas Bulman	Builder	1 St Cuthbert's Terrace	657 (17.5)
John Pearson	Gardener	Haugh Lane House	450 (12.0)
Total			3761

Can we establish reasons for this voting pattern? The record of a ratepayers' meeting prior to the election gives some clues (*HC* 31.3.1888). As one might imagine, there was much concern about the burden of the rates. Indeed a George Dixon proposed that 'it is not necessary to incur the expense of an election at the present time.' There were two major headings of expenditure facing the Board – the procurement of a decent supply of water for the town and the ownership of Tyne Green. For the former, there was the expense of taking a Bill through Parliament (*see* Chapter 11); while for the latter, it was pointed out that 'a road was to be made at a cost of £400; then a man was kept on the Green [to look after it] at the rate of £1 per week and there was the weiring to be done at the riverside'.

TABLE 6. *Distribution of votes for Stainthorpe in the 1888 election for the Hexham Local Board of Health. The names in the column on the left are those associated with Stainthorpe who were voted for on a particular voting paper. Plumpers gave all their votes to one candidate.*

Votes for Stainthorpe along with:	Actual vote	% total vote (1064)
Bulman and Pearson	356	33.5
Bulman and Robb	73	6.9
Bulman and Lisle	63	5.9
Bulman	53	5.0
Pearson and Lisle	22	2.1
Pearson and Robb	36	3.4
Pearson	10	1.0
Robb and Lisle	376	35.3
Lisle	9	0.8
Robb	22	2.1
Plumpers	44	4.1
Total	1064	100.1

In the light of what went on at the ratepayers' meeting, it is interesting to turn to three election addresses published in the *Courant* (24.3.1888). That of Robb speaks almost entirely about obtaining the new supply of water and his desire to bring the scheme to completion. He does promise to conduct the business of the Board 'in the most economical manner possible.' Stainthorpe, on the other hand, focuses much of his address on the financial aspects of the Board's operations, on reducing indebtedness, consolidating the loans taken on by the Board. The new water supply is only discussed in a somewhat oblique manner. Bulman's election address was published a week later (*HC* 31.3.1888). He is quite blunt, promising that

> I shall make it my care to see that the business of the Board is carried out with utmost possible economy, consistent with efficiency. I shall object to the employment of other Civil Engineers when we have one admittedly capable of doing his duty or even going to the unnecessary expense of having other Surveyors when such work can be done by an official.
> Having a thoroughly practical knowledge of all that pertains to plans and buildings, I trust I shall be able to render some assistance in their discussion.

One can conclude from these election addresses that Bulman's views chimed in with those of the electorate who were against spending public money if it meant raising the rates. Robb (and probably Lisle) believed that public expenditure was crucial to the undoubted need to produce a better water supply, the benefits of which far outweighed any disadvantages due to a rise in the rates. Stainthorpe stood between the two camps. As a retiring Board member, he had clearly demonstrated that he was in favour of continuing the spending programme of the previous three years. However, as both his speeches at Board meetings, full accounts of which were published in the two weekly Hexham papers, and his electoral address showed, he was continually pressing for a careful approach to expenditure by the Board. So, not surprisingly, Stainthorpe picked up votes from the camp of Bulman as well a great number from the camps of Robb and Lisle, thus ensuring that he came top of the poll.

Thus, for the 1888 election, the dominant issue was Board expenditure, particularly if it led increased rates. Indeed, there was a feeling that it was better to do without an election if money could be saved by doing so – one gets the feeling that persons were discouraged from being nominated so that an election would not take place. Though the evidence from previous elections is more fragmentary, there is sufficient to be confident that the major battleground over which an election was fought was Board expenditure. The battle between the clean and dirty parties with regard to sanitary reform reflects this (see Part II).

1894-1939

With the establishment of Urban District Councils in 1894, there were two major changes in the election procedure. There was the welcome introduction of a secret ballot, over twenty years after it had been introduced nationally for elections to the School Board. The other major change was the abolition of a property qualification for anyone standing for the District Council. Any person elected had to be a parochial elector of some parish within the district or had to have resided in the district during the whole twelve months preceding the election. The lack of a property qualification meant that women could now be elected to the District Council, though it would be 43 years before the first woman, Isabel Annie May Iveson, was elected unopposed as a member for Leazes Ward in 1937. In this respect, one should note that, provided they were over 30, the wives of male voters were given the vote in 1918. Ten years later, women were put on the same electoral footing as men. Sadly, there is no information as yet to hand to indicate whether the voting behaviour of women made any difference to the outcome of elections.

There was a further consequence of abandonment of the requirement for a property qualification, namely the increased possibility of a 'working man' candidate being on the electoral slate. The first appearance of such a candidate was in the election for the first School Board in 1874, for which there was no property qualification, when John Lisle was spoken of as a working man candidate (Jennings, 1996). The next such candidate was the rather remarkable R. B. Short who stood for the Local Board of Health in 1892. Bob Short had been for many years a cartman with various concerns – at the time of the election, he had already been employed by the railway as a rolleyman/cartman for a considerable period. The *Hexham Courant* had the honesty to admit that it looked upon Short's candidature 'in the light of a joke' (*HC* 9.4.1892). But the joke was upon the paper, for Short received 996 votes – 331 votes more than the candidate with the next highest total. Plumping by his fellow workers obviously made a contribution to his success but it also seems likely that many property owners must have been persuaded to support Short's candidature. He continued in office through the transition to the Urban District Council, retiring in 1901.

For the first election for the Urban District Council in December 1894, R. J. Conkleton threw his hat into the ring as a working man candidate. He claimed to be such in his election address, expanding on the point in an open-air meeting in Gilesgate before about 200 people. Then he talked about the removal of a property qualification giving 'working men the privilege of sending their own representatives'. Conkleton was in favour of allotments, public baths and wash-houses. It was five years before he was elected to the Urban District Council and then he had difficulty in holding on to his seat for any length of time. Nevertheless, he made an impact on the proceedings of the Council.

The term 'working man candidate' was recognition that elected members were not representative of the population at large. Doubts about the wisdom of having one single electoral area surfaced at the 1908 election. One of the candidates, J.H.P Whitehead, in his election address, indicated his support for having the district divided into wards. He came bottom of the poll but the *Courant* took up the proposal:

> There is one thing the recent election has forced to the front, the necessity of the division of the division into wards. It was put in the forefront of his address by one of the candidates. It is not a new proposal but it has been in abeyance for sometime. The recent growth of the town and its somewhat varying character, makes the division of it into wards of suitable area a necessity (*HC* 11.4.1908).

On 3 August 1908, at a meeting of the Council, James Robb, the Chairman, proposed

> That this Council petition the Northumberland County Council to make an order under section 57 of the Local Government Act, 1888, dividing the Hexham Urban District into Wards, and also to make an Order, under the same section of the Act, increasing the number of members of the Council (*HC* 8.8.1908).

Robb himself seemed to feel that increasing the number of Councillors ('spread the running of the town on a few more backs') was much more important than division of the District into wards. However the seconder, Councillor Ross, was in no doubt of the advantages of the ward system, since it would give more direct representation and that would increase the interest of the ratepayers in the work of the Council. Councillor Ainsley was against the proposal, as it could be seen as a means of dividing the fighting power of the labouring and working class. After a somewhat desultory discussion, the motion was passed by five votes to three. Proposed details of the scheme came forward in November from the officials of the Council. They had cleverly divided up the District into four wards (Fig. 2), each containing between 428-441 occupiers. The scheme (which included the proposal that there should be three councillors per ward, increasing the total number to twelve instead of the present nine) was discussed by the Council in Committee and the final scheme, differing little from the initial proposal was unanimously approved by the Council on 23 November. The proposals then went forward to the County Council that approved them in November 1909, in good time for the elections to be on a ward basis the following year (*HC* 13.11.1909).

TABLE 7. *The occupations of members of the Hexham Local Board of Health and Urban District Council during the period 1854-1939.*

Occupation	1854-93	1894-1914	1919-1939
Solicitor	5	2	Baker
Gentleman	2	3	Saw mill manager
Builder	3	3	Entertainment caterer
Surgeon/doctor	3	1	Bank manger (2)
Veterinary surgeon	0	1	Motor proprietor
Manufacturer	1	0	Merchant
Farmer	4	0	Dentist
Butcher	0	2	Newspaper employee
Grocer	3	0	Bookseller and newsagent
Provision merchant	1	0	Draper
Wine and spirit merchant	1	0	Medical Officer of Health
Ironmonger	1	0	Railway inspector
Draper	3	0	Retired builder
Painter	3	0	Tailor
Decorator	0	1	Gentleman
Joiner	1	1	Builder & contractor
Plumber	0	1	Consulting engineer
Miller	1	0	Coal & coke merchant
Roper	1	0	Civil servant
Tanner	2	1	Accountant/gentleman
Skinner	1	0	Retired chemist
Woolstapler	1	1	
Printer	1	0	
Nurseryman	1	1	
Gardener	1	0	
Gas engineer	0	1	
Chemist	1	1	
Auctioneer	1	1	
Parliamentary Registration Agent	1	0	
Sheriff's Officer	1	0	
Rolleyman	0	1	
Herbalist	0	1	
Engineman	0	1	
Market Gardener, etc.	0	2	
Innkeeper	0	1	
Clerk	0	1	
Hydro manager	0	1	
Total	44	29	

Whatever the arguments which led to the establishment of wards, there is no doubt that, with time, the elected representatives increasingly no longer lived in the centre of Hexham. By the period 1938-9, the great majority were residing in the periphery of the town (Fig. 3).

Finally, it should be noted that contested elections did not take place every year. In the early days of the Local Board of Health there was a feeling that elections should be avoided because they were thought to be expensive and a drain on the rates. Thus, in the period between 1854 and 1871, there were only five elections (in 1857, 1862, 1863, 1865 and 1868). In all the other years the three candidates were returned unopposed. After 1871, uncontested elections became increasingly infrequent, though the two elections before the Second World War were not contested.

Board members and Councillors

The qualification for election to the Local Board of Health was that the person had to be resident within the district and owning real or personal property of a minimal value to be fixed by Order in Council or Provisional Order but not exceeding £1,000 total value or assessment for rating of £30. After the Local Government Act of 1894, there was no longer a property qualification – all that was necessary was for the person to be either a Parochial Elector or resident in the area for the previous twelve months and included women. Even after 1894, the working man candidate was however very much the exception. Table 7 lists the occupations of members of the Local Board of Health and the Urban District Council for three periods: 1854-93 (the period of the Local Board of Health), 1894-1914 (from the start of the Urban District Council until the First World War) and from 1919-39. The period during the War has been ignored because there were no elections after 1915. In the first period, shopkeepers are well to the fore – nine such became Board members. Also, almost all were either owners of businesses or self-employed. Uniquely, four farmers were elected. During 1894-1914, the occupations of the councillors are less easily classifiable. It is in the period, 1919-39, that significant changes are manifest (Table 7). There are now a good number of persons elected with what we would now describe as managerial experience, although, as in all three periods, there was a builder and a gentleman (almost certainly someone living off his own income).

The length of tenure of elected representatives as a population hardly changed throughout the whole period under consideration. Between 35.4% of the total elected number elected remained in office for 1-5 years, 36.5% for 6-10 years and 27.1% for 14-26 years (Table 8). In almost all cases they either retired or were defeated in the polls; a few died whilst in office. Those Board members and Councillors who were defeated in the polls very rarely sought to fight again. But a medal for persistence must go to Lawrence Allen, bank manager, who lived at Burncroft. He was defeated in 1919 before being elected for the Priestpopple Ward in 1920 for three years; defeated again in 1923 to be re-elected in 1924. He was out of office until he was re-elected for Priestpopple Ward in 1937, having failed in the elections of 1927, 1929, 1932, 1934, 1935, for those in 1932 and 1934 he stood in Hencotes Ward. Usually, if candidates stood again after being defeated, it was because they wanted to be on the Board or the Council and knew that in order to do this they might have to fight one or two elections before the electorate became better acquainted with them.

Table 8 shows that a select few were in office for periods from 16 to 32 years. Inevitably, for good or ill, they exerted considerable influence on the deliberations of the body to which they had been elected. Pride of place must go to John Ainsley who was a member of the Urban District Council for 32 years. There was only one break when he was defeated in the election in 1930 for Gilesgate Ward. He bounced back in 1931 and was still in office when he died in 1933. He was a man of independent mind who spoke briefly but cogently. Seemingly, he was a systematic canvasser (*HC* 7.4.1906).

TABLE 8. *A summary of the length of service of those elected to the Hexham Local Board or Health/Urban District Council. The dates in column one indicate the period in which an individual was first elected. Those whose length of service was greater than sixteen years are named.*

			Years		
1-5	**6-10**	**11-15**	**16-20**	**21-25**	**32**
Pre-1894					
16	16	6	3	3	
			R. Robson	M. Smith	
			W. Alexander	J. T. Robb	
			R. Stainthorpe	J. Lisle	
Total	**44**				
1894-1918					
11	10	4	2	1	1
			G. Ross	J. Dodd	J. Ainsley
			W. C. Rollingson		
Total	**29**				
1919-1939					
7	9	6	1		
			J. W. Dent		
Total	**23**				

Total number of members 96

Politics in local government

Nationally, as the 19th century developed, political parties became well established. As a broad approximation, we can take 1880 as a date when they were fully operational (James, 1978). Nevertheless, although parties in the modern sense had not been fully established by that date, allegiance to a particular political philosophy appears to have been present within the population of Hexham by the 1860s. It would to hard to believe that this was not so, given that two newspapers with an overtly political stance were established in Hexham during that decade, namely the Liberal *Hexham Courant* in 1864 and the Conservative *Hexham Herald* in 1866. Of course, parliamentary elections had been fought on party lines since at least 1832 but the size of the electorate was small. Though it gradually increased, it was only after the Representation of the People Act of 1884 that there was a step change in the number of voters, nationally doubling from

2.5 to 5 million (Wright, 1970). Not only were there more potential voters in Hexham but at a parliamentary election they became more in contact with the candidates consequent upon the Redistribution of Seats Act of 1885. Instead of two seats, North and South Northumberland, the County was divided into four (Berwick-upon-Tweed, Hexham, Tyneside and Wansbeck). Prior to 1885, the South Northumberland Division, containing Hexham, had been a two-member division. Also, on only one occasion (in 1880) had an election been contested. At all other elections since 1832, the two MPs – a conservative and a liberal – had been returned unopposed. After 1885 when the great majority of seats became one-member, elections in the Hexham Constituency were always contested, such that any party with a candidate was very actively involved.

Yet, in spite of undoubted party activity in Hexham at Parliamentary elections, there is little demonstrable evidence of this permeating activity at the local government level. The only evidence that has come light that it took place, was in 1894, prior to the election for the new Hexham Urban District Council. Then we learn from editorial remarks in the *Hexham Courant,* which also deprecated the introduction of 'politics' into the election, that

> Conservatives have had many meetings and, we have heard, many squabbles with the result that the town is shortly to be flooded with polling cards bearing the names of candidates who the Conservative party...... have decided to put forward.

In view of this, it is surprising to find that, in the same paper (*HC* 8.12.1894), in the several election addresses, all candidates essentially saying that they hope to be of benefit to the community. All are keen to indicate that they are against unnecessary expenditure. None mention their political affiliations. Furthermore, the Liberals appear to have felt differently from the Tories. Prior to the election, the Hexham Local Liberal and Radical Association had met and had unanimously agreed the following resolution: 'That the approaching elections for the urban and rural district councils be not contested by the local Liberal party on political lines'.

Finally, it is apposite here to turn to that period, described in Part II, when the Local Board of Health was riven by those disputes concerning the provision of a better supply of water. While those who were members of the Liberal Party tended to be those who wanted to spend money on improving the water supply, there were two, Thomas Stainthorpe and Thomas Welford, almost always sided with those who wanted financial restraint. In contrast, one of the strongest voices in favour of improvement was Dr Daniel Jackson, a member of the Conservative Party, as was Lewis Lockhart, who for the short time he was on the Board could be considered a member of the 'clean' party. Further, it is often not easy to tell from voting behaviour to which party a member belonged.

Almost without exception, throughout the period 1854-1939, election addresses were almost uniformly anodyne, similar in kind to those, as described above, put forward in 1894. There is no better illustration than the election address of J. H. Bainbridge, railway clerk living at 'Balmoral' Elvaston Park Road in the 1939:

Hexham Urban District Bye-Election
To the Electors of the Priestpopple Ward

Ladies and Gentlemen,

In presenting myself as a candidate in the forthcoming bye-election, I wish to state that I stand for a basis of absolute honesty without compromise, and my task, if elected, would be to endeavour to lift the level of all proceedings and all policy above personal ambition, prejudice and party interest. I believe in the extension of social, educational and recreative amenities and town improvements and would support all such schemes consistent with a reasonable rate.

If chosen to serve, it will be my endeavour jealously to guard your interests and ensure that full value is received for every penny spent.

Bainbridge was elected with a majority of 85 in a three-cornered fight, 65% of the electorate voting (total 1,558).

One reason for the apparent lack of any party political activity with respect to local government elections would have lain with the fact that the electorate were the ratepayers. It seems very likely that such persons would probably belong to more homogeneous group than the bulk of the population. Certainly, circumstantial evidence, such as letters to the *Courant*, indicates that the concern of ratepayers was for financial probity in local government and law and order rather than party political initiatives.

The workings of the Local Board of Health/Urban District Council

From its inception the Local Board met fortnightly; the Urban District Council changed to a monthly cycle after 1910 (*HC* 6.8.1910). After 1864, much of the details of the business of the Board and the Council were dealt with in committee.

Initially, there were three committees – Finance, Sewerage and Highways and Lighting. Finance continued on as such until 1939. The other two disappeared in 1877 to be replaced by committees whose names changed according to the pressures on the elected body (Table 9). A Health Committee, probably a result of the report of John Hodgson on *The Sanitary State of Hexham*, was formed in 1877. Like the Finance committee it remained in being until 1939. When Tyne Green came into the possession of the Local Board, a committee was formed to develop it as a park. Then, when the Seal was leased by the Board, the Tyne Green and Mill Islands Committee was renamed as the Pleasure Grounds Committee. Three other committees merit a mention. When the Urban District Council took over the Cemetery from the Burial Board in 1911, a committee was established to run it. The Allotments Committee was established in 1917 following government pressures to grow more food during the First World War and, in 1934, the Establishment Committee was created to oversee the increasing number of staff on the payroll.

The operation of the committees, in many instances, was governed by the presence of byelaws. The first byelaws produced were based on those of Penrith Local Board of Health (NRO/PHU/A1/1). The details of these have not come to light. The Public Health Act of 1875 almost certainly provided, through its detailed consideration of all sanitary matters in the broadest sense, the framework for the type of byelaw that functioned at the end of the 19th century. Copies of notices are available that have been sent to owners of property fronting onto a street not 'levelled, paved or chanelled' requesting them 'in pursuance of The Public Health Act, 1875' to have this done 'to the satisfaction of the Urban District Council'. The first set of byelaws that we know about are those produced in the period 1885-1900. By end of that period, there were byelaws with respect to new streets and buildings, street cleaning, common lodging houses, pleasure grounds, dairies, cowsheds and milk shops and suchlike (NRO/B2/A1). Also at that time County byelaws started to make an appearance with a set for 'Locomotives'. From time to time byelaws were modified.

TABLE 9. *The history of the development of two committees – column one (Works Committee) and column 2 (Pleasure Grounds, Fire Brigade & Transport Committee) – that were in place in 1939 and column 3 (Lighting & Fire Brigade Committee) that was in place in 1931 but subsequently disbanded.*

Date	1	2	3
1877	Works Highways & Sewerage Committee		Gas & Lighting Committee
1885		Tyne Green & Mill Islands Committee	
1896		Pleasure Grounds Committee	
1899		Pleasure Grounds, Tolls & Market Committee[1]	
1900			Lighting & Fire Brigade Committee
1905	Works Committee		
1931	Incorporates Lighting Committee	Committee present in 1939 established	Lighting & Fire Brigade Committee disappears
1939	Works Committee	Pleasure Grounds, Fire Brigade & Transport Committee[2]	

[1]Tolls & Market Committee, originally separate, established in 1889

[2]Arose from the Horse Committee

Byelaws were, for the most part, uncontentious; they were an important part of the armoury by which sanitary improvements came about. Nevertheless, in 1895, two solicitors, George Dixon and Thomas Welford, separately wrote to the Local Government Board complaining that rule 54 of the bye-laws was not being adhered to (NA MH12/9067). That rule stated that

> Every person who shall erect a new domestic building shall provide in front of such building an
> open space, which, measured to the boundary of any lands or premises immediately opposite,

or to the opposite side of any street, which may not be less than twenty-four feet in width at the point where such building may front……

Dixon suggested a large number of recent buildings, such as the alms-houses at the bottom of Hallstile Bank, Robb's new shop and the *Courant* offices failed rule 54. But his ire was focussed on the plans for the erection of a bank (then for the Carlisle and District, now HSBC) where Fore Street joins Cattle Market for which 'the plans do not show any lateral space as required by rule 54'. Welford, as the reader will learn, wrote in customary intemperate style but in the process indicated that it was a personal interest in the matter ('my property opposite the proposed New Building') rather than 'the much dissatisfaction' amongst 'electors and owners' that prompted the letter. London refused to be involved citing that the complaint did not come within the scope of rule 299 of The Public Health Act of 1875. The matter was discussed by the Urban District Council, when Councillor Short observed that 'Mr Dixon's grievance seems to be that the Works Committee would not sanction his two shops down Meal market' (*HC* 7.9.1895).

The Board or Council could itself be agreed to be a committee in order to discuss confidential matters, the press and public being no longer privy to the proceedings.

Meetings of the Local Board and Urban District Council

On 1 May 1854, the Local Board of Health approved byelaws for 'regulating business'. There are no details of what are now called standing orders for the operation of the Local Board of Health. On the other hand, there is a copy of the Standing Orders that were produced when the Urban District Council was formed in 1894 (NRO/LHU/B2/A1). On the whole, Councillors and Board Members abided by the standing orders. But occasionally proceedings got out of hand. Thus, when debating the replacement of Ralph Robson, a member of the Board who had died in March, William Taylor took up the cudgels in ungentlemanly fashion on behalf of Thomas Cooke, a proposed replacement who, it had been decided, should not be allowed because the correct procedures had not been followed (*HC* 4.5.1878):

> Mr Taylor said that the motion appointing Mr Cooke required no notice because they all knew that Mr Robson was dead. Mr Cooke's election did not suit the books of certain parties and they tried to upset that motion. It was an ungracious act on the part of the Chairman [Mr Moffatt], who was almost the youngest member of the Board. They all knew that Mr Moffatt was pitch-forked on to the Board when he first got a seat upon it. ("Order order.")
> Mr Ridley: It is shameful.
> Mr Alexander: And it is disgraceful to interrupt a member.
> The Chairman: Mr Taylor is not using Parliamentary language; that word ought not to be used.
> Mr Taylor (warmly); I will not be interrupted. I say the present Chairman was pitchforked –
> Mr Catherall: That is not proper Language.
> Mr Ridley: We cannot allow that.
> Mr Taylor: Will you not.
> Mr Catherall: Mr Moffatt was elected by the votes of the members of the Board.
> Mr Taylor then gave a list of the number of votes given for himself, the late Ralph Robson, Mr Moffatt, and other gentlemen on several occasions when he had been elected to the Board, and then proceeded to say that the motion that evening [to elect Joseph Wray to the vacancy] was

disgraceful and an unparalleled act of impertinence in bringing it forward.
[*later in the proceedings*]
Mr Taylor again rose to speak when
The Chairman reminded him that he had already spoken, and other members ought to have an opportunity of speaking.
Mr Taylor still persisted in standing upon which
Mr Lockhart said he must object to Mr Taylor again speaking.
Mr Taylor: I have the right to reply.
The Chairman said that except the mover, any member could only speak once, except in explanation or in answer to a call from the Chairman. No member had the right to speak twice.
Mr Taylor: I shall maintain my right. Mr Lockhart has made an attack on me.
Mr Ridley: We must support the Chairman.
Mr Taylor was allowed to read the sections from the Act of Parliament, but on proceeding to make some observations,
The Chairman called him to order, and said he would not allow him to make a second speech.

The Board and later the Urban District Council were collectively both able to get over these spats. More important were those controversies into which both bodies could get enmeshed, generating much heat to little effect, the controversy over the water supply being an outstanding example. But there were others, a fine example being the controversy concerning the access to water at Whetstone Bridge. It all started in a seemingly innocent manner when the County Surveyor, J. A. Bean, wrote on 28 April 1906 to the Urban District Surveyor, that Mr Grant, manager of the Hydro and who was a member of the Council, was fencing in the land by the east side of Whetstone Bridge, then an actual bridge over the Cockshaw Burn which widened into a large pool, ostensibly a public watering place for cattle. The Works Committee recommended that the Clerk write to Mr Grant requesting him not to interfere with a right of way. In a statement to the Council, Grant said

> I wish the public to understand I don't want the land. As to its being a watering place it has been a public tip all the time I have been there and that is twenty years before that. I am the only one that tidied it up and I defy any beast to get water there. No cow or beast has gone to get water since I bought the property. I bought the land and paid for it...... It [the burn] is simply an open sewer and I defy any living animal to drink there, besides I hold it has never been a public watering place (*HC* 19.5.1906).

By December the temperature of the debate started to rise with one member of the Council, Ralph Conkleton, declaiming 'We are here to protect the rights of the public and in this instance we are the custodians of the public' (*HC* 15.12.1906) In the following May, the newly elected Joseph Alexander had joined forces with Conkleton and they persuaded a majority of the Council that it should direct its employees to remove the fence and other obstacles to allow the public right of way. A proposal to treat with Grant put forward by James Robb was turned down (*HC* 18.5.1907).

Grant's response was to re-erect the railings to which the Council responded on a four to two (Robb and Grant) vote by ordering 'all obstacles' at the site to be removed (*HC* 7.9.1907). Then Grant served a writ on the Council 'for an injunction to restrain the Council from pulling down, etc. the fence at Whetstone Bridge plantation and for damages and costs'. An extraordinary meeting was called that was not helped by a bad tempered Joseph Alexander. From the beginning he appeared to know that the Clerk to the Council (William Pruddah) was not keen to be involved in acting on behalf of the Council in any forthcoming action. Indeed, he accused the Clerk of being a friend of Grant. The Clerk stated it was otherwise. Though the Chairman, Robb, was most concerned that the integrity of the Clerk had been called into question, Pruddah indicated that, after what had taken place, he did not want to be involved. The remainder of the meeting was rather a shambles. Though nothing was settled, one important piece of information arose and that was that Grant had offered the land to the County Council (who it was known were responsible for the bridge) so that the bridge could be widened and the corner improved (*HC* 19.10.1907).

This extraordinary meeting had very considerable consequences. By the following ordinary meeting, three days later, the Clerk had resigned. The next issue of the *Hexham Courant* (26.10.1907) contained two letters containing very strong criticism of the Council, one of being scathing of Joseph Alexander's performance:

> The conduct of this member, not only at the meetings a week ago, but on former occasions, is only equalled by his conceit and ignorance. There was a fine exhibition of the latter at Friday's meeting when this man, who is prepared to put everybody to right on any and everything, made remarks about the writ which has been served on the Council, remarks which an office boy of a month's standing would have ridiculed as the chatter of a street-urchin

Also in the issue, was the news that a deputation wished to meet with the Council to put a point of view on the whole affair. It was to contain 35 persons and was led by Thomas Ellis, who had been a member in the 1880s. It believed 'the present case involves no principle worth contending for' (*HC* 2.11.1907).

But the intransigents on the Council stood firm, even though there were more letters in the press strongly in favour of the matter being settled through Grant giving land for widening the road and a memorial to the same effect signed by 660-700 ratepayers (*HC* 28.12.1907). There the matter in formal terms seemingly held fire. However, on 9 April 1908, J. A. Bean, the County Surveyor, wrote to the Clerk of the Council (now Mr John A. Baty) with the following proposal

> I am going to make the suggestion to your Council that, provided Mr Grant relinquishes his claim to the ownership of the portion of the land coloured red on the enclosed plan for the future widening of Whetstone Bridge, would not the Urban Council be content and also give up their claim to the remainder. The new boundary line shown on the plan would provide for widening the bridge to 40 ft. and I think, so far as the highway is concerned, it would meet the requirements of the public for many years to come. The remainder of the ground is practically useless to the Urban Council, so far as I am able to judge (*HC* 18.4.1908).

This essentially was the end of the matter. Of course there were further negotiations but the end result was as J. A. Bean proposed. Though Councillor Conkleton attempted a rearguard action it was without avail (*HC* 16.5.1908). It is probable that the achievement of an agreement in Council was helped by the absence of Jos. Alexander, who did not stand for election in April of that year.

In general, the Board and Council behaved well. It mostly moved slowly and with caution, partly because it was conservative by temperament but also because there was often little financial leeway for making big advances. But occasionally, caution was misplaced, as was the initial decision not to purchase the Abbey Grounds. With the 1914-1918 War, the Council became more positive in its decision-making as will be explained in Chapter18.

CHAPTER 4

Finance

Rates

Our starting point is the Poor Law Act of 1601 (43 Eliz. I, c. 2) that gave the parish registry the responsibility of administering relief. Section 1 of this Act imposed the liability to be rated on 'every inhabitant, parson, vicar and other of every occupier of lands, houses, tithes appropriate or propriations of tithes, coal mines, or other saleable underwoods', provided that the churchwardens of the parish, together two to four substantial householders, depending on the size of the parish, act as overseers of the poor by whom the rate was to be made (Crew, 1926). By the Act local rating had three distinctive features
1. The parish was the unit of administration for the purpose of the relief of the poor until 1925.
2. The relief of the poor was almost the only service for which rates were raised.
3. The overseers were the principal rating authority in every parish empowered to tax the inhabitants in such competent sums as they deemed fit.

The Poor Law Amendment Act 1834 (4 & 5 Will. IV, c. 76) transferred the duties of relief to boards of guardians elected by ratepayers annually. It must be stressed that the poor rate was not a charge on land, but a personal charge in respect of the land, i.e. on the occupier. This did not preclude the rates on a property being paid by the owner, e.g., this could be the case when tenants of houses or cottages were too poor to pay.

Property was the basis of assessment for the collection of rates for poor relief. The 1601 Act vested the whole responsibility for the administration of relief on the overseers. However, later Acts treated the vestry as the responsible body, since it was responsible for the appointment of overseers (Keith-Lucas, 1952). The parish vestry had originated as a meeting of parishioners to discuss Church business. Other responsibilities had been given to the vestry by statutes and custom, such as maintenance of the highways, suppression of nuisances, appointment of a constable and many others. This was so for Hexham (*see* Chapter 1), with the administration of the Poor Law dominating the proceedings of the vestry. Not surprisingly, since the rate burden was tied to property, it was the owners of property who were the decision-makers. Having made that point, it is not certain whether the right to attend vestry meetings belonged to all householders or all ratepayers. However, what is certain is that in the 18th century the poor rate became more burdensome. The majority of parishioners were willing to vote for generous relief if it meant that the most prosperous were to foot the major part of the bill.

With the new century, changes were to take place. In 1807, Samuel Whitbread, the brewer, introduced a Bill aimed at correcting the natural preference of the majority of the vestry for generous relief and heavy taxation of the minority of ratepayers. He proposed that a person 'assessed in a certain sum should have two votes, and in certain other larger sum, three votes and the largest four' (Keith-Lucas, 1952). The Bill not only failed but the clause proposing plural voting was withdrawn at the committee stage. However, eleven years later, the principle of plural voting by which the number of votes available to a voter was dependent upon his contribution to the rates was accepted. Following the findings of a Select Committee set up in 1817 under the Chairmanship of William Sturges, two Acts (58 Geo. III, c. 69 and 59 Geo. III, c. 12) were passed by Parliament concerned with parish vestries. They tend to be considered as one Act. When it was placed on the statute book, the Act regulated the procedures for running a vestry. It also established the procedure to be used in meetings.

Inhabitants rated at less than £50 were to have one vote; those rated at more than £50 were to have a vote for every £25 up to a maximum of six votes. Though the Act was generally unpopular, nevertheless plural voting was to continue as the basis for voting not only in the vestry but also for electing persons to such bodies in Hexham as the Local Board of Health and the Board of Guardians. As the 19th century progressed, the numerical scale for voting, based on the amount of rates paid, changed commensurate with increasing prosperity and changes wrought by increased inflation.

Having concentrated so far on the need to raise revenue for poor relief, we need to keep in mind that the County of Northumberland was also able to levy a rate. This power was first granted to the Justices by the Statute of Bridges (22 Henry VIII, c. 5) in 1530. It enabled the magistrates to summon all the parish constables of the county to a meeting. The magistrates could then, with the assent of this meeting, levy the necessary rate. In the following year, the Statute for Gaols (23 Henry VIII, c. 2) provided for the maintenance of gaols. Later rates also covered the salaries of officers, the expense of criminal prosecutions, conveyance of prisoners to gaol, coroners' inquests and provision of asylums (Taylor, 1989). The various taxes were consolidated in 1738, the Justices making the rate at the Quarter sessions – but without the assent of the representatives of the parishes.

Not only was there taxation without representation, but also there was a lack of transparency in accounting for the money raised. T. P. Dods, of Anick Grange, stated in a letter written in April 1870 to the *Daily News* that was also published in the *Hexham Courant*

> There is no law compelling an audit of the county accounts, and the magistrates of this important county (Northumberland) do not submit their accounts to an independent auditor, and there is no publication of their accounts, further than laying them on the table of the grand jury at sessions and sending a copy to the high constable (an office, by-the-bye, which should be abolished). The magistrates are an altogether irresponsible body, disbursing funds to which they do not contribute, and rendering no account of their intromissions to those who supply the funds (*HC* 26.4.1870).

On top of all this there was the increasing cost of county activities. At the start of the 19th century the costs accruing to the Justices were rising at a rate that was alarming to the bulk of the ratepayers, namely the occupiers of land. Keith-Lucas (1952) gives a measure of this rise – the cost of prosecutions in 1792 being £33,207, in 1832 it was £149,398, an increase of 359% in 40 years. Some help came from the Government in the form of grants initiated in 1832. The problems associated with county rates were resolved with the Local Government Act of 1888 (51

& 52 Vict., c. 41) and the County Electors Act (51 & 52 Vict., c. 10) that led to the formation of County Councils. From then it was the County Council that, in financial terms, became the major provider of services for those in Northumberland. Though the County was involved in education essentially from the start through its Technical Education Committee, it was the Education Act 1902 (2 Edw. VII, c. 42) that led to education becoming by far the biggest item in the Council's budget (Taylor, 1989). Roads were another very significant but insidiously increasing element in the Budget. Even before the Council was established, the Justices were responsible, not only for bridges but also for all those roads that had become disturnpiked since 1873 and which had, by statute, become main roads. By 1895 there were 563 miles of roads designated as main roads in Northumberland. As will be seen in Chapter 16, having roads designated as such was a way of reducing Hexham's financial burden. Not surprisingly, the county rate eventually outpaced those levied by the Guardians and Hexham Urban District Council. In 1890 the expenditure of the County was £66,000; in 1929, before taking over the functions of the Guardians it was £1,167,162 (HC 12.10.1929). The poor-rate and the county rate were collected as a combined sum. After 1929, the poor rate was assimilated into the county rate.

The making and levying the poor-rate was the chief duty of the 'overseers of the poor'. In Hexham the Vestry nominated the overseers, one for each of the four wards. The issue of 21 March 1885 of the *Hexham Courant* gives a lengthy description of the proceedings of a meeting leading to the nomination of J. S. Moffatt (Priestpopple), John Lisle (Hencotes), Jos. Johnson (Gilesgate) and E. Riddle (Market Street). The meeting also dealt with a considerable amount of business concerned with the activities of the overseers. Overseers were responsible to the Guardians. Though an overseer could be helped by an assistant overseer and payment was made to a collector, his job was not an easy one, as indicated by the Chairman of the above meeting

> Any one who had served in that office knew very well that there were more kicks than half-
> pence to be had. There was a good deal of trouble connected with the office, and they often
> came in for a fair share of ill will, as it was almost impossible to please everyone.

The impression that one has now is that increasingly the collection of poor rates was embedded in legal complexity. If one inspects *Hadden's Overseers' Handbook* one finds there are 19 pages of closely printed statutes as a prelude to 435 pages that are the guide proper (Dumsday, 1906).

Until well into the 19th century, the overseers were responsible for the valuation lists on which rates were assessed. The Union Assessment Committee Act of 1862 (25 & 26 Vict., c. 103) created the assessment committee consisting of 12 guardians and making it responsible for the valuation lists. The Committee, with the consent of the Guardians, might appoint some person to revise the existing valuation or make a new valuation. It is interesting to look at one example of this process. At the end of 1875, the Guardians of the Hexham Union decided to empower the Assessment Committee to employ a professional valuer to make a new valuation of the 'the rateable hereditaments [any property capable of being inherited] in the township of Hexham. It was sixteen years since the last valuation, then it totalled £15,000, at the start of 1876 it was £23,000 (*HC* 1.1.1876). Three weeks later, the position of external valuer was advertised in the *Hexham Courant,* whoever was appointed would have to examine between 1,100 and 1,200 assessments. Mr T. P. Dods of Anick Grange was appointed. The valuation was completed in 1879, seemingly not to the satisfaction of the Local Board of Health, which asked the Union Assessment Committee to reconsider the valuation 'on the ground of the great and continuing depression of Trade'. That dissatisfaction continued following a request from the Union Assessment Committee to the overseers asking for a new valuation list to be prepared and submitted to the Committee by 30 June 1880. There was a meeting of ratepayers to consider their position. The first part of the meeting generated a lot of hot air together with some degree of confusion as to what was happening. It was the Clerk to the Local Board of Health, Isaac Baty, who brought clarity to the situation, when he pointed out that the Hexham overseers had signally failed to take action for producing a new revised list in which inequalities were put right. Further the overseers needed help from the ratepayers. There was clearly lethargy all-round, not helped by a feeling that Hexham was over-rated. The net result was that the overseers were instructed to get on with the job and a committee of ratepayers was appointed to help the overseers. It is interesting to note that the valuation of the town was now £29,000 (*HC* 26.6.1880). One is left with the feeling that the procedures for assessing and collecting rates within the town were somewhat amateurish. Interestingly, it was only after 1882, that the overseers had any offices. Not long before that date, it seems that the overseers had had sometimes to transact their business in the Shambles (*HC* 6.5.1882).

With the passing of the Local Government Act of 1894 (56 & 57 Vict., c. 73), the powers, duties and liabilities of overseers for Hexham were transferred to the Urban District Council. This fact was brought to the attention of the Hexham Vestry in no uncertain terms by Alderman Stainthorpe

> It was a comprehensive section [in the Local Government Act] and included many important matters. One of these was the appointment of overseers and assistant overseers. He need scarcely say the meeting [of the Vestry] that appointed the overseers was a fossilised body, that would become almost extinct under the Local Government Act, and its days could not be very much lengthened. There was hardly any public notice given of this vestry meeting except the tolling of the church bell, and the meeting was held at one o'clock, a very inconvenient hour (*HC* 30.3.1895).

Interestingly, the overseers already had their offices in the Priestpopple building of the Urban District Council, the Vestry having agreed the move there from Thomas Ellis's building in Beaumont Street at the end of 1889 (*HC* 28.12.1898). The overseers were authorised to purchase a safe and furniture before making the move. The Urban District Council eventually took over the overseers in March 1896, appointing eight councillors as overseers; 'they were a representative body, they were supposed to know the requirements of the town, and they had in their possession a certain amount of information which did not come within the purview of men outside the Council' (*HC* 21.3.1896).

The consequence of the focus of local government on property not only as the source of money for the proper running of institutions but also on the manner of voting either in the deliberations of the Vestry or in the election of those to serve on the Board of Guardians and the Local Board of Health meant that the needs of the ratepayers could take precedence over the needs of others in the community. In all probability, those who paid the highest rates could be favoured because of the number of votes at their disposal. There is no doubt that the perceived rate burden played an important role in decision-making in the town. A number of examples of this can be found in other parts of the text. The many in Hexham in 1853 who were opposed to the formation of a third tax-raising body, namely the Local Board of Health is a reminder of a very significant example. It was only with the Representation of the Peoples Act 1918 (7 & 8 Geo. V, c. 64) that the payment of rates as a qualification for the vote disappeared.

On 1 April 1927, as a result of the Rating and Valuation Act of 1925 (15 & 16 Geo. V, c. 90) all the powers and duties of the overseers in Hexham in relation to the 'making, levying and collection of rates' was transferred to the Urban District Council, which became the rating authority. In 1929, the Hexham Board of Guardians was abolished and its function transferred to the Public Assistance Committee of the County Council, though the underlying structure was very similar. Public Assistance became a major financial burden on the county rates, particularly with rise of unemployment in the first years of the 1930s.

Spending and borrowing

Preamble This section concerns the period 1854-1914. Firstly it is based on the figures and balance sheets found in ledgers of the Local Board of Health/Urban District Council (NRO/PHU/A2 & NRO/LHU/C1). Second, all figures have been rounded up/down to the nearest pound. Third, financial years are denoted by the year of start, e.g. 1877-8 has been denoted as 1877. Fourth, in my considerations of Board/Council expenditure, I have been forced to ignore much of the information for the first twenty years, as there are no complete balance sheets of income and expenditure and income has been categorised under headings different from those in the following period. Ledgers for the years 1891-4 and 1903-15 are missing.

There were four sorts of rates in Hexham. – those levied to pay for the functioning of the Poor Law Union, that for the support of County activities and a general rate and a water rate both levied by the Local Board of Health. The first two have been discussed above. The water rate went solely to financing the water supply and sewerage system. It is the general rate that is of concern here.

Hexham Local Board of Health, from its very start, did not have a great deal of money to play with. There were a number of reasons for this. The relatively small population gave a small rateable base, which was exacerbated by the relatively low rateable input from commercial activity. As I have indicated elsewhere, the Local Board was averse to raising the rates, feeling right from the outset the rates were already too large a burden on the ratepayers. Whether this was true or not is a very difficult question to answer. What we really want to know is the financial background of individual ratepayers and I have been unable to think of a simple way to obtain the necessary information. Examination of wills is one way forward. However, it would be difficult, even if it were a matter discovering the amount of a person's wealth in terms of £.s.d., but, in Hexham, as elsewhere (Davidoff & Hall, 1987), many of those with disposable money invested it in property. Descriptions in the local press of property auctions make interesting reading from the point of view of the various local worthies who took part in the bidding. Details of anyone's property investments are likely to be difficult to track down today. As well as all this, inefficiency in rate collection, particularly in the first decades of the life of the Local Board, meant that frequently it had much less money from rates to play with than might be expected knowing the property valuations of all the ratepayers.

TABLE 10. *A comparison of expenditure by Hexham Local Board of Health for the years 1878 and 1888 and by the Urban District Council for the years 1898 and 1903 together with the income from rates for the same years.*

Item of expenditure	1878	1888	1898	1903
Sewerage		125	319	218
Street improvement	46	277	84	166
Scavenging and watering	417	357	668	436
Repair of highways		289	382	723
Lighting	200	183	351	411
Pleasure grounds		61	173	250
Fire Brigade		16	17	14
Town Clock			10	10
Election expenses	31	20	28	6
Law charges	233	89	29	713[c]
Salaries	213	273	413	453
Tradesmen's bills		104		
Instalments of loans	?	926	414	586
Interest on loans	?	405	213	200
Temporary water supply		86		
Sewage disposal			720[a]	49
Removal of refuse				327
Isolation hospital			456	371
Infectious diseases prevention			121[b]	160
Public conveniences				131
New horses, carts, etc.				128

a, septic tank
b, small pox
c, includes Parliamentary expenses

Money from rates	1572	3157	4549	6030

In the 19th century, most of the money coming to the Local Board and subsequently the Urban District Council was in the form of rates. However, as the decades passed, small amounts of money increasingly came from other sources. In 1898, for instance, £58 came from market tolls, £63 from the use of the pleasure grounds and £19 from the sale of manure (from scavenging and the Council stables). As well, Northumberland County Council paid £78 to the Council for scavenging and watering the main roads plus £75 towards the salaries of the medical officer of health and the inspector of nuisances. But the above amounts were trifling compared to £4549 collected as rates.

Essentially, as can be seen from Table 10, the money coming from rates went on maintaining services. Up to 1878, the services supported by the rates were limited, confined as they were to keeping the highways clean and reasonably maintained, street lighting and election expenses (a small sum of £31). Necessary for the maintenance of these services were the recurrent costs of the officers' salaries and legal charges. Ten years later, little had changed with respect to the services that were supported. However, in 1888, there is the first indication the general rates might be spent on a wider range of services. That financial year saw the expenditure of £61 under the heading of pleasure grounds, expenditure no doubt triggered off by the acquisition of Tyne Green and Mill Islands the previous year. Expenditure under the same heading increased in the following fifteen years.

Indeed over the next fifteen years the general rates covered a much wider range of expenditure, that was not necessarily recurrent, e.g., £750 spent on a septic tank in 1898. Similarly, the isolation hospital was completed in August 1898 (*HC* 20.8.1898), with £456 going towards its construction (Fig. 5). Public toilets were erected in 1903 in Priestpopple (no longer there) and on the Seal (still present) and which were opened in August (*HC* 27.7.1903 for a description) and the £131 under the heading public conveniences must relate to these two new toilets. The expenditure of £128 in 1903 on new horses and carts for use by the Surveyor must also come under the category of non-recurrent expenditure. On the other hand, new items of recurrent expenditure were taken on board, such as £327 on removal of refuse in 1903.

Finally, the greater the availability of money meant it became increasingly easier to deal with unforeseen, one-off items of expenditure. In 1898, £121 was spent combating an outbreak of small pox. On 25 May 1898, a family of four were admitted to the fever ward of the Workhouse on account of one of them having the disease. Three days later a woman with the disease was also brought there (*HC* 4.6.1898). Some of the money spent on combating the disease can be accounted for as follows in the following report of the Council's Works Committee:

> Small pox cases
> Mr Charlton be offered £25 in settlement of his claim of £66.15s.6d for clothes, etc., destroyed by the Council to prevent the spread of infection. This is in addition to £13.11s.6d spent on new bedding, clothes, etc., in place of those destroyed.
> Mr Urwin be offered £20 in payment of his claim for wall-paper-hanging for the two rooms where the paper was taken off.
> It is also recommended that notice be served upon the owner of Mr Urwin's house to strip and repaper any further rooms which may, in the opinion of the medical officer be thought necessary to prevent any further spread of infection (*HC* 23.7.1898)

The inclusion in the 1898 figures of the expenditure of £10 on the town clock demands amplification. The clock, of course, is that of the Abbey. At some stage, it seems the Local Board of Health were given the management of the clock (*HC* 13.8.1870). While the Board had made payments for repairs such as re-gilding the dials in 1875 (*HC* 27.11.1875), later, in 1883, it became clear that the Board could not pay someone to look after clock, otherwise the Board would be surcharged. On the other hand, it could provide a clock for the town and also keep it going (at the time the clock 'had been stopped for last eight or nine days') and in proper order. Given the concern of the Board to have a properly functioning clock in the town, it had the power to lease the Abbey clock from the churchwardens to be used as the town clock (24.3.1883). Agreement reached between them and the Local Board that the latter would lease the clock for one shilling on a yearly basis and also clean, repair and maintain it. This arrangement did not seem to work; it appears that the churchwardens wanted the responsibility of keeping the clock going. So, in 1888, the lease was raised to £10 a year to allow this to take place (HLBH 8.10.1888) – hence the item in the accounts (though the actual initial payment is in the 1889 accounts).

So far I have ignored consideration of what was clearly a major item of expenditure the servicing of loans raised by the Board for capital expenditure. During the period 1882-90, loan instalment and interest was at least 30% of the available income, indeed it could be as high as 47%, as was the case in 1887. (Fig. 4). Subsequently, the percentage dropped to no more than 20% in the period 1897-1903. The high proportion of income going on servicing loans was a consequence of the Local Board of Health in 1864 borrowing, on the security of the rates, £12,000 from the Atlas Assurance Co. for meeting the cost of constructing a better water supply for the town (HLBH 1.2.1864). Taking that loan on board left the Board with little room for manoeuvre financially. The situation was exacerbated by the fact that nine members of the Board had already signed a promissory note for £1,000 to get the construction work started; they needed to be paid back. In 1869, the Board was forced to advertise in the *Hexham Courant* for a loan of £650 for that repayment (*HC* 16.2.1869). William Wear was willing to loan the money for seven years at '£4.9s per cent per annum'. Subsequently the Board again advertised for loans. By 1876, the general loan account stood at £5,500. No details are available as to how that sum was made up but we know from the account figures for 1878 (£4,875) that it was made of loans of from £100 to £650 from those living in and around Hexham. There were eleven such loans in 1878.

By 1900, the loan burden was as follows – the major loan was £10,000 from the Prudential Assurance Co. with £10,840 in ten smaller loans, by far the largest being a loan of £2,510 from the Corporation of Burton upon Trent. Although the burden brought about by borrowing as a percentage of the rates gathered in had been reduced by the time Hexham entered the 20th century, there had been no proportionate reduction in road expenditure. Nevertheless, as I have indicated, there was more money for other items of current expenditure. That was because the rate income had been increasing from 1895 onwards (Fig. 4). This increase was not brought about as a result of the amount levied. Between 1893 and 1907, the general district rate stood at 1/6 in the £ for almost every half year (23 in total). There were eight exceptions to this: 1/4 in the £ for two half years (1895), 2/- (1898), 1/10 (1899) and 1/9 (1904) each for one half year, 1/8 for one half year in 1904 and two in 1905. The most likely explanation lies in the boom in new house building that took place around 1890 and continued until the 1914-18 War, bringing many new persons onto the list of ratepayers. Though there was more money coming in from rates, that this was so did not stop many from feeling that they were paying more than they need. The initial vote within the Urban District Council against purchase of the Abbey Grounds is testament to that feeling.

Fig. 5 shows the location of those buildings, etc., funded out of the Urban District rates before 1914. All were built in the period after 1900. The Abbey Grounds were purchased in 1910 but private as well as public money was required for that purchase (*see* Chapter 14). The only other building built with a significant proportion of public money was the new Grammar School but it was the County Council that funded that project with a significant sum coming from the Shaftoe Trust (Jennings, 1999). When one looks at the list of buildings funded by the Urban District Council, it has to be said that, objectively, what is on the list is not of huge significance. What the list does illustrate is the limited room for capital projects allowed by the income coming from the rates. I have already pointed out from an analysis of the 1891 census that the town had at that time a poor rateable base (Jennings, 2000). Seemingly, the situation did not improve over the next twenty years. In 1913 Sir Thomas Oliver, Professor of Medicine at Newcastle, when addressing the Hexham Aid Association, spoke of the slums of Hexham being as bad as in any larger town (*HC* 15.11.1913). He pointed out that the Housing Act of 1890 gave sanitary authorities the power to erect workmen's dwellings. But money was needed. Sir Thomas indicated that to do this there was a need to attract industry to Hexham, If the Council were to have more money coming from the rates. As will be seen in Chapter 20, the specific problem of financing council-built housing was solved after the 1914-18 war by direct government financing. But it will also be seen that financing other activities from the rates was still to remain a problem.

CHAPTER 5

The Workhouse

Introduction

When the monasteries were flourishing, they were a vital agency for the care of the poor. With the dissolution of the monasteries, this agency disappeared. With the Poor Law Act of 1601 (43 Eliz. I, c. 2) their place was to be taken by a civil unit, the parish. This Act made the magistrates, churchwardens and overseers responsible for the care of the poor and empowered them to give relief to the impotent, find employment to the able-bodied and to bind out apprentices. Those responsible were able to levy a poor rate, while the magistrates could send anyone to the common gaol. It is not my purpose here to give the history of poor relief. For my purpose it is sufficient to say that by the start of the 19ᵗʰ century the law was in a confused state and developments had been such that the rates levied had become burdensome. In 1832, Parliament, in order to cope with the complicated issues that had evolved over time, set up a Royal Commission. It reported in 1834 (Checkland & Checkland, 1974).

In the event, the Report made a highly significant recommendation, namely that there should be a central authority to control the administration of the poor laws. Importantly, this central authority could empower the combination of several parishes into a poor law union. Locally, poor law relief was to be the responsibility of poor law guardians who represented the parishes of the union and who were elected by the ratepayers. Local registered magistrates became Guardians ex *officio*. The Guardians were to build a Workhouse with salaried staff that was to house those seeking relief and thus be placed in a position less desirable than that of a man of the same class earning his living.

The Report was acted upon with great speed. On 12 April 1834 a Bill was introduced which soon became law. The resultant Poor Law Amendment Act (4 & 5 Will. IV, c. 76) took on board many of the recommendations of the Report. From the point of view of local government in England and Wales, it established some important principles – regulation of local administration by a central authority, the principle of payment for the executive officers and the election of those responsible for the local administration (the Board of Guardians) by the ratepayers. Poor law unions were to be established. Such unions were an important development from the point of view of local affairs because they showed that the single parish could be replaced as a unit of local government. In rural areas, unions were to be centred on the local market town, as was to be the case for Hexham. One reason for market towns being selected as centres was that the Guardians could meet and transact business on the market day – the day on which private business would have naturally brought them together (Redlich and Hirst, 1958). Though not so frequently emphasised, the introduction of an audit was another important reform, particularly after 1840 when the salaries of Poor Law auditors were made a charge upon the state.

What follows is a description of the workings of the Poor Law in the Hexham Union. If one were to treat the development of the town as an historical sequence, this chapter should have come before that concerned with the mechanics of local government. I have positioned this chapter after the former to emphasise the secondary role of the Board of Guardians in the life of the town. That said, the Board had an important influence on the town, particularly through its expertise about matters of health. In what follows I have been heavily dependent on the lengthy and illuminating work by G. A. Cadman (1976) on the administration of the Poor Law Amendment Act in Hexham during the period 1836-1929. Throughout this chapter, I refer to indoor and outdoor relief. For the former, the pauper was taken into the Workhouse; for the latter, the able-bodied pauper received relief in the form of financial aid or provision of goods or services while still living in the outside community.

The Guardians

The Hexham Union was formally established on 22 October 1836. It consisted of 71 parishes and townships, essentially located north and south of the Tyne valley from Haydon Bridge and Allendale in the west; to Simonburn, Chollerton and Whittington in the north; to Horsley, Wylam, Prudhoe and Shotley in the east and Hexhamshire, Slaley, Healey and Shotley Low and High Quarters in the south. The total area was 197,050 acres. The smallest of the 71, Dilston, had a population of five in 1851, rising to 7 in 1871. Allendale was the largest having a population of 6401 in 1861 and 5397 in 1871 and Hexham a close second with 5270 in 1861 and 5331 in 1871. Valuations were carried out in 1852 and 1876, the total valuation rising from £144,178 (£4.19 per member of the 1852 population) in the former year to £275,154 (£7.99 per member of the 1876 population) in the latter year. It is very interesting to note that of 71 parishes and townships, Hexham (£4.35) was quite a poor relation in terms of the rateable value of its property per member of the 1876 population. Only Allendale (£3.65), Shotley High Quarter (£3.1), Hexhamshire West Quarter (£2.2), Horsley (£2.1), Humshaugh (£1.7), Newbrough (£1.6), Mickley (£0.95), Prudhoe (£0.6) and High Fotherley (£0.4) had lower rateable values. Of course, rateable value is not necessarily a good predictor of the amount of money that can be raised but qualitatively the figures do give a relative indication of the rate that it was possible to raise.

The number of Guardians was dependent on the population. Initially, Allendale had six, Hexham five, Corbridge and Haydon Bridge two each and all the remainder one Guardian each. There were two *ex officio* (county) justices, making a total of 76 Guardians (NRO/GME1). Later the number of Guardians was reduced to 73. That was a result of amalgamation of a number of parishes in 1886, each new district only having one Guardian. In 1877, the Vestry of Hexham had sent forward a request to the Local Government Board that the town should have its representation increased from five to ten

> So that it [Hexham] may be officially and fairly represented at Hexham Union Board of Guardians Meetings according to the rateable value of Hexham (the present rateable value of £28,226) and population. Hexham, being the great centre of population, wealth, enterprise and property in Hexham Union and as such is insufficiently represented

In view of the above, this paragraph represents somewhat of a delusion of grandeur. Be that as it may, the Local Government Board put off a decision leaving it to the following year when it was clear that there was a need for some parish amalgamations. In the event both Hexham and Allendale were each awarded one extra Guardian.

43

TABLE 11. *Composition of the Board of Guardian of the Hexham Union for the years 1863, 1869, 1875 and 1892*

Occupation	1863	1869	1875	1892
Agent	1	2		2
Auctioneer				1
Brewer	2		2	1
Brick and Tile Manufacturer		1		
Builder				1
Butcher		1	1	
Clerk in Holy Orders	4	5	4	6
Colliery owner	1		1	1
Contractor				1
Draper			1	1
Farmer	41	56	55	not available
Gardener		1	1	2
Gentleman	2	4	8	3
Grocer		1		
Hydropathic Proprietor				1
Innkeeper		1	1	
Lead manufacturer	1			
Merchant				1
Miller	4	3	4	
Miner				1
Mining Engineer				1
Paper Maker				1
Road Surveyor		1		
Smelting agent			1	
Solicitor	1	1		1
Surgeon	1			
Tanner				1
Viewer	1			
Woolstapler	1			
Yeoman	6	4	2	
Total	66	81	81	26
% farmers	62%	69%	68%	

Elections for Guardians took place annually on 7, 8 or 9 April. The procedure for elections was very similar for elections to the Local Board of Health with some differences, an important one being that voting by all owners of land who were not inhabitants of the parish could be by proxy. In rural areas, such a landlord appointed his agent to act on his behalf. In towns, many landlords put the task in the hands of rent collectors and estate agents, allowing them to acquire a considerable degree of power in the election of Guardians. Otherwise, the voting procedure was that used for elections of the Local Board of Health. Cadman (1976) was unable to discover the rating qualification for election in the Hexham Union. Nationally, the qualification seems to have varied between £15 and £40 (Odgers & Naldrett, 1913), it it needs to be noted that the actual figure was fixed separately by the Poor Law Commission for each Board of Guardians. Table 11 shows the composition of the Board for the years 1862, 1865, 1875 and 1892. Throughout the period farmers dominated the Board, their membership being between 60-70%. Over the thirty years there was a variable range of occupations amongst the Guardians, only Clerks in Holy Orders and gentlemen showing anything like constancy

As has been indicated, the Guardians were to meet on market day, which, for Hexham, was on a Tuesday and they met fortnightly (at the very start they met weekly on Mondays at 11.0 a.m.). In July 1884, the Board agreed to move the day of its meeting to Monday, since it became apparent that many Guardians, farmers in particular, were too preoccupied with market business. However, that didn't work either, as farmers were loath to leave their farms on Mondays as well as Tuesdays. Not surprisingly therefore, not only because of such a conflict of engagements but also because of the travelling distances for many Guardians, particularly from the outlying areas, attendance at meetings could frequently be spasmodic. For instance in 1890, only eleven Guardians had attended twenty or more meetings (none had attended the complete 27), whereas twenty had attended fewer than five meetings. Ten had never attended a meeting throughout the year. Thus much of the responsibility for the operation of the Poor Law in the Hexham Union rested on relatively few people.

At first, the Guardians held their meetings in the Vestry Room at the east end of the Abbey. On 14 February 1846, because the building was dangerous and unsafe owing to its dilapidated condition, the Clerk asked permission from the Commission for the Guardians to hold their meetings in the Court House at the south west of the Abbey. The magistrates had agreed, charging a rent of £10 per year. The Commission attempted to make the Guardians meet in the Workhouse but that attempt was successfully resisted; it was argued that the Workhouse was too far out of town for meetings. In 1890, there was a move to build a committee room at the Workhouse. This came to nothing because of cost. In 1897, the Guardians moved into the offices at the north end of what is now the Queen's Hall when Lambton's Bank moved into different premises. At first the offices were rented but in the following year they became the property of the Guardians.

Administration and Workhouse staff

The Clerk – This was the chief officer of the organisation, fulfilling a role similar to the Clerk to the Hexham Local Board of Health. As was the case with the latter, the Clerk to the Board of Guardians was a solicitor who performed all the tasks of the office on a part-time basis. Between 1836 and 1929, four men held the office: John Ruddock (1836-38), John Stokoe (1838-74), Isaac Baty (1874-93) and J. H. Nicholson (1893-1929). Both Stokoe and Baty were Clerks to the Local Board of Health. The post became increasingly onerous not only because of the increasing complexity of the work of the Guardians but also because, as a result of the Public Health Act of 1872 (35 & 36 Vict., c. 39) the Board of Guardians also took on the role of Hexham Rural Sanitary Authority. This responsibility lasted until the Local Government Act of 1894 (56 & 57 Vict., c. 73) led to the formation of the Rural District Council. As with the Clerk to the Local Board of Health, the Clerk to the Guardians not only dealt with very considerable paper-work (not only with internal and local affairs but also with the central authority in London) but was also the legal advisor to the

Board and, further, he dealt with other matters such as supervising the election of Guardians.

Workhouse Master and Matron – These two persons between themselves were responsible for the day-to-day welfare of all classes of indoor pauper. Between 1839 and 1929, the positions of Master and Matron were held by six married couples:

Mr & Mrs England	1837-1867
Mr & Mrs Jameson	1867-1893
Mr & Mrs Newton	1893-1902
Mr & Mrs Elsdon	1902-1913
Mr & Mrs Keenleyside	1913-1919
Mr & Mrs Thirwell	1919-1929

The Englands' stay in post was brought to an abrupt end by the appointment of a new porter in 1866. He made several charges against the master such that he was not sober on the job that he had moved material out of the Workhouse in a suspicious manner and that he allowed people through the gates without the porter knowing. The Guardians didn't trust the reliability of the porter and dismissed his accusations. But the suspicions of the Guardians must have been aroused. It became clear that England was keeping his own ponies on the premises and feeding them with Workhouse porridge. There may well have been other ways in which he had been defrauding the Guardians. Earlier the district auditor had registered discrepancies in England's bookkeeping. England resigned before an enquiry could take place.

Jameson seems also to have been involved in various irregularities, such as making purchases that were not properly authorised. He appeared to ride these out as he did with the several cases of illegitimate births in the Workhouse. There was concern also that he had been spending time on developing a Patent Earth Closet instead of giving his full attention to Workhouse business. But in 1892 Jameson met his downfall through ordering excessive amounts of food for Christmas Day's dinner and New Year's Day tea. The Guardians passed a resolution in May 1893 that stated that they no longer had confidence in their master. In anticipation, Jameson resigned. In needs to be stressed that in both the case of England and Jamieson, the Guardians had shown themselves to be very inefficient in overseeing the work of both Masters.

The succeeding masters and matrons appear to have been more honest, though only the Keenlysides appear to have been free from involvement in any kind of misadministration. Emma Keenlyside was obliged in November 1919 to resign as matron because of ill-health. The Guardians decided that, as the appointment had been a joint one, they had no choice but to terminate her husband's appointment. William England avoided termination of his appointment when his wife died in August 1847 by remarrying in March 1848. Jameson's wife died in 1869 but in this instance he was able to have his sister, Eliza Robson, appointed Matron.

The Porter – This could be quite an important post, because he was expected to supervise all comings and goings at the Workhouse and to be responsible for vagrants. The first porter, William Rowe from Newcastle Union Workhouse, didn't last long. He came in July 1847 but was dismissed in the December for being drunk, for bringing drink into the fever ward and given it to the pauper nurses and for using abusive language to the schoolmistress when he was drunk. He was followed by the longest serving porter, George Hogarth, who when appointed was 60. A hatter by trade, he was retired on a pension in 1866 with an apparently unblemished record. We do not have records of the post after 1916 but, up to then, there was a succession of men who proved in some way or other to be not up to the job or found the pay inadequate. The Hexham Guardians seem not to have treated the position as important. Also it seems that the duties that the porter was expected to carry out seemed somewhat unpleasant. In 1895 it was decided that the porter should act as undertaker at the Workhouse and then act as barber after the resignation in 1895 of the person who did the job full-time.

Assistant matron – A post established in 1887. It was probably an important position, because of the insistence of the central authority on the Workhouse having proper staff. However, we know little about the post, except that the 1891 Census reveals that Jane Lizzie Jameson, aged 24 and daughter of the Master was in the post.

School teachers – In 1841, there were 49 children in the Workhouse. Of these 38 were illegitimate. Seven of the children were orphans, four were girls deserted by their fathers, two were children of people dependent on poor relief on account of mental or bodily infirmity, four were the children of able-bodied widows resident outside the Workhouse and four were children of widows resident in the Workhouse. Throughout the period 1841-1929, the number of children in the Workhouse hardly varied between a maximum of 65 in 1847 and 1861 and in the 30s and 40s in 1920s and 30s. Initially, it appears that the children were educated at an endowed school. However in 1840, the Guardians appointed Jane Rawlings as schoolmistress, so that the education could be delivered within the Workhouse. In 1843, the Guardians tried to appoint Joseph Coats, a pauper with only one leg but having had some education at Haydon Bridge, as schoolmaster. The Poor Law Commissioners objected. Two years later the Guardians made another attempt to appoint Coats and this time they were successful.

Coats was to remain as schoolmaster at the Workhouse until his death in 1881. Throughout the period when he was teaching there was a succession of schoolmistresses. The turnover is not surprising in view of the fact that only a small salary went with the post and, although the schoolmistress got double rations she shared accommodation with the children. In one sense, the Guardians were lucky to have Coats for such a long period. However, his teaching can from all accounts be only described as fair.

When Coats died in 1881, the Guardians decided that all boys over twelve should be sent out to Hexham Board School. Mary Robson, the schoolmistress at the time, was teaching both boys and girls up the age of twelve. When she died, all children over six went to the Board School. Prior to 1881, children at the Workhouse were taught the three Rs and given religious instruction. The children were exposed to some other subjects such as geography and history but there is evidence that the children gained little benefit. In preparation for the world outside, boys were employed on the Workhouse farm and had on hand a tailor, shoemaker and joiner who could instruct them in their respective skills. The girls received training in knitting, sewing, general housework and laundry work, though it is to be doubted that their training would fit them for domestic service.

The two schools one for boys and the other for girls also contained dormitories. In the 1914-18 War, as the Union was obliged to make space for military use as hospital and barracks, the Hexham children were moved out to various other unions, eventually ending up in Warrington. Between 1919 and 1923, the Urban District Council made several attempts to obtain the school building to use as local authority housing. The Ministry of Health vetoed the idea. In 1926, the children returned to the Hexham Workhouse to renovated school buildings, which became known as Dean Street House.

Chaplain – In January 1840, the Rev. Henry Peters, curate of the church of St John Lee, was appointed chaplain at the Workhouse at a salary of £40 per annum. Before his appointment, Anglican paupers had been obliged to attend the Abbey. Those who were not Anglican were allowed to attend their own place of worship and they continued to do this after the appointment of the chaplain. Throughout the period from when Peters was appointed until 1929, there was considerable hostility towards a salaried chaplain. Though not much is known about the post, it was clear that the central authority thought that the Workhouse could not afford to be without the services of a chaplain. It seems also that the filling of the post alternated between an Anglican and a non-conformist.

Relieving Officers

> The virtual suppression of the unpaid and annually chosen Churchwardens and Overseers by the salaried Clerk to the Guardians and a staff of Relieving Officers was an outstanding feature of the Act of 1834 (Webb & Webb, 1963).

All those seeking relief normally approached a relieving officer as a first step to acquiring it. The relieving officer was the officer empowered to give instant relief in cases of sudden or urgent necessity, without the approval of the Guardians, and the recommendations made by this officer often determined the kind of relief awarded to the applicant. Though only a servant of the Board of Guardians and obeying its orders, the relieving officer was in the peculiar position of being answerable to the Criminal Courts for any refusal, or even any negligence by which a destitute person suffers death, or serious damage to health. The practical effect of this criminal liability was to strengthen the position of the relieving officer against a parsimonious or strict Board of Guardians that might seek to prevent relief in kind being given in cases of sudden or urgent necessity (Webb & Webb, 1963, p.236).

As far as other duties were concerned, the relieving officers were responsible for ensuring that all paupers entitled to outdoor relief received payment regularly and that such assistance as they were afforded was not abused. Later, they acquired other duties:
1. From 1876, they were made responsible for the collection of all monies owed to the Union by paupers and their families.
2. In 1877, they became school attendance officers in their respective districts where no School Board was in existence.
3. In 1878, they were appointed enquiry officers.
4. In 1882, they were empowered to bury all paupers who died between meetings of the Board of Guardians without obtaining its consent.

When the Hexham Union was formed, four relieving districts were created, each with its relieving officer. Those for the Hexham District were: James Fairlam (1836-67), John Wray (1867-75), G.A. Shield (1875-1906) and Matthew Atkin (1906-30). The Hexham district was very large (52,956 acres).and it had the largest number of outdoor paupers. Thus the relieving officer was under considerable pressure, particularly as the 20th century progressed. However, in the mid-twenties Atkin's work was made easier by the possession of a car. However, an injury in a car accident meant that, for a short time, he was unable to perform all his duties properly.

Buildings

The workhouse was central to carrying out the new Poor Law of 1834. Disquiet with the working of the previous regime was such that, amongst other matters of concern, overseers were believed to be profligate with the distribution of outdoor relief. The Poor Law Report condemned all forms of outdoor relief to able-bodied men, on moral as well as economic grounds insisting on 'the restoration of the pauper to a position below that of the independent labourer' This proposed policy of 'less-eligibility' meant that the living conditions of paupers in the workhouse would be rendered less comfortable than those of the self-sufficient poor. As well as there being a loss of privacy in the workhouse, its Spartan conditions and monotonous daily regime would make it less attractive to the poor than the hardest existence they could sustain independently (Morrison, 1999).

The main instrument for this new policy was to be the 'well-regulated' workhouse. It was to contain at least four classes of pauper each to be segregated from the others, namely the aged and impotent, children, able-bodied females and able-bodied males. Some Unions already possessed workhouses that could be adapted to separate each class of pauper. In the newly formed Hexham Union there were workhouses in Allendale, Corbridge, Haydon Bridge and Hexham. The Guardians calculated that they needed to provide accommodation for at least 150 paupers, particularly because the new system was bound to increase the number receiving relief within the workhouse. At first, the Guardians felt this could be achieved by using the Corbridge and Hexham buildings, though it was to be accompanied by imperfect separation. However, this plan did not meet with the approval of the Poor Law Commission and the Guardians were encouraged to find land at Hexham on which to build a new workhouse. The old workhouse, on the south side of Priestpopple approximately where Commercial Place is now located, was sold on 26 May 1840 for £400 to Thomas Pratt, builder (NA MH12/9040).

In February 1837 land for the new Workhouse was quickly found at Peth Head but somewhat complicated ownership legalities resulted in delays such that it was only in September 1838 that three-quarters of an acre was purchased and in October a plan for the building was agreed (Fig. 6). As one can see, the plan of the building, dated 1845 (but almost certainly differing little from the original plan), is essentially T-shaped. Interestingly, it might have been possible to use one of the model plans, issued by the Poor Law Commission, which favoured three or four regularly-arranged courtyards separated by buildings and with walls or other buildings on the outer perimeter (Morrison, 1999). From the outset, it was cramped and said to be cold with poor ventilation, though it is not clear why this should be so, since sash windows were installed from the very beginning. Not surprisingly, for several decades following, the buildings were extended and modified, sometimes in small ways, while at other times there were extensive alterations and construction of new buildings. Without plans, it is very difficult to establish where a particular alteration or rebuilding has taken place. Here, I present what appear to be salient changes:

1. In 1842 a plan for a two storey building containing four rooms was approved by the Poor Law Commission to used for cases of infectious diseases.

2. In 1843, the Guardians purchased two acres of land on the south side of the Workhouse and, in 1849, slightly more than two acres on the north side. They had also rented in 1853 five acres from the Revd. Joseph Hudson to the south-east side (Fig. 7). This latter land was farmed. In 1854, the year after it had been rented it was planted as follows – $3^1/2$ acres potatoes, $1/2$ acre turnips, $1/4$ cabbages and $3/4$ acre 'a few' vetches and mangel worsel.

3. In 1864, a new school building one half for the girls and the other for the boys was built on the two acres of land to the south of the main buildings (Fig. 7). The old schools were converted into sick wards.

4. In 1870, a new bakehouse was built in the women's yard, a mortuary in the cellar and an eight foot high wall supporting a lean-to roof along the west side of the dining room and the chapel of privies for both men and women.

5. In 1872, the accommodation for vagrants was increased; there was a further increase in 1879 and again in 1884. Also in 1872, new fever wards were erected on the land to the south of the main buildings

6. In 1878, five acres of land at the west end of the Workhouse were purchased from Wylam Walker. In 1879, the guardians appointed J. H. Morton of South Shields, who was responsible for the Workhouse building there, as architect (*The Builder* November 16 1886, p. 785). After much shilly-shallying, in 1882, plans were agreed with the architect that provided a porter's lodge, new dining hall and kitchens and a Master's House (Fig. 8). Also included in the new buildings was the provision of new vagrant cells and something like 50 extra beds. It is not possible, because the drawn out nature of the planning process makes interpretation difficult, to determine what number of the extra beds were for the sick. Also, we are left to suppose that the space for such beds became known as the infirmary (a term which was often used but without any clear location). While the building was going on the Guardians decided that a new mortuary be included in the programme.

7. Except for minor alterations of one kind or another (a major one being the addition of bathrooms in the Workhouse schools; there had been none for the children before), there were no further changes to the Workhouse until it ceased to be run by the Guardians in 1929.

8. It is known that the Workhouse had a chapel and an infirmary but I have not been able to find out when or exactly where they were built. I think that the infirmary and sick wards might well be synonymous.

By 1929, the Workhouse was in a somewhat decrepit state. There had been a significant attempt to improve the buildings when, in 1903, Oliver Leeson and Wood of Newcastle were asked to report on the state of the building. They indicated that the buildings were out of date and also in an unsound state and provided a detailed plan as to how improvements might be made. In April 1904, the report went before the Board but it was turned down by a large majority. It seems that the Guardians were under pressure from the Ratepayers Association, though a request from it to meet the Guardians was turned down. Even on the Board of Guardians there was great concern about rising rates as exemplified by this statement by Joseph Alexander

If we look at the expenditure of public bodies why it is enormous. The indebtedness of the country today, with regard to the public expenditure of bodies similar to our own is £462,000,000. Before the South African War the national debt was only £700,000,000; and we are going to have a second national debt. The burden is pressing heavily on the ratepayers; in fact it is becoming intolerable. What I say, I say in the best of spirit. The time will come when we will be cross-examined on this question by those in authority who come here. While we must treat them as gentlemen we cannot be expected to meet the views of visionary people. If we have to spend the ratepayers' money cogent reasons must be given for so doing (*HC* 1.10.1904).

While Alexander was against spending large amounts of money on the buildings, he had chaired a committee of Guardians to examine the buildings and by tinkering with them obtained extra accommodation. I have tabulated the information coming from the report showing the rooms examined and the potential total accommodation that would be possible in each room (Table 12). The figures indicate the rather *ad hoc* arrangement of day-rooms and dormitories within the Workhouse. Though there had been new building in 1883, much of the Workhouse had developed in an un-planned manner. A leader article in the 30 October 1880 issue of the *Hexham Courant* describes the unsatisfactory development of the Workhouse buildings

To an outsider the spaces [of the Workhouse] all seem to be too restricted. One department is jammed up against another in improper proximity, and no two of them are in a right position as regards each other. The classification which is so essential in such an institution cannot be but imperfect under the present conditions

The Guardians held out against any major improvements, in spite of the very considerable concern of the Local Government Board that deplored the Guardians' inaction. In the first years of the 20th century, the possibility of installing electric light was turned down as was the installation of a telephone. The matter of electric light was looked at again in 1924 but no action was taken. Thus the buildings in 1929, when the Guardians were abolished, were much as they were in 1904. After 1929, as a result of the Local Government Act (19 Geo V, c. 17) the functions of the guardians were transferred to the Public Assistance Committee of the County Council.

Vagrants

Any discussion of the functioning of a workhouse requires something about vagrants, the large numbers of men and women walking round the country. From the point of view of the Poor Law Amendment Act of 1834, the Commissioners formerly recognised vagrancy in 1837 when they advised that 'wayfarers' or 'persons in a state of destitution who belonged to distant parishes' should be given shelter and a meal in return for a task of work, usually stone-breaking. Once officially recognised, they became a very significant recurrent problem. I have already indicated, when talking about the buildings of the Hexham Workhouse, that a vagrant ward was an early component and that the accommodation for vagrants had to be increased in 1872, 1879 and 1884. This indicates that vagrants were becoming an increasing problem for the Hexham Workhouse. This is confirmed by the figures in Table 13. We do not know exactly why the number of vagrants reached such high levels in the mid-1880s. Probably, it was due to the rise in unemployment during the period (Saul, 1972). Another possibility is overcounting, following the passing of the Casual Poor Act of 1882 (45 & 46 Vict. c. 36) by which a vagrant could no longer discharge himself after 11.00 a.m. on the morning following his admission but had to wait until 9.00 a.m. of the morning of the third day. Two reasons are given for this change. First, if the vagrant was released late in the day, as would be the case when he stayed one night, it was difficult to find work that same day. The second reason might be that the amount of work put in by the vagrant was greatly increased if he was in the workhouse for two nights. Thus the Local Government Board fixed the maximum quantity of stones to be broken at three to four hundredweights, if the vagrant stayed only the one night. If they were in for two nights, they had to break between ten and thirteen hundred weights. Whatever the reason for the two-night stay, the presence of the same vagrant might have been counted twice.

The large numbers of vagrants that were admitted put pressure on the vagrant wards, so in 1887 the guardians resolved to discharge vagrants on the morning after their admission. This decision in fact led to an increase in numbers, as the Hexham Workhouse was seen by the vagrant to be an easier touch as far as the amount of work imposed was concerned. A stricter regime followed in the 1890s though not for long. Vagrants remained a problem for workhouses until the very end.

Medical relief

> The medical provisions of the nineteenth-century PoorLlaw formed the nucleus for the development of the modern Welfare State. The story is one of optimism and sustained progress, pointing to gradual achievement, despite the act of 1834, its omissions and achievements (Hodgkinson, 1967, p. xv).

The above quotation comes from Ruth Hodgkinson's monumental survey of 'The medical services of the new Poor Law, 1834-1871' in her book *The Origins of the National Health Service.* Essentially, it is a story of doctors and nurses struggling for positive health measures against an unsympathetic background and with little legislative aid or guidance as, can be seen in the following Poor Law Acts:
1. That of 1834 did not specifically provide for a system of medical relief but section 54 did continue the power of the justices to order medical relief in cases of sudden and dangerous illness.
2. The Amendment Act of 1848 (7 & 8 Vict., c. 101) extended the provision of the Act of 1834 by allowing relief on account of 'accident, bodily casualty or sudden illness'.
3. The Amendment Act of 1851 (14 & 15 Vict., c. 105) permitted guardians to subscribe to 'any public hospital for the reception of sick disabled or wounded persons suffering from any permanent or natural infirmity'.
4. The Amendment Act of 1868 (31 & 32 Vict., c. 6) gave the central authority power to provide medical and surgical appliances in a workhouse without the consent of the guardians or ratepayers.

From 1868-1929 there were no enactments concerning medical relief. Undoubtedly, it was felt that the legislation already in place was sufficiently enabling to allow the appropriate developments in medical care to take place.

There are strong parallels with the developments of medical care within the framework of the above Poor Law legislation and the role of the medical officer in progressing the public health developments that evolved under the Local Board of Health/Urban District Council. The improvement of health in each of the communities for which the Poor Law Institution and the local authority were responsible depended very much upon the drive and strong wills of their respective medical officers.

TABLE 12. *Details of the space available for men in Hexham Workhouse based on a report on that accommodation produced by a committee of the Guardians chaired by Jos. Alexander (HC 1.10.1904).*

| Room | Dimensions (feet + inches) | | | Fireplace | Windows | Ventilators | Inmates |
	Length	Breadth	Height				
Wards							
Men's Receiving Room	16	13	9	1	2		? (2 beds present)
Men's Day room	14	12	10	1	2	3	12
2	18.5	12	10	1	3	4	14
3	15	12	10	1	3	3	9
4	21	16	10	1	4	4	22
5	21	16	10	1	4	4	22
Total	105.5	81					79
Mean Value	21.1	13.5					13.2
Dormitories							**Beds**
6	33	12	9	1	6	4	11
7	22	16	9	1	0	4	11
19	15.5	14.5	10	1	4	2	6
20	16	14	8	1	3	2	5
27	19	14.5	8	2	4	3	6
15	16	16.5	8	1	2	2	8
16	16	16.5	8	1	2	2	8
49	21	16.5	8	1	5	2	11
50	20	16	9	1	4	2	8
51	29	16	9	1	5	4	11
Total	207.5	152.5					85
Mean Value	20.75	15.25					8.5

As with ordinary relief, there was indoor and outdoor medical relief. Each union was divided up into medical districts to deal with outdoor relief. The Hexham Union started with eight districts, two being later subdivided because of their size. Here we focus on Hexham District that consisted of Hexham Township, Hexham Low Quarter, Hexham West Quarter, Acomb, Anick and Anick Grange covering an area of 12,754 acres and initially a population of 5,996. In 1842, Thomas

Stainthorpe was appointed medical officer of the Hexham District. Probably because of the shortage of properly qualified doctors, he was also appointed medical officer for the second and third districts.

TABLE 13. *The number of vagrants relieved at Hexham Workhouse per year in the period 1843-1903. The information for the years 1843-1874 inclusive relates to the actual number of vagrants in one year, the number per day being calculated. The remainder of the information is derived from numbers per day (HC 1.10.1904), the number per year being calculated.*

Year	Number of vagrants relieved	Number per day
1843	1814	5.0
1844	1907	5.2
1845	1215	3.5
1873	2010	5.5
1874	2011	5.5
1884	2647	7.25
1885	3727	10.3
1886	5899	16.2
1887	6174	16.9
1888	6219	17.0
1889	4384	12.0
1890	2770	7.6
1891	3004	8.2
1892	3462	9.5
1895	5326	14.6
1901	2357	6.5
1903	4528	11.1

The Workhouse medical officer was also the medical officer of the first and second medical districts of the Union. There were only three medical officers in charge of the Workhouse: Thomas Stainthorpe (1839-97), Duncan Stewart (1897-1920) and his son W. Mitchell Stewart (1920-30). In view of their other commitments, which included their own medical practices, the Workhouse position must be considered as only a part-time one. Nevertheless the position carried a significant workload. Thus the medical officer was required to give a medical examination to all the paupers on their entry into the Workhouse. This was not always done, especially in the case of vagrants. However, all paupers were classified and this was done by the medical officer.

He also supervised the diet of the paupers. It has to be said that the food provided was somewhat unvarying. Bread, cereal, milk and cheese formed the backbone of the diet, the monotony relieved by meat and vegetables. Fruit did not figure at all amongst the provisions supplied to the Workhouse. Invitations to tender for the position of supplier to the Workhouse took the form of advertisements in the local press. Suppliers were required not only for provisions but for other items such as blankets and clothing.

Though the medical relief was under the control of the medical officer, the quality of the care given to the sick and infirm within the Workhouse depended on the nursing staff. In fact, to speak of 'nursing staff' is to give totally the wrong impression for it seems that paupers were acting as nurses. This seems to have been common practice throughout the Poor Law system and the men and women who were employed were often illiterate, drunken and quite unsuitable for the kind of work they were expected to do. The fragmentary information indicates that, throughout almost the whole of the 19th century, nursing was carried out by paupers. We have almost no information about their effectiveness or otherwise. However, one incident makes salutary reading

> A letter from a pauper inmate, H. McGuiness, to the Local Government Board in August 1887 exhibited the inadequacies of the system of medical care which relied on paupers. McGuiness had been helping Denning, a pauper nurse, with patients in the sick wards. In dealing with a patient McGuiness claimed that Denning 'at last threw the poultice on the bed and told me to go to hell and put the poultice where I liked...... a nice saying to a dying man'. Denning was alleged to have said to another pauper assistant, McCabe, that if the patient died before he returned McCabe was 'to stretch him out' (Cadman, 1976).

There might have been some extenuating circumstances in that McGuiness was a difficult man to deal with, being frequently bad-tempered, but it is possible that he had cause to be as a result of the way he was dealt with.

In 1893, Emma Wear was appointed as a trained nurse at the Workhouse. At that time, there were 147 inmates, 29 on medical relief with 26 in the sick wards, 14 men and 12 women. Around 1900, an additional nurse was appointed. It proved very difficult to retain nurses. Initially, this was because of the unhelpful attitude of the other staff in the Workhouse, including the master; later, the cause was inadequate remuneration, the provision of poor accommodation and the conditions of employment. The duty hours were very long with a twelve and a half hour day shift for the day nurse and an eleven and a half hour night shift. Another reason could have been the nature of the invalids under the nurses' care. The majority of the cases were chronic, demanding almost constant care, and the fact that the wards being some distance apart did not help the situation. Some nurses were asked to leave because they proved to unsatisfactory – for instance one was dismissed for 'gross insubordination'.

Further care for inmates was provided through subscriptions paid by the Guardians to a number of hospitals and specialist institutions (Table 14).

Apart from infectious diseases, it is difficult to establish the nature of the disorders of those needing medical care in the Workhouse. In the 19th century, cholera, typhoid fever and small pox were the diseases of most concern. The Union medical officers were intimately involved in combating the cholera outbreak of 1853 (Jennings, 2002). Then five persons died in the Workhouse from the disease (NA MH/12/9402). But other diseases were also of concern. For instance, in 1880, there was an outbreak of scarlet fever in the Workhouse. Sometimes, when there was an outbreak of several infections at one time, the isolation facilities were hard-pressed to cope. One disease that we know little about in terms of prevalence in the workhouse is tuberculosis. Given the prevalence of tuberculosis in the town in the 19th century (Chapter 15), a significant number of the inmates must have contracted one form or another of the disease. We know very little, if anything, that is tangible about other illnesses and infirmities. Doubtless they would be of a kind and prevalence associated with pauperism, poor living conditions and old age.

TABLE 14. *Organisations used in the 1880s by the Workhouse for the further care of its inmates.*

Date	Organisation	Subscription (per year)	Note
1881	Whitley Convalescent Home Prudhoe	£2. 7s	
1886	Newcastle Infirmary	£5.5s	
1887	ditto (Prior to the building of the Royal Victoria Infirmary)	£15.15s	In 1904, 59 patients from the Hexham Union treated
1888	Newcastle Deaf and Dumb Institution	£3	
1889	Newcastle Eye Infirmary	£2.2s	

Paupers were moved into the Workhouse as the result of contracting some infectious disease. Possibly a few with other illnesses were admitted, though there is no available evidence that this was so. In 1871, the Workhouse purchased an ambulance for moving paupers to the Workhouse to replace a 'rickety sort of affair' that was at the end of its useful life. At a meeting of the Guardians

> Matthew Smith criticised the new ambulance in somewhat disparaging terms. In his opinion it was too smart and "dashing" for the Union, although the price paid for it was a reasonable one...... It was not so strong as Mr Smith would have wished it to have been and then it was three parts glass, and some refractory lunatic (see below) might take infinite delight in smashing it to pieces. Captain Nicholson pointed out that it was not for insane people to ride in it, but for fever patients, and that it was an advantage to have so much glass about it because glass was much less likely to carry infection than wood or cloth. Previous to getting this ambulance there was no means of removing fever patients from the town to the workhouse, is such was required to be done, as public conveyances are not allowed to used for that purpose (*HC* 11.3.1871).

The mentally ill and mentally handicapped

The 47th clause of the 1834 Act stated that lunatics and imbeciles were not to be kept in the workhouse for longer than fourteen days. Perhaps because of that workhouses did not have space allocated to the mentally ill. Yet, inevitably because they were taking in the destitute, workhouses took in many who were suffering in this way. Indeed, from 1840 the lodging of the mentally ill and the mentally handicapped within the workhouse became common and this practice continued until 1929. Increasingly, the more dangerous cases were removed to asylums. Although there was no separate accommodation for the mentally ill and the mentally handicapped within the Workhouse, a padded cell was provided and mechanical restraints were available in the charge of the master. Table 15 gives an indication as to the number of lunatic paupers for whom the Guardians were responsible around the middle of the 19th century. As one can see, somewhat under half of them were in the Workhouse. In 1847, the others were in licensed accommodation or with friends. By 1861, full use was being made of the County Asylum at Morpeth.

TABLE 15. *Returns from the Hexham Union to the central authority of lunatics or idiots under the care of the Guardians in 1844, 1847 and 1861 (Cadman, 1976). At the time of these returns term lunatic covered both mentally-ill and mentally- handicapped.*

	1844		1847	1861	
Location	Men	Women		Men	Women
Union Workhouse	9	12	19	12	6
Licensed houses*	2	5	9		
County Asylum				28	
With friends or elsewhere	14	6	15		

* Licensed to take lunatics under the Act for the Regulation and Care and Treatment of Lunatics (8 & 9 Vict., c. 126).

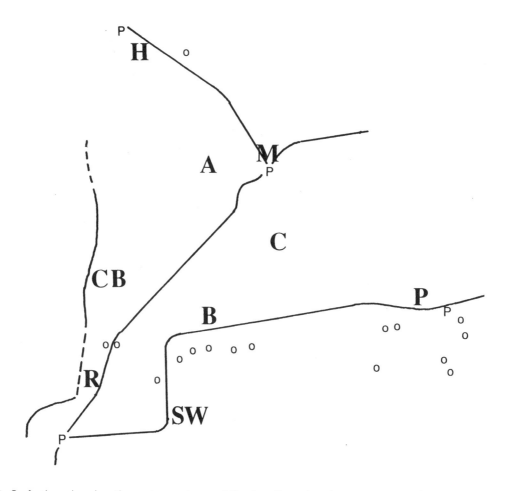

FIG. 9. A plan showing the water mains and the location of springs, pumps and wells in Hexham in 1853 – based on a map in Rawlinson (1853). The line associated with CB represents the Cowgarth (Halgut) Burn. The other lines represent the water mains fed initially from the Cowgarth Burn. One main ran along St Wildfrid's Road (SW) and then along Battle Hill (B) into Priestpopple (P); another main ran past the Roman Catholic Church (R), across the Abbey Grounds, splitting into two branches in the Market Place (M), one branch going to Hexham House (H) and the other going a short distance down Hallstile Bank. The small 'p' prefers to pants, while the small 'o' refers to a spring, pump or well; A, refers to the Abbey.

FIG. 10. The Seal Well, located on the east bank of Cockshaw Burn, a few metres south of the bridge across the burn into Cockshaw.

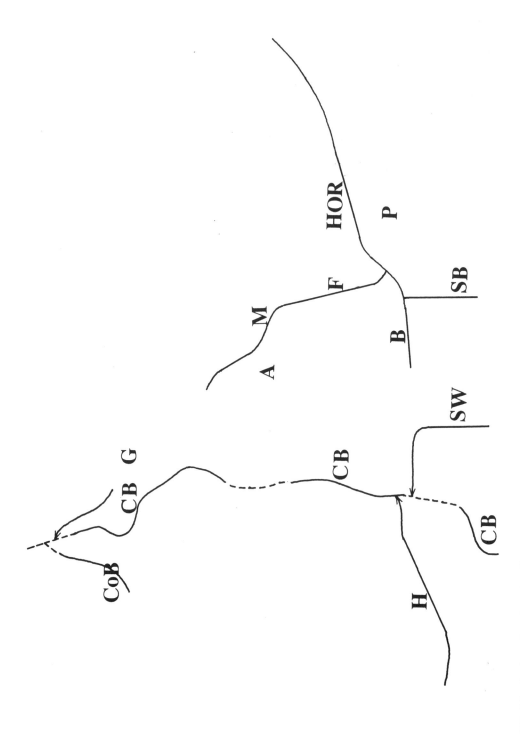

FIG. 11. A plan showing the distribution of sewers and drains in Hexham in 1853 – based on a map in Rawlinson (1853). There were three sewers feeding in to the Cowgarth Burn (CB) – one from St Wilfrid's Road (SW), one from Hencotes (H) and the third from Gilesgate (G). There was another sewer system based on Skinners Burn (SB) into which fed a sewer from Church Row, the Market Place (M) and Fore Street (F) and another from Battle Hill (B). A, refers to the Abbey; COB, Cockshaw (Hextol) Burn

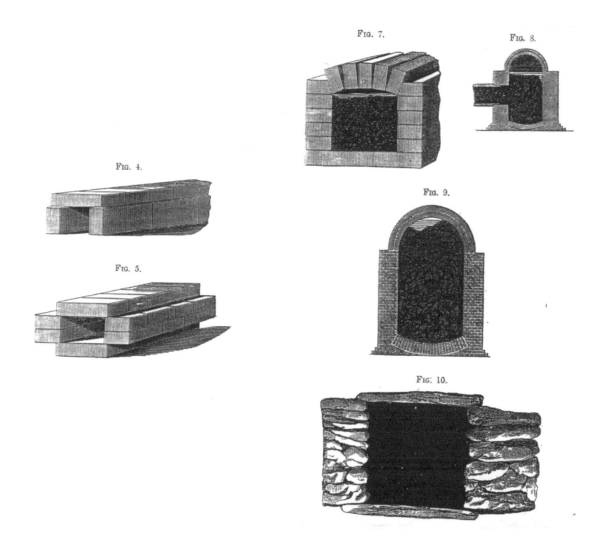

FIG. 12. Some examples of drains/sewers that were in use in England in the mid-19th century. It is likely that the drains in Hexham in 1853 were no better than the one illustrated by Fig. 10 (Latham, 1873).

Election of Local Board of Health

HEXHAM DISTRICT.

I do hereby Certify, that the Election of the Members of the Local Board of Health for the District of Hexham, has been conducted in conformity with the Provisions of the Public Health Act, 1848, and that the List hereunder written, contains the Names of the Candidates, together with the number of Votes given for each, and the Names of the Persons Elected.

Names of the Candidates.	Residence.	Quality or Calling.	No. of Votes given for each Candidate.	Names of the Persons Elected.
John Stokoe	Priestpopple	Solicitor	618	John Stokoe
Thomas Baty	Market Street	Sheriff's Officer	607	Thomas Baty
Matthew Smith	Loughbrow .	Farmer	604	Matthew Smith
Thomas Jefferson	Orchard Place	Surgeon	603	Thomas Jefferson
Robert Stokoe	Market Street, ...	Surgeon	579	Robert Stokoe
Thomas Pratt	Commercial Place	Gentleman	567	Thomas Pratt
William Lyon	Market Place ...	Manufacturer	552	William Lyon
Robert Bell	High Shield	Farmer	551	Robert Bell
George Robinson	Hencotes, near the Seal	Linen Draper	533	George Robinson
Jasper Gibson	Battle-hill, Hexham	Solicitor	404	
John Nicholson	Battle-hill, Hexham	Surgeon	38?	
James Kirsopp ..,.	The Spital, Hexham	Esquire	360	
Edward Pruddah	Hencoats, Hexham ,..	Printer	344	
Ralph Errington Ridley	Hencoats, Hexham	Tanner	336	
William Robb	Hall Garth, Hexham	Draper ...	335	
William Wilson Gibson	Fore Street, Hexham	Druggist	334	
Charles Head	Hackwood, Hexham	Solicitor	324	
Smith Stobart	Acomb	Tanner ...	312	

Given under my Hand, this second day of January, 1854.

JASPER GIBSON,

Returning Officer

FIG. 13. The result of the first election for Hexham Local Board of Health. Those elected met as a Board on 9 January 1854 with Matthew Smith in the Chair. Reproduced with the permission of the National Archives (NA MH13/91).

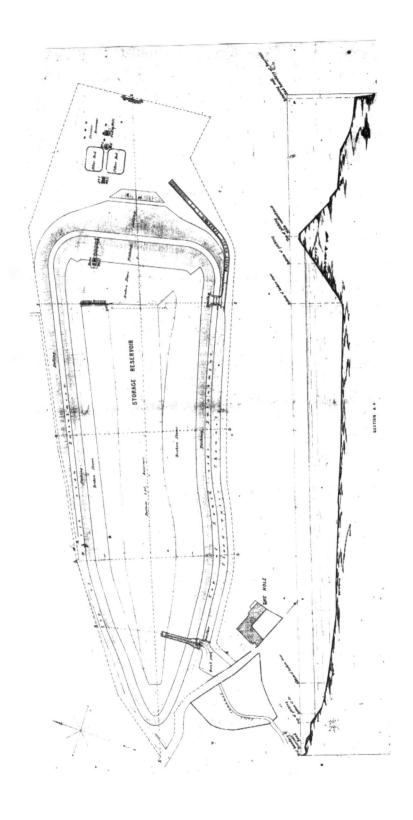

FIG. 14. Plan of the reservoir constructed at the Hole, filled with water from the Wydon Burn. The overflow went down the flood-water channel on the south side of the reservoir. Water was fed into the pipe taking water into the town via one of two filter beds, depending on which was being cleaned. Reproduced with the permission of Tynedale Council and the Northumberland Record Office (NRO/PHU/A5/8).

FIG. 15. The reservoir when full of water, photograph from the west, c. 1999.

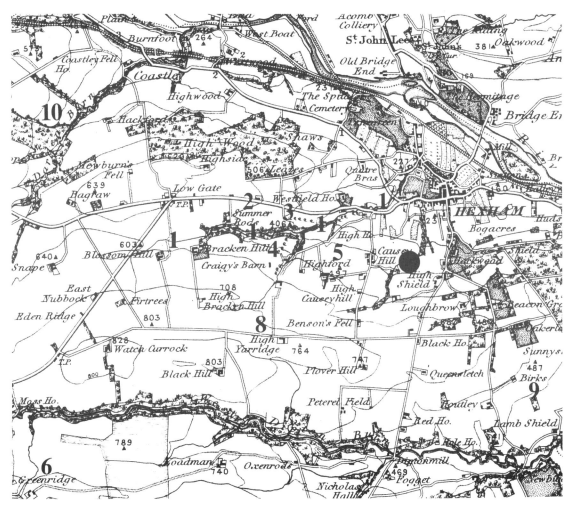

FIG. 16. Ordnance Survey map of 1866 showing the location of places, named in the text, with respect to the search for other sources for the supply of water for the town. 1, Cockshaw (Hextol) Burn; 2, Summerrods; 3, Woodley Field, 4, Breckon Hill (Bracken Hill on map); 5, Highford; 6, Greenridge; 7, probable location of Watty's Well; 8, Yarridge; 9, Barley Well and 10, Darden Burn.

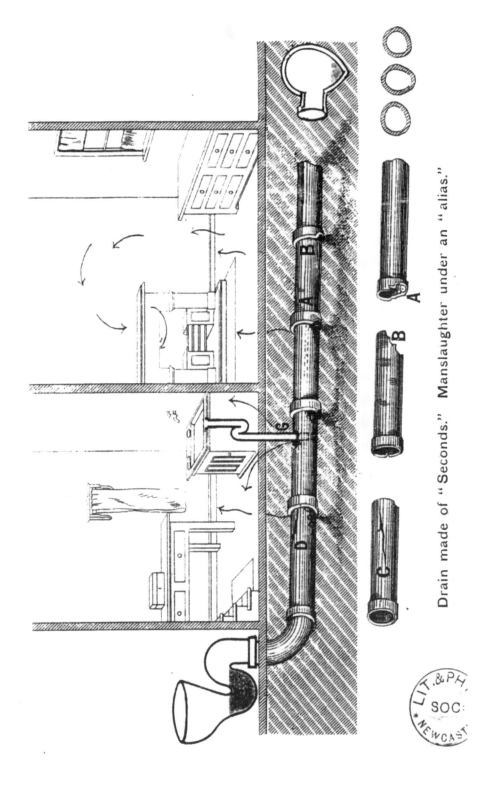

Drain made of "Seconds." Manslaughter under an "alias."

FIG. 17. Dawson's practice of breaking a hole in a drainpipe to make a connection with another pipe, which is referred to in the text, seems to have been commonplace as shown in this picture (see G). Making a hole as indicated allowed sewage could leak out of the system, as indeed could the use of 'seconds'. This picture and several others from (Teale, 1881) show that there were many other ways in which there could be leakage of sewage due to bad methods of laying pipes. Arrows refer to movement of vapour/smell.

FIG. 18. Portrait of Daniel Jackson, first Medical Officer for Health for Hexham. Born at Cambuslang on 30 March 1838; he was educated at Glasgow University. He came to Hexham when he was 24, becoming Medical Officer of Health in 1873. He retired in 1911, just before his death later that year. Reproduced by kind permission of Mrs Marion Prins.

CHAPTER 6

The history of Hexham's water supply and sewerage system from 1848 to 1868

Prior to 1854

On 12 August 1851, a committee of fifteen persons, appointed at a public meeting in the Moot Hall on 14 August, met to put into operation a report of Mr Robert Nicholson concerned with obtaining a better supply of water for Hexham (Rawlinson, 1853). At the meeting, the committee resolved that the best way forward would be to adopt the Public Health Act 1848. On 15 August a public meeting, again in the Moot Hall, agreed with this conclusion and resolved on preparing, signing and forwarding the petition referred to in Chapter 2. Subsequently the committee divided itself into sub-committees to consider the following topics – water supply; sewerage and drainage; sanitation; the burial ground; common lodging houses and the state of the roads. Rawlinson's report contains verbatim the reports of these sub-committees. Here I consider only the first two reports listed.

Water supply

The most populated part of the Township of Hexham, as much of it does today, lies on glacial deposits overlying millstone grit. Sources of water were frequent via springs, pumps or wells. A map produced by Rawlinson (1853) shows that a significant of pumps or wells were associated with the properties on the south side of Battle Hill, Cattle Market and Priestpopple (Fig. 9). Indeed, the readily availability of water for these pumps and wells may have been instrumental in the development of the town along the line of these three streets. However such sources, at the very most, could only provide a partial supply. The main source was the Cowgarth Burn. Skinners Burn was inadequate, while Cockshaw Burn was too low-lying to provide for the many buildings at a more elevated location. Cowgarth Burn was fed by several excellent springs, four of which – if not all – were on land owned by Matthew Smith. At a location close to where Cuddy's Lane crosses the Burn (the path from Priestlands Lane to Gaprigg Lane) at one time a very small dam (four foot high) had been built. At the time of the sub-committee's report, the small reservoir behind it was silted up. The water was then fed into a cistern, being 'filtered' by 'a few interwoven branches'. From there the water ran into another cistern immediately behind the Catholic Chapel. From there, the water ran down into town but the pipes used were of too narrow diameter, causing the cistern to overflow. One of the pipes entered the town via Battle Hill, descending to a pant, or public fountain, in the Cattle Market, which had an open cistern and thence a pipe continued to a close pant, working by a valve. The other pipe gave off a branch to a pant by the then Scotch Church, located next to what is now St Aidan's United Reform Church. The main pipe went across the Abbey Grounds to a pant in the Market Place (Fig. 9). The pant then being supplied had been erected by Robert Allgood in 1703, but seemingly replacing one already there. The water went into a large open cistern, which was of dubious cleanliness. At this pant the supply bifurcated, one pipe descending half way down Hall Stile Bank to another pant, while the other pipe went down Market Street and Gilesgate, apparently to just past Hencotes House where another pant was positioned.

There is little doubt that the system was very ineffective. Two of the pants were running continuously day and night, the water for the most part going to waste. The two main branches of the water supply (to the Market Place and Cattle Market Place) ran through pipes, which were said to have been in use since 'time immemorial' and when defects had been discovered, they 'had been remedied often by the readiest means and in the most inefficient manner'. Further the purity of the supply was of questionable quality:

> From the notorious want of purification at the dam it is no exaggeration to say, that during a considerable proportion of the year it is thoroughly useless even for the commonest purposes.

There were several reasons for this. Heavy rain brought down a great deal of sediment; decaying vegetation fell into the burn as it went through the wooded valley; within the recent period to the sub-committee reporting, a brick and tile works had started up near the source of the burn and, although, not referred to by the sub-committee, there was almost certainly contamination from farm animals.

But where the system failed was in the virtual absence of supply to households or businesses, either through a failure to make connections with the supply pipes or because of inadequate pressure. No more than 20-30 houses were connected to the main supply; even then there was insufficient pressure to raise the water above the ground floor. The net result was that the inhabitants of the town (who did not have their own well or pump) were forced to be content with the 'old and tedious mode of carrying it' from the public pants or from three other sources. Two were wells – one Penny Well in Skinnersburn-street (Eastgate), which is no longer present, and the other the Seal Well, which can still be seen on the edge of the Seal in the trees next to the bridge across Cockshaw Burn (Fig. 10). Many citizens fell back on the water from these two wells when the supply from the pants proved unsuitable or inadequate. The distance over which water needed to be carried by the users of these two wells therefore could be considerable. The third public source of water was the River Tyne, used primarily by those living on Tyne Green. If the water supply was inadequate for household use, it was almost useless for fire-fighting purposes. The pants could only supply the fire engine for an hour and it was a wonder that fire did not do more damage to the town than actually seems to have been the case. Having said all that, a considerable number of persons appear to have had access to pumps and wells. The *Courant* in a short note indicated that there were 74 sources of water that were said to be 'public' and 'never failing' (*HC* 1.3.1865). Whether or not the water was very pure must be questioned, in view of the unfavourable analytical figures obtained by the Surveyor in 1890 for water coming from a well at Fellside and a pump at Orchard Place. He recommended that both be closed (HLBH 14.7.1890).

The *ad hoc* nature of the water supply was an inevitable consequence of the way the development of the system was managed. According to the report of the sub-committee, there was a self-elected body in charge. Whatever improvements were made were financed by voluntary contributions. The accounts of the operation were never audited or published. There was a general desire for change and on 13 September 1852 there was a meeting of 'the Inhabitants of the Town' (ratepayers?) that resolved that a 'Pant or Water Committee' of thirteen named persons be appointed 'protect the proper supply of Water to the Town' (NRO/3064/EP/184/214).

Interestingly, the meeting made three other decisions – two of a general kind and one concerning a specific person, namely Matthew Smith, who had attached a pipe illegally to the Priestpopple pant pipe. But it was soon apparent that this new committee could do little to improve the water supply. When it was proposed to apply the Public Health Act to Hexham, it was not surprising that there were a number of leading citizens who saw the proposal as a way forward to administer for a better water supply.

Sewers and drains

The distribution of the sewers and drains in the town was very fragmented (Fig.11). All emptied into local watercourses. The two from Hencotes emptied into Cowgarth Burn, just before it ran through the Abbey Grounds; those in the Market Place, Fore Street and Battle Hill into the Skinner's Burn, which ran to the Tyne via Hall Orchard Road; that originating in the Back Row went down Bull Bank (Hallstile Bank) into an open channel and from thence presumably into the Tyne and finally the one originating at the top of the bank in Gilligate (Gilesgate) which ran into the lower reaches of Cockshaw Burn. These were the major drains; there were a few other drains but they were small. Significantly, the greatest proportion of Back Street, Hallstile Bank and Priestpopple were without drainage. But even those streets with drains did not have a system, which was any way reliable. The drains themselves were built of rubble stone without lime, being flat at the bottom (Fig. 12). In the view of the sub-committee considering drainage, the drains were 'better calculated as a deposit than for carrying away the sewage'. Skinners Burn, which was essentially a sewer as it ran through the town, was arched over as it ran under the streets and buildings 'but the arch was so imperfectly constructed that it has been repeatedly choked up'. Though one talks of a sewerage system, in fact the bulk of human excrement was for the most part conveyed from the household to the nearest ash-pit or accumulated in a privy-midden. At infrequent intervals, the accumulated excrement and any associated garbage were removed, either to be deposited in a dumping ground, which, as far as one can gather, could be anywhere, or used as fertiliser. We do not know who did the removing, though one presumes that it one or more of the several cartmen listed in the 1851 census.

Of course it wasn't just human excrement that had to be disposed of, there was excrement from animals, particularly pigs, as well as general refuse and most particularly the considerable quantities of offal and other animal waste from the several slaughter houses. The grisly consequences of the continued failure to cope with the disposal of all this refuse have been well documented (Jennings, D., 1998; Rawlinson, 1853). Today, the sanitary state of much of the town throughout the 19th-century is just unbelievable. The sub-committee's view that 'considered as a whole the sanitary state of Hexham is of the lowest class' appears to our eyes a mild view of the situation, which was not to be properly resolved until the 1930s when proper sewerage systems had been established and the slum property in the centre of the town had started to be removed. A proper sewerage system should not only dispose of the sewage from houses and other buildings within the town but also treat the sewage so disposed, so the eventual end-product was innocuous. While legislation was an important driving force for an effective system for treatment, so too were a wider understanding of microbiology and an increasing concern about the pollution of the Tyne.

Early years after 1854

It needs to be realised that, while those petitioners who wanted a Local Board of Health had a successful outcome to their efforts, they were roundly defeated in the first elections to the Board, the results of which were announced on 2 January 1854. The voting appears to have been, almost without exception, along (for want of a better word) 'party' lines. What came to be known as the 'dirty party' (Jennings, R. 1998) obtained between 533-601 votes for each of its nine candidates; those who were in favour of sanitary improvement only obtained between 312-404 votes (Fig. 13). The views of those who were to run the Local Board are clearly expressed in the 'Petition against the Act' sent to the Commissioners of the General Board of Health in 1851:

> The town, from its peculiar situation, has always been, and still is, unquestionably, one of the healthiest towns in the kingdom....... We further respectfully submit that the town of Hexham, situated as it is in an agricultural district, and depending on the district in a great measure for support, is not at present in a position to pay any further amount of taxation.

Not increasing the rates was a guiding principle for the operation of the Local Board of Health, particularly in its early years when the dirty party held sway – though such sentiments did not seem in any way apparent in those meetings following the first one held on 9 January 1854. Thus from the minute book of the Board we read 'Ordered that Mr Lawes' *Treatise on Public Health* be procured for the use of this Board' (HLBH 23.1.1854) and

> Resolved that proper and efficient sewerage and drainage with necessary water works be carried out by this Board in the Township of Hexham, the plans and arrangements to be determined upon.
> Resolved that application be made to the General Board of Health for information as to the best mode of proceeding to have a proper Survey and Plan made of the Township of Hexham for sewerage and waterworks and as to the probable expense likely to attend such survey and plan (HLBH 6.2.1854).

In its early days the Board could be forgiven for not striving to fulfil these Resolutions. There were other more pressing matters to deal with such as drafting the bye-laws and setting the rates. But at the 9 October 1854 meeting, the Board began to show its true colours. A letter from Charles Guthrie, an upholsterer, to the General Board of Health was received by the Local Board (NA MH13/91). That letter contained a scathing attack on the Local Board in general and its Chairman, Mr Matthew Smith, in particular, over the failure to empty the middens in the vicinity of Guthrie's house in Battle Hill (of which Mr Smith was the landlord) (Jennings *et al.,* 2004). The situation was such that, according to the letter to the General Board of Health.

> this filthy Landlord of mine is Chairman of the Said board with a friend of his a pig-jobber for inspector as for the yard where it is rain for want of Spouts and drainage it is a complete cesspool...... he keeps this yard of ours as a kind of depot of filth for his land [Smith was amongst other things a farmer].

The Clerk of the Local Board wrote back to say

......the Inspector of Nuisances having been interrogated respecting it [the letter] when he reported to this Board that the charge made that the Middens and Soil Pits being suffered to remain unemptied for such a length of time that the accumulation of filth were the cause of serious illness to the Inhabitants was incorrect and without foundation and all the Middens and Soil Pits were all regularly and properly emptied.

The comment of Charles Guthrie on learning from the General Board is succinct, if not very grammatical:

......your communication with the Hexham Board of Health has no effect for my Landlord the chairman of that Board is a man of that kind if you can do. Nothing stronger than communication you may save yourselves the trouble for there is nothing done for the filth is worse.

In the early years, hardly anything, if at all, seems to have been done to improve the water supply and almost nothing to the sewerage system. In fact the first major initiative came in 1858 from a private individual, when it is reported (HLBH 5.7.1858) that Mr Joseph Ridley proposed erecting a fountain or pant in Gilligate and to bring water into the same (from the Seal Well) at his own expense for the public at large. On 11 October 1855, he attended a meeting of the Local Board and presented to it 'The Glovers Pant' for public use. Thereafter the system was tinkered with – a pipe laid here, a pant altered there. The minutes of the Board are for the most part unclear as to what precisely was being done and where, but the general impression is one of inactivity over bettering the supply of water. A sewer had been laid down in the Market Place, along Back Row and then down Hallstile) Bank, where it went to from there cannot be established. Another went from the Market pant, through the Hall Garth into the Skinners Burn. There were very few connections with houses and the sewers were essentially drains (HC 8.3.1865).

The new water supply

In 1863 there was change. That year saw the election of three men to the Board strongly in favour of sanitary reform, namely (in the order in which they headed the poll) Thomas Stainthorpe, Charles Head and William Robb. There had been two previous elections, in 1857 and 1862, but the dirty party candidates still had been clear winners. The results of the 1863 election were known on 6 April; on 25 May William Robb moved and Thomas Stainthorpe seconded – 'That a Report on the best means of extending and improving the best means of extending and improving the present supply of Water be immediately obtained.' There was a caveat – the means used be contrived 'to preserve the present supply to the Public Pants.' A committee of three (Matthew Smith as Chairman, William Robb and Thomas Stainthorpe) were to consult Messrs Ridley about the matter. On 22 August 1863, Messrs Ridley reported to the Board that

a sufficient supply of water will not be obtained by the present Borings to warrant further expense and further that it is very problematical whether in any other place in the neighbourhood water can be obtained by Boring, in sufficient quantities to rise to the surface and be made available to the Town.

Though some of those against sanitary reform fought a rearguard action, it was evident that something must be done to improve the town's water supply, both in terms of quality and quantity. With the improvers holding the initiative, it was decided that not only should the water supply be improved but also the sewerage system. Mr John Lawson, of 34 Parliament Street, Westminster, was 'engaged to make a survey, prepare plans and estimates with a view to carrying out the water supply and sewerage of the town' (HLBH 14. 9.1863). On 30 October, Mr Lawson produced his report for the Board. Quickly thereafter, the Clerk proceeded with the necessary steps for the compulsory purchase of the land required for the contemplated water and sewerage works. The reservoir was to be at the Hole, interestingly most of it was constructed on land belonging to Matthew Smith; the sewage works was to be on Tyne Green. Because the watercourse was already in use for public purposes, there was no need to obtain permission for its further use from the owners of the land bordering the banks of the Cowgarth Burn – something that was to cause difficulties when the town required a much larger supply. After the plans had been approved by the General Board (Robert Rawlinson being involved in the process; NA MH13/91) and the Home Secretary had given his consent to the Local Board borrowing £12,000 for defraying the costs of the work, Mr Lawson was put in charge of the operation of making his plans a reality. Tenders were sought, the selection made, such that around April 1864 work commenced on the reservoir. It was to have an earth embankment as a dam and two small filter beds, through which was fed the water supply to the town (Figs. 14 & 15).

But matters did not run smoothly. The Local Board minutes of 10 October 1864 include a letter from George Dixon, contractor for the reservoir:

> Gentlemen – I am under the necessity of stating to you that I find I am unable to execute the Main Embankment and side Embankment with carts for the sum set forth in my schedule the whole of which is excavated from within the Storage Reservoir.
> I may state that when I made out my tender I based my calculations upon removing the earth with <u>Wagons</u> and in stating to Mr Laws that I would endeavour to remove it with carts I find that I have committed an error.
> My object in addressing you now is to ask if you will grant me an additional four pence per cubic yard – this will meet my requirements and I can only assure you that nothing shall be wanting on my part to carry out the works to your satisfaction. Trusting you will give this matter your earnest consideration – I am &c., George Smith, Contractor.

The request for the four pence per cubic yard was granted, the Board appearing sympathetic to George Dixon's problems (HLBH 17.10.1864). But that action by the Board was not enough and in the Board minutes of 15 February 1865, George Dixon is reported as being 'unable to continue with the Works of his various Contracts under the Board'; on 4 March he was declared bankrupt (*HC* 22.3.1865). Mr Lund, newly appointed as the Board's Surveyor, was instructed to take possession of Dixon's 'Horses materials and implements...... in the construction of the said Works' and proceed with the works himself. Clearing up the financial fall-out from George Dixon's failure took some months. By May, it was clear that the Board were facing financial problems of its own, as it was resolved that application be made to the Home Secretary for his sanction to borrow £7,000 in addition to the £12,000 already borrowed (HLBH 31.5.1865). Negotiations with London resulted in a revised application being made, based on the advice of John Lawson, for the sum of £5,600, which sum was reported as having received the sanction of the Secretary of State on 27 November 1865.

It is not clear when the reservoir and associated pipe systems were completed. We can be certain they were completed by 18 June 1866, when the Local Board:

> Ordered that a handbill be printed and issued stating that the Board is about to put the Streets of the Town into a State of thorough repair and that all parties who have not yet obtained a Water Supply or whose House Drainage is still incomplete must apply to Mr Marshall surveyor to the Board who will see to the proper execution of the Works and thus avoid the damage and expense of disturbing the surface of the Streets after the same have been completed. And also that after the expiration of two months from this date several of the Public Pants will be discontinued and removed.

When the Local Board considered the need for additional money, it was estimated that there was a need to make connections to 522 houses. The 1861 Census shows the town to have had 785 dwellings. A good number would have been outside the built-up area; nevertheless it is probable that a good number within the town would still have to depend on the old sources of supply, wells and pumps. Further, as the above resolution indicates, it seems likely that not all the 552 houses scheduled for a connection did in fact receive one. Indeed this is a likely supposition in view of the fact that anyone, whose building was beyond a 100 feet from the water main, had to pay for a connection to it, the cost by special agreement with the Board (HLBH 2.1.1866). Also, once any connection was made the owner of the property had to pay a water rate.

We have little idea what was entailed by a connection. Certainly, it would not be to an internal plumbing system, as we know it, or even a very simplified version. Most probably the connection was to a tap, which could well have to be shared between a number of families and even quite possibly to some sort of water closet. It is difficult to establish what kind was installed. There are indirect indications that there were water closets, which had a piped supply of water for flushing away the excrement. But more general evidence suggests that pan closets were the more likely, in which excrement was flushed into the sewerage system by hand-poured water (Muthesius, 1982; Reid, 1892). However the presence of any such a closet was of little use without it being connected to an effective sewerage system. It is not at all clear that the Local Board were able to do little more than extend the system to an outfall to the north of the station. The extent to which individual dwellings were connected is uncertain, though there was some effort by the Board to ensure that all properties in the town had water closets (HLBH 8.10.1866). On 13 July 1868, the Surveyor reported to the Board that there were 230 water closets in the town. However, there is plenty of evidence from later years that ash-pits and midden privies were a major feature of the sanitation scene until the turn of the century. The Local Board of Health was responsible for clearing out the ash-pits and privies. Originally their contents were taken away in a wooden cart. But later, specially designed carts may have been used. On 4 December 1865, we find the Local Board ordering 'that the Surveyor [Mr Vardy] procure an iron cart according to the plan submitted by him to the Board'. Altogether, the sewerage system at this time, though seemingly improved, was still primitive and not very effective.

In spite of the better supply of water, some of the pants were kept going after modification, confirming that not all had access to piped water in the immediate vicinity or within the building in which they lived. Glovers pant was attached to the mains, while the pants in Market Street and Fore Street were restored (HLBH 12.2.1866 & 16.7.1866). A new pant was erected in Priestpopple; that in the Market Place was taken down (HLBH 9.12.1867). The criteria behind these decisions are not clear but in the case of the pant in the Market Place it almost certain that, as it flowed continuously, its removal would reduce the loss of water. Considerable concern was expressed in the Board about the consequences of the removal of these public water supplies for many people in the town (*HC* 16.6.1868). Nevertheless, a month later the pant in the Cattle Market was removed. At around the same time, the Board agreed to extend the water mains to Maiden Cross, Haliwell Dene, Tyne Green and Quatre Bras. The sewerage system was also being extended.

It is about this time that the imperfections of the new water supply as built began to show. It was becoming clear that the supply was finite and there could be shortages. Eighteen sixty-eight was the year that an attempt was made to introduce water metering. There may have been a financial motive as well as the need to make users more economical. On 30 November, the Board learnt it was £1600 in debt. But those who had to pay, and they were essentially businesses, soon found arguments for not doing so, one particular one being that the amount of water that they used would generate less money for the Local Board than the sum that was being paid for the hire of a meter. A lot of hot air was generated over the issue but what was probably more troublesome for consumers was the decision to turn the water supply off at nights (HC 27.10.1868). Of particular concern was the ensuing greater damage if fire broke out and a supply of water was not available (*HC* 31.10.1868). Of less concern, but a considerable irritant (both psychologically and physically from the large amounts of dust generated in the dry weather), was the cessation of watering of streets (*HC* 4.7.1868). But even when the supply was sufficient, the quality could be poor. At the extreme, a dead ewe was in the reservoir (*HC* 10.3.1868), while on 1 August 1866 the *Hexham Courant* reported

> Much excitement was created in Hexham in the early part of the week on it being discovered that the new reservoir was in a most impure condition and quite unfit for drinking purposes, the stench arising from it being patent to the least susceptible noses.

While this particular problem appears to have been cleared up relatively speedily, one cannot have much confidence in the overall purity of the water supplied to the town from the reservoir. Dr Thomas Stainthorpe, was a voice of continuing complaint in the Board for many in the town about the quality of the water. Much, if not all, of the problem seemed to be due inadequate maintenance of the filters. Essentially, the town seemed to suffer from not having someone who had the proper experience of managing the supply.

CHAPTER 7

The fight for a better water supply and an improved sewerage system

The problems mount up

The years from 1869 to 1889 brought forth to public attention the increasing inadequacy of the water supply. All through this period, the town was growing, albeit at a slower rate than the national average, with the well-off becoming wealthier (Jennings, 2000). The actual connection of the source of supply to a dwelling or business in itself increased usage. Thus the inception of a water supply from the reservoir increased water use from 6 gallons per day prior to 1864 to 20 in 1870 (*HC* 3.9.1870). This period saw increased house-building, particularly in the west of the town, the new properties often having amenities, demanding increased water usage. Thus the *Hexham Courant* of 27 July 1871 carried an advert for the sale or letting of three 'new-erected' dwelling houses at Leazes Terrace:

> containing front Sitting Room with Bay Window, Scullery, Pantry and Five Bed Rooms; fit with proper sewers, Water, Gas, Bell and every convenience.

It may be significant that there is no mention of a bathroom, or, indeed, toilet facilities. William Robb, speaking that year as Chairman of the Local Board, observed that there would hardly be more than a dozen people in the town with private bath (*HC* 11.1.1870). However he believed that water closets were not only a luxury but also an absolute necessity. Not surprisingly, because of their sanitary efficacy, the installation of water closets was encouraged, though it would be many years before privy middens disappeared, especially from the poorer parts of the town and those outlying properties not yet connected to piped water supply.

It was the more wealthy citizens who were able to take best advantage of the new water supply. Thus they not only had piped water into their houses but they were able to indulge in more sophisticated horticulture, in which the hosepipe played a major role. By 1869, there was sufficient use of water in gardens, both commercial and private, for the suggestion to be made that such usage be subject to a charge (*HC* 27.7.1869). In October 1868, it was decided that manufacturers using water from the public supply should have it metered and charged accordingly (HLBH 5.10.1868), though it was 7 March 1870 before agreement was reached in the Local Board as to the scale of charges and then only after much public discussion, because the initial attempt at a scale encouraged rather than discouraged use of water. A leader in the *Courant* put it succinctly

> We repeat, we would like to know on what basis this ingenious table has been compiled. On small consumers the scale will tell with unwanted severity, whilst those using larger quantities of water almost receive a premium for doing so...... it appears more like a practical joke out of place.

It is not entirely clear the extent that manufacturing increased water consumption. Evidence from water charges suggests that water usage by manufacturing was relatively limited (Jennings, 2000).

This is borne out by some figures given at the second Local Government inquiry into the water supply held in August 1878 (*HC* 31.8.1878), at which Edward Brown, the engineer who was advising the Board, indicated that about nine per cent of the total water consumption during 24 hours earlier in the month was used for 'trade' purposes. On other days, the figure might be somewhat higher, because during the period of measurement the North Eastern Railway used only 100 gallons on that day, when their average daily consumption was 3,500 gallons, while Thomas Pearson, brewer, used a negligible amount. Perhaps of greater concern, at least in terms of the town's future prosperity was a statement made at the first inquiry by Joseph Catherall (*HC* 14.4.1877) that

> it was not so much what was really used at present for trade purposes but what might have been used had tradesmen been guaranteed a regular supply of water.

Catherall knew several who would have been using water at the present time if they could have been certain of a constant supply. In support, Edward Pruddah said that until 1870 he used water for hydraulic machinery for the printing the *Hexham Herald* but in that year the water was taken from him at a week's notice and he used a steam engine instead.

The institution in the town using the most water was routinely the Workhouse. The other main users in 1884 (towards the end of the period with which we are concerned here) were the North Eastern Railway, Hexham Gas Company, John Ridley's tannery, J. B. Thompson's Steam Laundry and Dye-works and the Tyne Saw Mills. The next on the list was Mrs Alexander's ladies' boarding school in Battle Hill, the high position on the list supporting the view that industry and manufacturing in themselves did not impose any excessive demand on the supply. Though we do not have figures, the Board itself must have been a significant user of water for flushing the sewers and for watering the streets. One other significant call on the supply, often referred to in Local Board minutes was the loss of water during the winter months due to persons leaving the taps running to prevent pipes from freezing.

With each succeeding year, the inadequacy of the water system made itself felt. The battle was on between those who felt there should be minimum expenditure on increasing the supply and those who wanted a supply which was in keeping with the times in terms not only of quantity but also quality. The fundamental issue under debate was the catchment area for the supply of water. The larger the area, the greater the quantity of water supplied for any given rainfall. But for purity we can do no better than quote from a 19th-century text (Greenwell & Curry, 1896):

> Purity of source...... is of paramount importance. The most satisfactory area to impound water is where there is a sparse population, scant herbage, and an absence of cultivated land. The nearer these conditions are approached, either naturally or artificially, by collecting and diverting the pollution, the nearer will an ideal water-shed be realised.

Within the period, there was a succession of crises, each triggered by inadequate rainfall. While the annual rainfall figures make it obvious that a crisis was inevitable, it is not always the case. To determine how each crisis developed it is necessary to have monthly figures for rainfall together with the routine guagings of the amount of water in the reservoir. Guagings are often available but relevant monthly rainfall figures have not been tracked down.

Attempts to increase the water supply (1868-77)

What follows is an account of the various proposals for increasing the water supply to the town. The precise details of what was being proposed are not always clear. Debate about any one proposal was often confused, old arguments being frequently re-iterated, particularly by a significant number of members who continually fought any possibility of increased expenditure by the Board. But often those anxious to increase the supply of water were less forceful than perhaps they ought to have been, because they too were concerned about the expense of what they were proposing. Consequently an air of indecision frequently hung over the proceedings of the Board.

TABLE 16. *Rainfall figures obtained by the Newcastle and Gateshead Water Co. (NRO ZCL/F/15/3). Though the watershed feeding the Wydon Burn, is some distance away from where the rainfall figures were collected, they appear to give a reliable picture for the whole area under consideration in view of the few figures obtained from the* Hexham Courant *for Hexham. Figure in bold indicate the amount of rain (in inches) above average and a minus sign the amount below average.*

	Whittle Dene Reservoir Rainfall		Hallington Village Rainfall		Hexham Rainfall	
Year	Year total	From average*	Year total	From average*	Year total	From average**
1863	29,94	0.68	32.66	1.75		
1864	25.93	− 0.33	27.70	− 3.21		
1865	23.39	− 2.87	25.46	− 5.45		
1866	25.22	− 1.04	33.44	2.49	31.48	2.09
1867	23.35	− 2.91	24.86	− 6.05	24.52	− 4.87
1868	23.77	− 2.49	28.49	− 2.42	29.02	− 0.37
1869	22.23	− 3.39	28.54	− 2.37	24.91	− 4.48
1870	19.43	− 6.83	26.20	− 4.71	20.79	− 8.60
1871	27.01	0.75	30.32	−		

* from figures for 27 years
** from figures for 7 years

The year 1870 was one of crisis, with the rainfall between 70-85% of the average, exacerbated by the below average rainfall during the three preceding years – indeed there had been water supply problems in 1868 (Table 16). The *Courant*, in a leader in its 8 September issue, expressing great concern about the situation particularly if a fire broke out, pointed out that 'Newcastle and similar towns were under a limited supply'. The same column gave three suggestions for eventual improvement of the situation. The first, was put forward by Mr Lawson, who engineered the original supply, in which he suggested that a wall be built along the main embankment of the reservoir, high enough to allow the water to rise to the top of the bank, and yet prevent the spray from this higher level being driven over to the danger of the whole structure. The increase in depth would only be 21 inches. The second possibility was to build a new reservoir further up Wydon Burn to catch the water from winter floods, such that ten million gallons would be stored. Even at this stage, cost was already ruling out this option. The third course of action, which had already been in the mind of Mr Lawson when he advised on the building of the reservoir, was to take water from the Cockshaw Burn at a point near Summerrods and pipe along the hillside to the reservoir. The cost was estimated to be £400. It was thought to a very satisfactory way forward especially accompanied by the erection of the wall at the reservoir.

The Local Board held a number of meetings in September and October of 1870, which focussed on the crisis. It was decided on 19 September that water for trading and manufacturing purposes be cut off and that a committee be appointed to consider 'the propriety of obtaining an additional water supply and as to the means and expense by which such supply could be obtained if deemed necessary.' That decision was not accepted by Thomas Welford, a tireless opponent (both in the Board and in letters to the press) of any activity likely to increase the rates. At this juncture he argued for stopping the supply of water to gardeners and others, who used it 'most lavishly for a few pounds a-year'. Nevertheless he was put onto the committee. At the next meeting, a Mr Rome was appointed to survey the land and estimate the cost of conducting water to the reservoir from 'certain springs'. The committee reported to the Board on 17 October. Springs at Yarridge and Highford appeared to be promising sources of supply for the existing reservoir (Fig.16). However financial considerations loomed large, not only because of a shortage of money but also because of possible pending legislation with respect to river pollution through the discharge of sewage. The use by Hexham of the Tyne for such purposes could have considerable future financial consequences for the town and as the report put it 'ought to prevent any but the most absolutely necessary expenditure'. It was proposed that no action be taken, other than water used for trade be metered. Essentially, the Board put its trust in winter rainfall.

The following year, at the 17 April meeting of the Board, the Chairman, William Robb, brought up the matter of the need for more water. He took a new tack, governed by a need for the town 'to save all possible expense' (later in the year it became clear that the town was in debt). He was concerned that a considerable portion of the water from the drainage area on West Causey Hill was being channelled into the bye-wash, the stream by-passing the reservoir, because a certain quantity of sewage was coming from three or four houses in the vicinity. He proposed that the sewage be removed in some other way. The Sewage Committee, which took up the matter, both confirmed that the Yarridge scheme proposed the preceding year was too expensive, and reported that, by use of cess-pools and diversionary channels, the sewage from the properties could be prevented from entering the water running into the reservoir. But no action seems to have been contemplated.

The very high rainfall in 1872 took the need for an improved water supply off the agenda of the Board. But the year is not without importance to the sanitary history of Hexham. On August 23, William Robb, as the Chairman of the Board, at the start of the proceedings of the Board, 'in pursuance of the Public Health Act of 1872', declared meeting to be the first of the Urban Sanitary Authority. A tangible consequence of the passing of the Act was the need to appoint a Medical Officer of Health. The actual appointment was deferred twice before Dr Daniel Jackson was favoured over a Dr Haining and appointed to post on 28 April 1873, at a salary of £20 per annum. His appointment was part time but he proved to be a doughty fighter for better sanitary conditions within Hexham.

Below average rainfall in 1873 led to the rationing of water in the autumn. The disappearance of water from the reservoir re-focussed the minds of the Board on how to solve the problem. At the meeting of the Board on 1 September a committee was set up, the main recommendation of which was that an engineer be appointed to make a preliminary survey of the district. After a debate about the matter the Board engaged John Tone of Newcastle, to make a preliminary survey. The following year saw Dr Jackson making a short but highly critical statement on the sanitary condition of Hexham (HLBH 19.1.1874). He left no doubt as to the need for an improved water supply in his remark 'wherever water supply is deficient disease is sure to follow.' On 23 February, Tone presented his report to the Board on increasing the supply of water. He based his thinking on the need to supply the town with 200,000 gallons per day, upwards of twice the amount yielded by the present water works. This requirement immediately ruled out Cockshaw and Causey Hill Burns and the Yarridge springs. Tone therefore concentrated on the Dipton Burn focussing on its watershed above Greenridge. The height of the place, where impounding was proposed, meant that water could be brought by open aqueduct to Nubbock and thence by aqueduct or pipe to the reservoir. The water-collecting area according to the Tone's report 'is remarkably free of population and the land is almost wholly used for pasturage, thereby avoiding contamination from sewage or manures.'

For the next stage, the Board decided to set up another committee that would procure an analysis of the water at Greenridge and obtain any other information, which would allow the Board to come to an informed decision as to whether or not to proceed with the proposal. On 27 April 1874, armed with some more information, the Board debated Tone's proposals. William Robb gave the lead. He expressed concern about the cost of the scheme (estimated to be c£1,500) as well as the difficulties of obtaining easements, that is the right to lay pipes across a considerable distance of land and securing agreement with those having riparian rights, which were the result of their land abutting on the banks of the stream, to the water of the stream. Negotiating easements and obtaining permission over riparian rights would entail financial compensation. Robb therefore did not want to press forward with the scheme. Instead he proposed that it would be much better if they took water from much closer to hand from the Cockshaw Burn at Summerrods. At the Board meeting a fortnight later, seemingly as a result of a survey carried out by James Marshall, Surveyor to the Board, the proposed location for impounding water was moved eastwards to Woodley Field. to the stream running into the Hextol Burn (Fig. 16). The reason for the decision was undoubtedly the prevailing conditions of drought. The closer proximity of Woodley Field to the reservoir was such that less piping would be required (and the cost proportionately reduced), allowing the scheme to be carried out without delay. The year 1874 saw a long dry summer, which was of national concern, the Local Government Board issuing a circular to sanitary authorities about the need for care over using other supplies which might be polluted and to adopt every precaution for the storage of 'wholesome water' (HC 11.7.1874). Hexham like the rest of the country was up against a shortage of water. But legal difficulties over permission to use the water prevented the desired swift action. W Cunningham Glen, a London lawyer and asked to advise the Board on the matter, indicated that compulsory powers would be required to obtain the water (HC 13.6.1874). The Board immediately authorised the laying of 3-inch pipes from Watty's Well to the Intake Burn. The exact location of this particular well is uncertain but must have been relatively close to the reservoir. At an earlier date, in order to increase the supply of water in the Cockshaw area of the town, the Board had resolved that the Seal Well be repaired and the Glovers Pant be reconnected with the

Well. It is not clear when these sources of supply were brought on stream – there was some question as to whether the Board still had rights to the water from Watty's Well under the Award of the Hexham Commons – but on 17 August the shortage of water was such that it was decided to cut off the supply to the town from 8 p.m. to 6 a.m. A fortnight later, the time when water was not available was increased, the water being turned off at 4 p.m. and not coming on again until 7 a.m the following day.

William Robb was unwilling to let short-term measures divert the Local Board from a search from a long-term solution to its problem of providing a satisfactory water supply. On 6 July, he persuaded his colleagues to agree to a motion

> That a gentleman acquainted with the strata of the neighbourhood and the water which may be found in such strata, be engaged to survey the Southern Hill Side with a view to obtain increased supply of water by gravitation.

It was also resolved that John Roscamp, the Manager of Acomb Colliery, be engaged to make the survey. He responded quickly. He went over the terrain with two unnamed Board members. In his report he pointed out that many springs in the area close to the reservoir would not provide effective supplies because they are in strata, which dip down into the hill. On 19 September, Ralph Robson rose in the Board to propose

> that the principal Riparian Proprietors on Summerrods and Dipton Burns be communicated with a view to obtain their consent to take water from their streams for the purpose of increasing the Town Supply and report at the earliest possible period.

Both Robson and the seconder William Robb stressed the need to go further afield for the supply of water now that it had been shown that there was insufficient close to hand. The motion was passed *nem. dis.* Whether such discussions took place is not clear but on 26 October Robson and Robb proposed that water be taken from the Dipton Burn at a point near Greenridge and, when this was agreed to (only Matthew Smith dissenting), they proposed that some qualified person be appointed to produce a detailed survey and estimates. Edward Brown, Engineer, of Newcastle provided a report, which was read to the Board on 13 November. Knowing that the Board was satisfied that the Greenridge Burn could supply the necessary quantity of water of the required quality he devoted his report to the best route for the water to reach the reservoir. Using pipes to convey the water, the estimated total cost was £1950.10s.0d. The following day, in the *Courant*, the Local Board gave notice (in somewhat complicated legal jargon) of its intention to get the necessary permissions to take water and to purchase land as given in a schedule and required for the 'purpose of supplying water for drinking and domestic purposes to the said District of Hexham'.

The Chairman of the Board, Dr Thomas Stainthorpe was anxious to proceed with the scheme and on 7 December proposed that permission be obtained to lay a significant length of pipes be laid before seeking permission to abstract water. William Robb urged caution, since the Board would lose money if they were unable to get permission to abstract water from the Greenridge Burn. It was decided that the whole matter be held over for six months. That decision seems not to have been adhered to, for on 1 February 1875 the Board resolved that the Clerk write and report to the

Home Secretary that the Board was now in a position to meet an Inspector for the purpose of carrying out the proposed additional water supply. Though no Inspector had come to Hexham, the Board on 21 April petitioned the Local Government Board to authorise the local Board to Purchase the lands required for improvement of the water supply. Once again, when the vote was taken, Matthew Smith was in a minority of one.

Then, for reasons that will be made apparent later, matters held fire until March 1876. In the interim, there was an indication that the way forward might not be smooth. On 25 March there was a meeting of the ratepayers in the Moot Hall 'to take into consideration the present water supply and sanitary condition of the town' (*HC* 27.3.1875). Matthew Smith was elected chairman and spoke at length against the plan to extend the water supply as proposed. He thought that the very dry conditions of 1874 'might not occur for many years to come'. He felt the Local Board should try another year and avail themselves of all the resources of the district. Until that experiment had been tried he was opposed to any expenditure. He condemned the water in Dipton Burn as being 'injurious', since it would bring animal and vegetable matter into the reservoir and spoil the pure water they were getting from the pure springs in the district. In saying this, Smith had studiously ignored an analysis carried out by the Medical Officer the same month from which he reported that the outflow of a duck and horse pond at the Intake into the rivulet, which supplies the reservoir as being 'hurtful to health'. Admittedly the rivulet was to be diverted to avoid the outflow, but it is clear that Smith was ignoring the unsatisfactory nature of the area from which he wanted water to be collected for the use of the town. Almost all those reported spoke against the proposed expenditure to improve the water supply. Only Edward Snowball expressed doubts and that was in terms of an inadequate supply of water to flush the sewers, leading to ill-health of the inhabitants. But at the end of the meeting, a long resolution, which in essence supported Matthew Smith's view that the proposed scheme should only go ahead if all local sources of water had been brought into use and found insufficient, was passed unanimously.

On 13 March, 1876, Matthew Smith attempted to have the resolution passed to ask Parliamentary powers for bringing increased quantities of water from Greenridge and Nubbock be rescinded, the application for increased Parliamentary powers be quashed; and water within their present range be added to the general supply without delay. Interestingly, the Chairman, the medical doctor Thomas Stainthorpe, seconded the motion. But everyone else was against and, as a strong expression of their opinion, they instructed the Clerk to write to the Local Government Board and request an Inspector be sent down with as little delay as possible to examine the Greenridge scheme. All the old arguments were trotted out by Smith but without effect; those who were against could not see where the additional water, envisaged by Smith, would come from. Ralph Robson thought Smith was just electioneering.

Robson was almost certainly right. The election of four new members (usually three but William Robb had tendered his resignation in January and replacing him was held over till the election) that took place in April was hard-fought affair. Ruth Jennings (1998) has described the campaigning in some detail. Essentially, it was a battle between those (the so-called clean party) who wanted to spend money and improve the sanitary conditions of the town (both improved water supply and a better sewerage system) and those (the so-called dirty party) who were content with the *status quo*. Those who wanted sanitary reform came out of the election with a strong mandate for progress with their aims. Matthew Smith was thrown off the Board. But, as we shall see, the hold of the clean party on power was tenuous.

Signs that all was not well came on 8 May, when the decision of 13 March (see above), seemingly not acted upon was deferred for another month. When the time came for the matter to be reconsidered, the proposal to request the visit of an Inspector was defeated (Ralph Robson and Lewis Lockhart who would have supported the motion were absent from the meeting). This decision was followed by a resolution that applications be made to the owners and occupiers of land south of the reservoir in the High Yarridge/Breckon Hill and High Causey Hill areas for their consent with respect to obtaining water and laying pipes to the reservoir.

One of the landowners contacted was Mr. Beaumont. His agent John Kaye, echoing what experts had expressed previously, wrote to say that, while Mr Beaumont was willing to give a 21 year's lease for power to put down pipes provided sufficient water was left for the farm, he (Kaye) feared that the supply would be inadequate for the town (HLBH 25.9.1876). However, other landowners refused to sanction pipes crossing their land. The Water Committee of the Board, reporting on obtaining water from Breckon Hill (HLBH 9.10.1876) – Causey Hill had been ruled out because of possible pollution – made clear the legal route, which needed to be followed:

> In order to interfere with or acquire land or water rights of any proprietor or tenant the necessary compulsory powers must be obtained and in order to borrow funds required permission must be had from the Local Government Board, and that the Board must in any case be satisfied on investigation that the proposed extension is such as they ought to sanction.

The Committee were undoubtedly convinced that there was insufficient water close at hand to the reservoir and thus recommended that 'the Board acquire forthwith the powers required for the purpose of carrying out the scheme contemplating the scheme of Mr Brown......' 'All powers should be obtained as soon as possible......' The plain speaking throughout the report was almost certainly a consequence of it being produced in the middle of a water crisis

> On Sunday and Monday, scores of people visited the reservoir, and many were the exclamations of surprise which broke from the lips of those who visited it for the first time for some weeks past, as they gazed upon the very scanty supply of water (HC 7.10.1876).

Four days before that report the Local Board had resolved that 'during the present scarcity of water the supply to the town be limited to four hours in the morning viz from 7 to 11 and two hours in the evening from 4 to 6......' This must have caused great hardship, particularly for those institutions that required a continuous supply of water. A notable one was the Workhouse, as we have seen, almost certainly one of the larger users of water, if not the largest, which was in difficulty over the supply of water to its steam boiler which was used for cooking and other purposes (HC 14.10.1876). A restricted water supply continued into November.

Mr J. W. Jamieson, who had reported on this problem to a meeting of the Board at the same time suggested that the Board hired a 14-horse power engine standing unemployed at Hexham Ironworks and pump water from Barley Well near Birks (Fig. 16). They could get 86,000 gallons a day, at a cost of £200, with pipes running c 600 yards to the reservoir laid on the surface. At a later meeting (HLBH 6.11.1876), Barley Well was added to the list of possible sources of water, though it was not as satisfactory as seemed at first sight, since it was at a lower level than the reservoir. Water could be fed directly into the filter beds, just below the dam of the reservoir (Fig. 14) that were 32 ft 8 inches lower than the Well.

The key decision during this crisis period for the Board was the re-engagement of Edward Brown of Newcastle to advise the Board (HLBH 1.11.1876). As before, he didn't waste time. On 8 November, he reported to the Board. He was extremely disparaging of the idea of using Barley Well. It would only yield, at the most, 40,000 gallons per day, the distance to be travelled to the filter beds (which would only hold one day's supply of water) along the contours was 3.1 miles, the fall would be eight feet per mile and 1³/₄ miles of that pipe would have to be laid wholly through wood and rocky strata. (At the next meeting, the proposal to use Barley Well was rescinded – Thomas Welford nevertheless arguing that Brown's report could not be trusted and attempting to rubbish the Greenridge scheme.) Having disposed of Barley Well, Brown made clear to the Board that they should carry out the Greenridge Burn scheme. He also spelt out most clearly the steps that had to be taken to obtain Government approval of the scheme. Though as we shall see below, the Board had been made well aware of what needed to be done by the Local Government Board.

January 1877 saw some real progress. A Petition, prepared by the Clerk, in which the members of the Local Board 'humbly pray…… be allowed to put in force the powers of the Lands Clauses Consolidation Act 1845 with respect to the purchase and taking of lands otherwise than by agreement' after being signed and sealed was transmitted to the Local Government Board. Interestingly, in spite of what had been decided in the Board meeting reported above, the Petition was concerned not only with the acquisition of land for a reservoir to be built at Stublick (the Greenridge Burn scheme) and for a pipeline to the storage reservoir at Wydon Burn but for a pipeline from Barley Well (NA MH12/9050).

But behind the above picture of events from February 1875, culled from the minutes of the Local Board of Health and reports in the *Courant* of seemingly satisfactory progress towards the provision of a larger water supply, the Hexham Local Board of Health was in very considerable trouble. The Local Government Board had become increasingly aware of the unsatisfactory state of the sanitary state of the town. It all began with the first annual report of the Medical Officer of Health, Daniel Jackson, presented to the Local Board of Health on 18 January 1875, which he also forwarded to the Local Government Board. To obtain the full picture of what happened, there is a need to recount what is known about development of the sewage system in Hexham between 1854 and 1876 and this will be done in the next chapter The reader should note that it was the arrival of the Petition, referred to in the previous paragraph, which brought everything into the open.

CHAPTER 8

An interlude about sewage

The problems of dealing with sewage

What we know as sewage disposal is a very specialised operation. Indeed it is something that rarely impinges on the great bulk of the population, except when there is the occasional blockage of a sewage pipe. The disposal of sewage now demands engineering and biological expertise, no longer carried out by local authorities but by the water companies. But in 1848, when the first Public Health Act was passed, sewage disposal was part of the large body of sanitary matters coming under the purview of the Local Board of Health.

Throughout the nineteenth century the town had only two paid officials to deal with sanitary matters – the Surveyor and the Inspector of Nuisances. Sometimes the two posts were combined, sometimes separate. Undoubtedly, the person or persons holding these posts were under pressure, not helped by tendency of Local Board members to treat them as servants, there to do the bidding of the Board. This is illustrated by the following exchanges at the second Local Government inquiry in 1878 (*HC* 11.8.1878):

> Mr Baty (Clerk to the Local Board): In flushing the sewers and watering the streets, have they been as sufficiently and frequently done as they ought to have been?
> Mr Dawson (Surveyor): No.
> The Inspector: Why have you not done so?
> Mr Dawson: Continual complaints were made by members and ratepayers that I was wasting water.
> The Inspector: If the Board came to a decision and give you instructions, you have no right to attend to the directions of individual members, either of one or more of them.
> Mr Dawson: I have been told that any member of the Board has a right to interfere with me. They have interfered with me repeatedly.
> The Inspector: Very improper.

Dawson went on to say that 'they went on to such a pitch interfering with my duties that at the beginning of the month I resigned'. The actual incident which led to his resignation was his decision to sweep the streets on a Saturday night, after 9.0 p.m., when 'all the windows were open'. What is surprising is that, after the position was advertised, it was Dawson who was appointed back into his old post (HLBH 30.9.1878) – much to the disgust of John Hodgson, who wrote a highly critical letter to the *Courant* about 'The Hexham Surveyorship Fiasco'. He outlined Dawson's many faults most strikingly illustrated by the method of making connections between public sewers 'by the reprehensible method of breaking holes in their [pipes] sides' (Fig. 17). This particular appointment is illustrative of the fact that the method used for appointment to these posts was a surprisingly hit-or-miss affair. One problem, in the early days, was obtaining candidates who had anything more than a superficial understanding of the problems (engineering and biological) that they were facing. Not surprisingly, the Board members, especially if the person was a builder, often knew as much, if not more, than the two officials – hence their status vis-à-vis the Board. It has to be said that, even when the Surveyor was a competent engineer, such as Robert Grieves (see below), a Board member could take a high-handed attitude with regard to sanitary expertise. A striking example was the acrimonious correspondence in the Courant between a Board member, Robert Stainthorpe, and Grieves over the relaying of sewers in Skinnersburn (Eastgate). The evidence that eventually included testimony of W. Geo. Laws, City Engineer of Newcastle, came down heavily in favour of Grieves. A lengthy letter by John Hodgson to the April 16 1879 issue of the *Courant* provides a critical and detailed commentary on the inability of the Board to manage its sanitary affairs with any degree of efficiency. He had no hesitation in concluding that 'the fault lies with the Board, who have chosen to exercise their powers of amateur supervision over the town's work in preference to relying upon skilled advice, such as is, of course under the circumstances, not represented on their staff.'

A change of attitude came in 1873 with the appointment of the Medical Officer of Health, Daniel Jackson (Fig. 18), who, as we shall see, reported (with great effect) to the General Board of Health and to the Local Government Board. He always spoke with authority, using statistics to good effect. He was a good ally to surveyors and inspectors of nuisances and probably helped to inculcate a more professional approach within the Board to sanitary problems. Undoubtedly, the several experts called in for their advice during the first decades of the Board also contributed to this professional approach. Eventually, the appointment on 16 January 1882 of Robert Grieves, from South Shields, to the post of Surveyor brought the required professionalism to the sanitary side of the Board's activities. Following the dismissal of the previous Surveyor, because he could not cope with the demands of the post, Grieves demonstrated his authority with an initial incisive report on some of the sanitary problems of the town. From then on he submitted a formal report to each meeting of the Board, a tradition carried on by his successors. A good measure of the stature of Grieves was his ability to deal in a satisfactory manner with questions put to him in the consideration of the Hexham Water Bill by a committee of the House of Lords in 1888.

Early on, we indicated that much of the sewage ended up in pits (middens) associated with privies or associated with the ashes and other household waste material – all of which had to be carted away. Material of similar kind had to be removed (scavenged) from the roads as the result of the considerable traffic of animals, horses for carrying people and haulage and cattle and sheep, on their way either to be sold or to be slaughtered. Gradually flush toilets came in and of course they required pipes to take away the effluent. Finally there was an increasing need to take away rainwater, as extensive showers could damage the road-surface and lead to blocked drains.

We know, only in a general way, how all this material was dealt with. As has been indicated earlier, the extent of the pipe system required for transporting liquid sewage and associated suspended material was limited. It was some time after the formation of the Local Board was formed that steps were made to deal with disposal. In 1866, it was planned to purchase Harbottle's (Broonhaugh) Island from W. B. Beaumont for the 'purpose of conveying the town's sewage beneath the surface of the Tyne'. As far as one can gather, there was to be a cesspool, to be used 'for collecting and deodourising' the sewage, which, after this primitive treatment, was to leave the cesspool for the river by an outfall (*HC* 14.11.1866). The cesspool was undoubtedly built but it seems not on the

Island and, further, it has not been ascertained whether or not the sewage reached the river from the cesspool by a pipe or by passing over (by 'irrigation') the land. As we shall see this latter uncertainty is rather academic.

That said, the auguries for a much-improved system for dealing with the sewage were not good. Matthew Smith remained as Chairman of the Board until 1866 and throughout that period and after set a very bad example. We have earlier learnt of his attitude to the conditions of his tenants with regard to the disposal of human waste. But events were to catch up with him. In 1872, he was forced by the Board to take better sanitary care of his property, in which, we now know from a letter from William Robb to the Local Government Board, there were three privies 'so notoriously defective and kept in a state so vile that a detailed account is impossible' for 130 persons (NA 12/9047). Nevertheless, the improvement seems to have been short-lived, since, in 1876, he was warned once again by the magistrates about his property, eventually being fined the following year for failure to comply (Jennings, 1998). It is not surprising that, if a leading citizen could behave in this way, other members of the community were slow to make improvements to the sanitary aspects of their property. Equally the Local Board moved only slowly with regard to improving the sewage system.

The sanitary situation in Hexham at that time is best summarised in an extract from Daniel Jackson's second annual report to the Board on 2 January 1876. He is bitter about the very high annual death-rate of the town, the rate for 1875 being 34.7 per thousand, when he is convinced that, 'considering the great natural advantages of its [Hexham's] position', it could be much lower, indeed under 20 per thousand (see Chapter 15). Jackson, lamenting the lack of any action by the Board, describes the town as follows

> The system of cleansing the town by contract may be economical, but in a sanitary point of view it has signally failed in Hexham. The defective structural arrangements of many of the houses remain unchanged, huge middens still exist, uncovered and unprotected from leakage by non-porous flagging and lining. The removal of daily refuse from dwelling houses takes place at all hours in open defiance of your by-laws. Houses remain unspouted, the streets are almost impassable on foot on account of the numerous pools of stagnant water, and the ventilation and cleansing of the public sewers are left to the precarious action of the rainfall. As a necessary and inevitable consequence the town is rarely free from fever and other preventable disease......

One particular problem which added to the difficulties of cleansing the town were the several slaughterhouses, which with one exception 'are most prejudicial to health, both from their defective construction and from being situated in the midst of crowded tenements'. Jackson could not conscientiously sanction their existence and was disturbed that at the meeting to which he presented his report that the Board put off building public slaughterhouses. In fact they were not built until 1902 (HC 25.10.1902).

It is difficult to discover what improvements were made to the sewage system in the period from 1854 when the Local Board of Health was established and 1877, when the unsatisfactory nature of the sewage system took on a much higher profile.

The Local Government Board demand action

The minutes of the meeting of the Local Board on February 16 1877 cryptically report

> It was resolved on the motion of Mr Welford and seconded by Mr Taylor that a Committee of the whole Board be appointed to take into consideration the letter received by the Clerk from the Local Government Board dated February 13 1877 and the Report of the medical Officer for Health dated November 1876 and to take such steps as my be determined by meeting, and that this meeting be adjourned until Monday evening next.

The minutes give no details of the contents of the letter but hey were made apparent in the press the following Saturday. Essentially, the Local Government Board accused the Hexham Urban Sanitary Authority (the Local Board of Health) of failing to execute the provisions of the Public Health Acts, such that the Local Government Board were seriously considering dissolving the Hexham Authority under the terms of section 170 of the Public Health Act of 1875 and merging it with the Rural Sanitary Authority. The communication from London focussed the town on its sanitary problems with an intensity not apparent since the inspection of the town by Robert Rawlinson in 1853.

As will be made clear, the letter should not have caused any surprise for the Local Board of Health. Although its minutes give hardly any indication of the fact, the Local Government Board had, since the start of 1875 become increasingly irritated with the indifference shown by the Hexham Board to the sanitary problems of Hexham. We only know that this was so from the files of Local Government Board now in the Public Record Office (NA MH/12/ 9048, 9049 & 9050).

The starting point for the Local Government Board's concern was the arrival in mid-January 1875 of a copy of Daniel Jackson's first report to the Hexham Board that, like his second report from which I have quoted above, contained damning statistics about the health of Hexham. Shortly afterwards, the Local Government Board were writing to the Clerk, Isaac Baty, expressing concern about the sanitary state of Hexham and asking what steps the Board were taking or proposing to take 'to provide for the efficient flushing and ventilation of the sewers and to improve the water supply of the town'. Before that letter had been received, the Clerk, Isaac Baty had written to the Local Government Board informing them that, in accordance with the Lands Clauses Consolidation Act of 1845 (8 & 9 Vict., c. 18), notice had been given to take certain lands in the District to increase the water supply and 'requesting an Inspector be sent down to report on the advisability of the scheme'. As a result of this latter letter, London had two matters of concern about the approach of the Hexham Board to sanitary problems – the state of the sewage system and the manner in which the Board were going about improving their water supply. On learning what was proposed about a new water supply, the Local Government Board requested a petition of the kind referred to earlier, together with evidence that the action envisaged by the Board was being properly advertised in local newspapers. In spite of three reminders, there was no reply from the Hexham. The only letter that the Local Government Board received was the following anodyne communication from Isaac Baty dated 20 April 1875:

> I beg to acknowledge the receipt of your letter of the 25th March last respecting the Report of Dr Jackson to this Authority on the Sanitary state and mortality of their District and am

instructed to say in reply that the sewers have been efficiently flushed and steps are in progress for the proper ventilation of the sewers and to improve the Water Supply of the town.

Who authorised the Clerk to write, as he did, cannot be ascertained. There is no mention in the Board minutes of any instruction, nor, for that matter, is there any indication of sewer flushing. Indeed, at a meeting of the Board seven days earlier Dr Jackson in his quarterly report is stressing the need for an abundant supply of water for sewer flushing. He also drew attention to the practice of those connecting houses to the main sewers 'to knock a rough hole in the main pipe and thrust the end of the connecting pipe into it, instead of making the proper water tight junction'. There is no evidence in the minutes of any great efficiency with regard to the care of the sewers.

The problem for the Hexham Board was that the Local Government Board continued to learn from Daniel Jackson, through his quarterly reports, about his views on the sanitary state of the town. After three letters from the Local Government Board repeating the request for the presentation of a petition with respect to obtaining land for an improved water supply and another one expressing the continued concern about the high death rate in Hexham (which Jackson had drawn attention to), the Clerk replied on December 14 1875 with such phrases as 'The high death rate which has prevailed in their [the Board members'] district...... has urged them to measures to abate the nuisances', 'awake to the general principals [sic] that the public health is mainly dependent upon pure water and air, the Authority are putting in force all the powers which the Sanitary Acts have rested in them'. The Clerk argued that the problems have been due to 'a succession of droughty summers' but the sewers are to be 'thoroughly flushed and examined from the highest part of the Town to Outfall', an Inspector of Nuisances is 'actively engaged in seeing that yards, ashpits and privies are kept in cleaner condition', a Provisional Order application 'is being made' with respect to increasing the supply of water and the fact that the Local Board had purchased land 'upon which to erect a Common Slaughter House' (NA MH/12/9047). Much of what was said in that letter was stretching the facts, if not untrue. Standing out was the fact that, while there were on-going discussions to build a common slaughterhouse (the suggested site being in Broadgates), no land had been purchased – indeed no public slaughterhouse was ever built there.

The Local Government Board almost certainly must have read this letter with a considerable degree of scepticism, because on 13 December 1875, the day before Isaac Baty was penning his letter, the Board had written to him about a report from their Medical Inspector, Dr Stevens, who had reason to visit the district in connection with a proposal that patients should be sent by the Hexham Board to the fever wards of the Workhouse. That particular issue need not detain us. Stevens was dismayed by what he found about the discharge of sewage from the 'fever block' – it flowed into the town sewerage system and without modification into the Tyne. He was concerned about 'the very many persons living in detached cottages and isolated hamlets' taking their water from the river. The covering letter, requesting the observations of the Hexham Board, pointed out that the settling tanks for dealing with the sewage were disused.

The following year, 1876, was outstanding for the number of letters from the Local Government Board attempting to get action over the following i) the sanitary improvements indicated in the Clerk's letter of 14 December (two letters); ii) the disposal of sewage (four letters); iii) the re-appointment of the Medical Officer (three letters) and iv) the need to send forward a petition with respect to the proposed water supply (five letters) This stream of letters continued until September. In the period from January until then, there were only three letters from Hexham. There was one from the Chairman, Thomas Stainthorpe, asking permission i) to have on the voting paper an indication that electors can vote for four candidates (in the past the number has been three but, due to the resignation of William Robb in mid-term, there was an additional vacancy) and ii) not to have the names of all the nominators on voting paper because with the number of candidates (seven) to do so would make the paper unwieldy. This letter was courteously answered but it was clear that the Local Government Board should not have been troubled; the matter was one for the Town's Returning Officer. Of the other two letters, there was one from Matthew Smith querying the validity of the Local Election that had just taken place (he lost his seat). That was again a matter for the Returning Officer. The final letter, dated 10 May, was a terse communication from the Clerk, saying that at a meeting of the Local Board 'the consideration of forwarding a petition to your [Local Government] Board asking for an Inspector to be sent down was deferred for one month'.

The reply of the Local Governing Board to that last letter showed the Board's patience was wearing thin. The letter pointed out that the Hexham Board, since February 1875, had been dragging its heels over the matter of the petition. The Local Government Board regarded 'the proceedings as very unsatisfactory'. Finally the Board's patience snapped. On 2 September 1876, J.H. Rotton, on behalf of the Local Government Board sent a long letter indicating the Board's considerable displeasure at the failure of Hexham to answer its letters. The last paragraph spoke in no uncertain terms:

> It appears that the Board are unable to obtain from the Local Board any information with respect to several questions of importance in relation to the sanitary affairs of their District and they cannot help feeling grave doubts as to whether these affairs are being properly administered. A Local Government District is only established for proper sanitary administration and the Local Government Board are empowered by Section 170 of the Public Health Act, 1875, to dissolve any such District by Provisional Order, if they think it expedient to do so. The Board feel it incumbent upon them therefore to consider whether the power should be exercised in the present case and unless they receive within a month from the date of this letter some satisfactory communication from the Local Board with regard to each of these several matters referred to, they will proceed to direct an official enquiry with a view to determining whether a Provisional Order should be issued to dissolve the District of the Local Board and to merge it with that of the Rural Sanitary Authority (NA MH12/9049).

The response of the Clerk to the Local Board, Isaac Baty, proved not to be acceptable. The exact nature of the reply is difficult to establish because of the present damaged state of the letter that was sent. The comments of the civil servants written on the letter make it clear that they know from other sources that, in spite of the apparent protestations of the Clerk, all is not well with the sanitary state of the town. One comment led to the agreed response of the Local Government Board:

> Would it not be well to say that the letter is unsatisfactory and ask for a special report from the Medical Officer of Health (who I believe is a good man) on the Water Supply, Ventilation of sewers, disposal of sewage, conditions of the Slaughter Houses and generally on the sanitary condition of the town (NA MH12/9048).

A letter dated 1 November 1876 to the Clerk contained this request and, for once, this fact was reported in the minutes of the Local Board of Health. Jackson quickly obliged and, on 20 November it was sent to London. The report, which was seen by the Local Board pulled no punches, amplifying at length what had he had written at the start of the year. When the report is read, it is difficult to see how one can conclude other than the town was in a parlous state from the sanitary point of view. When the Local Government Board received the report, it was commented upon as follows

> The report confirms everything that has before been reported or suspected as to the neglect and incapacity of the Local [Hexham] Board. It will be observed that it was asked for to assist this Board in its consideration of the necessity of superseding the Local Board and giving the same function of the Local Board to the Rural Sanitary Authority. Apparently it furnishes no reason against such a step (NA MH12/9048).

The Local Government Board did not immediately come to a decision about how to pursue the matter. Fortunately for Hexham, the Local Board paid attention to the report of Edward Brown, presented in November 1876, on how the Town might be better supplied with water. In that report, he had 'strongly' advised to the Local Board of Health to submit the necessary petition to the Local Government Board for a provisional order leading to the compulsory purchase of land for the proposed new water supply. The necessary petition was submitted at the start of 1877. Because the Local Board had for once done something that the Local Government Board had been wanting, the letter of 13 February, which caused such alarm in the town, was in fact less catastrophic than might have been predicted, because, the letter as well as mentioning the possibility of the dissolution of the Local Board, also informed the Local Board that an Inspector was to be sent

> with regard to the water supply but also for the remedy of the other grave sanitary defects (especially in the condition of the sewers, the disposal of sewage, and the removal of refuse) which have from time to time been brought to their [Local Government Board's] notice

Hexham was thus being given the opportunity to present a convincing case that matters on the ground were not as bad as they seemed to be from the various reports that had been emanating from those who had looked closely at the sanitary conditions of the Town.

Before returning to the narrative of events in Hexham, we need to digress to consider why Hexham took its stance that it did with respect to the letters from the Local Government Board. There is no doubt that the Town had an antipathy to outside interference. This is shown strikingly by the response of the newly elected Local Board of Health to the report produced by Robert Rawlinson such that it had little intention of bringing about sanitary improvement. But throughout the 19th century and indeed to a lesser extent in the last century, there is plenty of evidence from the transcripts of discussions in the Local Board of Health/Urban District Council that members took umbrage over decisions made in London. However, the stance taken was never of such strength as to prevent eventual acceptance of what London was wanting. There is no doubt that during this period when the Local Government Board were chasing Hexham over the sanitary state of the town, there were sufficient hot-heads on the Local Board to feel that London could be faced-down. Yet, as we have indicated, there were also on the Board, during this particular period, several members who were committed to sanitary reform and one would be inclined to doubt that they would have supported treating the requests for information from the Local Government Board in the manner described. There is thus a tantalising situation that needs explanation. I think we can rule out an explanation based on the inefficiency/wrong-headedness of the Clerk, Isaac Baty. During the same period, he was also Clerk to the Guardians. One has only to see the massive number of communications to London from Isaac Baty, when acting in the latter capacity, compared with the very few he sent on behalf of the Hexham Local Board.

A possible explanation lies in the financial state of the Board. Correspondence in the files of the Local Government Board indicates that the Hexham Board had got behind with the repayment of its loans and perhaps all members were, to a greater or lesser extent, fearful of the consequences of the consequence of an increase in expenditure. If this is so, there must have been collusion between all the members of the Board that letters from the Local Government Board should not only not be answered but the letters themselves and any replies should not be made public. There is some slight circumstantial evidence for this view. Joseph Catherall, who was editor of the *Hexham Courant*, was at this time a member of the Board. He was an enthusiast for sanitary improvement, yet when the February 13th-letter arrived in Hexham, the response of the *Courant* was surprisingly muted; there was no leader on the matter, the news of a possible takeover by the Rural Sanitary Authority of the Hexham Local of Health being given in a short paragraph, printed in small type.

The response of the Town to the Local Government Board letter

Regardless of whether the Board were surprised or not, the inhabitants most certainly were. Amongst the first responses was a long letter in the 24 February issue of the *Courant* from *Pro Bono Publico* in which the letter from the Local Government Board is

> an indignity to the town, which never previously suffered, even in the palmiest days of dirty water, and it is difficult to conceive a lower depth of degradation and humiliation than is indicated by the indirect threat to subject the town to the control of the Rural Sanitary Authority.

Nevertheless, the author admits that with respect the Local Board 'folly has prevailed and nothing has been accomplished.' The next week's issue contained the advertisement for a Public Meeting of 'Ratepayers and Inhabitants...... to consider the threatened dissolution of the Local Board...... and to take such steps...... to avert the threatened calamity.'

We need not go into the details of that meeting. Old arguments were rehearsed and much heat was generated. Indeed, there had been a similar meeting the previous week, ostensibly to hear the three retiring members of the Board give an account of their three year's stewardship in preparation for the forthcoming election. In actual fact, two candidates, John Moffatt and Ralph Robson, seemingly were not invited – the meeting turned into one to further the candidacy of William Taylor. Not surprisingly, the meeting, which should have been concerned with the possible dissolution of the Board, degenerated into an election debate.

Mr Hodgson's report

Fortunately, the Board itself had got the message and at an adjourned meeting on 19 February 1877 decided to take action. The resolve of the Board was probably strengthened by a letter to the Board from Major Nicholson, who had chaired 'a private meeting of a few leading ratepayers held that afternoon in the Town Hall Building', in which letter he urged the Urban Sanitary Authority to 'immediately take such steps as may be required to enable them to conform thoroughly with the wishes of the Local Government Board', hoping that the town would be put into a satisfactory sanitary state before the Inspector arrived. Not all the action proposed was very sensible. Dr Jackson was requested to carry out a number of tasks, which were essentially a repeat of what he was doing already. But the Board did have the sense to recommend that 'some competent Engineer be asked to visit Hexham and make a full and thorough examination of the Sanitary arrangements of the Town......' On 26 February, John Hodgson of Haltwhistle was recommended for the task. His report of six closely-argued printed pages was presented to the Local Board on 25 March (NRO/PHU/A6/1).

Hodgson's report makes salutary reading. He refers to the 'very great and unusual distance to which, almost throughout the town the buildings yards, etc., of individual properties extend from the front street.' this and the lack of back streets made for difficulty in carrying out sanitary measures. He points out that those properties as they have 'decayed and deteriorated' are no longer houses 'of a superior class' but tenemented properties, let and sub-let, such that 'one room constitutes the sole domestic accommodation of a sometimes large family'. Hodgson finds it difficult to conceive anything 'more useless and extravagant than the prosecution of sanitary measures in such low-class property as is to be found all over the town.' Nevertheless he does his best to provide helpful advice. Much of his report is concerned with the sewerage system. He is critical of the lack of inspection, the far-too-seldom flushing of the system, the excessive amount of material from the roads filling the sewers and the lack of ventilation of the system. The method of sewage disposal being used at present is inadequate and some simple measures for its improvement are suggested. The present system is one of *clarification*, i.e. removal of solids; Hodgson warns that the Local Government Board may demand that the sewage be *purified*, either chemically or by pumping it onto land. From a criticism of the sewerage system, Hodgson devotes almost two pages to the sanitary failings of private property. Much of criticism repeats the complaints already made by Dr Jackson. Here we need mention that 'not only are the water-closets of the commonest and cheapest pattern...... but the character of the fittings is also inferior' and 'another glaring defect in the sanitary arrangements of Hexham is the large number of middens which have been allowed to remain in use in spite of the sewerage system having been so long completed'. Finally Hodgson condemns all but one of the slaughterhouses and supports the application to the Local Government Board for an additional supply of water.

A committee was appointed to consider the report and recommend what steps, as deemed advisable, should be taken for carrying out the scheme. On 9 April 1877, having had discussions with Mr Hodgson, the Committee reported to the Board. The message was short and to the point. In general terms

The Committee confidently expect that many of the subjects of complaint noticed in the report [of John Hodgson] will now be removed by the efficient and systematic removal of refuse; cleaning of streets and roads; attention to gullies, water closets and water taps, etc.; and by due fulfilment of other work of like nature which the Board will now it is believed be able to carry out effectually by its own staff of men. The Committee recommend the Board to take into immediate consideration the propriety of obtaining as soon as possible the necessary carts, horses and other plant with the view of entirely dispensing with contract work and of placing the responsibility of the execution of the regular work of the Board upon their own Surveyor (NRO/1150/240).

As far as specifics were concerned, the following demanded attention:
1. Sewer ventilation – the provision of 60 additional openings with gratings, together with the alteration of the present man holes by the substitution of gratings for covers
2. Provision of 36 flushing valves in the places enumerated in the Hodgson's report.
3. Construction of the following new sewers – from Fore Street behind Priestpopple to Wentworth Place; in Church Row; from Wentworth Place to the Railway Tavern and from the Moot Hall to the top of Wentworth Place (depending on the condition of the present sewer there, which could not be inspected in the absence of man-holes).
4 Attention to be given to the state of private drains, surfaces of yards and spouting of buildings.
Action over the provision of slaughterhouses was deferred in consequence of the submission of plans for their erection in Haugh Lane.

On 13 April, the Board strengthened its response to Hodgson's report by proposing to apply to the Local Government Board for £1000 to carry out the work identified by the Committee and agreed unanimously that Mr Hodgson carry out the work. Yet, at the same time and in spite of the great value of his report, there was a move in the Board to renege on what was agreed verbally with Hodgson as to what he should be paid for advising on sanitary matters (HLBH 30.4.1877; 7.5.1877; 28.5.1877). Nevertheless, on 10 December, the Works Committee were able to report that the works, as specified by the Committee responding to John Hodgson's report, had been completed. The excavation and laying of the four new sewers were carried out by William Carr of Temperley Grange, the iron pipes being supplied by the Hexham firm of Pattinson, Davison & Spencer, the sanitary pipes by Messrs Harriman & Co. of Blaydon. However in the process of carrying out the work (HLBH 16.5.1877), the Surveyor to the Board, Mr Dawson, who was overseeing the work, reported on the almost universal defective condition of private sewers. Also, when pipe sewers had been put in, the old stone culverts had been left in place, becoming cesspools in the process (HLBH 11.6.1877). Dr Jackson, in his report to the Board of 23 July, brought to the attention of the Board further inadequacies present in the old system. Several of the sewers were 'mere rubble drains of unknown antiquity' such that 'the adjacent soil has become soaked and sodden with sewage.' Of particular infamy was the Skinners Burn. Jackson described it as running under the houses in the street of the same name, 'receiving the filth and excreta from many of these houses.' It then crossed the head of Priestpopple, going under the stables of the White Hart Inn, emerging from the tunnel at the back of the houses in Wentworth Place. Before emerging the stream had been joined by sewage from these houses as well as that coming from rubble-built sewers that lead through Hall Gate. It is not clear if these problems brought to light were properly rectified. Nevertheless, the indications are that the sewerage system was much improved. The only matter still requiring attention was sewage disposal at the outfall, by the railway station. For that, the surveyor had been authorised to make improvements, the significant ones being the provision of wire screens for use in the tanks to remove solid matter and the planting of trees in between the tanks and the railway.

Hodgson had another task, which was to suggest improvements to the water supply (HLBH 9.7.1877). First he recommended that the water entering the reservoir be screened to remove solid matter. Second he was scathing about the condition of the filter beds, making recommendations about their proper construction. The present system of cleaning the beds was, in his view, performed 'in the most negligent and incomplete manner'. A Mr Lynch, who was responsible for the management of the reservoir and filters, seems, all too frequently, to have been brought into the town for other duties. Also, he appeared to have had no idea about how to manage the filter beds, filling them up with an indiscriminate mass of sand and gravel.

CHAPTER 9

Much huffing and puffing about the water supply (1878-1886)

Two inquiries

By 1879, many considered the sewage problem was solved – though it has to be said that, in all probability, the maintenance of the system was far from perfect. Thus, in August 1879, we find John Hodgson writing to the Local Government Board about the lack of flushing of the sewers and their inadequate aeration, as well as a failure to record where new sewers had been laid down (HLBH 25.8.1879). These allegations were totally refuted by the Hexham Board.

Hodgson was concerned that nothing had been done to increase the supply of water to the town. An Inspector from the Local Government Board, John Thornhill Harrison, C.E., had held two inquiries (HC 14.4.1877 and 31.8.1878). Though the first (the forthcoming nature of which was contained in the letter from the Local Government Board of 13 February) was also concerned with the general sanitary state of the town, it was also concerned with the proposal to increase the water supply to the town from Stublick Syke (Fig. 19). Following that particular inquiry, the Hexham Local Board of Health received from the Local Government Board a Provisional Order enabling it, as the Urban Sanitary Authority, compulsorily purchase of the necessary land associated with using the water from Stublick. The second inquiry was exclusively concerned with improving the water supply, being triggered by the need of the Hexham authority get sanction to borrow £3,500 needed for establishing a new water supply. In both inquiries, there were criticisms raised (Thomas Welford being particularly vociferous). Apart from complaints that an increased supply was not wanted, essentially there were three criticisms of the scheme. The first was that the water-collecting area was used at certain times for washing/dipping 400-500 head of sheep, the second was that there was iron contamination from mine-workings (Fig. 20), third that Thomas Gibson Leadbitter, one of the riparian owners would not give his permission for water to be used. Harrison dismissed the first criticism, feeling that other suitable arrangements could be made for washing the sheep; he ignored iron contamination problem. His comments about the lack of agreement with Leadbitter (it appeared that negotiations were going on which revolved about the appropriate sum to be paid to him) suggested that he thought it a minor issue. The upshot of the inquiries was that the Local Government Board did not consider further transferring the sanitary responsibilities of the town to the Rural Sanitary Authority and, more positively, gave its blessing to the Stublick Syke scheme.

We do not know precisely why the Local Government Board did not carry out its threat to transfer the authority for sanitary matters from the Urban Local Board to the Rural Board. The seemingly lucky break of getting a Petition to the Local Government Board, before it had decided to act, undoubtedly helped, as did the decision to employ John Hodgson to produce his report. But there could be other factors. One kindly act by William Robb probably, in its small way, helped. No longer a member of the Local Board of Health (he had resigned the previous year), nevertheless he clearly felt morally obliged, for the good of the town to write to the Local Government Board on February 19. He did nothing to disabuse the Local Government Board of the unsatisfactory state of the Town, which he put down to 'vis inertiae' and 'false economic notions' but he finished

> I must candidly say that (though it hardly appears logical after all my remarks) I would be sorry to see the Town merged with the Rural Sanitary Authority. As I remember I told you in my last [communication] that I had not much confidence in the present mode of election or even the franchise returning men fitted by intelligence and general culture to undertake the governance of the town, yet the disgrace of passing into the hands of a few farmers not to mention the increased cost, is rather trying to the feelings (Excuse this little piece of sentimentality).
> If you could find a way to get the Authority to do all your inspector thinks should be done with due 'guarantees' the 'atrocities' should not be repeated, you would secure the two ends desired, that of a healthy town and that of a self-governing town.

Whether or not this letter had any influence, the hope of William Robb expressed in the last paragraph represents what seems to have been the satisfactory outcome to a potentially unfortunate episode in the Town's history.

It is appropriate to end this stage in the development of Hexham's water supply that at the second inquiry, the Surveyor, George Dawson, reported that there were in the town, 57 hydrants, 60 baths, 512 water closets and 771 taps in kitchens, yards and gardens – for a population of just under 5900.

The next steps in the water supply saga

The Stublick Syke scheme never materialised. On November 7 1878, Hugh Owen Jnr., for the Local Government Board, wrote to the Clerk giving the Local Board sanction to borrow £3,500, but only if the Board 'have entered into provisional agreement for the purchase of lands required and the water rights are requisite to enable them to divert the water from its present channel'. But well before that date, all momentum for an improved water supply had been lost. In part, that was due to the then membership of the Board but progress was very considerably hampered by attitudes within the Town. In July 1877, only two months after John Harrison's first inquiry, certain members of the town had sent a memorial to the Local Government Board petitioning against the Stublick water scheme (NA MH12/9050). The central argument put forward was that enough water could be provided by the present system if waste was considerably reduced. The quantity of water going to waste was said to be 37.6 thousand gallons daily. This would appear to be a figure of considerable magnitude, since it was over a third of the daily consumption from the reservoir of 94,280 gallons. If this wastage could be reduced, there ought to be no problems, since, according to the figure which the memorialists used from the report of Rawlinson (1853), the amount of water provided by the collecting area for the present water system was thought to be 128 thousand gallons daily. It was not clear how the above figures were arrived at. If they were correct, the town would never have any water, since the throughput of water from the reservoir would never be matched from input from rainfall. While there may be doubts about the figures there are no doubts about the reason for the dispatch of the memorial. One clause within it makes clear the real concern of the petitioners

> Your much oppressed Ratepayers submit that their industry is already taxed too heavily the present Local Board Rate is 4/- in the £ and 2/- in the £ Poor Rate beside other imperial taxes land tax and tithe and rentals high

The petitioners also stated that 'the increased water supply and Sanitary Improvements have not decreased the death rate'. The increased mortality 'is to be attributed to overcrowding and want of ventilation and damp walls, defective House drainage and want of House accommodation *and not want of water* [my italics].'

In 1878, there were two more memorials (received in May and September) to the Local Government Board, both trying to make the case that there was a very large waste of water. This time, the figures were based on the gauging of water leaving the reservoir. If we take the first memorial, the petitioners would seem to have a strong case, as it was based on actual measurements (made by Edward Brown in April and May 1877) and not on theoretical estimates. The rate of loss of water from ill-fitting junctions, leaks, etc. was taken to be the lowest reading during the night, it being assumed that at that time the rate of water use by the community would be extremely low. We are fortunate that the actual hourly figures for the gaugings made by Edward Brown in 1877 are still present in the Local Government Board archives (NA WO/374/34726). Inspection of those hourly figures indicates, firstly, that in taking the gaugings there was a significant measurement error and secondly there must be considerable uncertainty about the value for the rate of water due to leakage. Crucial values in this respect are those obtained between midnight and 6 a.m. on 12th April 1877, when the gauging found the following sequence of hourly measurements (in gallons):

4,534 (1 a.m.)	5.127 (2 a.m.)	1,172 (3 a.m.)
334 (4 a.m.)	5,509 (5 a.m.)	4,986 (6 a.m.)

Because of the high values at one, two, five and six a.m. (which were only about one to two thousand gallons per hour below the rate found during the previous and following day-time values), John Harrison, who presented the results in his report of 1 May 1877 to the Local Government Board gave the impression that the lowest values, e.g., 3 a.m. and 4 a.m., were spurious, as similar low values were not obtained on three other occasions. Indeed he suggested that the wastage due to leakage was around 5,000 gallons per hour (*HC* 16.5.1877). The second memorial of 1878 repeated the arguments.

While one cannot deny leakage was taking place, there is no clear case for arguing, as the memorialists did, that the leakage was more than the amount consumed. One has the feeling that the memorialists were very content to view the figures in the worst possible light. Irrespective of the extent of the leakage, action was possible to reduce water loss from known sources. John Hodgson directed his energies on dealing with taps and fittings, many of which were of inferior standard. This attack on the wastage of water seems eventually to have borne fruit. Edward Brown, who advised the Board on matters relating to the supply of water, was able to report to the Board on March 4 1878 that the consumption of water had dropped from 133,606 gallons per 24 hours in April 1877 to 112,027 in February 1878. Brown felt that the frequent inspection of taps and fittings had had a good effect – though whether the inspection led to much improvement in the nature of the fittings must be questioned (on November 15 1880, the Surveyor reported that he was in the process of renewing 78 stop taps). For those petitioning the Local Government Board, the information about inspecting the fittings and evidence that it had had an effect on water loss did nothing to allay their concerns over water loss from leakage. In retrospect, the Board were remiss not to follow the advice of Edward Brown to ask the permission of the Newcastle and Gateshead Water Co. for the loan of their trained staff for the purpose of detecting waste in their mains and house service and to get them to test the whole of the mains. Mr Main, Secretary of the Company, offered to supply two men to do the job in four to six weeks at a cost of £150. The Works Committee felt it not prudent to spend that particular sum of money, feeling that, if there were a significant loss of water, it would manifest itself on the surface (HLBH 24.6.1878). Of course, since no such manifestation took place, the arguments about the large loss of water by leakage fell rather flat.

Personalities

The fourth of April 1873 saw the election of Dr T. G. Stainthorpe to the Chairmanship of the Local Board. He held this position until April 1877. Thus he chaired the Board throughout the period leading to the debacle of Hexham being considered for takeover by the Hexham Rural Sanitary Authority. Though, in the period before the Local Board was established and in the early days of the Board, he obtained the reputation for being a leader in sanitary improvement, in part that may have been due to the fact that his seemingly forward-looking approach to the problems of the Town appeared so much better than the views of those medical men, who felt that Hexham was an healthy town. Certainly, even in those early days of the fight for sanitary improvement, it was made apparent in a profile in the *Hexham Courant* of 24 February 1877 that 'Dr Stainthorpe had not the suggestive or even constructive genius which in those early struggles were invaluable in the work in Hexham, novel in its nature and startling in its dimensions'. When he became Chairman

> Nearly every nuisance is now defended and all sorts of difficulties are put in the way of every motion for reform. He does not give the great works in which he had so honourable a share a chance to work out their proper results, and the consequence is, the sanitary party are being blamed for evils which have only risen out of the non-doings or mis-doings of that Board whose debates Dr Stainthorpe guides and inspires.

The writer of the profile thought that Thomas Stainthorpe was more interested in the trappings of the Office of Chairman of the Board ('the more ornamental part of the work'). What was wanted of the Chairman was not to return thanks for a toast to the Town at the end of a Farmers' Club dinner but

> a man whose heart is in the work of health reform, whose ready and cheerful impulse and wise and regular supervision are guarantees that the right work shall be ordered and done.

This medical man was opposed to the use of water for the disposal of sewage. His views on the matter were clearly presented at a meeting of the Local Board on 29 December 1879

> He thought that the time would come, if water closets continued increasing in number in the way they were doing, when they would require an increased quantity of water. He had already said elsewhere that that his opinion had materially changed as to the beneficial effects of water closets as a whole. His former opinion, in theory, was that they would be very useful; in practice

he had found them thoroughly useless, and as such he could never consent as one of the members of the Board to do anything for an increased supply of water, if it was simply to supply a want caused by an increased number of these pestiferous places. It was well known that water was not a destroyer of sewer gas, it was a mere conveyor and only moved it from place to place. He thought they might do well as ratepayers, to thoroughly transform their water closets and have nothing but earth closets. (*HC* 3.1.1880)

But what is even more revealing about his attitude, was the fact that as a member of the Local Board – and the only one at that – he saw fit to sign both memorials which were sent to the Local Government Board complaining about the wastage of water by leakage, yet seemingly making no effort as a member of that Board to attempt to reduce it. It is difficult not to conclude that he was siding with the petitioners not because of the wastage *per se* but with the main thrust of the memorials that was to get the Stubblick Syke water scheme stopped, thus ruling out the expenditure of public money.

In the election of 1879, two sanitary reformers, Lewis Lockhart and Joseph Catherall lost their seats. From a letter that Lockhart wrote to a Miss Dodd, on 12 April 1879, shortly after the result was known, it is clear that the dirty party were out in force before the election. In his letter, he drew attention to the effort that that party put into canvassing, 'in which about 40 of their ardent supporters were employed'. But as far as Lockhart was concerned he lost the election because his heart was not in it. 'I wished to be done with it [membership of the Board], and could not retire without bringing down upon me the blame of forsaking my post' (NRO/HLK/I). Of the three members who were elected, William Alexander, John Pearson and Thomas Welford, the latter two were against spending money on increasing the supply, Welford certainly believing that the present supply was ample for the town's needs, especially if the problem of waste was rectified. Furthermore, Welford was almost a law unto himself, caring little about niceties, if he thought that due economy was not being adhered to. A temperamental person – in August 1868, he was censured for being drunk a second time at a Board meeting (HLBH 17.8.1868) – his characteristics are best described in a letter from 'Mumbo Jumbo' to the *Hexham Courant* on 25 January 1879

> Did he [Mr Welford] not, as a poor-law guardian, by his 'sound and fury signifying nothing', his meaningless motions and interminable preachings at the ratepayers, prove himself an intolerable bore, which his fellow guardians were thankful to get rid of, and the electors in the first instance acquiesced. Was he not, as quondam member of our Local Board, a most extravagant time-waster; and not withstanding all his tirades on economising the ratepayers' money, did he not add very considerably to the expense and delay of carrying out schemes which were really dictated by true economy and not by the empty bombastic 'fudge' which he so furiously preached.

Then there was the seemingly ever-present William Taylor. He was first elected to the Local Board in 1868, then topping the poll. He continued to be re-elected, only once – in 1874 – not heading the poll, until 1883 when he stood down from the Board. He died on 17 December the following year. A man of few words, but ready jokes, he had a *laissez faire* approach to the problems of the town. A profile of Taylor in the *Courant* (17.2.1877) said that 'he does not bring to those vital questions [relating to the sanitary state of the town] the gravity, thoughtfulness and wisdom which they demand'. His attitude is well illustrated by the following statement made to the Local Board in February 1879 (*HC* 8.2.1879)

> [there have always been] some croakers in the town making querulous remarks about the state of the town. He did not believe there was a more healthy town in the counties of Northumberland and Durham than Hexham. A good deal of the illness that did prevail in the town was brought upon the people themselves; at any rate it was sickness for which they as a Local Board could not be held responsible.

These four members (Stainthorpe, Pearson, Welford and Taylor) of the Board formed a bulwark against sanitary progress.

Keeping a brake on public expenditure was central to those who did not want a new water supply, as otherwise the rates would become too burdensome. But we need to give the lie to the off-stated view that Hexham was too heavily taxed. While it is not possible to give meaningful figures for the amounts paid in taxation (rates) in terms of the wealth available to individuals, a leader article in the *Courant* throws light on the extent to which the so-called high taxation/rates was affecting the financial capabilities of some of Hexham's leading citizens

> Not the least curious of the inconsistent positions in which the 'dirty' party has placed itself, is that of having, in spite of its Cassandra-like prophesies of awful disaster to Hexham in consequence of the pressure of taxation taken advantage...... to lay out a goodly proportion of capital with excellent prospects of remuneration in buildings of many kinds...... in a town where every facility has been given them for such expenditure, even though handicapped by four shillings in the pound. An ex-Chairman of the Board [Stainthorpe] has built a fine mansion in Battle Hill; a very persistently obstructive candidate has been a party to erecting a whole dozen houses in Hellpool Lane [now Alexandra and Leazes Terraces]; several gentlemen of well-kown Conservative views have built terraces in the west end, an old fellow-townsman from Carlisle who certainly does not believe in Stublick Syke increases his house property every year, and a member of the Board purposes to make the handsome addition by and bye of some 200 houses at the east end of the town...... Necessarily a very large expenses has been incurred for water, sewerage, and gas had at a cost of many hundreds to be carried to these speculations of our acute friends. They might have been assessed by special improvement rates, but the Board, with generous and encouraging wish to give its advantages all possible enlargement have paid for such extensions out of the common fund. (*HC* 30.3.1878)

Finally, as a good example of the tinkering by the Board with the control of the use of water rather than attempt the find a bold solution for its water supply problem, it decided that all houses having baths should be charged 10s.6d a year extra (HLBH 5.5.1879). Significantly, it was welcomed in a letter to the *Courant* by 'A Ratepayer' as 'a step in the right direction', finishing with 'It must be admitted by all who have an elementary knowledge of sanitary science that the exclusion of human excrement from sewers is a public benefit.' (*HC* 10.5.1879).

Muddling through

On 29 December 1879, the Board had decided to take no further steps in the matter at present.

The *Courant* reported (*HC* 3.1.880) as follows:

> The facts are simply these – the Medical Officer strongly urges the Board to take action to increase the water supply, and the Local Government Board have approved the scheme for taking an additional supply from Stubblick Burn. The engineer has testified to the plentifulness of the supply obtained from that source, while Mr Pattinson of Newcastle, has analysed the water and found it to be good household water with only about a third of the hardness that is found in the present reservoir water. The preliminary steps have been taken, and if the Board could secure the written consent of the new owner of the Paise estate [formerly T.G. Leadbitter, who had died the previous year], and were determined to carry out the scheme, steps could be taken for securing the desired supply. The opponents of the scheme contend that at the present time the town is groaning under taxation, and there is no need for any further supply.

At the start of February there was no more than a fortnight's supply in the storage reservoir. Though the problem was to an extent transitory, those who were in favour of economy with regard to expenditure on increasing the water supply, rushed into action. Welford was the driving force. His pet project was to use more of the water from close to the reservoir, that was otherwise running into the by-wash, which skirted the reservoir. This water had been disposed of in this manner, because it was believed to be polluted from farm waste. On 5 April 1880 the Chairman of the Board (William Taylor) reported that he had visited the reservoir and 'had the pleasure of seeing purer water and more of it going into the reservoir than from the usual source. He had tasted the water – 'was very pure'. Welford was ecstatic; 'they had for a trifling outlay obtained sufficient supply. Hitherto the Board was held back by the party of obstructiveness.'

Needless to say Dr Jackson was appalled and wrote to the Board in no uncertain terms, saying that the scheme 'showed a want of proper consideration for the health of the inhabitants' (HLBH 27.4.1880). Also he forwarded the letter to the Local Government Board. The Chairman's response was to think that Dr Jackson, though 'a man of authority' did not have 'the wisdom of the Board and he [Taylor] thought it unparalleled impertinence to write such letters to them.' At a later meeting of the Board, Jackson pointed out that the water was coming between a pigsty and a farmyard midden. Seven to nine feet to the north of that source of water was a cesspool to gather the liquid manure out of another byre (*HC* 3.5.1880). John Hodgson also wrote to the Local Government Board, in no uncertain terms and along similar lines to Jackson. Amongst his many points of criticism was that the volume of water from this new source was of minor significance – 2,970 gallons per 24 hours compared with 38,927 from the original supply. On receiving this letter via the Local Government Board, Taylor's comment was 'a more impertinent letter I never read' (*HC* 18.5 1880). In the end wisdom prevailed; at the Board meeting on 12 August 1880, we find Welford moving and Pearson seconding that the sewage be prevented from going into the reservoir from Intake and Hexham Fell, Mr Cruddas' property.

Significantly, the denigration of Jackson continued into 1881. When Jackson presented his usual rightly critical report on the sanitary state of the town, it was greeted by the Chairman (again Taylor) with 'Most unmitigated lies.', 'A most one-sided false report.' and 'The man should not be made a tool of to write such stuff.' (*HC* 12.2.1881). The following meeting was devoted in large measure to a tirade against Dr Jackson, with most of the Board members (of those speaking only John Ridley not joining in) taking up a self-satisfied stance – summed up by the final remarks of the Chairman

'I don't set myself up as a medical authority, but I consider the town to be very healthy and the water as pure as it can be.' Later that same year, not surprisingly, there was a contested election for the post of Medical Officer of Health. A Dr Cottingham Farmer was the other candidate, who had no experience of public health. Fortunately for the town, Jackson squeaked back by one vote. The *Hexham Courant* expressed amazement, particularly that in view of 'all the hard things said of him by indignant critics', should have even permitted his name to go forward but that he had received votes from those who had strongly criticised him earlier in the year.

While the matter of sewage running into the reservoir was being debated, an initiative for action came from a group naming themselves the Association of owners and occupiers and property. A deputation, headed by Mr R. Cook, met the Board on 18 May 1880 to put forward a specific proposal for increasing the supply of water for the town. They had met Mr Beaumont for the purpose of obtaining his consent 'to the Urban Sanitary Authority availing themselves of two streams flowing at Blackhill and Yarridge.' The Association had done its homework, indicating the possible collecting area and suggesting how the water might be fed into the present system. They indicated that both Beaumont and his agent, John Kaye, had both expressed their willingness to assist the project forward. It seems to have taken time to persuade the Board of the wisdom of this suggestion. On 18 October 1880, the Surveyor reported that the water works had been extended to Yarridge at a cost of £437.12s. 6d. There was an element of triumphalism in the letter, which the Hexham Board agreed to send to the Local Government Board. This particular letter was in reply to a request from the Local Government Board both for the Hexham Board's views on the criticisms of John Hodgson (see above) and for details about what the Board was doing to improve its water supply. The Board wrote

> [in an earlier letter] we anticipated that the extension of works to Low Yarridge would obtain a plentiful supply of water, ample and sufficient to meet the requirements of the town, we are glad to say that those anticipations have been more than realised, for from the 26th July last, with slight variation, our reservoir has been full and has not been able to contain for some time the whole of the water available for the Board's supply, a large quantity flowing down the bye-wash (HLBH1.11.1880).

The degree of self-satisfaction was almost certainly not justified. We know from earlier correspondence of the Board with John Kaye that he did not think that the Yarridge supply was very large – something confirmed in a leader in the *Courant* of 29 May where it was stated that the new supply would contribute only 4,500 gallons per day, in contrast to the old supply of 33,000 gallons per day. The same leader talked about the 'amateur engineering' in progress at Yarridge and the fact that 'many intelligent ratepayers...... have in strong terms expressed their indignant astonishment at the large and almost useless expenditure of the Board's money'. A leader written towards the end of the dry summer of 1882 spoke of the amount of water supplied from Yarridge as being 3000 gallons per day (*HC* 23.9.1882).

Nevertheless, apart from the close call in 1882, when the level of the reservoir dropped to eleven feet – and that depth measurement was for the deepest part (*HC* 21.10.1882) – the town was able to survive with its water supply until 1885. There was little discussion in the Board on increasing the supply. Indeed the time was devoted to, what were thought then, matters of more immediate concern. Some significant issues during the period were the purchase of the market tolls, obtaining Tyne Green and Mill Islands for the town (*see* Chapter 14), negotiating a more favourable price from the Hexham Gas Company. The water mains were extended to new housing, as indeed were the sewers – a major extension of the latter being to Quatre Bras. The Board carried out a major road scheme, the improvement of Loosing Hill, for which they obtained the sanction of the Local Government Board to borrow £400. The work entailed reducing the gradient, increasing the average width by twelve feet, forming a granite tramway up the centre of the road (to allow horses to get a better purchase as they went up the hill) and building a substantial wall on the south side (*HC* 10.10.1885; *see* Chapter 16). The work was completed by May 1886. That same year it was proposed to replace the sewer from Maiden Cross to Cockshaw, because of the unsatisfactory nature of the levels of the old sewer (*HC* 15.5.1886). Behind this constructional activity, one can detect the more professional approach of the Surveyor, Robert Grieves. But as well, there were elected to the Board more men with commonsense and a wider public outlook than hitherto. 1882 saw the election of Robert Stainthorpe (who was to become a County Alderman when the County Council was formed) and James T. Robb. Edward Snowball was elected the following year and John Lisle in 1885. I have picked these men, because they seem to stand out in the discussions of the Board. Stainthorpe, Robb and Lisle all became Chairmen, a measure of their status amongst their peers. However, it must be said that discussions in the Board became far more constructive and less confrontational – they were undoubtedly carried out in a more civilised manner. Altogether, the Board of this period was better equipped to face the problems ahead.

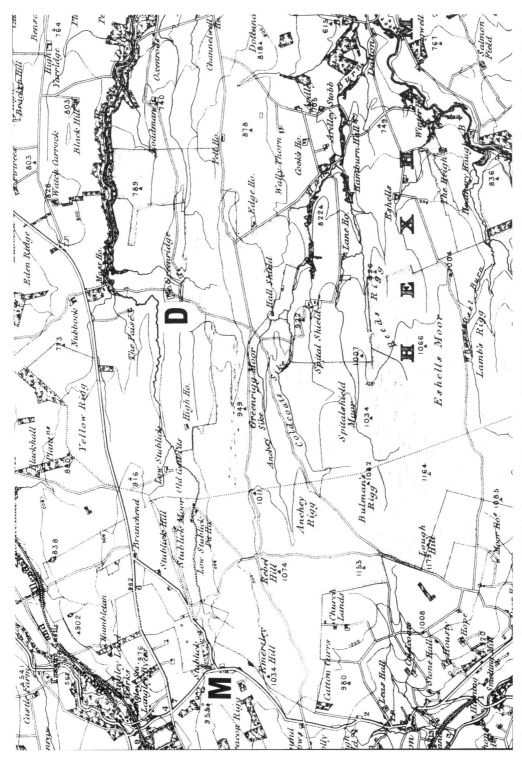

FIG. 19. Ordnance Survey map of 1866 showing the stream (Stubblick Syke) running east through the valley to join the Dipton Burn, in the wooded dene at the right of the map. D, general location of the proposed small dam; M, colliery (still present) at Stublick, though it can be seen that mining was taking place in other parts of the adjacent area.

FIG. 20. Stublick colliery (see Fig. 19) standing over a small coal mine, near Langley smelt mill. It is extremely unusual for such a complete group of early 19th-century colliery buildings to have survived almost intact.

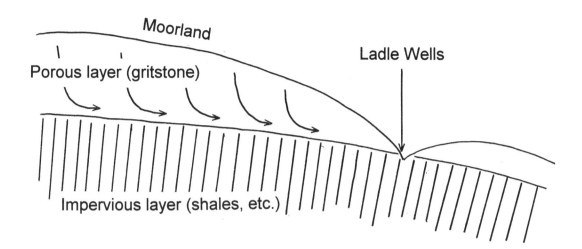

FIG. 21. Section through the hills above Ladle Wells to show how rainwater enters the porous (gritstone) layer and replenishes the springs, as a result of the water being unable to penetrate the impervious layer of shales and other rock below the gritstone.

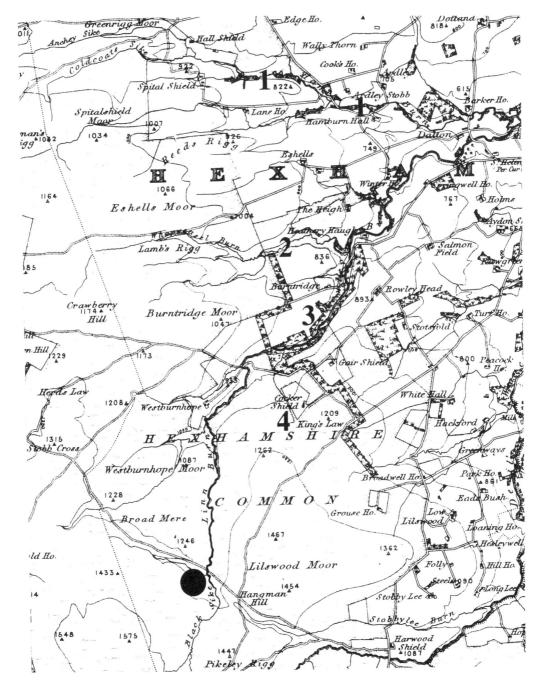

FIG. 22. Location of the five sites in Hexhamshire that Hubert Laws felt were capable of providing a satisfactory supply of water for Hexham. 1, Ham Burn; 2, Burntridge Burn; 3, Rowley Burn and 4, King's Law Springs. The fifth site, Ladle Wells and the one that was selected, is represented by a black circle

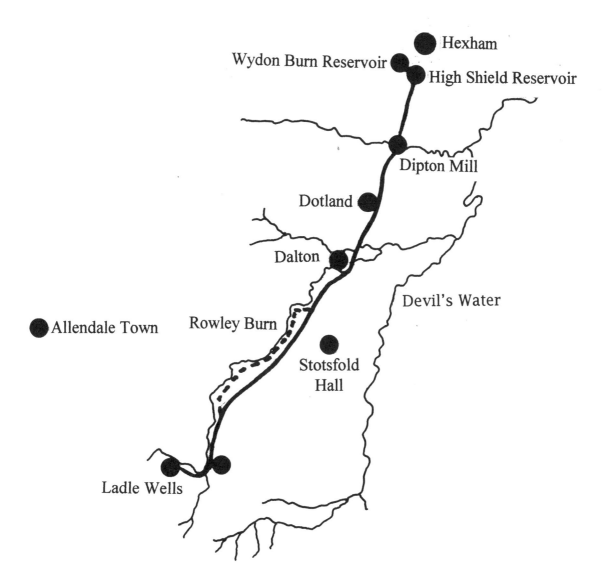

FIG. 23. The route of the pipe line from Ladle Wells to the Wydon Burn reservoir via the new service reservoir at High Shield. The dotted line represents the road that W. B. Beaumont required be avoided when the pipes were laid.

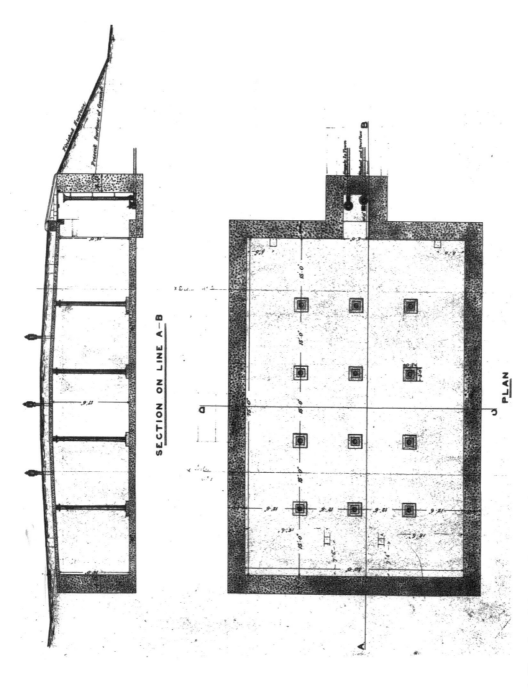

SECTION ON LINE A—B

PLAN

FIG. 24. The plan of the service reservoir eventually built at High Shield. As one can see, it is a covered structure, which, though reconstructed, is still in use today. Reproduced with the permission of Tynedale Council and the Northumberland Record Office (NRO/PHU/AS/9).

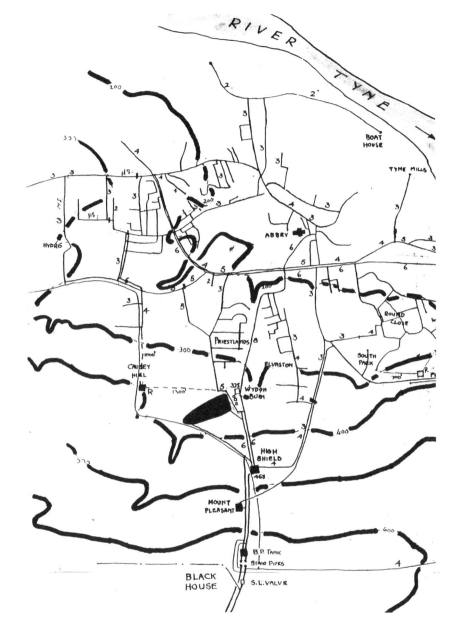

FIG. 25. A rough plan of the water pipe system within Hexham, drawn probably around when the system was taken over by the Newcastle and Gateshead Water Co. in April 1959. The high service pipeline can be seen on the left of the plan, where it runs from High Shield down Causey Hill to the Hydro. The pipe taking excess water from Wydon Burn through the fields to St Wilfrid's Road for street watering is that on the plan with 8 (inch) next to it. B.P. tank at Black House – break pressure tank to equalise the pressure in the water in 6 inch and 8 inch pipes bringing water from Ladle Wells. Reproduced with the permission of Tynedale Council and the Northumberland Record Office (NRO/PSU/AS/9 but with reservoirs and contours highlighted).

FIG. 26. The two pipes, taking water from Ladle Wells to Hexham, crossing Black Syke, close to the source of the water. The pipe on the left is the new 8-inch pipe referred to in the text; the original 6 inch pipe is on the right.

FIG. 27. One of 17 cast iron posts marking the route of the 8-inch pipe. On one side is 8 INCH; on the other HUDC. The post illustrated is on the moors close to Ladle Wells.

CHAPTER 10

The faltering steps to an increased and better water supply

The first signs that the Board were aware of the need to improve the water supply was not concern about the lack of water but about its quality. The Surveyor, Robert Grieves, expressed concern that the water supply was still being contaminated from farm waste (HLBH 13.10.1884). Next year, T.L.T. wrote to the *Hexham Courant* about the condition of the water supplied to the town

> My experience may not be shared by everyone, but I find the water to contain much vegetable matter and great numbers of animals, dead and decaying, the species I know not, and which impart an offensive smell...... it transpired at a recent meeting of the Board that one of the filter beds had not been renewed for five years. Think of the accumulation of filth through which our drinking water had been passing. Surely it must have poisoned instead of purified (*HC* 30.5.1885).

These findings were confirmed in a report by John Pattinson of Newcastle to the Board, in which he indicated the water was of somewhat doubtful quality, since 'microscopic examination showed spores and moving organisms' and 'more organic matter than should be in good drinking water'. Russell (1996) gives an excellent account of the type of measurements that were made to come the latter conclusion.

Stimulated by a Board member, John Trotter, there was a flurry of interest in artesian wells (HLBH 12.10.1885). But the geological experts who were consulted were not very optimistic. On January 4 1886, the Board decided to re-open negotiations with the 'riparian and landed proprietors to secure all the necessary rights of land and water supply for the town from the Greenridge Burn' (equated with the Stublick Syke scheme referred to in last chapter; also see Fig. 19) and to carry out the works of water supply, borrowing £3,500 for the purpose, given that the required sanction could be obtained from the Local Government Board. We have no information as to the negotiations with these proprietors. It is only on 14 March in the following year that we learn that the Board decided that 'negotiations be re-opened with Major Leadbitter for the purpose of carrying out the Greenridge scheme' (Fig. 19). A week later, the Board agreed to accept the price offered by Major Leadbitter's lawyers, namely £700 for 'the land required for the reservoir with a right of way thereto and the right to lay down pipes and take the water' (HLBH 28.3.1887). It should be noted that the term reservoir is misleading. Edward Brown had not intended to build such but merely form a dam across the syke, $2^1/2$ feet high of 'concrete cement', so always to cover the mouth of the supply pipe.

Though there were still doubts in the town about the Stubblick Syke scheme to the extent that a deputation met with the Board on 14 May 1887 to argue against the scheme, one item of evidence being an unsatisfactory analysis of the water in the syke (a small stream) carried out by a Mr Routledge. But Mr Hubert Laws CE of Newcastle, who was appointed to advise the Board on the scheme and Mr J. Patterson, who carried out an analysis of the water, gave approval to the scheme.

Seemingly, the water collected by Routledge for analysis had come from a site lower down from where the water would be collected and likely to be contaminated by farm pollution. The 4 June issue of the *Courant* carried a public notice detailing what was proposed and the action the Board was to take in making the Stublick Syke scheme a reality.

But time was not on the side of the Board. It was to be a year of unprecedented drought. As the level of water in the reservoir fell, it was clear that action must be taken to seek out an additional source, which could be quickly taken into the system. The first thought was to take water from Woodley Field. Agreement was obtained from the owners and a pump installed but the supply was found to inadequate. Two other suggestions were made (HLBH 11.6.1887). One was to make an open cutting so that water could be brought from Stublick Syke. This could be done in three weeks. The other alternative would be to take water from the Darden/Coastley Burn, which was found (from a number of guagings during 1887) to supply even more water than Stublick Syke (Fig. 19). Mr Laws was asked to pronounce. He came down firmly for the latter scheme; he felt the former would require time for water to flow in sufficient quantities into the town's water system. As for the Darden Burn scheme, it could be done in two stages – water pumped from the Burn into the Cockshaw Burn, from which it could be then taken into the water system at Woodley Field, using the pump already in place. With some more time, pipes could take water directly from Darden Burn into the system. Mr Laws offered that advice to the Board on 13 June. A week later, the Chairman reported to the Board that water from Darden Burn would be running into the Woodley Field Burn and thence into the reservoir by the next day. He was over-optimistic, because they had difficulty obtaining a pump and boiler. However, the severity of the drought – the rainfall from 1 January had been little more than one-third of the amount which fell in a corresponding period during the previous year and that was by no means a wet period – meant the Board were unable to defer the cutting off of water to field and garden. However by 25 June 1887, water was being pumped from the burn, as was strikingly clear from a letter to the Board from Mr F.J. Snowball, agent of Mr J. C. Straker:

> I might add that Mr Straker was surprised and annoyed that the Hexham authorities should be as you say actually now purifying and conveying water from Darden Burn (which runs entirely through his property) without either asking his leave or even applying to me and thus rendering the Town liable to damages in consequence.

The emollient letters from the Board did not soften the heart of Mr Straker. In a letter from his solicitors Clayton and Gibson, reported to the Board on 4 July, it was clear that Mr Straker was very annoyed. Nevertheless, he was willing to allow 'the temporary supply of water for the use of the inhabitants of Hexham to continue and [he] has no wish to place unnecessary obstructions in the way of that being obtained'. But he was adamant on one matter

> We are requested to point out that if the Board had proceeded with the Stublick Syke scheme eight or ten years ago when arrangements were first made for it instead of year by year temporising and putting off the present lack of water would not have occurred and we have to intimate that Mr Straker's permission to continue the pumping of water from Darden Burn is temporary only and that if steps are not taken by the Local Board for the purpose of carrying out some scheme for obtaining a permanent supply of water Mr Straker will consider himself at liberty to remove the pipes and steam engine at any time on his giving fourteen days previous notice to do so.

At the meeting after the Board had received on 6 July a letter of similar kind from Clayton and Gibson, the Chairman moved that the application to the Local Government Board to borrow £5500 to carry to carry out the combined Darden and Stublick schemes (the most recent proposal of Hubert Laws) be rescinded. Relations between Mr Straker and the Board were further strained when, without a request being made, a shed was put up to protect the pump. On 2 September, the Chairman, James Robb, reported that he and Mr Trotter had seen Mr Laws and instructed him to examine the whole district with regard to water supply.

Hubert Laws presented his report to the Board on 4 October 1887. It is a noticeably balanced one. First he re-assesses those sources previously considered. He is clear that the combined Stublick and Darden Burns scheme is the best of these, having been proved during a very dry season of supplying 230,000 gallons a day. Going further afield, he dismisses the north side of the Tyne, since he did not find anything to trouble the Board with. However to the south west of Hexham he speaks glowingly about the millstone grit formation.

> To the south west of Hexham is a very extensive area of hill pasture and moorland on Millstone Grit formation the surface being very porous and remarkably free from peat moss. The rain sinks immediately into the ground and passing through a natural filter is collected in a subterranean reservoir to come up again to the surface at a lower level due to impervious bands of bands of shale. There are several burns, fed almost entirely by springs, affording copious supplies of the most beautiful water (HLBH 4.10.1887).

The geological situation is shown diagrammatically in Fig. 21; while Fig. 22 shows the location of five sites selected by Laws for detailed consideration. Taking the sites in order of their closeness to Hexham, their features are as follows, finishing with the cost of the works to use the supply in brackets:
1. Ham Burn – This source of supply was not thought to be such a desirable a supply as the others but was still thought to be worthy of consideration (£2,330).
2. Burntridge Burn – This name was used for convenience to describe the collection of water from Whapweasel and Lambs Rigg Syke. These two burns were known to be fed by springs from the millstone grit and maintain a summer flow beyond the requirements of the town (£3,617).
3. Rowley Burn – Considered to have similar characteristics to Burntridge Burn (£3,540).
4. King's Law Springs – A number of springs of very pure water at an elevation of 630 ft. (192 m) above the reservoir. There was uncertainty as to the quantity of water that could be obtained and also the permanence of the supply during a dry season (£3,413).
5. The Ladle Wells Springs – Though eight miles from the reservoir Laws reported that at 1,300 ft (396 m) there were twelve considerable springs within 200 yards. Three of the springs were capable of collecting 254,000 gallons a day. The water could be collected readily (£4194). Laws says about the springs

> They are stated to be of a very permanent character, as is no doubt the case, considering the nature and extent of their gathering area. That they are deep seated is shown by the extreme low temperature of the water, as it issues from the rock, namely 38o F [3.3o C]. I have not hitherto met with a spring of such low temperature.

Laws based his final decision as to the best source of supply on three criteria - purity of water , the quantity which could be relied upon with certainty and the cost. Laws focused on King's Law and Ladle Wells. He would have chosen the former if it were not for the uncertainty of the quantity of water which could be obtained. If there had been a plentiful supply, one guesses that cost would have decided in favour of King's Law. However, Laws was in no doubt about Ladle Wells

> [they] not only offer sufficient quantity of water to enable you [the Board] to discontinue the use of water from your present gathering area but to supply a much larger demand than at present should it hereafter be required.

He also commended the supply for its 'extreme purity and 'extreme softness'. Though the Ladle Wells scheme was the most expensive, to be set against this was the large quantity available and, further, there would be a saving in expense by the absence of any need for filtration. Because of its elevation, given that the same sized pipe were being used, Ladle Wells with its greater elevation would supply more water per unit time than Kings Law. Irrespective of which of the two sources of supply was used, it would be possible to construct a new service reservoir to supply the higher parts of the Hexham district.

If there was any doubt about the purity of the water coming from Ladle Wells, it was dispelled by a report of an analysis of it by John Pattinson of Newcastle. He was extremely enthusiastic about its properties

> This water is of remarkable purity, perhaps the purest sample of natural water, I have ever examined. It is very 'soft' water. It is evidently well suited for the purpose of a domestic and manufacturing supply (HLBH 4.10.1887).

CHAPTER 11

The fight to obtain water from Ladle Wells

The first steps

The Board unanimously agreed to take action, the first step being a request that a deputation be received by W. B. Beaumont, who owned the land from which the water would be taken and over which much of the pipework would be laid, with a view to obtaining his consent to carrying out the scheme. On 26 September the Board instructed the Clerk to write to Mr F. J. Snowball (in response to a letter from Mr Straker who wanted a definite answer about whether or not the Board was proceeding with the Stublick Syke scheme) saying that 'steps were being taken to obtain a supply of water from Hexhamshire'. Further, the minute describing the line of action to be taken indicated that conversations had already taken place with Beaumont's agent, John Kaye, about the route to be taken by the pipes through Beaumont's land.

Beaumont did not accede to the request to meet a deputation but left it to his agent to talk the matter over with the Board. John Kaye met the Clerk and Hubert Laws and the following was reported to the Board (HLBH 18.10.1887):

> 1. Mr Beaumont does not feel justified in deciding upon a scheme for the Town, he does not wish to lead opinion but awaits it.
> 2. Mr Beaumont's views are that a Private Bill ought to be obtained and he does not say he will oppose it.
> 3. After the question has been fully considered by the Board and the Towns people, Mr Beaumont is prepared to further consider the decision arrived at by them and the requirements of the Town, at the present he does not express an opinion for or against the scheme.

The Board took the logical step and called a meeting of ratepayers in the Town Hall for the evening of 24 October. The *Hexham Courant*, on learning that such a meeting was to be held, published a leader strongly deprecating the decision to hold such a meeting, 'in which party and personal bitterness and narrowness would only be equalled by the ignorance of all the essential elements of the question......' (*HC* 17.9.1887).

But the *Courant* was wrong. When the meeting did take place, James Robb set the tone with a masterly introduction, putting the Ladle Wells scheme in context and explaining the reasons for the Board's choice of source of supply. William Alexander, often critical in the past, spoke next and analysed in detail the financial consequences of the scheme – a wise move, since cost had been the major stumbling block in the past. According to his calculations about the rates to be levied, Alexander believed

> If they could have an abundant supply of pure water and the Board could furnish it at 11d in the pound, they ought not to have a croaker in the town or a croaker in the neighbourhood.

At the end of his speech, Alexander proposed

> That the ratepayers of the township of Hexham in public meeting assembled express their approval of the Ladle Wells water supply scheme, and would urge upon the Local Board of Health the importance of carrying it to completion without delay, and with a view to obtaining the consent of Mr Beaumont (he being the principal land and riparian owner to be affected), a memorial to him and the other owners interested be drawn up, and the signatures of the owners and ratepayers to the township obtained thereto.

John Moffat seconded the motion. The Chairman allowed further debate before putting the motion to the meeting. But the debate itself on the issue was non-existent. Not unexpectedly, after a period devoted essentially to technical matters, when James Robb put the motion to the meeting it was carried unanimously. The *Hexham Courant*, if one makes a comparison with its leader a fortnight earlier, was ecstatic, feeling that 'the matter of the town's side may be considered settled.' Further the paper confidently anticipated there should not be 'any very great difficulty with Mr Beaumont', though it indicated that, on the basis of past experience, any negotiations might be protracted (HC.29.10.1887).

Now that the Board had the town behind them, there was a flurry of activity. There was a special meeting to produce a resolution, the main function of which to promote a Bill in Parliament for securing the Ladle Wells water supply, followed by a meeting of owners and ratepayers, later the same day, to support the resolution. The *Courant* published in its advertisement columns formal details of what had transpired at both meetings as well as the details of the scheme, which also stated that, before 21 December, printed copies of the Bill would be deposited in the Private Bill Office of the House of Commons. On 19 December, the Clerk reported to the Board that the Bill had been deposited in the House of Lords.

In the meantime, the first steps were taken to ensure that all parties who might be affected by the proposals were in agreement about their going forward. To that end a meeting was advertised to be held for all such persons at

> Mr Hogarth's, The Fox and Hounds Inn, Woodside, Hexham-shire...... for the purpose of their appointing a Committee to treat with the said Local Board for the compensation to be paid for the extinction of such commonable rights in or over such parts of the said Stinted Pasture [allotted for grazing]...... in such Wells or Springs or Streams which arise there from, and in any other rights or easements in, through or over the said Stinted Pasture as the said Local Board may require for the purposes of their additional Water Supply undertaking (*HC* 10..12.1887).

The start of 1888 saw the Clerk informing the Board that the meeting had gone well and 'they had every reason to hope that an amicable arrangement satisfactory to all parties would be carried out' (HLBH 3.1.1888). A week later, he reported that he had had a very satisfactory meeting with Mr Beaumont's agent 'who had met him very fairly and openly' and there was every indication that 'an amicable arrangement' would be reached. Also he had learnt that the Local Government Board had approved of the Bill as far as it could.

Then the difficulties began. On February 13 the Clerk reported that the 'position had not changed much for the better since the last meeting'. That was an understatement. There had been a meeting between Mr Kaye and Mr Thompson (of Dees and Thompson – solicitors for Mr Beaumont) and Mr Laws and the Clerk at which it was clear that it was almost certain that stringent conditions would be laid down with respect to obtaining water from Mr Beaumont's land. The extent of those conditions only properly became clear on 25 February when the *Courant* published the details of a petition presented by Mr W. B. Beaumont to the House of Commons against the Hexham Local Board Bill. He claimed, as lord of the regality or manor of Hexham, to be 'injuriously affected by the bill and objects there to.' His position is described in a long-winded statement written in legalese. The major matter of concern can be put simply – the mines and minerals on his land, forming the catchment area for the water to be abstracted by the town, are of great value to him and 'an ample supply of water is essential for their working'. But Beaumont was also concerned about his sporting rights (both shooting and fishing) and about the laying of pipes along the road (which today we would call a track) built by him, leading from his Mansion House in Allendale to his Mansion House at Dipton. As might be expected, his action 'caused considerable indignation in the town'. Mr J. S. Baty in a letter to the *Courant* referred to the 'additional powers which our defective land laws may bestow upon him as Lord of the Manor are merely remnants of Norman tyranny' (*HC* 3.3.1888). The only good news to brighten the gloom was given by the Clerk to the Local Board on 12 March when he reported that its Special Water Committee had come to terms with the Commoner's Committee, whose establishment is referred to above.

Soon, at a Local Board meeting on 26 March 1888, further details of Beaumont's position with respect to the Bill become clear. He proposed the following amendments to the Bill
1. To limit the town to take no more than 250,000 gallons per day from the springs and streams on Hexhamshire Moor.
2. The town had not to lay their pipes within a certain distance of the road and only to interfere with the road where it was absolutely necessary.

After these terms had been received, the Clerk reported that Mr Beaumont expected the Local Board to pay the whole of his costs. Strangely, in view of past history, the reaction of the Board was muted; there being no impassioned speeches. But it was of one mind. While Hubert Laws could suggest another line for the pipes, albeit at greater cost, the Board was adamant that they needed much more water than Beaumont was prepared to allow. Also they were not disposed to pay his costs now that his petition was going to incur a serious outlay for the Board. Prior to the petition, the Board were prepared to meet his costs.

If the Board had any doubt about Beaumont's intransigence, they were dispelled on 23 April in a letter from his Parliamentary agents, Sherwood & Co., to Messrs Dyson & Co., Parliamentary agents for the Board:

> We have submitted to Mr Beaumont your letter of 14ᵗʰ inst., from which we gather your opinion to be that any further meeting or discussion, for the present time at all events, would not be advantageous, a view in which we have no difficulty under the circumstances in advising our client to acquiesce.
> The information he is now receiving leads him to greatly doubt whether the Bill is necessary or

desirable for the town and district, in which he has so considerable an interest; and certainly the Bill if passed into law in the shape you propose, would be very injurious to him. The clause you propose to insert for the benefit of Mr Beaumont is, in its main features, entirely useless. We trust when your clients had a little time for further reflection they will with Mr Beaumont come to the conclusion that it would not be well for them to further to proceed this year with the Bill before Parliament; but should they unfortunately take a different view we are instructed to say that you must reckon on the most strenuous opposition both in preamble and clauses in the Lords.

The reaction of the Board was to 'urge and empower the Special Water Committee to prosecute with the utmost despatch the securing of an ample supply of water from Ladle Springs.'

Contrary to what was said in the above letter, Mr Beaumont's agents requested a meeting with the Board's advisors in London. Isaac Baty, the Clerk, and Hubert Laws went but the impasse over the amount of water the town would be able to abstract remained. When the results of the discussions had been reported to and discussed by the Board on 7 May the Chairman said that 'they were in for a contest with Mr Beaumont before the Lord's Committee' ('after Whitsuntide'). In the meantime 'the Water committee were taking such steps as they thought necessary to be prepared for that contest'.

It is not clear why Beaumont took his petition to the House of Lords rather than the Commons. The *Courant*, in a hard-hitting leader that described him (on the basis of the evidence of his actions) as

> a petty, quibbling, selfish spirit, whose object...... is to delay, mutilate, or entirely defeat a measure essential to the welfare of a Town which he actually in one of his missives assumes to be his own peculiar inheritance

And the paper was of the opinion that

> His views and modes of action we know are not to be measured by those of the common run of men and hence we were hardly surprised that he allowed the Bill to pass through the Commons reserving the final struggle for the more aristocratic lists of the Upper Chamber (*HC* 5.5.1888).

Whatever the correctness of this particular opinion, the paper was in no doubt about its general feelings about Beaumont that were amplified in another leader on 26 May. It was written as the result of a meeting (in Leeds, close to the family seat at Bretton Hall) called by Beaumont (in response to a personal letter to him from James Robb, the Chairman of the Board) with representatives of the Board (Chairman, Clerk and Hubert Laws). Both parties stood by their positions. The *Courant* believed Beaumont's arguments about the amount of lead available to him in the Ladle Wells area and the amount of water required by Hexham were of 'the flimsiest and most untenable character'.

The House of Lords Committee

The Committee met on Monday, 18 June 1888. There is a transcript of the proceedings in the

Courant of 23 June; the printed version of the official transcript is bound in the minutes of the Local Board of Health (NRO/PHU/A1/6). The Earl of Jersey presided, the other members being Viscount Powerscourt, Lord Windsor, Lord Manners and Lord Herries. Mr Pope QC and Mr Mcrae and the Clerk of the Board, Mr Baty, appeared for the promoters of the Bill, The Local Board. Their Parliamentary Agents were Messrs Dyson and Co. Mr Bidder QC and Mr Worsley Taylor appeared on behalf of Mr Beaumont. Their agents were Messrs. Sherwood and Co.

Mr Pope opened with a presentation that at first sight seems lengthy, but was nevertheless a concise statement of the history of the water supply problems for the town and an analysis of the various alternatives. He also critically analysed Beaumont's petition, using the opportunity to put his lawyers on the defensive. Pope was highly critical that the road across the moors 'constructed partly upon his [Beaumont's] own land and partly upon common land' could not be used as a right of way to Ladle Wells as well as the supposition that once the pipe had been laid Beaumont's shooting and fishing rights would be interfered with. He summed up the petitioner's approach as follows

> this is just one of those cases in which a gentleman largely interested in property places in the hands of his parliamentary agent his case, he says, I object to their taking all these springs, I do not know what use I may make of them, and the Parliamentary Draftsman drafts the petition including everything which he can possibly conceive can arise. Who on earth would dream, except a parliamentary draftsman, that by putting a certain tank to collect these springs and taking the water away in a pipe to Hexham – a sort of simple waterworks which every gentleman has who has a spring in his own wood and takes it down to supply his private mansion – that that is to interfere with sporting rights and fishing rights of the lord of the manor?

There followed a period with Mcrae questioning James Robb, essentially about the history of Hexham's water supply and the efforts that were made to increase the supply – all of which have been described in an earlier section. The day finished with Bidder raising questions and Mcrae responding.

Tuesday saw more of the same, with Bidder questioning the procedures of the Board, asking about resolutions. Bidder probed the unwillingness of the Board to spend money on increasing the water supply at some length. His aim was best exemplified by a question to James Robb

> Has it ever occurred to your Board before spending a large sum of money in going so far afield for fresh water supply to see whether they were utilizing their existing water supply?

Thus he was trying to make out that the Board were profligate in the use of water and did not need another supply. Though he spent a considerable time on this line of questioning, the impression on reading the transcript is that Bidder was not successful in extracting any serious admission of profligacy or serious mismanagement by the Board of its water supply. The rest of the day was devoted to the lawyers for the Promoters of the Bill questioning a number of expert witnesses – Dr Jackson, the Medical Officer for Hexham; Mr Robert Routledge, analytical chemist to the North Eastern Railway Co.; Dr H. E. Armstrong, Medical Officer for Newcastle and Mr Robert Grieves, the Surveyor for the Hexham Board. Essentially it was a matter of drawing from these witnesses the case for an increased supply of water for the town. If anyone had any doubts about the poor quality of the present water supply to the town, they must have been disabused by Dr Armstrong, who had been over the gathering ground:

> The land nearest the reservoir was the most highly manured of all. There were many cattle there. On one farm he observed a manure tank which was overflowing into the burns that supplied the reservoir. All the burns were open and were watering places for the cattle. At one point the general sewage from a farm went into a burn. It was a matter of absolute certainty that the water at present was contaminated with sewage, and it was the duty of the local authorities to find a fresh source of supply, in the interests of the health of the population.

Beaumont's solicitors did not question Armstrong. Indeed they seem to have been caught out, having been under the impression that the present supply to the town was only insufficient, being otherwise satisfactory. Jackson and Routledge got off relatively lightly with respect to their being questioned. But the Surveyor, Bidder, again pursuing the matter of waste of water, gave Robert Grieves a hard time.

The final expert witnesses were two water engineers Hubert Laws and James Mansergh of London, whose partner, John Lawson was the engineer for the original (1864-5 scheme) and four mining engineers – Mr Millican of Newcastle, Mr Burns, Mr Paull and Mr Hutchinson. There was little doubt from Laws' testimony that Ladle Wells was a highly suitable supply of water, while the mining engineers were unanimous that there was little lead in the area and if there was it would not be profitable to mine it.

Towards the end of the third day, Mr Bidder started on the case for the petitioner. His aim seems to have been to demonstrate the importance to Beaumont of the mining potential of the area. Bidder's witness was Thomas Bewick, formerly mining engineer to Beaumont for nearly twenty years. It becomes clear, as one reads the transcript of the questions and answers, that there is little evidence to support the view that there might be significant amounts of lead worth mining in the area. Cobbler's Venture Mine is stated by Bewick not to have been a success. He appeared circumspect about the possibility of success were another shaft to be sunk. Altogether, Bewick's testimony appears to have done little to reduce the value of the evidence given by those mining engineers acting as witnesses for the promoters of the Bill. The other witnesses called were unable to help Bidder's case. Indeed, during the cross-examination of Thomas Fenwick, of the firm Martin and Fenwick, coal engineers, Pope drew forth some very revealing statements – one being that, even if the Hexham were to abstract 300,000 gallons per day, there would still be enough water for running a lead mine further down the valley; the other being that Beaumont was a petitioner not only because of the need for water for any mining operation but also because he was the biggest ratepayer in the district and the cost of a new supply could seriously affect the rates that he paid.

Bidder's summing up adds almost nothing to an understanding of the petitioner's case. At the end, the Chairman asked the parties to withdraw before he and his colleagues called upon Mr Pope. After a short time, the Counsels and parties were called back before the Committee. Thereupon, the Chairman stated 'I do not think, Mr Pope, I need call upon you to reply, because the Committee are of the opinion that the Bill should proceed.' There was a caveat 'We think however that the amount of water taken should be limited to 350,000 gallons [per day].' The Chairman would brook no discussion on this point. However, he did agree to the request of the petitioners that there must be some kind of measuring device; 'Mr Beaumont ought to have an opportunity of knowing how much water they [the town] really did take.' The promoters also obtained a concession that was of considerable importance:

> Mr Mcrae: that I will leave with one observation to the Committee. My Lord, at present it is agreed that we are to have permission to use the Moor road for the construction of those pipes which are to be laid alongside. Surely it is reasonable if the pipes at any time here after require repairing that we may be at liberty to enter the private road for that purpose. Is it not reasonable? Are we to go to the expense of making a fresh road for the purpose? I think it is too ridiculous.
> The Chairman: I think that is so.

Consideration had to be given to the wording of the clauses making up the eventual Act (51 & 52 Vict., c. 154). These detailed the protection that would be given to Beaumont in addition to a limitation as to the amount of water taken on any one day. Thus, the road referred to above was not to be used for the pipe-line (as Laws had intended originally), except where it was necessary to cross the road. No pumps were to be installed on the stinted pasture and the Local Board of Health were not to supply water beyond the limits of their district. The sporting rights on the land were to remain with Beaumont. The works were to be finished within a year. The final Act deals with a number of other matters, such as the location of the service reservoir (see later) and the borrowing of money for the project. It is not appropriate to go into detail about these matters; they are overshadowed by the achievement by the town of its aims.

One has the feeling that the Committee were readily won over to the case for the town. Rightly the Town felt it had gained a victory. Indeed it was more than just the winning of the case in the Committee of the House of Lords. For once the town had pulled together as one. As a leader in the *Courant* put it 'When it [the Ladle Wells scheme] was first mooted...... the Board were unanimous in its adoption; the ratepayers gave their acceptance of the scheme with one voice – a harmony as unusual in Hexham as it was important'. When the Chairman of the Board (James Robb) and the Clerk (Isaac Baty) arrived back at Hexham Station on 22 June, after attending the Committee, they were met by a large number of townspeople, including many town notables. The two men were taken in a procession (headed by the Mechanics' Institute band and brought up at the rear by the fire engine with the firemen in full uniform) to the Market Square via Priestpopple and Fore Street. In the Market Place William Alexander fulsomely thanked the Chairman and the Clerk. Both James Robb and Isaac Baty responded. The latter 'hoped in the future, that out of a supply of pure water, they would have better health, that their population would increase and that wealth would come pouring into the town (cheers)' (*HC* 23.6.1888).

Naturally, the project having been given the all clear, the Council moved quickly to get it underway (Fig. 23). Hubert Laws, now in charge of the project, reported that work on it had started on 6 September 1888 (HLBH 2210.1888). A new service reservoir (Fig. 24) had to be constructed and $8^1/_2$ miles of pipe to be laid. But all proceeded apace and on the 'cold' Thursday, 17 January 1889, James Robb performed the ceremony of turning on the water from the Ladle Wells. 'After the first tank had slowly filled and as it flowed over the partition and into the main pipe, three hearty cheers were given by all present' (*HC* 19.1.1889). In the evening, there was a celebratory dinner at the Royal Hotel. This was followed on Friday, 23 February, by a complimentary dinner to the Chairman and Members of the Local Board at the Tynedale Hydropathic Mansion. 'The repast was of a most elegant and excellent character and exceedingly well served' (*HC* 23.2.1889). As was typical for the time, both events were all-male, the latter of the two being the larger, when 'about eighty gentlemen sat down to the spread.'

In actual fact, one could say that the two dinners were slightly premature. On 16 June 1890, the Clerk reported to the Board of Health that Mr Laws had found that the new service reservoir was leaking and that he had served Mr Carr the contractor with formal notice requiring him to make good the work. The Board minutes of 30 June indicate also that the laying of pipes from Ladle Wells might not have been totally satisfactory, for Laws reporting that he thought there could be a serious leak in the Dotland area. But these initial teething problems seemed to have been rectified and we hear of no further problems. However, it is not completely clear when the new supply of water was properly functioning. It must have been sometime in the middle of 1890, because the *Courant* reported on 17 May that the new reservoir is 'gradually filling with water'. What the Board minutes do record is that, at the meeting on 15 June the following year, the Chairman announced the death of Hubert Laws.

As if to remind everyone of past history, an issue arose in 1889, which harked back to the time when the Cockshaw Burn was a major source of water for the town. On 30 December the Surveyor reported to the Board that 'Messrs Bell and Sons were found supplying one of the tannery pits in Gilesgate with water by a rubber pipe attached to a tap'. The firm continued with their use of the piped supply. We then learn that the Clerk informed the Board on 10 February 1890 that a writ has been served on the firm, claiming an injunction 'to restrain with their manufactories...... without the Board's consent'. However the case was no as simple as it seemed. It hinged on the use of Cockshaw Burn as the supply of water. It had been used by the town and subsequently by the Board, after the reservoir had been built in 1866. But Bell and Son had equal right to the water, since they too had used water from the burn before the reservoir had been built. This historic right to the water from the burn was embedded in the eventual agreement. Based on the premise that the Board were not then taking any water from the burn, the agreement laid down that Messrs Bell pay for, by meter, such water as they may use from time to time from the Board's mains for manufacturing purposes *but*, if at any time the Board materially diminish the supply in the burn, Messrs Bell should be supplied *gratis*. Further, until a meter was fitted the company would have a free supply, 'unless the Board shall represent to them that the Ladle Wells scheme is falling short'.

The purity of the new supply was almost immediately seen as a great benefit to the town. It is from this time that we read about 'Hexham as a health resort'. The town began to see itself somewhat akin to Harrogate or Scarborough. When the Local Board of Health was to be superseded by the Urban District Council, John Lisle, the Chairman of the Board, when reviewing its achievements, said this about the new water supply

> This was the golden act of the Board, which brought health and prosperity in its train; in a word
> it was the town's greatest boon. Since its completion, they had extended the town's water main

106

to the extent of 3,600 yards, and the town's sewers to the extent of 2,400 yards, showing that pure water had created a demand.

The demand was not only from property already in the town but also from that which was newly-built. In the decades from 1841 to 1891, only in one decade (1861-71) had over a hundred houses been built in Hexham, a total of 112 compared with the average per decade of around 60. Between 1891-1901, the number was 391 between 1901-1911 it was 307 (Jennings, 2000). The provision of a reliable supply of pure water must have made that increase possible. Certainly advertisements for new houses after Ladle Wells had come on stream now draw attention the presence of hot and cold water. Whatever was the actual underlying cause of the increase level of house building, there is evidence that the 1890s saw an increased pressure on the housing market. The *Courant* of 18 June 1892 said

> On every side I hear complaints as to the general lack of houses to let in Hexham. No sooner is it known that a house is likely to become vacant than there is a rush to secure it. One or two that have come under my notice could have been let many times over. This of course, speaks for the popularity of Hexham, but I am sure it would be better if a few more of those who are desirous of taking up their abode here could have their desire gratified. There is a demand for houses of three rooms and up to eight rooms.

Most significantly for our story, with the Local Board of Health, and subsequently the Urban District Council possessing a reliable source of good water, it meant that their members could devote their energies to matters other than those that had governed many of their earlier deliberations. Also, not only did the new water supply extend the length of the water main within the town as the result of increased house building, but also this latter activity increased the length of the sewerage system. Not surprisingly, the increased use of water and generation of sewage within the town led to much more sophisticated thinking about the functioning of both systems.

CHAPTER 12

The two decades following on from the development of the Ladle Wells supply

Enhancing the water supply

The new supply consisted essentially of the cisterns for collecting water at the various springs at Ladle Wells itself, the pipe-line to the original service reservoir and to a new service reservoir 'nine chains or thereabouts to the west of High Shield House' (Hexham Local Board [Water] Act, 1888).

Once the new water supply was functioning, the system was almost at once expanded. The sequence of pipe laying was as follows (information from Board minute books): Maiden's Cross to the Hydropathic (1889); Black House to Oakerlands (1889); Fellside (1893); the Dene to Monks House and Hudshaw House (Mr Tweddle to contribute one-half the cost) (1893); Pearsons Terrace to Portland Terrace (1893); Hudshaw House to Kitty Frisk (1899). The new supply stimulated improvements of the old pipe system. Thus in 1890, the supply to West Cockshaw and Pearson's Terrace from Portland Cottage was up-graded from a 1-1¼ inch pipe to one of 3 inch diameter, because the narrower bore could not cope with the amount of water required to extinguish a fire if one was to arise in the locality.

While the Hydropathic was at last connected to the Local Board of Health supply (until that occurred that institution appears to have been dependent on its own private supply) the proprietor, Mr F. G. Grant, complained of the 'irregular supply' provided by the Board (HLBH 20.3.1889). The problem could not be solved without a major addition to the system. On 7 January 1895, County Alderman Robert Stainthorpe gave notice that at the next ordinary meeting of the Council he would propose

> That this Council meet in committee [in private] to consider the expediency of adopting a High and Low Independent Water Supply in order to reduce the unnecessary pressure on old fittings in the town and causing the abnormal waste of water.

As became clear when Stainthorpe spoke to his motion, a high pressure was necessary to drive the water up-hill to such places as the Hydro, the 'irregular supply' referred to by F. G. Grant being presumably due to a drop in pressure. At the same time, pressure in the Market Place was 300 ft vertical pressure, which meant 120 lbs per square inch in the pipes, a pressure that seemingly could cause problems. Stainthorpe quoted from a letter written by Hubert Laws on 15 March 1889 (*HC* 26.1.1895)

> With respect to the supply of the higher districts by an independent main, though not as essential as a high service reservoir, I am of the opinion that it would add very materially to the convenience of the supply. It would enable you to reduce the pressure in the lower parts of the town to what it was under the old system. Another advantage of this independent main is that the existing reservoir could then be utilised as part of the scheme, giving an additional reserve of 150,000 gallons.

108

The motion was passed, though further details were required before the scheme could be got under way. The matter was discussed further both in the Council and in the Works Committee of the Council but eventually on 7 January 1896, it was resolved

> That the Council recognising the present undue pressure upon our water pipes, valves, etc. and the immense advantage to our otherwise excellent water supply and the great saving of water that would ensue if we adopt High and Low water mains, we are agreed that the sum of £800 required to carry out this alteration be added to the application now before the Local Government Board for a loan to be paid for the Council's water undertakings.

The Surveyor quickly drew up plans for the scheme. Essentially, it involved taking a pipeline from the new High Shield Reservoir in a westerly direction to Wydon Burn, down Causey Hill road to the Hydropathic and then across to Leazes Lane (Fig. 25). The first and third stages were to be, for the most part, across private lands; the road was the property of the Council. In an easterly direction there was to be a pipe down the Dipton Mill Road to join up with the pipe going to Fellside. However, the actual scheme had to await Government approval for the funding. By the start of 1897, that had arrived. In July, Alderman Stainthorpe inaugurated the high service system by turning on the sluice valves that were placed a little below the High Shield Reservoir. There was no doubt about the effectiveness of the scheme. The pressure on fittings within the system was reduced from 100-150 lbs per sq. inch to something like 50-90 lbs per sq. inch. The greatest pressure in the system before the high service system installed was at the Railway Station where the value was 153 lbs per sq. inch; after installation, the value had dropped to 92 lbs per sq. inch. As a result of the high service system via Causey Hill it was now possible to carry water with sufficient pressure to the Leazes, located c 100 ft above the old reservoir. All the high-lying places were to be served by water supplied by the new reservoir, the lower parts of the town from the old reservoir (*HC* 17.7.1897).

At the Board meeting on 7 March, another element entered the planning process for extending the water system within the town. Apparently, there had been conversations amongst the Councillors about the use of water that was in excess of that supplying the old reservoir, i.e. that which went down the bye-wash. It had been concluded that if this water could be piped off, it could be most profitably used for watering the streets (Fig. 25). A resolution to that effect was passed. The Surveyor estimated the cost of the pipe-work to be £148. Since no account had been taken of way-leaves (strictly, a mining term but here used for the rights of way, granted on payment of a fee, to allow the excavation work to take place), it was recommended that £250 be added to a sum, earmarked for extending the water mains within the town, being put before the Local Government Board for its sanction as a loan. The 'unfiltered water main', as it came to be termed, was to come through the fields into St Wilfid's Road. It was commenced in January of 1897 but its completion depended on Government approval of a loan for the money. The obligatory Local Government inquiry was held in July 1898 but it was little more than an exposition of the details by the Clerk, William Pruddah. When the Inspector from the Local Government Board, Walter A. Ducat, asked if anyone present wished to ask any questions, Alderman Stainthorpe said 'We are all members of the Council and we are pretty unanimous on the application.' The proceedings then terminated (*HC* 23.7.1898). All this was in marked contrast to the disunity shown by the Local Government Board in the 1870s and early 1880s. When a loan was sanctioned in September, the unfiltered main was taken along Priestpopple (to supply the auction marts, flour mill, steam laundry and flushing the public cattle market in Priestpopple itself) and down Beaumont Street and thence down Market Street and Gilesgate.

As indicated earlier, the bulk of the loan was used for extending the water mains within the town and a long list of streets are given in the proceedings of the enquiry, such as the Allendale Road, Eilansgate and the Burswell House estate. The town was well on the way to being properly supplied with water. Thereafter, for the most part, it was a case of extending the pipes to specific sites, particularly where new houses were being built. Of course within many houses in the town there was much to be desired with respect to the water supply (and the removal of sewage) but, for the most part, that was a problem for the owners of the properties. Until the late 1920s, the management and extension of the water supply had become very much a routine matter.

It would be a mistake to believe that, from then on, everything ran perfectly smoothly. As early as May 1894, people in the town were talking about 'a long and protracted drought', such that Thomas Temperley, of South Park, wrote to the Board expressing aggravation that many 'thousands of gallons per day are being wasted watering the streets, cleansing the auction marts, etc.' (HLBH 15.5.1893). More importantly, he was concerned that 'inferior water from the old reservoir is being used for drinking and domestic purposes'. It seemed just like the bad old days, when he stated

> The water from our taps this morning contains much matter in suspension, becomes brown or yellow [denoting the presence of organic matter] when permte [permanganate] of potash is dissolved in it , and in a hot water tank lively minute creatures are to be seen disporting.

Seemingly, there is no evidence that until that letter, the Board was taking the matter with any seriousness. However, two weeks later at the next Board meeting on 29 May, the Works Committee is recommending that there be night inspections by two men with a water meter to note waste taking place, with a follow up during the next day by another man, who will have the power to turn off the supply and not allow the supply to return, until the owner has remedied the source of any waste. Also waste at the site of the Ladle Wells springs and along the pipeline from them was to be investigated. Meanwhile there was discontent simmering in the town, such that on 13 June a deputation, containing many well-known names, waited on the Board. With Lewis Lockhart as their spokesman, they expressed concern about the supply of water, 'especially since a large sum of money had been spent on it'. The Board was subjected to a list of questions, mostly about the running of the water supply since the Ladle Wells supply started, to which the deputation wanted answers. The Chairman of the Board (John Lisle) gave an unambiguous response. The Board would meet two nights later to consider its answers to the questions; and there is the suggestion that another meeting would follow this with the deputation. In the end, the answers to the questions were published in the *Hexham Courant*. The Board did not wait to learn what the deputation felt about the answers; there was a need for action to deal with problems facing the Board at that particular moment. At an extraordinary meeting on 21 June it was decided that 'all garden taps be cut off' and 'that the use of Town's Water by means of hose pipes when washing of carriages, carts, horses yards, etc. be prohibited' and 'that a general notice be issued asking Inhabitants to be as careful can be with the use of Water'.

It is not appropriate to go into the details of the questions and answers. Sufficient to say, the rumours about the use of water at that present from the old reservoir were exaggerated. Though water from that source had been used, it was predominantly in January when, during a period of frost, taps were left running to stop the pipes from freezing. On no occasion did more than one-tenth of the night's supply to the town come from the old reservoir. The water had been continually analysed by Dr Jackson, who pointed out 'that during the present year the town has not suffered from any disease attributable to impure water'. He also pointed out that it was not good to use a supply very intermittently, something he had warned about in 1874 when there were two deaths due to enteric fever, which were the direct result of an intermittent supply. On receiving the answers by the Board to their questions, those masterminding communications with the Board called a meeting of ratepayers to formulate a response to the answers of the Board. Those answers focused on the detailed management of the supply, emphasising the decade-old matter of detecting and cutting down of waste. The details need not detain us; there were a number of sensible suggestions (HLBH 26.6.1893), though one cannot ascertain the extent to which they were acted upon. At that particular time, the Board's attention was upon dealing with the present shortage of water. Concerned about the adequacy of the present supply of water, on 10 July the Board decided to apply to 'W. B. Beaumont Esq. and Robert Dixon Esq. for permission to take water from the Cockershields Springs' that are about two miles north of Ladle Wells. Mr Dixon declined to allow water to be used, 'until he sees for himself from where the water will be taken'. Yet again, the Board appeared to have jumped the gun, because it seems as if its workmen have been on land not owned by the Board without the owner's permission. Dixon complained of ground broken by laying pipes, walls pulled down and stones taken to be used elsewhere, without his leave or that of his tenant. It does not seem that this supply was ever tapped (HLBH 24.7.1893). By October, the crisis was over, Ladle Wells was supplying 15.000 gallons a day more than two weeks previously (HC 21.10.1893). In the autumn of 1904, according to the Surveyor, 'there had never been such a continued period of drought since you [the Council] got water from Ladle Wells'. Then it seems that Cockershields Springs was used as an additional water supply (*HC* 10.12 1904).

After bringing the Ladle Wells supply on stream, one matter remained outstanding for a number of years. While the performance of the supply was not in any way jeopardised, the matter gave the Hexham Local Board of Health (then the successor Urban District Council) considerable concern until it was eventually resolved. That matter was the compensation to be paid to Mr Beaumont for taking the water from his land. Compensation to other landowners, through whose land the pipes passed, seems to have been dealt with relatively swiftly. But that to be paid to Mr Beaumont was only settled around fourteen years after the completion of the scheme. It is not apparent why it took so long. Though the Local Board were clearly preparing themselves for negotiations, in that they had re-appointed John Davidson of Belmont House, Haydon Bridge (he had acted with respect to the other claims) to act on its behalf with respect to the amount of damage to be claimed against the Board regarding the road across the moor and the pipe track, it was Mr Beaumont's Agent who made the first moves. Indeed, the matter initially seemed to be urgent if the tone of the letter from Kaye, reported to the Board of Health on 14 July 1890 is taken at face value. 'Mr Beaumont would like now to have the question of compensation settled. What do you propose to do with respect to it?' The Board took a measured view. It 'will carefully consider any claim for compensation that Mr Beaumont may be advised to make in respect of the Hexham Water Supply.'

A fortnight later, on 28 August, the following was reported to the Board:

The statement of W. B. Beaumont's claim for compensation in respect to land taken, pipe easement, road and game damage.

	£	s	d
For purchase of site of tanks at Ladle Wells	25	0	0
For easement from Springs to Lightside Road and through Mr Simpsons and Mr Johnsons fields	1,327	0	0
For damage to sporting rights during construction	45	0	0
For damage by use of road during construction	55	13	0
Total	1452	13	0

Note - nothing is included in the above statement in respect of water rights. It is proposed to leave any claim to compensation for interference with them to be made and dealt with hereafter if necessary – John E. Kaye

Not surprisingly, the Board requested Kaye to furnish details of any further claim, as indicated in the footnote, 'so that the whole question between Mr Beaumont and the Board may be fully gone into and finally settled.'

It was then that matters started to become complicated, for the next significant communication to the Board was the copy of a letter from Mr Beaumont to his solicitors, Messrs Dees and Thompson, asking them 'to see the Clerk of the Local Board' to see if they could effect a compromise 'on the basis of allowing mining water rights to stand if it ever does' (HLBH 8.8.1892). But nothing then seemed to happen. It was 1894 before negotiations restarted. Then the Board took the initiative by offering £374.12s 4d to Mr Beaumont in discharge of his claim (HLBH 26.5.1894). Dees and Thompson replied saying 'that our client cannot accept the Board's offer'. Nevertheless they suggested that 'to settle the matter in a friendly way and with as little expense to the Board' Mr Kaye and the Board's representative, Mr Davidson, were to meet to reach a settlement, with a Mr Gow, acting as final arbiter. A letter from Dees and Thompson, dated 30 November, indicated that Kaye and Davidson could only agree about some minor matters (HLBH 10.12.1894). Further, Dees and Thompson were still trying to get the Board to agree to have Gow as the arbiter. The next year, 1895, saw more of the same with the Board making offers that were unacceptable. The Board were not happy with suggestion of Gow as arbiter, so there was a flurry of letters containing other suggested names. In the end Mr W. J. Bolam emerged as the agreed person (HLBH 14.5.1895)

And so it went on. The matter was only resolved in 1904. The previous year, the chances of a resolution of the problem seemed distinctly unpromising. When asked to report their views on a letter from Dees and Thompson received in June, the Finance Committee in August responded 'Your Committee do not consider that Mr Beaumont has sustained any damage by the Council taking water from Ladle Wells' (HC 1.8.1903). This led to Dees and Thompson requiring arbitration. The Council agreed and, even when, at a later date, Mr Kaye made an offer, it still allowed arbitration to proceed. On 2 July 1904, the *Hexham Courant* reported the proceedings of the previous Council meeting. In them the Award of the Umpire, Sir Ralph Littler, KC, with respect to Mr Beaumont's claim was given in full. To the end, Mr Kaye and the Council's representative, Mr Thomas Gow, were still disagreeing. So it was left to Sir Ralph who fixed the compensation at £4563 10s, which was undoubtedly a considerable shock to the Council. The Chairman felt that the sum should be paid as soon as possible. He felt that, if the Council was prepared to economise for a short period, the resources of the town were such to meet this claim till such time as further developments of the building trade gave them further resources. At a later meeting the Council agreed to apply to the Local Government Board to sanction a loan to help pay off the above sum (*HC* 13.8.1904).

CHAPTER 13

The sewage problem revisited and the final addition to the water supply

The demand for an improvement of the sewerage system

The most striking change in outlook following the establishment of the new water supply in 1889 was probably the emergence of a genuine concern about the most unsatisfactory nature of the then system for dealing with the disposal of sewage. First, there was a need to improve how sewage was managed within the town, which meant not only the provision of better and more sanitary appliances but also laying pipes and associated structures which could cope with the amount of material entering the system. Those responsible for the system had become much more aware of the need to take into consideration the entry into it of run-off water from rain and other sources. Even the design of the system needed to be more sophisticated. Thus Robert Grieves, reporting to the Local Board about the many complaints of the smell of sewer gas in the town, said the problem was due to the sewage pipe at the outfall allowing free passage of air into the system, thus forcing gas out of the higher sewers. He recommended that a tidal valve be fitted at a cost of £10. Second, there was an increasing awareness of the need not only to remove sewage from domestic and other premises but also to treat it. Initially, sewage was disposed of either at an outlet close to the station or into the Cockshaw Burn on Tyne Green; essentially it was a matter of disposal via the Tyne. But pressure for change came with the Rivers Pollution Prevention Act, 1876 (39 & 40 Vict., c. 75) which stated

> every person who puts, or causes, or permits to be put or to fall, or be carried into any stream, so as to interfere with its flow, or to pollute its waters, the solid refuse of any manufactory, manufacturing process or quarry, or any rubbish, cinders, or waste, or any putrid or solid matter, will be guilty of an offence.

The Act specifically contained prohibitions against allowing solid or liquid sewage matter to be put, or flow into any stream of water. If this did not signal to a sanitary authority that river pollution was a matter of serious concern, the amending Act of 1893 (56 & 57 Vict., c. 31) left sanitary authorities in no doubts about their responsibilities:

> If any sewage matter falls or flows or is carried into any stream after passing through or along a channel vested in a sanitary authority, the sanitary authority shall be deemed to knowingly permit the sewage so to fall, flow or be carried.

One has the impression that the River Pollution Act at first made little impression on Hexham. The *Hexham Courant* drew attention to its publication (*HC* 14.10.1876) and earlier in 1876 the same paper published a long article on 'The Disposal of Town Refuse', indicating possible ways of treating sewage (*HC* 1.4.1876). But those running the town were distracted away from these issues by the political controversy over the supply of water (R. M. Jennings, 1998). However, as time went on it is hard to believe that these two Acts did not influence thinking within the town about the way it dealt with sewage disposal. Indeed, also, the growing knowledge of microbiology must have had some influence. By 1890, Pasteur, Lister and Koch had established the germ theory of disease, making possible the widespread understanding of its implications for public health. 'The investigations [of men such as these] have exposed dangers to health formerly unthought of, and already fresh legislation has been the result' (Reid, 1892). Thus, in 1890 the Public Health (Amendment) and the Infectious Diseases (Prevention) acts came into force. It became increasingly clear that not only had sewage to be disposed of from domestic and other buildings but there was a need to treat it so that it became both harmless and its unattractive nature eliminated.

After the building of the Ladle Wells water supply, pressures began to build up for sewage to be treated before disposal. Some pressures were of quite long standing. One was the close proximity to the railway station of the sewage outfall, from which passengers were often treated to most unpleasant odours and the site itself was most unattractive. In its issue of 11 September 1869 the *Courant* was to write

> As many of my readers are aware the outlets or pits for the sewage of the town near the railway station are an eyesore to many travellers (to and from the east)...... could not the North-Eastern Railway Company erect a boarding in front of the pits? It would be most agreeable to travellers if they would do so, and besides that, the boarding might be used as an advertising medium, for generally the train goes very slowly opposite that particular place...... the cost of which would only be trifling.

Second, as one moves into the second half of the 19th century, pollution of the Tyne by sewage and industrial waste becomes of increasing concern. Thus, four days later than the date of the extract just quoted, the *Courant* was reporting on the visit of the Principal Health Officer of Bombay, Mr Hewlett. He was a pupil of Robert Rawlinson and he

> very decidedly objected to the midden steads...... Last of all he visited the outfall of sewage at the railway and stated his surprise at our wastefulness in allowing so much good manure to run into and pollute the river. He cited Banbury, Croydon and Reading...... as instances of the great fertilizing power of sewage when applied to land...... He hoped it would soon be illegal to permit town sewage to run into a running stream.

The paper itself took up the theme on 10 October 1869 in an editorial devoted to sewage. It is not appropriate to go into the arguments propounded for its use as an agricultural fertiliser. From our point of view it is the premise that 'Rivers flowing as they do through populous land cannot long continue to be the huge *cloaca* they have become' that needs the emphasis. The issue of sewage disposal into the Tyne took on special significance later in December when it was reported that 'it is the intention of the Newcastle and Gateshead Water Company...... to erect a new works in the parish of Ovingham for the purpose of pumping water from the river.' The article pointed out that 'the poison of infectious disease' might be transmitted from Hexham's sewage into 'the stomachs of the inhabitants of Newcastle upon Tyne'. But as we shall see it was some time before those in Hexham were to recognise that they had responsibilities towards other communities as well as themselves.

At the last meeting of the Local Board for 1869, the Chairman read out two letters (HLBH 27.12.1869). One was from D.D. Main, Secretary of the Whittle Dean Water Company, responsible for supplying water to Newcastle and Gateshead. He was concerned about the sewage of Hexham being allowed to flow into the Tyne.

> I may state however unwillingly we may be ourselves to interfere with any public body our relationship with the Towns of Newcastle and Gateshead with reference to the River Tyne will impose upon us the duty of seeing that it is kept as far as possible free from Sewage water. We shall be glad to hear that you propose taking immediate steps to carry the Sewage elsewhere.

The other letter was from William Cuthbert, Chairman of the Tyne Salmon Conservancy, who spoke in terms very recognisable today

> We know that the health of mankind is far more important than the propagation of fish and when we ask you to stop this flow of Sewage into the Tyne we are supported by the conviction that we are doing more for the benefit of Mankind than for the Salmon.

The reaction of the Board to these two letters was to set up a committee of three who were to report to the meeting of the Board on 24 January 1870 and the Water Company and the Conservancy Board be 'informed about the appointment and objects of such a Committee'.

There is no evidence of any report. One has the feeling that the two letters were not taken very seriously. In a rambling discussion in the Board at its meeting of 7 March 1870 about the issue of sewage disposal, there was a reference to a speech that Mr Cuthbert made to the Tyne Salmon Conservancy the previous Saturday. Matthew Smith commented 'Mr Cuthbert had stated that Hexham had only put sewage into the river for the past 40 years, but it had run into it from time immemorial'. Nevertheless, the *Courant* in a leader warned that

> the present easy-going system of pouring it [sewage] into the nearest running stream will no longer be tolerated......Many years will not pass by until it will be wondered at, that a time like our own, professing so much love of progress, should have hesitated in seeking any and every means to preserve at the same time the health and save the pockets of the nation by treating the sewage of towns (*HC* 11.1.1870).

On 15 December 1866, the Board of Conservators for the Tyne Salmon Fishery District met for the first time in Hexham (Marshall, 1990). The Board, as well as granting licences for salmon fishing, was to be involved in taking proceedings 'against any person or persons acting in contravention of the Salmon Fisheries Acts 1861-1865'. By 1869, the year of the letter above from William Cuthbert, the salmon fishery proprietors were only mildly interested in the matter of entry of sewage into the river, as it had been found that sewage 'did not materially interfere with the health of the fish' unless the sewage contained toxic matter from chemical works and the like. By the next year, they had taken a different tack (*HC* 8.3.1870). They were now particularly concerned about the detrimental effect on fishing on the abstraction of water from the Tyne by the Newcastle and Gateshead Water Company. However, 'the pollution of the town of Hexham will also be detrimental to the fishing interest of the river'. The Chairman, William Cuthbert, was desirous of having the attention of the Royal Commissioners, who were enquiring into pollution of rivers, called to the Tyne 'at this critical juncture'. There is no doubt that, based on the fairly recently acquired understanding of the spread of cholera, authorities were right to be wary of any water to be used for public consumption if it might have been contaminated by sewage. From Hexham's point of view however, those who ran the town had little to fear. The reason was simple. Contamination could only be demonstrated chemically and the volume of water flowing down the Tyne was such as to dilute any sewage contamination beyond the limits of any analytical methods, as pointed out by Richard Burdon Sanderson, the Chairman of (what was now) the Newcastle and Gateshead Water Company, in a letter to the *Hexham Courant* of 22 February 1870. Nevertheless, the matter of sewage contamination of the river raised the public awareness of the dangers of disposing untreated sewage into watercourses.

Pressure for change was to come from a third direction. When County Councils came into being in 1888, they were authorised to appoint, if they chose, a County Medical Officer, though the powers and duties of such officers were not defined (Taylor, 1989). At the time it might have seemed that the County Medical Officer might not have much influence, since the County Council lacked direct authority in health matters. However, significantly, when the new Sanitary Authorities, such as the Hexham Urban District Council, were formed in 1894 the County Council became able to advise and admonish the new authorities and could take legal action against any who persistently failed to discharge their responsibilities. Furthermore, County Councils were able to take steps to enforce the Rivers Pollution Act, 1876, as if it were a sanitary authority. Fortunately for the future health of Hexham, the County Council decided in 1894 to appoint a Medical Officer, Dr J. W. Hembrough to the post. He served until 1919 and appears to have been a most successful appointment.

But it was probably the Local Government Board in London that provided the strongest motive force for change with respect to the most effective means for the disposal of sewage. By the 1880s, there were a number of ways by which sewage from a town could be disposed of more or less effectively, without having a significant detrimental effect on water-courses (Reid, 1892). These were:
i) Precipitation with lime and aluminium salts, such that a sludge was deposited, but the clear fluid remaining needing further purification. The sludge could be laid directly on the land which was eventually cropped, or pressed into cakes to be sold or given away as manure, or burned and manufactured into cement.
ii) Intermittent downward filtration via effluent drains laid 5-6 feet below the soil surface. The clarified sewage irrigated the surface for about eight hours with an interval of about sixteen hours before the next interval. We can probably speak of this as a microbiological method, the organisms in the column of soil above the pipes breaking the sewage down.
iii) Broad land irrigation. The sewage was discharged over a larger area of land by irrigation channels, seemingly without the same underlying pipe system in ii) but in principle with the same mechanisms involved. Untreated sewage could be used but the prognosis of successful treatment over the long term was not good.
iv) The best system appeared to have been artificial filtration. The precipitant was a material called *ferrozone*, which acted quickly but also appears to have broken down the dissolved organic matter. There was a filtering medium called *polarite*. This was a specially-prepared iron ore, which was credited with oxidising organic matter. The effluent from precipitation tanks first passed through a layer of first sand and then gravel laid above the polarite to remove any suspended matter. After a period, the layer of sand has to be replaced

Now that information about these various possible ways was within the public domain, the Local Government Board felt well able to request of the Hexham Local Board of Health

> to be informed of the arrangements in operation in the district for the disposal of sewage. A plan and description of the system of disposal should be supplied in illustration as well as a statement of the exact area of land, if any used for the purification of the sewage (HLBH 21.4.1890).

It seems the Board ignored this request. At an inquiry in Hexham, instigated by the Local Government Board to consider the application from the Local Board of Health for sanction to borrow money for new offices and 'works of sewerage' (see below), the Inspector, Colonel Luard, questioned the Surveyor about the nature of the outfall works. When the Surveyor said that they 'simply screened the ashes and passed the sewage over it', Col. Luard said 'it was possible the Local Government Board might not sanction these loans for new sewers on the ground that the filtration was not as good as it should be.' (*HC* 13.6.1891). However in the end, the total amount to be borrowed was sanctioned (HLBH 19.10.1891).

There is no evidence that the Board reacted formally to that comment but the Surveyor, Robert Grieves, was clearly forced to think about the matter. On the 16 October 1893, he presented a detailed report to the Board in which he recommended the 'ferrozone' process. After detailed questioning from members of the Board, the Chairman moved 'that the Board stand adjourned until Monday evening next and in the meantime Mr Grieves would do his best to get further information.' That meeting was deferred to enable him to visit one of the places where works for the purification of sewage similar to what was being proposed for Hexham was taking place. As it happened, James Robb and George Bell of the Board accompanied Grieves. They visited Condon, in County Durham; on the way, they were joined by Charles Bell, Chairman of the Durham Rural Sanitary Authority. When they were at Condon they were impressed with what they saw. 'Effluent came out in such a pure state that some of the members were persuaded to take a mouthful of the water. One member said it had the taste of iron.' A sample of sewage sludge was brought back to Hexham; 'it was of a dark colour but not the slightest degree of an offensive smell.' The delegation expressed satisfaction at what they had seen (*HC* 28.10.1893). There is little doubt that this visit had converted any doubters and the Surveyor's scheme was approved at a meeting of the Board on 25 October. The Local Government Board had already received on 6 April 1893 an application from the Hexham Board of Health a request for a loan of £700 to be sanctioned for a number of sundry works in the town, but including £350 for sewage works and a culvert to take effluent across Tyne Green. Subsequent letters from the Local Government Board indicated that it had concerns about the scheme being proposed.

The Local Government Board demanded that there be a local inquiry with respect to borrowing £350 for the sewage scheme. That took place in the first week of the 1894. Reading the report of the inquiry (*HC* 6.1.1894) it is clear that the total scheme was ill conceived. The problem was that sewage of the town was going to two separate treatment sites. There was the one to the east of the station, with settling tanks but no chemical treatment before being passed over ashes. It was only at Tyne Green that the sewage was to be treated by the ferrodoxone (ferrozone) process, the effluent going by the proposed culvert to the Tyne. The Inspector, again Col. Luard, was not impressed. With regard to the eastern outfall he said 'that would not satisfy the Local Government Board'. He pointed out that the Tyne at Hexham was not tidal and the Hexham Board was subject to the River Pollution Act. From amongst the audience there were expressions of concern about the right of the Council to build a sewage works on Tyne Green. While these concerns were certainly misplaced, they did not engender a favourable atmosphere. The response of the Local Government Board made it clear what had to be done. Assistant Secretary, Alfred D. Adrian wrote

> Board are advised that the proposed treatment of the sewage will not secure an effluent sufficiently pure to allow of its discharge into a non-tidal river and they are therefore unable to comply with the application.
> I am to request that the Local Board re-consider the question of the disposal of sewage of their district with a view to the connection of the western outfall with the eastern outfall and the acquisition at or near the latter of a sufficient area of land upon which to purify the sewage by filtration.

Thereafter the matter of sewage disposal hung fire for nearly eighteen months. It wasn't as if the Hexham Board were not being pressed to resolve the matter The Local Government Board wrote twice (in April and June) to it to find out what consideration it was giving to the matter of sewage disposal. Then, in October, Charles D. Foster, Deputy Clerk of the County Council, sent a report of the County Medical Officer about sewage pollution of the Tyne, which emphasised the primitiveness of the Hexham disposal system. The major cause for the lack of action was probably the resignation of Robert Grieves in April 1894 on his appointment to a similar post with the Cowpen District Local Board (*HC* 21.4.1894). His replacement, appointed in May was Richard Thomas Surtees of Morpeth. He must have needed time to establish himself and become properly acquainted with the sanitary and other issues for which he had responsibility. But the lack of action could also have been due to the problem of joining up the two outfalls, owing to the distance and the very small gradient that imposed itself along the most suitable line for the pipe connection to take. A final factor was the replacement of the Local Board of Health by the Urban District Council that held its first meeting on 31 December 1894. The establishment of the Council meant an election for all nine places on it. Understandably, there was probably a tendency to defer some decision making to the new local authority.

Whatever the reasons for delay, it was not until 14 October 1895 that the matter of sewage disposal came back onto the agenda. Then, the Health Committee recommended 'that another committee be appointed to make enquiries concerning the town's sewage'. Shortly afterwards, at the 11 November meeting, it was agreed 'that the members of the Works Committee along with the Medical Officer, Clerk and the Surveyor be appointed a deputation from this Council to visit such places which they deem necessary where sewage works are in operation and to report upon such works'. That decision can be considered the start of what can be taken to be a long journey by the Council towards providing Hexham with a sewage system that could be described as efficient in terms of both the purity of the effluent and the capability to cope with the volume passing through.

Solving the problem

Two factors affected progress towards better systems of treatment. One was the fact that sewage treatment had become very much a new technology. One can see in the reports of the proceedings of the Urban District Council the difficulties that the Councillors had over making decisions about several different possible systems when they were not conversant with the principles underlying them. Further, at the time we are considering, many systems were undergoing change. Decision-making under the circumstances was not easy. A heavy burden was put on the Surveyor, who had the best understanding of what was needed.

The other factor affecting progress were the pressures on the Surveyor from other aspects of his responsibilities. Hexham was seeing a boom in house building. It was up to the Council to ensure that the various building sites had the necessary supply of water and that there were the necessary pipes for taking away the sewage. Throughout the period we are considering, much of the effort of Richard Surtees and his successor in 1902, G. L. Murray, was spent in coping with these particular problems. Also, whatever improvements were made to the systems for treating sewage were carried out by the Surveyor's own labour force. One wonders whether it was because of the critical report on sewage disposal following the enquiry in 1893 that the Council continued with the policy of doing the work 'in house', as it was the most economical way of getting the work done. In this way, the need to request a loan from the Local Government Board was minimised and thus pressure on the Council from that Board to have only one sewage treatment plant was obviated. At any rate, an application to the Local Government Board for a loan for the purpose of dealing with sewage was not made again until 1912 (NA HLG/1/465).

A measure of the uncertainty of the Council as to how to proceed with the treatment of sewage was the fact that in November 1897, the Council, in order to improve their expertise, embarked on another tour of sewage works in other parts of the country. Whereas, previously, except for Nuneaton, the places chosen for visiting were not of great consequence, *viz*, Royton, Cheadle, Failsworth, Pye Bridge, the next tour took in Exeter, Hendon, Sutton, Oswestry and Winsford (in Cheshire). This latter tour appears to have focussed particularly on the septic and bacterial systems about which they were to obtain very good reports (HUDC 6.12.1897).

On the basis of the findings of the visiting group, the District Council agreed that septic and bacterial systems be installed to deal with the sewage coming down to Tyne Green. It was necessary to have land on which to build the sewerage system and this was purchased from William Ridley, next to his manure works (HUDC 8.2.1898). The new works were completed and in operation at the end of 1898. Just over two years later, Dr Hill, the Medical Officer of Health for Durham, expressed considerable satisfaction with their working (HUDC 11.3.1901). However, the larger works at the Railway Station were in a less satisfactory state as can be seen from this report of the County Medical Officer

> The Urban District Council some time ago laid down some sewage disposal works for the purpose of treating experimentally the sewage from a portion of the district, in liquefying tanks and bacterial beds [at Tyne Green]. In the meantime the works [at the station] for treating the rest of the sewage have been considerably improved, and a better effluent is obtained than was the case before the recent alterations were carried out. The effluent, however, though greatly improved in appearance, is in a putrescible (*sic*) condition, it is four to five times as impure as that obtained from the bacteria beds of the other system, and is not such as should be discharged into the river (*HC* 26.9.1903).

Even by 1912, Hexham was without a completely satisfactory system for dealing with its sewage. In that year, the Council decided to borrow £420 for extending the sewer up the Allendale Road to Duke Willey. Hexham was visited W.O.E. Meade-King, a Local Government Board Inspector with respect to the application. He visited both sewage works and approved of what he saw (NA HGL/1/465). He was somewhat concerned with the Tyne Green works, feeling it was overloaded. However, he was reassured by the fact that the Council was proposing to buy land (just across the railway) from Lord Allendale for the purpose of increasing the capacity of the sewage works. A detailed description of the two sewage works, at the Railway Station and Tyne Green, as they were functioning at the start of 1911, is given in a report by R. M. Bicknell, another Inspector, also concerned with the same application to borrow money (NA HGL/1/465).

Whatever the state of the sewage works, there was little doubt of the need to extend the sewer up Allendale Road from Whetstone Bridge, as was indicated by Bicknell's report

> Any houses in a Westerly direction beyond that point [Whetstone Bridge] drain either into cesspools which overflow into the ditch on the side of the main road or directly into that ditch without passing through a cesspool. The nuisance caused by the sewage stagnating in the ditch is, at times, very considerable and the land on the North side of the Lowgate Road (which is the main road leading from Hexham to Carlisle) is now ripe for building, but people are chary of erecting houses owing to the fact that there is no sewer to which they can connect.

Later it became clear that the Local Government Board was far from satisfied with the situation at Tyne Green. Before coming to a decision about the request for a loan of £420, the Local Government Board requested that it 'will to be furnished with a resolution of the Council that the proposed new sewer will not be connected to the existing sewerage system until the proposed alterations to the sewerage system...... had been completed.' Several other improvements to the system were also indicated (*HC* 18.2.1911). The Chairman intimated that the required alterations might take some time. Indeed, it was 1914 before the sewage works at Tyne Green were completed (HLBH 5.1.1914). However, even before that date, the Urban District Council decided to press on with the extension of the sewer up the Allendale Road, deciding to pay for the work out of revenue and to ignore the way forward via a loan (*HC* 7.12.1912). But the sewer never got further than Duke Willey. Low Gate had to remain unconnected to the town's sewerage system until as late as 1930-31, when the Unemployed Grants Committee recommended a loan of £850 for carrying out the work. The Public Works Loan Commissioners advanced the money and the work was carried out by contract (*HC* 9.8.1930).

Water for Low Gate

Probably stimulated by knowledge of Hexham's new water supply, concern surfaced about the supply of water for Low Gate. The supply came from a well that was legally accessible to the public, made so in the Enclosure Award of 1755 (*HC* 23.7.1898), but located on private land. The Urban District council had no jurisdiction over the well, except if it were to be polluted and, if this were the case, the Council could close it. The problem was the well was not only accessible to the public but also to cattle. There are several reports of cattle drinking the water supposed to be for human consumption.

The District Council made various attempts to have the well railed off but all of them angered the owner of the land Mr J. S. Young of Brecon Hill, who was emphatic that 'never during a period extending over twenty-five years have I received from the tenants the slightest complaint about pollution at this water supply'. In 1897-8, there were a series of letters in the *Hexham Courant* complaining from Young of what he considered the high-handed action of the Council. One has to say that, at first sight, Young had a case. Thus, Council workmen had been on his land in an attempt to rail off the well, without his permission; the Surveyor and Medical Officer of Health had visited the well and made recommendations without consulting Young and his letters to the Council seem not to have been answered or dealt with (*HC* 11.9.1897, 18.9.1897, 25.9.1897, 26.3.1898, 3.9.1898). Nevertheless, as the correspondence progresses, one feels that he will only co-operate on precisely his terms. The Council at its meeting on 12 September agreed with the suggestion of Young, namely that

> [he] will allow the Council to erect a single rail around the trough four feet from the edge of the water, so as to keep the cattle off, a suitable watering place for my cattle being provided at a convenient place some distance from it. The whole work to be done in a satisfactory manner at the expense of the Council and an acknowledgement made (not necessarily a money payment) for the erection of the fence on my land &c., during the continuance of the arrangement surface damage to be arranged for.

Young seems to have agreed the erection of the railing but he was adamant that the well was not a public one, agreeing only to an understanding that the present rights of either party should not be affected. However he also seems to have turned down the idea of a wicket gate or stile to allow easy access from the road to the well. Whatever the case, matters seemed to have quietened down for a good number of years.

It all boiled up again in 1907 when it was reported that the Low Gate well was in an abominable state (*HC* 25.3.1907). This led to a petition, signed by notables such as Lewis Lockhart and Henry Bell, being submitted to the Council about the well that 'is dangerous to the community and in a dry season no supply at all'. What followed seems to have been protracted discussions with Mr Young. It was at a meeting of the District Council on 27 June 1910 when the Surveyor submitted plans for a supply from the well to be brought to the roadside for ease of access by those using the supply. There was to be a trough, with a ball cock, for the cattle. The inlets to the trough and the public water supply were to be at the same level, so that an equal supply of water was given to each. It took a year for agreement to be reached with Mr Young (*HC* 10.6.1911), with the work being got under way almost immediately afterwards.

Even then the somewhat upgraded supply could never have been more than very much second best. At this phase of the story, Low Gate, though a small place, had (in 1915) over a hundred persons depending on the supply. It was known from past experience that when there was a drought, the supply ceased, such that the inhabitants of Low Gate had to go half a mile for an alternative supply. This was increasingly not an appropriate alternative. Also, it was to become clear that the supply could become polluted. On 5 October 1914, the Medical Officer of Health reported to the Urban District Council that the water at the well at Low Gate had been contaminated with enteric fever that had spread to Hexham in milk such that five cases had been reported in a tenemented property at the Gilesgate end of Haugh Lane. All were removed to hospital, one dying there. The Medical Officer had no doubt that it was a matter of urgency to provide a proper supply of water to Low Gate.

This time the Council were abreast of the problem. It had become clear that water could not be abstracted from the area round Low Gate through bore holes, nor could the town's supply as it was at that time, produce sufficient pressure to drive water up the hill to Low Gate. Since this was so, the Surveyor had been investigating how that pressure could be generated. It is difficult to be certain of the details of the eventual supply system. However the general features are clear (NA HLG/1/465). Water from Ladle Wells was piped into a reservoir on land recently purchased at Black House. Water from this reservoir was to reach Low Gate via a new 4 inch main running past the south-west corner of the storage reservoir and running down Causey Hill. At 183 m, the end of this new main was 24 m lower than the reservoir. The work was financed by a loan sanctioned by the Local Government Board and was probably completed in the early years of 1916.

Improving the Supply from Ladle Wells

The final chapter of this story of the development of Hexham's water supply prior to 1939 concerns the further increase in the volume of water reaching Hexham, to meet the growth of the town and the increased use of water. Between 1889, the year of the inception of the Ladle Wells scheme, and 1931, the population of Hexham had increased by 50% to 8888. As I have indicated, that increase in population was accompanied by a rise in house building. The rate of house building slowed down immediately after the War but water usage almost certainly continued to increase, because of the greater emphasis on personal cleanliness and probably also greater use of water for commercial purposes. According to the Surveyor, there was an increased usage through the watering of gardens and washing of cars (*HC* 15.9.1928).

The Surveyor sounded a warning of the need for more water in his report to the Urban District Council on 5 July 1915. He indicated that there was only sufficient water to ensure a full supply to the town until the end of October. In the previous year, the springs did not increase in volume until November, implying that it might be later in 1915. The Works Committee up took the matter immediately and at the next council meeting it was proposed that work be commenced on connecting up the additional springs to the supply system and additionally proposed that 'as this work will involve considerable supervision' a motor cycle and sidecar be bought for the use of the Surveyor. This work could not have been set in hand had not ongoing negotiations been successfully completed with Lord Allendale for the lease of eleven additional springs. The wisdom of this action by the Council was seen in 1919, when the yield from the springs was the lowest on record. It was reported at the Council meeting of 3 November 1919 that had not the new springs been added to the water supply, the storage reservoir would have been empty for more than two months.

The problem was not that the Ladle Wells were not able to supply enough water but that the rate of supply was high at the start of the year and thenceforward declined (*HC* 5.9.1928). The Surveyor, W. G. Landale, provided a quantitative analysis of the problem. He reported that for four months of the year there is an overflow from the springs of 18 million gallons, namely 150,000 gallons a day. For the remaining eight months there is an average deficiency in the daily consumption of 50,000 gallons. Thus, if the overflow could be captured, then the deficiency was easily met. However, to capitalise on this increased supply, it was necessary to have an increased flow of water to the storage reservoir. The original six inch diameter pipe from Ladle Wells could not provide this increased supply. Landale therefore proposed that an eight inch diameter supplementary pipe be laid from Ladle Wells to Black House alongside the existing main (Fig. 26 & 27). Although not stated explicitly in the Council minutes, it seems that Lord Allendale had now allowed the Council to have unlimited access to water from the springs and, further, the gauge that had been put in originally to control the amount supplied was to be removed.

There were two dissenters to what was being proposed, Councillors Rollingson and Ainsley. Their attitude to this relatively large capital project bore a resemblance to those in the previous century to any big scheme for bringing a better water supply to the town. This time, such dissenters could do nothing to stop the progress of the scheme.

At the meeting of the Council on 1 October 1928, two resolutions were passed. One was that application should be made to the Ministry of Health to sanction the borrowing of £18,500 for the scheme. The other was a Provisional Order under the Public Health Act of 1875 be asked for to partially repeal, alter or amend the Hexham Local Board (Water) Act 1888, and the Hexham Orders 1896 to 1905 to give the required powers to borrow the necessary money, to take the water by agreement and to make and maintain the required pipes and other works. None of this could be done under the 1888 Act as it stood. On 12 December, Mr R. C. Cox, an Inspector of the Ministry of Health, conducted the necessary inquiry into the details of the proposed scheme that also encompassed the two resolutions. Councillor Rollingson's concerns fell on deaf ears, while Mr H. Taylor, a consulting engineer of the firm Taylor and Wallens, spoke approvingly of the scheme.

From then on, it seems there had to be much tortuous negotiations with all the parties involved. Over a year later, a leader in 1 February 1930 issue of the *Hexham Courant* indicated that agreement still had to be reached. It was at this time that the Council decided to press ahead with the application for a Provisional Order (detailed in an advert in the 22 March 1930 issue of the *Hexham Courant*). That application met quickly with success going through Parliament and receiving Royal Assent at the beginning of August (*HC* 9.8.1930). It was then that the Council applied to the Unemployment Grants Committee for financial support for the scheme. Though one would have felt it was a very appropriate scheme, involving as it did a significant work force, it seems that persuasion was necessary to obtain the grant. The Council learnt it was forthcoming at the beginning of January 1931, as it also learnt of the approval of the scheme by the Ministry of Health. The work had to start on 2 February and be completed within ten months. Indeed, it was completed well within that time period. On Thursday, 17 September, at 3.0 pm the water was turned into the new main by Lt-Col. J. R. Robb, Chairman of the Council.

FIG. 28. Part of the 1865 Ordnance Survey map of Hexham showing the then area of Tyne Green and the so-called Mill Islands, that were on the north east side of the Mill Race (or fleam). Fleamside Road that ran closely parallel to the race, is marked on the map by arrows. Jacky's Hole, one of the bathing spots on the race, is identified on the map.

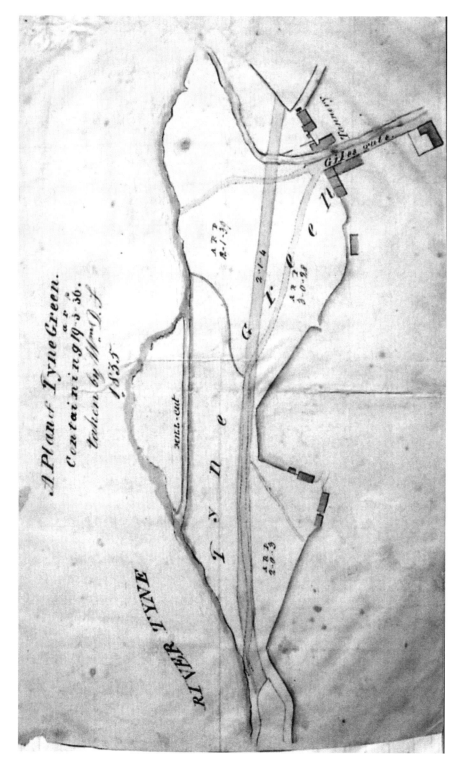

FIG. 29. A plan of Tyne Green made in 1835 showing the proposed line of the Newcastle to Carlisle Railway. Reproduced by kind permission of Dr Jim Hedley.

FIG. 30. The medieval (pointed arch) bridge, connecting the Priory with the Seal across the Halgut (Cowgarth) Burn, showing the 19th-century eye-catching parapet above.

HEXHAM, FROM THE WEST, NORTHUMBERLAND.

FIG. 31. An early 19th-century print of the Seal in summer showing the path across from Cowgarth to Cockshaw. At this particular time of year, the remainder of the Seal would not have been accessible to ordinary citizens.

FIG. 32. The Seal photographed from Seal Gate, showing one of the shelters.

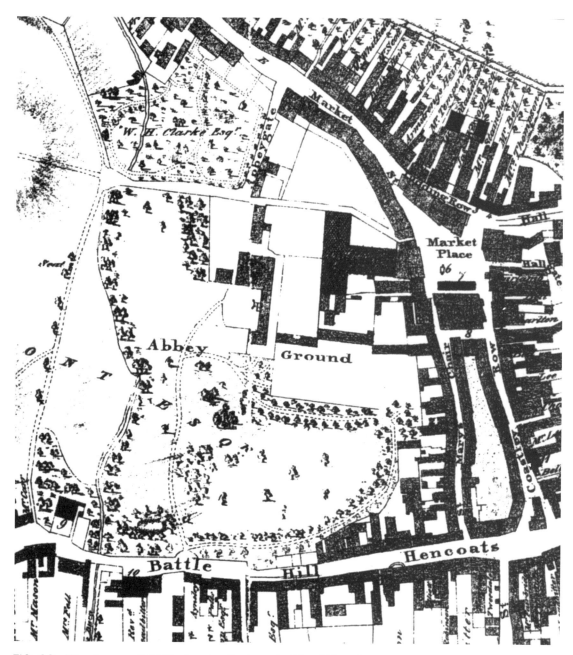

FIG. 33. Wood's map (1826) showing the layout of the Abbey Ground (later plural) in a picturesque manner, with informal walks and a boundary of trees to screen off the buildings and public.

Hexham and Tyne Vale.

FIG. 34. Hexham's public slaughterhouses (abattoirs), which were opened on November 1902, are shown in the centre of the foreground; to the right are Bogacres farm buildings. Hexham Middle School buildings were eventually built just to the west of both sets of buildings. The use of the plural slaughterhouses indicates that individual butchers (seven when the building was opened) were allocated space for their work.

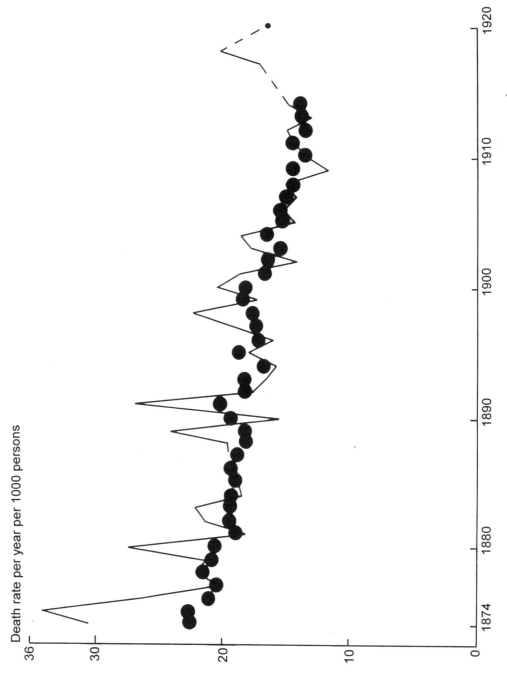

FIG. 35. The yearly mortality figures for Hexham (line) together with the average yearly figures for England and Wales (solid circles) during the period 1874-1920. A dashed line indicates that no figure is available (Hexham Medical Officer of Health, 1874-1930; Registrar-General, 1919).

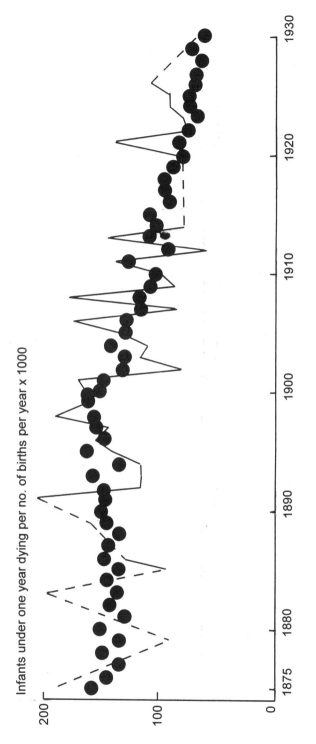

FIG. 36. The yearly infant (children under one year of age) mortality data for Hexham (line) together with the average yearly figures for England and Wales (solid circles) during the period 1875-1930. A dashed line indicates no figures are available (Hexham Medical Officer of Health, 1874-1930; Registrar-General, 1919; Chief Medical Officer, 1939).

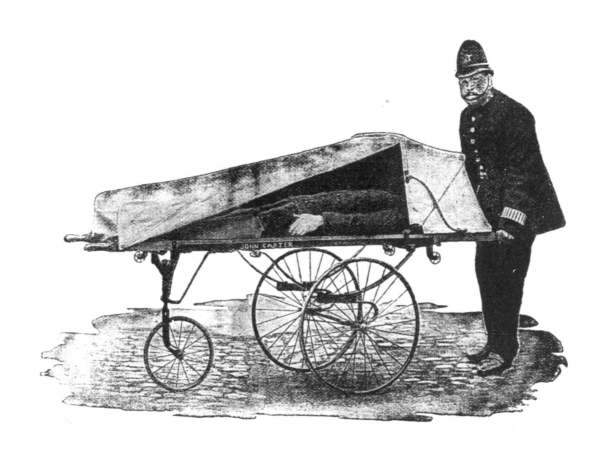

FIG. 37. The likely type of the ambulance used in Hexham to convey a person suffering from injuries such as those described in the text (Riddell, 1894).

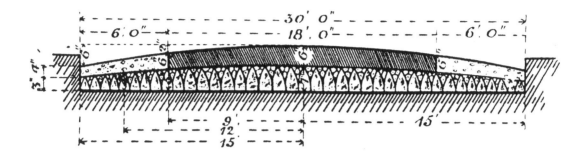

FIG. 38. Diagram of the cross-section of a 30 foot (9.1 m) road constructed according to the specifications of Telford (Aitken, 1900). A trench is first excavated and a bottom course or layer of stones is set by hand (the process of 'penning') in the form of a close firm pavement. On top is a layer of stone chips filling the spaces in the bottom layer and above that is a 6 inch (15.24 cm) layer of nearly cuboid stone pieces, capable of passing through a 2$\frac{1}{2}$ inch (6.35 cm) ring. In the case of Beaumont Street, this was whin or limestone. The layer of stones is then covered with gravel and well rolled. Note the strong convex surface to the road to allow good drainage, water running into a 6 foot (1.83 m) border of fine gravel at the edge of the road. In Beaumont Street, there was a 3 foot (0.91 m) channel on either side of the road, water being led into the drainage system.

Chapter 14

Securing open spaces

Introduction

Hexham is most fortunate in having three open spaces of long standing – the Abbey Grounds, the Sele (*see below* about spelling) and Tyne Green – each differing in character and visual attraction but of great value to the Town for the provision of leisure activities. Though they seem a permanent feature of the townscape, their acquisition by the town has not been without difficulty. Two of them were cut through with transport arteries – the Abbey Grounds by Beaumont Street, Tyne Green by the Newcastle to Carlisle Railway – while the Sele nearly suffered in the same way from the Newcastle to Carlisle turnpike (Jennings *et al.*, 2004). However, a portion of the Sele was lost as open space when the new building for the Subscription School was built in 1854. Each open space has made its own contribution to the cultural and recreational life of the town. Here I concentrate on the events leading up to the acquisition of each space by the Local Authority.

Tyne Green

Tyne Green was common land available for grazing, with soil (and mineral rights), being owned by the Lord of the Manor. At the start of the 19th century, Tyne Green was considerably different from what it is today. The original open space was more to the west. While the only reliable map is 60 years later (Fig. 28), there is no reason to believe that very much had changed during the period from the turn of the century. The 1860 map shows that the area to the north of the road running to the Alemouth Road along the boundary of Tyne Green was much reduced compared to what it is today. A race/fleam that was close to this road (Fleamside) and running to a mill on the eastern side of the Alemouth Road, was separated from the river by islands. This topography led to the area, which today we know as Tyne Green, as being known as Tyne Green and Mill Islands. Of course, the islands and the race have all now disappeared as a result of land being claimed from the river.

In 1836 that section of the Newcastle to Carlisle Railway between Hexham and Haydon Bridge was opened, the track cutting through Tyne Green (Fig. 29). While, regrettably from the present-day perspective, the railway cut the space almost in half, as will be seen in Chapter 17, the Town gained financially from the building of the railway. The route of the railway was to a degree inevitable because of the topography but it seems likely that Hexham was very accepting of whatever were the wishes of the Railway Company. The scattered evidence indicates that the area was seen more as a source of building material, such as sand and gravel (HLBH 19.12.1864) and a site for dumping rubbish (*HC* 7.11.1866). Charles Head, the then Chairman of the Local Board of Health called the area a wasteland. On the more positive side, the area was used for bathing, either in the Tyne (Burn, 1855) or in the race, where there were various bathing spots such as 'Sandy Dandy', 'Jackies' and Cuddy's Plonge', though close to the road, they were hidden from passers-by by a thick growth of willows (*HC* 8.6.1935). Bathing apart, the area was not seen as an amenity. When, at the end of 1864, the Local Board of Health turned its eyes first on the general area with a view to making a purchase of land, they rested on Harbottle's (Broomhaugh) Island as the site for making it their major sewage outlet (HLBH 19.12.1864).

There was an attempt in 1836 when the Newcastle and Carlisle Railway Co. were in the process of buying the land for their railway line across the Green to get them to buy all the rest of the of land and sell it back to the Town (NRO/EP/184/171; *HC* 7.11.1866) But it came to nothing, as did an approach to T.W. Beaumont in 1841, for him to forego all claim to Tyne Green if some of the money coming from the Railway were diverted to covering the Skinners Burn as it ran through Hall Orchard (*HC* 11.5.1872). The first concerted moves towards purchasing Tyne Green and the Mill Islands came in 1866.

> The Board being of opinion that the improvement of Tyne Green and Mill Islands would prove highly beneficial to the Town in many ways <u>Resolve</u> that the Chairman and Messrs Gibson, Robson and Robb be and hereby are appointed a Committee to collect information on the following matters in relation to such improvement and report thereon to the Board at the first Board Meting in September viz
> 1. As to the parties having claims on Tyne Green and Mill Islands, their rights and privileges and the best mode of dealing with them.
> 2. As to the fordable (*sic*) cost of defending the Green from encroachments of the River and of levelling fencing and preparing the Land.
> 3. As to the best use to which it can be put when so prepared and the probable Revenue to be obtained from it.
> 4. As to the most suitable place on Tyne Green on which to place Slaughter Houses, the cost of erection and the Income likely to accrue from them (HLBH 16.7.1866).

It is clear that, from the start and not surprisingly in view of the fact that the Board had only recently taken out the very large loan for the building of the new water supply, Tyne Green was seen as a source of revenue. Nevertheless the decision to put slaughterhouses on the land was to a degree altruistic, as, ever since Rawlinson's (1853) Report, the unsatisfactory location of the slaughtering of animals for butchering purposes, most of which took place cheek by jowl with other property including ordinary houses, had entered the consciences of those who wished for sanitary improvement.

There is no information of what this small group reported but on 5 November 1866, the Board initiated action via the Land Clauses Consolidation Act of 1845 (8 & 9 Vict., c. 18) for the purpose of purchasing 'the Island belonging to Mr Beaumont' (presumably Harbottle's Island) and for 'embanking fencing improving and cultivating' Tyne Green and Mill Islands. Even before that decision by the Board, influential people in the town had heard what was afoot and a public meeting was called. Also a notice was to be inserted in the *Hexham Courant* convening a meeting of the Vestry with respect to compensation of those who held 'Commonable and other rights' to the same land.

The public meeting was essentially concerned with informing those present about the Board's plans. It became clear that, as well as what was proposed at the Board meeting, as itemised above, it seems that the Board also planned to extend the nursery gardens onto the land and raise revenue by doing so. While there seems to have been general agreement with what the Board was proposing, there were some dissident voices. A Mr Dinning, who seemed not to be a resident, wanted the land made into a park, while George Robinson, 'an ancient freeholder entitled to some part of Tyne Green' said 'he would not part with his share of the land until he knew the whole sum of what was to be done with it.' Nevertheless the meeting gave unanimous support to what the Board was trying to do (*HC* 7.11.1866).

The Vestry meeting allowed the commoners their say. Though the number attending was small, it became clear that the Local Board would not have its own way. The use that it proposed to make of Tyne Green did not find favour. It was felt strongly that, since it was common land, the area should be devoted to recreational activity. The Rev. F. Kirsopp was emphatic about

> What were other towns doing? Why, some actually buying land, while in others generous people gave land, in order to have public parks made. Here they had land, and though he knew the Board wished to have it enclosed for the benefit of the town, yet they should have a guarantee that they would not cultivate it for the purpose of realising a profit, and it must be the wish of every right-minded gentleman amongst them to have it put into proper order and made into a pleasant place for the people, especially the poor.

Though the meeting agreed to the proposal 'that all commonable rights on Tyne Green shall and hereby extinguished', resolution of the matter would only come after negotiation between the Board and the Commoners. The former had already selected their representatives; the final act of the Vestry meeting was the selection of those to represent the latter (*HC* 28.11.1866).

It would seem that the Local Board were not too worried by the possibility of opposition for over the next months as efforts were focussed on the purchase of the 'right in the soil and commonable rights in Tyne Green'. In May, the Board resolved that the Clerk prepare a memorial to the Home Secretary for his authority to put in force the powers of the Land Clauses Consolidation Act 1845 for the purchase of Tyne Green and Mills Islands for the purpose of making a public park, erecting slaughterhouses and for constructing 'a reservoir or cesspool for collecting and deodourizing sewage' and for sanction to borrow up to £4,500 to make the purchase. The Board realised it might not be financially plain sailing, since they also asked for permission to extend the period of their major loan of £17,600 from thirty to fifty years (HLBH 6.5.1867).

But then matters began to get a little more complicated. The Local Government Board sent Arthur Taylor to make 'an inquiry, and hear objections against' the purchase of Tyne Green. It led to all sorts of complaints being raised. As the *Hexham Courant* put it

> It was expected by not a few of our quiet steady-going, unobtrusive townspeople that the inquiry would be merely a formal affair...... I was, indeed not a little astonished when I heard the opposition of the Lord of the Manor...... at the eleventh hour opposition appeared from a most unlikely quarter and from gentlemen, too, who had ample opportunity of attending and discussing their objections at the previous meetings.

It appeared that W. B Beaumont, through his solicitor, R.R. Dees, had objected to the proposed scheme and threatened his utmost opposition to it. That from the 'gentlemen' was equally fierce and almost every criticism of the scheme that could be brought forward was brought forward. Typical of the criticism was that of J.O. Head, who complained that one would have to walk through some of the worst housing in Hexham to the park and about the closeness to it of the gas works and manufactories. Not surprisingly the *Courant* thought the improvement of Tyne Green was doomed to delay.

On 22 July 1867, the Clerk read a letter from R. R. Dees, which appears to have written in less strong language than the two to the Home Office. The first part dealt with matters of detail, such as the boundary of the land to be purchased, fishing rights and the supply of water to the mill, which could be settled by further negotiation. But Beaumont was more concerned about what the Board had in mind for the future of Tyne Green. He questioned whether the Board had the capability to maintain the land in the proper state for recreation. He was not enamoured with idea of slaughterhouses located there and he wondered what other buildings would also be located on the land. As far as the deodourizing works, which the Board had planned to locate on Harbottle's Island, were concerned, he felt that this particular matter should be kept separate from that of the purchase of Tyne Green. This caught the Board on the back foot, so that a long, detailed and conciliatory letter of reply was quickly dispatched back (HLBH 22.7.1867).

Though one might not have anticipated it, from the nature of the inquiry conducted by Arthur Taylor, the report submitted to the Home Secretary was, apart from the matter of the use of Harbottle's Island, so satisfactory that he inserted Hexham's requirements in the usual Government Bill. But the threatened opposition was so grave that it was found necessary to postpone the application to the next session of Parliament. Another attempt was made to generate an agreement through the good offices of Joseph Cowen, MP for Newcastle, but to no avail. The stumbling block was the Mill Islands below Tyne Bridge (*HC* 9.10.1867). The Local Board was adamant that they needed them as an approach to Harbottle's Island and as a foundation of any bridge that they might wish to build across to the Island and also as the site for slaughterhouses, baths and washhouses and possibly a market for store cattle. But Beaumont was equally adamant that he should not give up these islands (*HC* 6.11.1867).

However, these problems had brought about one change. A Vestry meeting, with 'very numerous attendance', unanimously supported the motion

> That this meeting having heard the correspondence between Mr Dees, Mr Beaumont's agent, and the Local Board of Health, read in reference to the further action of the Board as to Tyne Green and Mill Islands, advised the Board to proceed to acquire these lands in the manner provided by the Acts, even if it should be necessary to support a provisional order before a Parliamentary committee (*HC* 23.10.1867).

There is little doubt that Hexham's citizens rallied round the Board because they felt it was being put upon. However, the Board itself had changed its position, as a result of it deciding to use the Mill Islands to the east of the Bridge for slaughterhouses, etc. This decision meant that all the part of Tyne Green west of Tyne Bridge was to become a park, which was very much to the liking of everyone.

In spite of the seeming obduracy of both the Board and W. B. Beaumont, there was still room for manoeuvre. Indeed in the New Year, the Board waited on Mr Beaumont to discuss the matter. On 24 January, the Board received a memorandum of the terms agreed with him. It is not appropriate to spell out all the details. The striking feature was the flexibility of the arrangements. But essentially, Beaumont was to retain possession of the Mill Islands east of the bridge, allowing the Board to have access to Harbottle's Island. He would provide land for a lean cattle market between the railway and the river. And he would allow slaughterhouses to be built on Tyne Green. It seems the plan to build washhouses on the Mill Islands had been discarded (*HC* 25.1.1868).

It appeared from the discussions with W. B. Beaumont that there was a way out of the impasse. However, the affair began to unravel. First the Board had become concerned that no Provisional Order was forthcoming from the Home Secretary. Then negotiations with the Commoners became almost farcical. They had appointed a Committee to treat with the Local Board and, indeed, it had settled terms of agreement with the Local Board for the purchase of the Common rights. However, before the purchase could be completed four out of the five members ceased to act as such. As the law requires that there must be at least three signatures on the receipt of the compensation money, the transaction could not take place. It seems that those who had resigned had done so because they were concerned that the Local Board, on taking possession of Tyne Green and Mill Islands would enclose the land (*HC* 22.2.1868). There was also dissatisfaction with the terms of the agreement between the Board and Mr Beaumont. In reality, the resignation of the four members of the Commoners Committee was a symptom of a growing unease amongst a number of influential inhabitants. This became apparent in the run-up to the elections for the Local Board of Health in April (*HC* 4.4.1868). Not only was there a concern that Tyne Green and Mill Islands was not to function solely as a park but there was increasing opposition to the amount of money required to purchase the land. Thus, Thomas Welford, one of those elected, had actively campaigned 'to prevent the Tyne Green and Harbottle's Island Schemes from being carried into operation'. The concerns about the financial aspects of the transactions were genuine. As we have seen in Chapter 6, in building the new water supply, the Board had committed itself to very sizeable loans. Indeed, towards the end of 1868, there was serious concern within the Local Board of the state of its finances (HLBH 20.11.1868). Not surprisingly, a little later, in the following month, a discussion between a deputation from the Board and Mr Beaumont about taking over Tyne Green left the matter in abeyance.

Not surprisingly, Tyne Green continued to deteriorate. Flooding by the Tyne was causing serious problems. As Ariel wrote in the *Hexham Courant*

> The recent floods, I perceive, have made further inroads upon Tyne Green. In a short time the railway will be compelled to take active measures towards protecting their property, which in the course of time will inevitably suffer from the encroachment of the river...... Some take a malicious pleasure in seeing this pleasant spot slipping from under our feet, as it were, and not content with the ravages made by the angry floods, are aiding the work of destruction by stripping off its turf in cartloads, and this without a single word of remonstrance on the part of the Lord of the Manor or commoners, to whom the herbage properly belongs. One individual, when I told him he ought to be punished for his vandalism, replied that the highest penalty that could be inflicted for his offence was a fine of sixpence for each cartload he cut and carried away, and this, he added with a grin, was to obtain 'sods' at a cheaper rate than he could get anywhere else. (*HC* 27.2.1869).

The writer of 'Local Gossip' in the Hexham Courant described it in equally graphic terms:

> I had a walk round by the 'Debatable Land,' yclept [called] Tyne Green, the other day, and really the inroad that old Father Tyne in his winter frolics is making on the Green is something alarming. At the west end of it, and on the south [?] side of the railway, near to that well known residence 'Neddy's Cabin,' vast quantities of earth may be seen which has only recently fallen off the side, and the other portions are seemingly ready for a break away. In fact every flood brings down several cwts. of earth from the side of the Green. Could not a weir be put up so as to prevent any further inroad...... Tyne Green had a miserable appearance when I saw it, with heaps of refuse emptied down just where fancy or chance dictated. There was every kind of soil and rubbish – picturesque they may be, but certainly not pleasant...... (*HC* 15.1.1870).

Surprisingly, Mr Beaumont made the next step in the saga by deciding to put a bill before Parliament for the Hexham Manor (1792) Amendment Act. The first that Hexham knew about this was a letter from Mr J. Newall, Beaumont's Parliamentary agent to the Clerk of the Local Board informing him that the bill would include in it 'clauses for carrying out those objects which may save the Local Board from the expenses of an application to Parliament for an Act or provisional order' and enclosing a notice about the bill that would appear the next day in the local papers (HLBH 27.11.1871). The flavour of the reply from a small committee of the Board to Mr Beaumont indicates that the Board was stunned by his move. While concerned about some of the detail within the bill, the Board was willing to accede to its main thrust. Beaumont reassured the Board that there would be plenty of time to alter the bill in committee to suit its needs.

The major concern of the bill was

> to extinguish compulsorily all rights of Pasture upon the lands commonly called 'Hexhamshire stinted pasture' and 'Allendale stinted pasture' and to provide for the allotment thereof, compulsorily all other common rights ...... (*HC* 25.11.1871).

The first nine clauses deal with the stinted pastures. Only Clause 10 concerned Tyne Green. The bill proposed that Commissioners 'be appointed [by the Home Department] to deal for the purpose to determine upon a scheme for selling, leasing or otherwise of disposing of Tyne Green or any portion thereof......'.

Once the details of the proposed bill were in the public domain, there was much discussion. As might be expected, the Commoners were put out that they had not been involved in any way (*HC* 13.1.1872). The Board itself became heavily involved in producing clauses relating to Tyne Green and Mill Islands to be inserted in the proposed bill (*HC* 23.3.1872 *et seq.*). There was a visit of William Robb, the Chairman of the Local Board to London to put its views to Mr Newall, the bill's Parliamentary agent, the Home Department and Lord Redesdale, Chairman of the Lords Committee, responsible for scrutinising all private bills. Following those discussions, it became clear that there would be storms ahead, since Beaumont emphatically indicated that he would not be dictated to as to how he should proceed with the distribution of his land. It had been proposed [by Lord Redesdale] that the distribution be done through a commissioner and Beaumont was totally against that. However, the bill was having a far from easy ride. The stintowners had been opposed to the bill. Nevertheless, it was the Admiralty that was the major opponent. It vetoed the bill, as it related to their Greenwich Hospital estates. A leader in the *Hexham Courant* of 9 March 1872 warmly greeted the opposition to the bill, referring to the arbitrary 'exercise of the prerogative claimed by the Crown', and indicating that if the bill had been passed 'the terms [for the distribution of land] were too hard and the bargain too close.'

It was a victory for the stintowners of Hexhamshire and Allendale but it did nothing for the Local Board and an emasculated bill was to continue on its way through Parliament. However, the nature of the objections of the stintowners carried over into the considerations of those the parts of the bill concerned with Tyne Green and the Mill Islands, because the Committee of the House of Lords 'strongly objected to the Bill on the ground that the assent of the Commoners has not been obtained' (*HC* 20.4.1872). Shortly afterwards the bill was withdrawn (*HC* 11.5.1872). The leader in the *Courant* announcing this news, spoke of the 'Heart of England' beating more freely. More significantly, it went on to say

> It is really wonderful how the value of Tyne Green has increased since the Bill was first mentioned, and every day has added to it an importance few ever imagined previous to Mr Beaumont's attempt to get a definite settlement of the question as affecting the Green and the Islands. As an earnest of their feelings in the matter, a subscription list has been drawn up, and upwards of £30 realised towards a fund for putting Tyne Green right; removing the accumulated rubbish heaps, and weiring the western portion of the Green, which has been left to the rough mercies of the winter and spring-tide floods......

Unfortunately, one has to say that all that was generated was hot air, for little seems to have been done to improve Tyne Green. Yet there was much talk. The problem, of course, that Beaumont's permission was needed if soil was to be levelled and the river bank weired (*HC* 14.12.1872). It was also questioned whether or not the Local Board could remove rubbish, since there was doubt that it could constitute a nuisance within the meaning of the Public Health Acts. From then on, all desire to sort the matter out seems to have been dissipated. It was over ten years later before concerns about the state of the Green resurfaced. In May of 1883, members of the Board had visited it with purpose of viewing the sewer outlet and must have been highly disturbed by what they saw (HLBH 28.5.1883).

Thus began another series of meetings with the Commoners, more letters in the papers about the matter and more correspondence with W. B. Beaumont, mostly either through his solicitors, Dees & Thompson, or through his agent, John Kaye. The Commoners were now prepared to negotiate with the Board, though only on a provisional basis. Any final agreement waited on the Board agreeing with the Lord of the Manor for his rights to the soil of Tyne Green. Nevertheless given that the Board reserved Tyne Green and Mill islands solely for 'Recreation and Pleasure Grounds', the Committee of the Commoners would be willing to accept the sum of £200 'as full compensation for their whole rights to or over Tyne Green and Mill Islands' (HLBH 14.8.1883). Meanwhile, Beaumont kept up an appearance of intransigence, still refusing to give up land to the east of the bridge and access to the river. His mineral rights must continue to be respected.

However, with considerable prodding, Beaumont seems to have been willing to move, almost imperceptibly, forward. So negotiations continued through 1884 and into 1885. But they were to collapse in March of that year. A leader in the *Courant* angrily described the situation:

> The negotiations between the Lord of the Manor and the Local Board about Tyne Green and Mill Islands have again collapsed. They never gave more favourable promise of a satisfactory conclusion than on this last occasion, but just when the finishing touch was about to be given to a prolonged, minute and tedious 'arrangement,' Mr Beaumont's agents intervened with demands which, if implemented would have robbed the lands in question of their chief attraction (*HC* 21.3.1885).

The agents had demanded that the Lord of the Manor retained his right over that half of the river extending from the shores of Tyne Green and the Mill Islands. Access to the river would be denied – swimming, boating, fishing by the citizens of Hexham would therefore be impossible. The leader writer became incandescent:

> How, in the name of common sense did ever such ridiculous distinctions arise as have cropped out of this Tyne Green business. The herbage belongs to the Commoners, it is legally insisted upon but the soil to the Lord of the Manor, as if the latter is not essential to the former, and the former a necessary consequence of the latter. The lord is a Commoner, along with the tailors and cobblers of the town, for the surface, but absolute and alone in his proprietorship of all matters below, down to the Antipodes. The fish which swim in the river, the bird which flies across the Green, are his. The fuel by which we are warmed are his; the stone our houses are to be built are his. His too are our buying and selling in the public market, and of some kinds of property we cannot dispose without his permission. In fact, we are hemmed around with bonds as absurd and oppressive in their nature as they are dubious in their origin (*HC* 21.3.1885).

Though the negotiations had reached an impasse, letters still continued to pass between the Clerk to the Board and Beaumont's solicitors, Dees and Thompson. The difference between this new correspondence and what had passed previously to and fro, was the presence of a new topic for argument, namely the exact location in the Tyne of the boundary between Acomb and Hexham townships.

The matter drifted on through 1886 and into 1887, with the Board becoming increasingly worried by the state of the Green. Rubbish continued to be dumped there, while turf and sand was taken without permission. Flood damage continued to be extensive – a tract of foreshore a hundred yards long by four or five yards wide seems to have disappeared in this way over a short period (*HC* 20.3.1886). However, suddenly, and without warning to the outside world, at the Local Board meeting on 25.2.1887, the Clerk reported

> That Mr Wentworth Beaumont had offered to hand over to the Board all his interest in the soil of Tyne Green and Mill Islands above the Bridge (exclusive of the Mineral rights) upon the condition that the Board grants to him the land below the Bridge extinguished from all Common or other rights, to commemorate the Queen's Jubilee which offer the Tyne Green Committee on behalf of the Board had accepted.

The Board unanimously approved the action of the Committee. There were loose ends to be tied up and that took time. However the 8 June 1889 issue of the *Hexham Courant* was able to report that the Clerk of the Local Board had exchanged deeds for Tyne Green (as Tyne Green and Mill Islands will be now called) with Dees and Thompson, and that a cheque had been signed payable to the Commoners' Committee for their rights to the herbage.

Though there had been a delay in completing the legal formalities, almost immediately after it knew of Beaumont's gift of Tyne Green to the Town, the Local Board took a proactive stance to the running of its new possession. At the meeting of the Board on 8 August 1887, it adopted regulations for Tyne Green. Camping by itinerant hawkers was forbidden, as was the removal of turf. People were to be compelled to deposit rubbish only in places as the officers of the Board may direct. Likewise sand, loam or soil and stones were to be taken from approved areas. No-one would be allowed to erect any structure such as a hut or tent. The owners of the two buildings already there, one for boating and the other for the Rowing Club, had to enter into a formal arrangement with the Board. Also, no wool, hair or 'spetches' (animal hides used for making glue) were to be spread out for drying without the permission of the Board. At the same time that these regulations were approved, the Surveyor was asked to prepare a plan for laying out the Green.

It was to be almost thirty years before Tyne Green was to become anything like the open space that is enjoyed today. Nevertheless, there was steady improvement in the use of the land and the facilities that became available. Here are a few of the highlights: the menagerie of Mrs Manders allowed on the Green (1881); Messrs Fell & Co. present fifty trees for the Green (1888); golf course opened (1889); a boat landing built (1890); new boat house built for the Rowing Club (1897) and tea room (1915). But the major change that was wrought was the recovery of at least two acres of land from the River Tyne. Weiring was the term used for the operation – for the most part that of building a retaining wall with piles and back-fill with 'large-size rubble stones' but it seems brushwood was also used. This work, started in 1898, continued on well into the first decade of the 20th century. Mr G. L. Murray, the Surveyor, designed the method of weiring. When he left for a post in South Africa in 1913, the bulk of the weiring had been completed and the two acres of land had been added to the park. A comparison of today's map with that of 1863 forcibly demonstrates the achievement.

The Seal

The Sele or Seal is formed from a hillock of glacial alluvium in the centre of Hexham. The name is Old English for hall. While 'Sele' is the present preferred spelling, in the 19th century and into the 1930s, 'Seal' is by far the most frequent spelling in written material. Because of the frequency of the latter spelling during the period under consideration in this book, I have used 'Seal' throughout.

When the Priory was functioning, the Seal was part of its farmland. To reach it, the canons crossed the Halgut (Cowgarth) Burn by a bridge that is still exists under the present one (Fig. 30). After the dissolution of the Priory, the Seal came under the control of the Lord of the Manor. It remained as farmland, but not always as grassland, there being evidence of ploughing prior to the 19th century. Probably for centuries, there has been a public path across the Seal to Cockshaw. As well, there have been paths round the periphery, which were improved in the eighteenth century by the then Lord of the Manor, Sir Walter Calverley Blackett. Four seats were placed to enhance the enjoyment of the fine views that these paths provided (Wood, 1826).

The Seal has been jealously guarded as an open space by the town. When it was mooted to run the Carlisle to Newcastle turnpike road across it in 1823, Diana Beaumont, Lady of the Manor, successfully opposed the scheme (HC 1.3.1865, 31.12 1999 supplement). Her action was stimulated by the demand in a petition signed by over 60 persons that T. W. Beaumont (Lady Diana's son) change his mind. Lady Diana commanded the surveyor to meet her at 7.0 a.m. on 27 September to explain the different routes the road could in fact take. She is said to have told those residents of Hexham waiting for her to learn the outcome of the meeting

> Gentlemen, I have examined the different lines of the intended new road, and am fully of opinion, that the Temperley line [that eventually followed and the present road out to Carlisle] is decidedly the best. I doubt not they [the Commissioners] obtained my son's consent to the line passing through the Seal, by representing to him that it was for the general good; but though he has the rents and proceeds of the property in the neighbourhood, yet I am still Lady of the Manor, and no power on earth shall induce Colonel Beaumont and myself to do anything to deprive the inhabitants of Hexham of the comforts and privileges they have so long enjoyed on the Seal.

'She then returned to her carriage followed by the good wishes of all present; and the bells rang many a merry peal throughout the day.'

In spite of the allusion to a seemingly free access to the Seal, the reality seems to have been somewhat different. Wright (1823) speaks about 'the beauty and fashion' 'promenading' along the paths. One should be careful in assuming the elegance that Wright seems to indicate, since the term promenading was used in Hexham in the 19th century to describe what today we call a stroll – thus a walk along the Carlisle Road to the Cemetery at that time was termed as such. We know that by the start of the 19th century the public were excluded from the Seal after Wednesday in Easter week until the autumn. This exclusion certainly referred to the present central area of grassland, which was apportioned (stinted) for a fee for grazing. But it probably did not apply to the walks round the periphery of the Seal. Certainly, as one can see from an old print (Fig. 31) the path across the Seal to Cockshaw could be used during the summer months. Finally, there is little doubt that visitors to the Seal were not confined to those with refined manners. The 6 June 1869 issue of the *Hexham Courant* carries the following complaint that on Sundays the Seal is

> infested by a number of blackguard boys who wrestle, blaspheme in the loudest tone of voice and seriously among all respectable persons who may be passing on their way......worship......I was sorry to observe that a great number of grown-up girls nearly women, in fact, were last Sunday participating in a very questionable species of romp with some hobbledehoys of their acquaintance.'

Although what I have just said indicates at least a major portion of the Seal was closed to the public during the summer months, there could be events not of a promenading kind. William Robb (1882), writing of the period 50 years speaks about

> [when] I was as a boy, a spectator of regular pugilistic combat on the Seal a summer evening. Notice of its coming off had been widely spread, there was no authority to prevent it. Hundreds assembled to witness the sport. I still think I see the surging to and fro of the excited crowd as

they followed 'the current of the heady fight,' and I still seem to hear the brutal shout from the maddened multitude 'which hailed the wretch who won.'

However, it is possible that such fights took place on the land now occupied by the Seal School. Before that, on the same area of land throughout the year, 'all sorts of games were played on it, carpets were dusted on it and holes dug, without any interference from anyone' (*HC* 24.4.1878, 27.4.1878).

The first building, of what is now the Sele School, was erected in 1856. It was occupied by the then Subscription School, the land being given by W. B. Beaumont, as described in Chapter 17.

The year of 1868 is notable for a change in the policy of access, for it was then that the lessees of the Seal, led by Charles Head, decided that it should be open to all the citizens of the town throughout the year (*HC* 7.4.1868). The following year, at the annual meeting of the lessees 'the pleasing aspect of the Seal during the long bright summer evenings of 1868, from the numerous and varied and happy groups which made it their playground' was alluded to with great satisfaction (*HC* 29.6.1869). At the same meeting, it became clear that the philanthropic gesture of the lessees amounted to a significant sum, for those days, of £15-20 of lost revenue from stints that could not be taken up. Thereafter, the use of the Seal for formal activities, such as battalion drill for the Rifle Corps, cricket team games, start to take off. From then on, the Seal began to be properly seen as an asset to the active life of the town. To an extent, it is not surprising that the Local Board felt that the Seal should be under its control. While it is possible that the Board had had informal information that the lessees were finding it difficult to maintain their generosity, it was the Board that initiated discussions about it taking over the lease of the Seal (HLBH 16.2.1885).

In fact nothing appeared to develop from this overture. It is possible that the negotiations concerning the acquisition of Tyne Green had stalled any negotiation with the Lord of the Manor about other matters. It was 1891 when another contact was made with the lessees through one of them, Lewis Lockhart. He responded most favourably:

> The lessees are quite willing to assign their tenancy to the Local Board if the consent of the lessor can be obtained on the Board paying any balance which may be required to clear the lessees accounts. The Board will of course take over the existing seats, fencing, etc. (HLBH 23.3.1891).

John Kaye, Mr Beaumont's agent, responded by saying that Mr Beaumont thought that the Seal was already managed satisfactorily and that it was not the custom to sanction transfers of tenancy. When asked by the Clerk if the lessees were to surrender the lease would Beaumont transfer it to the Board, Kaye said 'Mr Beaumont cannot be asked what he will do with the property' under such circumstances. Kaye's attempt to throw a wet blanket over the idea must have deterred the Board, because another four years were to elapse before the matter was re-opened. At a meeting of (what was now) the Urban District Council on 29 April 1895, Joseph Alexander, Chairman of the Board, drew attention to the unsatisfactory state of the Seal. There are no details of what he said but it is clear that it had an effect on the Council because it resolved that 'application be made to the lessees of the Seal, asking them to assign their lease of that place to the Council.' A fortnight later a letter was received indicating the lessees were agreeable to the request. This time no barriers were put in the way; by 1 January 1896 the tenure of the Seal was in the hands of the Urban District Council (*HC* 28.12.1895). A condition was laid down under the agreement, namely that the ground not be allowed to be broken up for obtaining gravel for walks (*HC* 18.5.1895). Seemingly, those other conditions that applied to the former lessees also applied to the new one. On 1 January 1903, the lease was renewed for a further seven years (*HC* 16.8.1902).

Once in control, the Council reassured the public that 'privileges previously granted would continue as heretofore'. There was however to be a close time, from 8 April to 6 May to allow the grass to recover after the football and before the cricket seasons. Further, it was recommended that A Company of the 1st Volunteer Battalion of the Northumberland Fusiliers should have the use of the Seal for the purpose of drilling on the same terms as before, but no blank cartridge firing was to take place (*HC* 4.4.1896). The Council started on a programme of putting the Seal in good order, commencing with the improvement of the paths. Slowly other changes took place, the first significant one being the opening, in front of the Subscription School of a drinking fountain, erected by the Hexham Abbey Church of England Temperance Society in September 1899. This was followed by the replacement of the old bridge across the Cockshaw Burn by the present 'ornamental' one in April 1902 and public toilets (along with those in Priestpopple and based on designs of those in Scarborough) in September 1903 , for the erection of which the Local Board had to obtain permission of W. B. Beaumont.

In 1904, the District Council branched out in allowing entertainments on the Seal. For two years running, troupes of Pierrots had applied to the District Council to be able to perform on the Seal. In 1903 the applications were turned down, because it seemed that some sort of platform was required (*HC* 18.6.1904), which was not permitted by the agreement with W. B. Beaumont. This understandably annoyed the two populist councillors, John Ainsley and Ralph Conkleton, who felt that the town had a duty to put on such amusements not only for the inhabitants but also visitors. However, the following year the troupe making the application indicated they only wanted some surface (seemingly very temporary) to dance on. It was agreed that the troupe could perform on the Seal at a charge of 10s per week. Pierrots continued to perform on the Seal until the 1930s. More than not, in the early days, they often seemed to be in disfavour with many on the Council, who felt the moral welfare of the town's inhabitants was being endangered, either from the nature of their performances or their tendency to go on after dark. At one stage, the Chairman of the Council, expressing concern about the performance extending beyond the allotted hours, darkly stated 'there would be danger coming at once. They know from past experience what took place under such conditions and the same might occur if the hours were lengthened out after dark' (*HC* 10.7.1909). W. B. Beaumont, ennobled in June 1906 as Lord Allendale of Allendale and Hexham, died in February 1907. His son, Wentworth Canning Blackett Beaumont, who was also MP for Hexham succeeded to the title. At its meeting of the Urban District Council on 20 July 1908, the Chairman read out a letter from John Kaye that contained the following:

> I am directed by Lord Allendale to intimate to you as Chairman of the Hexham Urban District Council his desire to present 'The Seal' which for many years has been leased to your Council for the public benefit, to the local authority as a recreation ground for the enjoyment of the inhabitants.

> Lord Allendale has for some time had this in contemplation, but so long as he was
> Parliamentary representative of the district he hesitated for obvious reasons, which no doubt
> you will appreciate, to give effect to his intentions. As these reasons no longer exist, he sees no
> object in deferring his proposal (*HC* 25.7.1908).

Naturally there was jubilation at the news of the gift, 'a fitting memorial of himself and his family of which he is head, a memorial more enduring and more appropriate than any other that could be devised', as put by the leader of the *Hexham Courant* of 25 July 1908. The gift was celebrated on the night of 7 January 1909 with a commemorative banquet in the Town Hall when Lord Allendale presented the deed of gift of the Seal to James Robb, Chairman of the Urban District Council and his Lordship was presented by Lewis Lockhart with an oxidised silver casket, with on the front the arms of Lord Allendale, flanked by a view of the Moot Hall on one side and the 'Manor Keep' on the other, as well as an inscription and other decoration, containing an address on vellum.

Now that the Seal was in the hands of the Council, more substantial improvements could be made. Fine gates at the Hencotes entrance, commemorating the gift of the Seal by Lord Allendale and designed and built by Messrs H. H. Martyn of Cheltenham, were erected in 1912. The way down to Cockshaw was greatly improved by the path with railings, less steep gradients and tarred surface, which is still present. Two shelters were erected in 1915 (Fig. 32), while tree planting was started, culminating in the planting of the common bank in the 1920s. However, a move to have tennis courts at the top of the Seal was stymied by opponents outside the Council and the views of the then Lord Allendale.

The Abbey Grounds

Wood's map of Hexham published in 1827 shows the Abbey Grounds landscaped in a picturesque manner typical of the 18th century. There was a walk encircling most of the southern part of the grounds with trees planted round the whole periphery and informal plantings elsewhere (Fig. 33). This landscape was broken when, in 1866, W. B. Beaumont drove the street named after him through the Grounds (Jennings, 2003). The 1897 OS map shows a very unstructured landscape.

Beaumont Street was a commercial development, inaugurated by the building of the Town Hall and Corn Exchange in 1866. But development went slowly, the street frontage on the east side not being completed until 1909 with the opening of the Primitive Methodist Church (Payne, 2002). There were also to be developments on the other side of the street in the Abbey Grounds. On a number of occasions, the town attempted to gain control of the Grounds. In 1889, no doubt greatly encouraged by the success of obtaining the lease of the Seal, the Clerk of the Local Board of Health was asked by the members to approach W. B. Beaumont with a view to putting the cattle market, then in Priestpopple, on the Abbey Grounds. John Kaye, Beaumont's agent, wrote back, the letter containing the key phrase 'my instructions are to put the land into the market for building purposes' (HLBH 17.6.1889). The next year, it seems that it was learnt that the then present lessees (who probably used the area for grazing cattle; *HC* 20.5.1911) were willing to give up their occupancy in favour of the town obtaining the Grounds as a public park. This generated a harsh reply from Beaumont via Kaye:

> Mr Beaumont regrets that he does not see his way to accede to your application, his intention being to deal very differently with this property, to open out which Beaumont Street was made at a considerable cost. It does not appear to him that there is any necessity for a further park, for if the Board were to develop and lay out Tyne Green for the purpose for which it was given to the town, there would be with it and the Seal ample ground for the population of Hexham (HLBH 30.6.1890).

The request was repeated in 1902, when the Board probably mindful that W. B. Beaumont had transferred Tyne Green to the Local Board in commemoration of Queen Victoria's Jubilee, resolved to approach him again for a lease of or to purchase the Grounds. The idea behind the resolution was to 'safe-guard the interests of their fellow-townsmen and to secure for them and future generations a permanent recreation ground'. The answer from Beaumont (via Kaye) was blunt – he was not prepared to enter into negotiations either for a sale or lease of the Abbey Grounds. What was essentially confirmation of this view came in a meeting that took place between Kaye and the Chairman of the Council, William Alexander, in December 1905 that seems to have been triggered by rumours of house-building in the Abbey Grounds. At the Council meeting held afterwards, Alexander said

> All that we asked was that if at any future time Mr Beaumont wished to sell this land the Council should have first offer of it. We have not got a reply to that effect [only an anodyne letter from Kaye to the Clerk about the matter] (*HC* 30.12.1905).

The leader article in the 25 July 1908 issue of the *Hexham Courant* warmly welcoming the gift of the Seal suggested that the next step would be for the town to purchase the Abbey Grounds. On 1 February 1909, following the banquet in January commemorating the gift of the Seal, the Council, sensing that the new Lord Allendale had a perspective on the commercial viability of the Grounds now different from his father, instructed the Clerk to write to John Kaye with a view to ascertaining on what terms the Council might acquire the Grounds (*HC* 6.2.1909). There is an indication that James Robb, the Chairman of the Council, had already discussed the matter with Lord Allendale. In May, Mr Kaye came to Hexham and on the 4th had discussions with the Council. By then support for the acquisition was already building up a head of steam. A deputation went to the Council to express its support, while in the week following the *Hexham Courant* published a leader urging the acquisition (*HC* 15.5.1909). A further interview with Kaye took place but no definite result was obtained owing to the fact that those involved felt unable to give the price asked. Further negotiations were deferred until the Chairman had returned after a 6-7 weeks holiday in Canada to see his son in Winnipeg.

On 14 February 1910, the Council published a report on the several discussions that had taken place to resolve the issue of the appropriate price for the grounds. The distinguished local land agent, C. H. Sample, was appointed to value the land, which confirmed the view that the Council should offer £1,000 per acre for the Grounds. An offer of £5,500 was eventually made, accompanied by the promise that only 3/4 acre would be reserved for the erection of public buildings. As the Council was going to deprive itself of building land, Lord Allendale reduced the asking price to £6,000; but he would not budge from this figure. There was an impasse, the reaction of the Council was to request that Lord Allendale extend the time for the offer to stand open from 31 March to the end of May (*HC* 19.2.1910). One reason for requesting the extension was the feeling that it would be more appropriate to first dispose of the Council elections to be held in early April.

With the completion of the election, which according to the *Hexham Courant* gave strong support for the purchase, the impasse was broken by James Robb. At the meeting of the Council on 9 May 1910, he gave notice that at the next meeting he would move

1) That this Council agree to the purchase of the Abbey Grounds from Lord Allendale at the price which he asks for the same, i.e. £6,000, subject to the approval of the Local Government Board;
2) That in the event of the motion as to the purchase of the Abbey Grounds being carried, the sum of £500 (the difference between the Council's offer for the Abbey Grounds and the price asked for by Lord Allendale) and the vendor's costs and stamp duty be raised by public subscription.

At the next meeting a fortnight later, there was an eloquent speech by James Robb in support of his motion (*HC* 28.5.1910). However, reading the transcript of the debate one cannot fail to be impressed by the gloomy financial view of the future painted by those against the purchase, with impending expenditure hanging over them, according to one councillor, 'like a sword of Damocles'. The motion was lost by 5 votes to 6. In making this decision, the Council turned down the munificent offer of £1,000 that had just been made towards the purchase by County Alderman T. W. Benson of Allerwash. The leader article in the *Hexham Courant* called the defeat of the motion 'the greatest civic blunder in the history of the town and there have been not a few'. The article went on with 'the parrot cry of increased rates has once again prevailed over the dictates of common sense.' And later, while stressing that expenditure of public money by public bodies should be sustained but not extravagant, the leader went on to say 'on the other hand a policy of parsimony is absolutely ruinous to a progressive community'. Scorn was cast on the half of those who voted against the scheme, who by keeping quiet during the debate, failed to make clear why they did not want the scheme to go forward (*HC* 28.5.1910). The following week's leader article suggested that the opposition had been co-ordinated by a number of 'secret negotiations' over the previous weeks.

The reaction against the vote was almost instantaneous (*HC* 4.6.1910). Three councillors, John Dodd, George Ross and John Farbridge (the first two supporters of the purchase; Farbridge was not present at the Council meeting), called an extraordinary meeting of the Council. Possibly they had been spurred on to do so by the more wealthy of the town, thirty-four of whom wrote to the Hexham Courant guaranteeing £500 towards the purchase price. Another letter, this time from Alderman Benson to say that his brother, two sisters and himself were willing to add £500 to the £1,000 already offered. The information in both letters was known to the Councillors before they met again to debate the purchase of the Abbey Grounds. Naturally, this knowledge had an effect on the result of that debate, which according to the leader article in the Hexham Courant, led to 'one of the most remarkable reversions of policy in the civic history of the town', namely the resolution to purchase being carried unanimously.

On 11 March the following year James Robb proposed that the seal of the Council be attached to the conveyance deed of the Abbey Grounds. Once the Grounds had been purchased, a number of events quickly followed that led to the formal landscape of the Grounds that we see today. Following agreement of plans prepared by the Surveyor by the Council on 4 December 1911, the Grounds were beautifully landscaped. In 1912, there was the presentation of both another munificent gift from Alderman Benson, namely the fine Edwardian Gates at the corner of Beaumont Street designed by Messrs H. H. Martyn of Cheltenham and also the presentation of the elegant bandstand by Henry Bell. On Thursday, 25 August 1912, the Grounds were formally opened, with new gates built and the bandstand in position. Before 1939, the Grounds changed little; the only significant addition being the erection in 1921 of the war memorial designed by Sir Reginald Blomfield and dedicated the same year.

FIG. 39. Stand-pipe, still present at Holy Island, that was used for watering the road and probably also in the event of a fire.

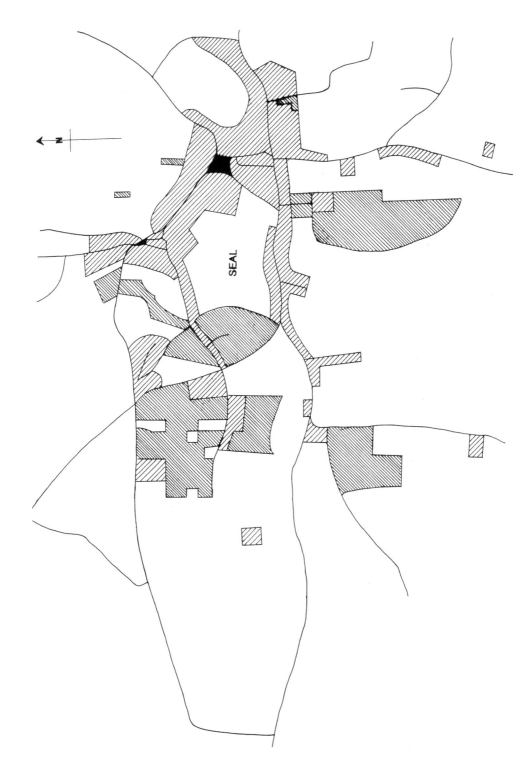

FIG. 40. Map showing the location of new houses built in Hexham in the period 1896-1921. Housing built prior to 1896 – shading rising from SE to NW; in the period 1896-1921 – shading rising from SW to NE.

SEAL

Fig. 41. Elvaston Road, photographed probably before the 1914-18 War, the houses being part of what was called the Elvaston Estate. Rodney Higgins (1995) has described how land for an estate was built on land bought by a speculator who would split it up into building plots, selling them off to builders. Such was the case with the Elvaston estate built on land purchased by William Maugham of Gosforth. Note the presence of iron railings, sadly to disappear in the Second World War. Reproduced with the permission of Beamish.

FIG. 42. Whitby Avenue before a road was built. Reproduced with permission of Newcastle Libraries and Information Service.

FIG. 43. Argyll Terrace showing the terrace on the east side, where a wall with railings was built in place of a path in front, the erection of which led to controversy between the owner and the Board of Health.

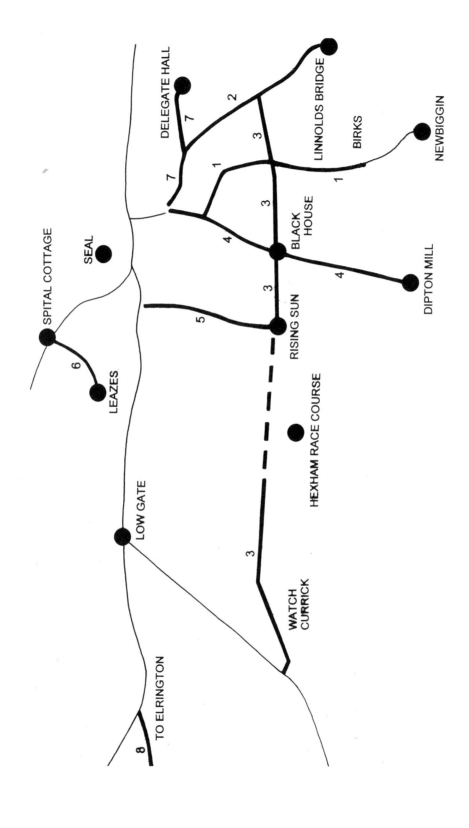

FIG. 44. Map showing the location of the *ratione tenurae* roads mentioned in the text. 1. Houtley Road; 2. Linnolds Road; 3. Yarridge Road; 4. Dipton Mill Road; 5. Plover Hill (Causey Hill) Road; 6. Shaws Lane; 7. Gallows Bank/Tyneview Terrace; 8. Ellrington Road. The dashed section of the Yarridge Road indicates that it was traversing part of Hexham West Quarter.

FIG. 45. The building on St Cuthbert's Lane, now flats, but originally built for the Proprietary School which was opened in 1855. After 1895, it was no longer a school; the subsequent history is described by Jennings & Rossiter (1999).

FIG. 46. The original Subscription School at the top of Eastgate.

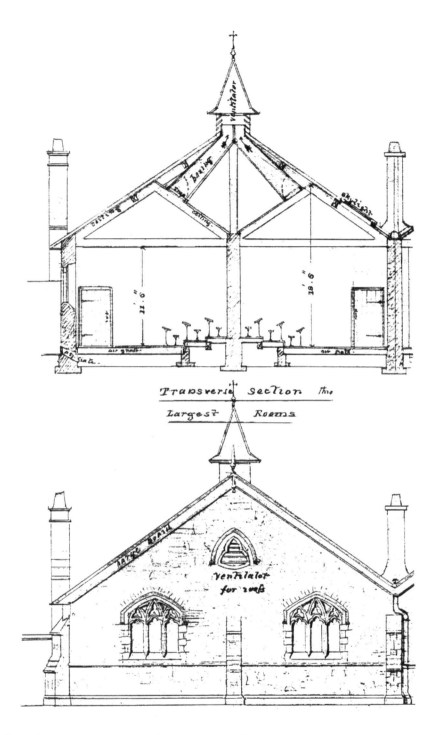

Fig. 47. Part of the architect's plans for the new building for the Subscription School erected in 1856 on the Seal. Reproduced with the permission of Tynedale Museum Service.

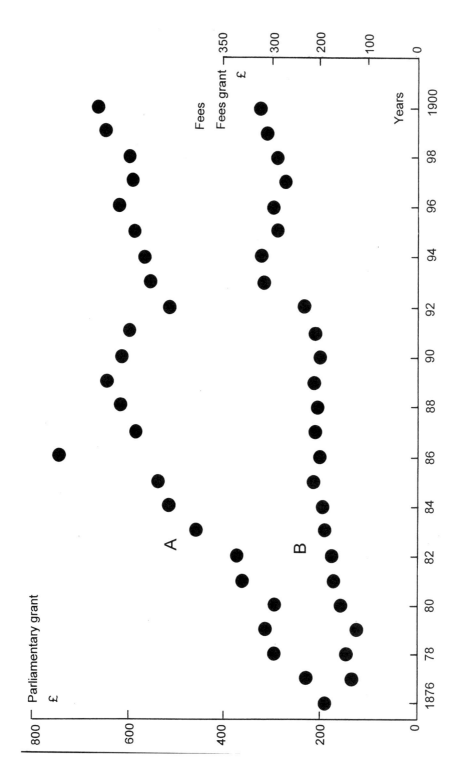

FIG. 48. The change in the Parliamentary Grant, fees and fees grant to Hexham Board Schools over the period 1874 –1900. **A.** Parliamentary Grant – the outlier for 1886 is due to circumstances leading to a grant for 16 months; **B.** Fees then fee grant after 1892. Please turn to the text for further information.

CHAPTER 15

Health

During the first part of the 19th century

We can get a (somewhat restricted) picture of the health of Hexham in 1853 from Robert Rawlinson's report. Within it, four doctors (surgeons) give their views. Thus:

> *Thomas Jefferson* – There is generally more or less fever, but this is not peculiar to Hexham nor does it prevail more in one part of the town than another.

> *Mr Robert Stokoe* – Epidemics are common, endemics are not common in the district. There is generally more or less of small-pox and scarlet fever. I have always considered the town healthy, being seldom visited with contagious or infectious diseases, and never of long duration. A strong proof of the town being considered healthy, is the number of families resorting to it from Newcastle, Shields and Sunderland, and various other places; many of the people being sent by their medical advisers. Local deaths are increased by the influx of sick strangers, four old invalids having died in one lodging-house within the last three years. I consider the list of deaths before you today to be considerably above the general average, and this has been caused by certain epidemic diseases prevailing during the period when the list was taken.

> *Mr William Pearson* – Finds most disease in the distressed parts of the town amongst the poor; has no doubt that if the filth were removed, and pure air was allowed to circulate, there would be less sickness, and less parish relief required.

> *Mr Thomas Stainthorpe* – Considers the town very unhealthy – this view was confirmed by *Mr John Nicholson* and *Mr J. B. Maughan*

Stokoe's statement indicates a fatalistic approach to disease in the town. That is understandable in view of the fact that the germ theory of disease had yet to be formulated. Rawlinson's comment is apposite here:

> It has been said that no physician above 40 years of age would believe Harvey's circulation of the blood. The senior surgeons in Hexham will not believe in sanitary improvement.

If we look at the mortality figures for seven years preceding Rawlinson's visit to Hexham (Table 17), they present a very gloomy picture of the health of Hexham. In five out of the seven years listed, the death rate was worse than in England and Wales. In the other two years, though the death rate in Hexham was lower, the difference between the Hexham value and that for England and Wales was very small. In Rawlinson's report the unfavourable statistics from previous years are given support. For instance, it is reported that, during the previous winter (1851-2), Stainthorpe attended 217 cases of small-pox. The locations of these cases are detailed in Rawlinson's report. Those reaching double figures are as follows: 65 in Gilesgate, 10 in Cockshaw, 21 in Skinners-burn, 13 in Back Street and 20 in the Workhouse (many of these particular cases had been brought to the fever wards of the Workhouse from other parts of the town). Ignoring the last figure, over 50% of the small pox cases were from four parts of the town, which we know were very crowded. Surprisingly, there is no mention in the report of pulmonary tuberculosis (phthisis) which later statistics was to show was a major cause of mortality in Hexham.

TABLE 17. *Mortality data for Hexham and England and Wales 1845-51 (Registrar-General, 1856).*

Years	Number of deaths	Death rate (number per year per 1000 population)	
		Hexham	England & Wales
1845	106	21.2	20.9
1846	149	29.2	23.1
1847	156	30.7	24.7
1848	116	22.7	23.1
1849	145	28.1	25.1
1850	124	23.9	20.8
1851	114	21.8	22.0
Total	910	177.6	159.7
Average		25.4	22.8

The figures for small pox cases seem terrible now; it is likely that matters were worse a decade or so earlier and, of course, much worse prior to Jenner's discovery of the prophylactic power of vaccination against the disease at the end of the 18th century. An Act of Parliament of 1840 gave the privilege of free vaccination to all those who applied for it. The Poor Law Guardians were charged with implementing the Act (Hodgkinson, 1967). The next year another Act made it clear that there was no pauperising stigma associated with free vaccination, which was performed by a medical officer of the Union (see Chapter 5). An Act passed in 1853 made vaccination of children compulsory on parents and penalties could be imposed if the children were not vaccinated within a few months of birth. We do not know how effective the Guardians were in carrying out compulsory vaccination. However, the Act of 1867 tightened the administration of compulsory vaccination throughout the country, with each union divided up into districts. For the Hexham Union these were the same as the medical districts with medical officers carrying out the vaccinations (Cadman, 1976). In 1871, The Guardians appointed William Stainthorpe to the new post of Vaccination Officer, to oversee the whole process of vaccination both via the Union and private doctors. Thus Hexham, like the rest of the country, was to see a decline in the incidence of small pox, though it was not until the end of the 1920s that the disease was eradicated.

It is difficult to assess the extent of medical care in Hexham in the first part of the 19th century. As Wright (1823) has it a dispensary 'was instituted on 15th of May 1816'. At the time Wright was writing the Hexham Dispensary was lodged in a house rented for the purpose near Hall Bank Head. When funds became available it was planned to erect a separate building. The 'projectors of this admirable institution were the Rev. Sloughter Clarke, the Rev. Robert Clarke, the Rev. John Wilson, Colonel Carr, and James Kirsopp. Its objects were to afford medical assistance to those, who, having barely sufficient for their common maintenance, are unable, in case of sickness, to bear any additional expense

[and to be a useful] auxiliary to the objects of the truly excellent institution, the County Infirmary; to relieve sickness in cases where the patient cannot, without great inconvenience, be sent to a distance; and to check the progress of disease in its earliest appearances.

Wright describes the government of the dispensary. There was a board of control of nine governors and a committee of fifteen governors, together with the 'medical gentlemen' who were *ex officio*. Later history suggests that, with time, only the committee remained properly functional, the treasurer also becoming *ex officio* (*HC* 24.5.1890). The qualification to become a governor and to vote at general meetings, was an annual subscription of 10s 6d which gave the person the right to recommend one patient in the year. This right increased in proportion to the amount of the subscription. An overseer might become a governor on behalf of his parish or township on the same conditions. In 1890, there were 32 subscribers; there are no figures for earlier years.

There was free medical attendance at the dispensary; patients unable to attend would also be visited free. All who benefited from the institution did so following a letter of recommendation from a governor. In cases of accident and 'necessity' letters of admission could be dispensed with until the next day. Patients who refused medicine or who resisted an operation were discharged and a printed notice transmitted to the recommending governor. No mention is made of those who were unable to obtain a letter in the first place. Patients who were cured were expected to return thanks to Almighty God, in their usual place of worship. There were printed rules for the conduct of patients. The dispensary seems to have been a way of avoiding what a leader column in the *Hexham Courant* (23.10.1886) referred to as the stigma of the 'pauperised feeling that must attend an application to the Parish Doctor'. Not only did the dispensary provide the sick with medicine but, in the 1890s, provided those recovering from illness with tickets (vouchers?) to allow them to spend short periods at convalescent homes at Silloth and Whitley (Bay?) at the seaside.

Though the dispensary seems to have gone into limbo around 1886, a contributory reason may have been that the offertories taken at the Abbey on Hospital Sunday were no longer given to the Dispensary (20.5.1899). It made a spirited recovery in 1890, continuing until at least 1936, still being of assistance to the poor in pre-NHS days (*HC* 16.5.1936). At the AGM that year, it was reported that there 56 patients and 737 prescriptions made out. It was agreed to ask the doctors involved not to recommend prescriptions of Bovril, Ovaltine and other proprietary articles except for acute surgical cases.

The second half of the 19ᵗʰ century

There were many advances in medicine during the 19ᵗʰ century that gathered pace as the century progressed. However, it is not clear to what extent the new knowledge generated fed down into the practice of medicine in Hexham. The increasing number of advertisements for patent medicines in the *Hexham Courant* as the century progressed suggests that medicine could do little to cure a great number of ailments. We need to remember that the germ theory of disease was not formulated until the last quarter of the century. It was only in the period 1860 to 1876 that investigations were made to prove that bacteria by themselves could initiate disease in a healthy body (Dubos, 1951). The compelling evidence came from the work of Robert Koch working on anthrax who demonstrated for the first time that a microbe grown outside the body was directly responsible for a disease. Until 1876, when Koch made his demonstration, and, indeed, for some time after, disease was believed to be caused by 'miasms' or polluted air, and that 'contagia' were miasms that had developed in the human body. Consequently there was a focus on minimising the production of removal of foul air within the community. As we now know, even when the microbial basis of many diseases had been established, the fight against many diseases did not start to succeed until well into the 20th century.

Though there are indications that the town had bye-laws from the inception of the Local Board of Health, we have few details as to their content, particularly those with respect to new streets and buildings. They appear to have been revised in 1878 (HLBH 16.9.1878); again we have no information as to their contents. The earliest printed bye-laws are those of 1897 (NRO/LHU/B2/A1). But we can get some idea of those in force around the 1870s and 1880s from the reports of the Medical Officer of Health and the Works Committee. There was much emphasis on getting rid of nuisances and also on the need for fresh air and removing gas from the sewers, indicating the belief in Hexham that disease was spread by miasms. Nevertheless, though the germ theory had yet to take hold, we can interpret the benefits of many of the sanitary improvements in the town in terms of their ability to reduce microbial infection.

It was Dr Daniel Jackson (Fig. 18), Hexham's first Medical Officer of Health, who was the driving force behind these sanitary improvements. It is instructive here to refer to his first annual report to the Local Board of Health, produced after nearly three years in office (*HC* 8.1.1876). In his introduction he says

> In my first quarterly report I pointed out the principal nuisances that tend to cause and perpetuate an excessive high death-rate in Hexham, indicated the remedies to be applied, and urged the speedy action of your Board. In my successive quarterly reports have repeated my advice and warnings, but I regret that my suggestions have not been carried out, and in consequence of this neglect the death-rate of the district, of which the sanitary condition has been to your care, instead of decreasing has been steadily increasing until it has become higher than that of any other place similarly situated in Great Britain.

He went on to speak of the 'foul state of the town' and the fact that 'long continued sickness and slow lingering disease prevail among the inhabitants of every locality rendered unhealthy by filth and neglect'.

Jackson throughout his career as Medical Officer continued to lash the Board or the District Council with criticism, if he thought that either was not moving forward with sufficient vigour to resolve sanitary problems. As we will see, his son, Dr John Jackson who succeeded him as Medical Officer of Health, was equally forceful.

In the rest of the his first annual report Daniel Jackson lists the sanitary matters that need attention

144

1. The need to construct a public slaughterhouse, pointing out that, apart from one exception, they were all of defective construction and were situated in the midst of crowded tenements.

2. The system of cleaning by contract had signally failed from the sanitary point of view, with removal of daily refuse taking place at all hours in 'open defiance of the bye-laws'.

3. The presence of huge middens, uncovered and unprotected from leakage by non-porous flagging and lining.

4. Almost impassable streets on foot on account of the numerous pools of stagnant water.

5. Houses that are unspouted.

6. Failure to systematically flush and ventilate sewers.

Jackson must have stimulated action over the slaughterhouses almost as soon as he was in post because at the meeting of the Hexham Local Board of Health on 1 September 1873, William Robb proposed that the same committee that had been appointed to extend the water supply consider the best means of abating the nuisances caused by the slaughterhouses (*HC* 6.9.1873). In proposing the motion Robb pointed that nine butchers would be brought before the magistrates next day for frequent and serious breaches of the bye-laws. Further, he suggested that the whole of the slaughterhouses be removed out of the town, a site found and a proper building erected. Indeed, 'A Butcher' had written to the *Hexham Courant* the previous week making this suggestion, at the same time complaining that the butchers were being victimised, while the tanners and tallow chandlers were untroubled even though they produced 'noxious odours'. It was to be nearly two years before 'it was resolved that common slaughterhouses be built with as little delay as possible' and that a suitable site be sought (HLBH 30.8.1875). A list of possible sites was put forward, from which a garden in Broadgates belonging to Mr W. A. Temperley was chosen (HLBH 27.9.1875). Though the site passed the critical inspection by the Medical Officer of Health, the decision to build a slaughterhouse on the garden was, after a long debate in the Board meeting was only passed by four votes to three (HLBH 8.11.1875).

There was an outcry. Thomas Welford, who that year failed to be elected to the Local Board, came out with all guns blazing with a letter, overflowing with typical histrionics, to the *Hexham Courant* (20.11.1875):

> What has the Urban Sanitary Board [another title for the Local Board of Health] done for the sanitary purpose of the town? It has encumbered the ratepayers with a debt that can never be repaid, by ill-judged and imperfect sanitary arrangements, and made Hexham once the garden of Eden and the heart of all England, the dirtiest town in the Kingdom and also the most unhealthy. Are we ratepayers to submit to this local tyranny and abuse of power by permitting our local senators to sow the seeds of indebtedness by the erection of slaughter-houses in an improper place......

The decision to build in Broadgates was confirmed by the Local Board on 20.12.1875 after what the *Hexham Courant* described as a 'lively scene'. A fortnight later the situation was completely reversed by Ralph Robson, who, in proposing that the original decision to build be rescinded, presented figures that purported to show that the town would make a loss of £53 each year on the operation. Questioning of the figures by Thomas Bulman and a thoughtful speech by W. S. Kirsopp seemed have little effect and the original decision was rescinded. Strangely, William Robb, who was not at the meeting, had sent a letter tendering his resignation as a member of the Board. There are indications that he had himself had become too involved in the negotiations, though with the approval of the Board, and that he felt personally responsible for pursuing, what he had now anticipated was a failed scheme. At any rate the affair was 'very painful' to him (NA MH/12/9049).

The matter of public slaughterhouses rumbled on for nearly thirty years. They were eventually built on Wanless Lane and opened in November 1902 (Fig.34).

The idea of contracting out street cleaning and highway maintenance was first mooted in 1869 in the Local Board of Health by Thomas Welford as a way of reducing costs. He presented a detailed case comparing the previous year's costs with some assumed figures for contracting out. Part of his argument for doing this would be that one could dispense with the services of the Surveyor (HLBH 5.4.1869). The saga of contracting out is discussed in Chapter 16. One notes here the system disappeared in 1877.

Daniel Jackson's shopping list contained one other item, namely the need for an isolation hospital in the town. The initial proposal was put to the Local Board of Health at its meeting of 29 January 1877 by the Chairman, Thomas Stainthorpe. He pointed out how outbreaks of small-pox had been contained by cases being removed to the Workhouse hospital. However, for those persons who were not paupers there was no appropriate place. In fact, in this respect the Board, at its meeting of 6 December 1875, had received a letter from the Clerk to the Guardians saying that the Local Government Board had refused to allow non-pauper cases of infectious disease to be admitted to the Workhouse. Stainthorpe thought that

> If they could get a suitable cottage, it would not need much furniture, say, a table, a bed, and a chair or two, so the expense to the ratepayers would be very small. All that would be necessary in case of a disease breaking out, would be to send a woman to light a fire and to wait upon the patient, and then translate the case to the cottage.

This proposal was agreed. Yet it would be 1899 before the town would have a functioning isolation hospital, this in spite of badgering by Jackson and letters of enquiry by the Local Government Board (HLBH 3.8.1886, 28.3.1887, 4.4.1892 and 23.1.1893). The hospital, properly fitted out as such with baths and other facilities (HLBH 18.3.1899), was built just off Maiden's Walk and added to in 1902 (*HC* 19.7.1902).

It is not easy to obtain figures to measure the health of Hexham as it has changed over the years since around 1854. First, the Registrar General's figures for Hexham are clearly for an area larger then the area administered by the Local Board of Health. Second, as succeeding years passed since each decadal census, errors occurred in calculating rates of mortality (deaths per 1000 per year). This was because the mortality rate for any one year in a decade was almost certainly calculated using the population figure obtained from the census carried out in the second year of that decade, 1841,1851, etc. This means that as the decade passed the mortality rate became increasingly an over-estimate. It should be noted that such over-estimates relate to mortality rates whatever their source, whether they be local or national.

Fig. 35 gives the mortality rates for Hexham and England and Wales plotted as a function of year over the period 1874 to 1930. The figures for Hexham are those of the two Medical Officers of Health for the period – Dr Daniel Jackson for the years 1874 to 1910 and Dr John Jackson for the years 1911 to 1930. Concentrating on the period 1874-1910, it can be seen that for both Hexham and England and Wales the death rate declines, roughly speaking at the same rate. The fact that the death rate as a function of year for Hexham tracks the rate for England and Wales indicates the decline in overall rate are due to general factors, that are having their effect nationally. Thus the overall decline in the death rate over the period 1874-1914 cannot be ascribed to anything special that is being done in Hexham.

It can be seen also that there are a considerable the number of times when the death rate in Hexham was higher than the figure than that for England and Wales. Particularly striking examples are 1874-6, 1880, 1882-3, 1889, 1897-8, 1900 and 1903-4. The only instances when the death rate in Hexham was obviously, but not markedly, lower are 1890, 1893, 1902 and 1909. However, it is the occasions when the death rate was higher that demand our attention because of the their much more frequent occurrence. These particular occasions must be due to special circumstances in the town. Only for 1880 is it clear what might be that circumstance, namely a scarlet fever epidemic. The fever ward of the Workhouse was full of cases. Isolation of cases was therefore not possible for cases outside. However, the fact that one cannot point to other special circumstances would make it not be unreasonable to assume that the many sanitary failings of the town, Daniel Jackson continually drew attention to, are the cause of the much higher death rates in the occasions alluded to.

Interestingly, though there is considerable fluctuation in the rate of infant mortality, the figures for Hexham are on average similar to those for England and Wales. Nevertheless we should be cautious about this similarity, not only because of the wide fluctuations of the Hexham figures but also because of under-recording, uncertain in magnitude, that is known to have taken place nationally (Woods & Shelton, 1997). That said, it is very interesting to see that the rate of infant mortality remained substantially constant not only in Hexham over the period 1875-1900 but also in England and Wales. This is in keeping with the view that the Victorian sanitary revolution had a little demographic impact on infants in England and Wales. In 1900, the national rate begins to fall; there is a similar fall for Hexham but there is a suggestion that it occurs a decade later. If this is so, and it needs examining further, the Town must be lagging behind many places in England in bringing about the changes necessary for reducing infant mortality. At present, one can do little more than hazard a guess as to why this could be so. It is believed that the national decline in infant mortality was brought about by a number of factors, such the supply of cleaner milk, better trained midwifes and the institution of Health Visitors (Bruce, 1961). The arrival on the scene of the latter in Hexham will be considered below. We do not know anything like enough about the milk or midwife provision in Hexham in the first decade of the 20th century to say whether or not either or both were inadequate. Indeed, the decline in infant mortality could well have been due to the increase of new houses in the town, allowing families to benefit from indoor sanitation, particularly washbasins and baths supplied with very clean water from Ladle Wells.

Finally, reference must be made to the rate of deaths from pulmonary tuberculosis in Hexham for the period 1881-1938. The relevant figures are given in Table 18 and show between 1881 and

1910, deaths from pulmonary tuberculosis were around $1^1/_2$ times the figure for England and Wales. This confirms the correctness of the great concern of Daniel Jackson about the extremely poor living conditions for many in Hexham, since pulmonary tuberculosis is a disease that flourishes in crowded and damp conditions (Dormandy, 1999). Indeed, it is not only pulmonary tuberculosis that flourishes but also other respiratory diseases, particularly pneumonia, bronchitis and pleurisy. Deaths by all respiratory diseases over the period 1879-1910 ran at an average of 26% of all deaths.

TABLE 18. *Pulmonary tuberculosis deaths in Hexham compared with those in England and Wales.*

Year	1881-90	1891-00	1901-10	1911-20	1921-30	1938
1	–	15	23	9	-	
2	–	9	8	11	11	
3	27	10	11	11	–	
4	21	12	24	14	–	
5	–	13	8	0	5	
6	9	11	19	0	9	
7	–	10	18	4	–	
8	14	11	10	15	–	
9	13	15	12	0	–	
0	18	14	9	9	4	
Total	102	120	142	73	29	
Per year	17.0*	12.0	14.2	10.4	7.2*	6
Population	5919	5932	7071	8417	8843	9292
Deaths per million population per year						
Hexham	2,872	2,023	2,008	1,235	820	646
National	1,810	I,418	1,143	1,007	768	476
Ratio	1.59	1.43	1.76	1.23	1.07	1.36

* calculated from an incomplete set of figures

Earlier, I referred to the difficulty of establishing the extent of infant mortality due to under-recording. The Registration of Births Act of 1874 made it the duty of the Guardians to appoint and pay a Registrar of Births and Deaths. In public health terms this was not satisfactory since the information did not readily reach the medical officer of health so that he could provide help about infant care. At the start of the 20th century, Huddersfield led the way in providing support for the mother and new child through properly organised supply of milk and through health visiting. The town strengthened its support for infant care in 1906 by promoting a private Act for the compulsory notification of births within the borough. This was so successful that the Notification of Births Act was passed the following year. This Act allowed local authorities to adopt similar powers. One of the chief advantages of the act is that it allowed the development of health visiting (Bruce, 1961). Hexham did not adopt the Act. Significantly, Councillor Conkleton, speaking in Council, indicated he was not against notification but he was concerned that it would mean a 'district' visitor who would be out of place in Hexham. They did not want such a person who would go into peoples' homes telling parents how children should be brought up. 'In all probability these visitors would be spinsters without any practical knowledge' (*HC* 30.11.1907).

Two years later the Council's attitude changed. At its meeting on May, the Council agreed that it should appoint Miss M. A. Spurr of the Milford Milk Depot near Derby as Assistant Sanitary Inspector at a salary of £75 to work under the superintendence of the Medical Officer to visit houses where there a birth had been notified and advise 'in a homely and practical manner' on the questions of feeding and rearing children. She also had to visit properties as directed by the Medical Officer, calling attention of the occupiers of any unsanitary conditions and also houses where there had been infectious diseases, particularly where children under five had died. She had to keep a journal with a full record of what she found. Nurse Spurr's (as she came to be called) appointment was met with some dissent in Council, particularly from Councillor Ainsley. Indeed it is possible that the appointment may not have been made had not been for the been for the influence of the Hexham Nursing Society under the chairmanship Mrs J. C. Straker and which contributed £35 towards Nurse Spurr's salary. Her appointment, in the first instance, was only for one year but, when the time came for her reappointment, it was clear that she had shown her worth and her post was made permanent. Significantly, John Ainsley, who was against her appointment originally (he had been against having another official to harass people, who were not in a position to stand any more harassing), was now in favour of it. Nurse Spurr was to remain in post until her death in 1920; she had made an important contribution to the welfare of Hexham.

The Hexham Nursing Society was an important example in of voluntary involvement in the health and welfare within the town. As far as I have been able to find out, the Society had its origins in the Hexham and St John Lee branch of the Cathedral Nurse and Loan Society for Sick Poor around 1889. Fortunately we have a good account of the kind of work this Society supported at that time:

> The nurse begins her duties, say at 9 o'clock. Away she goes her satchel filled with bandages, lint, plaster ointment, &c. The first she has to visit is the case of a bad burn, she at once begins and dresses it properly, makes the patient's bed if necessary, and sees that the patient has what the doctor has ordered, such as beef tea, &c.; if the home is too poor to have such a necessity she gives them a line [?] and they can get some beef tea ready made if milk is ordered they get milk...... and away she goes to another case, it may be a mother who has just been confined, who has no one to look after her or the baby; well the nurse begins at once, washes the baby and dresses it. If she thinks the child's dress not sufficient, she allows them some warm clothing from the Loan Society, gives them some instruction how often the child should be fed and how to dress it. Now what an advantage will this alone be, seeing 30 to 50 percent of our children die before they are five years old (*HC* 12.4.1890).

In view of this it is not surprising that the Society supported the Council over the appointment of Nurse Spurr. In 1893, the Newcastle Cathedral and Loan Society built a nursing home in Hexham towards the top of Hextol Terrace. The building still stands, converted into flats.

Concern within the town about the need for a health visitor reflected a greater awareness of the need for better medical care within the town. For instance,1889 saw the advent of ambulance classes in Hexham (*HC* 14.12.1889). 93 ladies and 93 men (all the candidates) had taken the separate courses run by Dr Duncan Stewart. Lady Aline Beaumont presented certificates to the ladies at a special occasion in the Town Hall (tea, flowers and speeches as well as the presentation (*HC* 15.3.1890). A second set of classes was held later in the year.

Duncan Stewart had a deep concern for the improvement of health of Hexham. He had used his influence towards the building of the infectious diseases hospital (*HC* 2.6.1894). But it was he, more than anyone else, who kept the need for cottage hospital to the fore. His ideas, which were far from grandiose, were conveyed in a letter to the *Hexham Courant* of 15 October 1910

> If an Hospital were built or a house and garden rented, you must not forget the upkeep for a hospital of 6 beds would be something over three hundred pounds. It would be a great advantage if the District Nursing Association and Hospital will combine; it would lessen expenses and there would be less overlapping. If some lady or gentleman would give us a site or give us sufficient money to build a hospital, it would be done at something like £200 per bed perhaps less. What an advantage an hospital would be to patient, nurse and doctor.

Hexham needed a hospital, though at a higher standard than suggested by Duncan Stewart. Being without a hospital meant that anyone in Hexham requiring hospitalisation, particularly those with serious injuries and needing surgery had to go to Newcastle Infirmary. The *Courant* of 21 June 1902 records an accident, the outcome of which was probably typical. Two men were injured, when scaffolding bridge, being used in the repair of the bridge taking the Carlisle Road over the Cockshaw Burn in 1902, collapsed. Both were conveyed (it is not clear how) to Dr Jackson's surgery (presumably at Carntyne, opposite to the Abbey Grounds). Robert Henderson, of Morpeth, with a broken arm was said to have walked home. Robert Brown of Cambo, who in addition to a broken arm was hurt about the head and legs and conveyed to his lodgings by police ambulance (Fig. 36). We know that after the Royal Victoria Infirmary opened in 1906, 23-26 cases had been admitted from the Hexham area (*HC* 27.6.1908). in view of what has just been described, these must have been serious cases.

The 1920s and 30s

It was the 1914-18 War that catalysed the move towards providing Hexham with a hospital. As early as 19 May 1917, the *Hexham Courant* was saying 'and we do not think this memorial [to the war] could take a more permanent or more beneficent form than the erection of a cottage hospital'. The Medical Officer of Health put forward the same suggestion to the Urban District Council in his report for 1916 (HUDC 18.8.1917). In 1919, the Council called a public meeting for 4 February to be held at 7.0 p.m. in the Presbyterian Hall, Hencotes to discuss the proposed War Memorial. There was a 'large and representative gathering' that after listening to an impressive survey by James Robb of the contribution of Hexham men to the war effort 'of these, alas, about 230 to 250 would never come back', heard an impassioned speech from Dr Stewart for the hospital that he had in mind. It was to cost £20,00 but, given the sacrifice of those who had died, it should be possible to raise the necessary money. He was strongly supported by Mrs J. C. Straker. No other suggestion came forward to the meeting. At the end of the meeting, a committee was appointed to look into the matter and report back (*HC* 8.2.1919). On 19 April, the committee presented its report that proposed that a cottage hospital was 'the most suitable method of commemorating the dead' in addition 'a monumental memorial' should be erected in some central position in the town. It was also learnt that St Wilfrid's, the residence of the late Mr Jasper Gibson, had been offered to the committee (*HC* 3.5.1919). From then on donations flowed in and St Wilfrid's was converted into what was to become the Hexham and District War Memorial Hospital. H.R.H. Prince Henry opened it on Thursday, 29 September 1922 (*HC* 1.10.1921).

Almost immediately the hospital made an impact on the medical provision in the town. Within eight months it had dealt with 174 cases and 117 operations had been carried out (HC 13.5.1923). Improvements were continually being made. In 1924 alterations and extensions were carried out, a male medical ward being added named the 'Duncan Stewart Ward' (HC 15.3.1924). A sun-ray clinic added in 1928, x-ray equipment in 1936 and a new operating theatre in 1937 were some of the further improvements made before 1939.

Chapter 16

The early decades of roads under Local Authority control

Introduction

The minutes of the Hexham Local Board of Health for 24 December 1866, has the following entry:

> The Road through the Abbey Grounds from the Market Place to Battle Hill having been made [by W. B. Beaumont] in accordance with the Specification accepted by the Board dated 23rd February 1866 and the Surveyor having expressed his satisfaction with the Work the Board hereby agrees to take the said New Road or Street into their charge and maintain it henceforward.

The entry goes on to specify details about the formation of pavements, the permanent nature of which were to depend on the occupancy of building sites along the 'New Street or Road'. On 11 February 1867, the Board decided to call it 'Beaumont Street'.

There were two systems of road building in vogue at the beginning of the 19th century – that of Thomas Telford and that of James Macadam (Fig. 38). It appears that the Surveyor was basing his specification on the system of Telford. For our purposes the similarity of the two systems is much more important than the differences. Both systems were based on a hard-core of broken rock the interstices of which were filled with much very small diameter material, which through friction helped to enhance the stability of the system while at the surface the same material when compacted provided the required smooth surface. However, in contrast to modern road materials – concrete and bitumen – the forces holding the materials together were not very strong, such that movement of vehicles along the road would be more likely to displace the underlying road structure. Of course, unlike modern roads, the roads of Telford and Macadam, though an advance on what had been present before their systems were relatively permeable to water and this agent could be as severe as traffic on road structure. A pithy letter, dated 12 October 1896, to the Hexham Urban District Council from James T. Robb, then living in Haining Croft, graphically indicates the consequences of the action of water:

> I beg draw your attention to the state of St Wilfrid's road. It is not safe for any vehicle on springs – the ruts in one place being quite a foot deep. At the top of the new terrace the mud is lying so thick that it is almost impossible to get across the road. I trust you will have it put right at once.

Though there are indications that St Wilfrid's Road was of lower quality of construction than Beaumont Street, it is not difficult to see that the combination of traffic, both animal and vehicular (Table 19), and running water over the road surface would mean its more frequent repair than is the case for modern roads. The difficulty of crossing a thoroughfare due to the presence of mud was avoided in the main streets by the forming of paths across them with setts (small rectangular blocks, often granite, laid together to form a durable surface).

Building roads to such a standard of Beaumont Street was labour intensive. Not only had the stones to be closely packed, particularly those in the upper layer, but also they had to be broken to size – and the more uniform in shape and dimensions of the resultant small stones the better they were for making a good road. Because of the requirement for considerable numbers of men, road-building was frequently used as a means of alleviating unemployment. Other labour costs came from having to water the roads in dry weather (Fig. 39), to keep down the dust, and from having to clean the road surface of animal droppings (scavenging) – the amount of such droppings can be guessed from the figures in Table 19. While scavenging was labour intensive, the droppings so collected were sold as manure, thus bringing in a small amount of money into the coffers of the Local Authority.

TABLE 19. *The results of a traffic census carried out over a twelve-hour period on Tuesday, 9 October, 1910, at the Fox and Hounds corner and at the bottom of Loosing Hill* (HC *15.10.1910*).

Category	Loosing Hill	Fox and Hounds Corner
Foot passengers	1758	3,202
Horses and carriages	933	506
Motor cars	103	69
Traction engines		2
Bicycles	249	242
Cattle	298	81
Sheep	40	38
Total animals	1271	623

It is not difficult to see that upkeep of highways within a small community, like Hexham, in the nineteenth and the early years of the last century could be a considerable drain on local finances. As I have shown in Chapter 4 (*see* Fig. 4) as much as 50% of the income from rates could go on the upkeep on highways. Such expenditure put considerable pressure on other heads within the annual budget, and contributed to the considerable political tensions of the 1870s and 1880s, when there was the prolonged debate about the pros and cons of spending money on an enhanced water supply and thus increasing the financial calls on the ratepayers (*see* Chapter 9). Furthermore, maintenance of roads in the more rural parts of the Local Authority district presented some seemingly intractable challenges. This chapter will steer a short course through the tangle of facts underlying over forty years of negotiations aimed at meeting these challenges. However, before we start on that particular story, there is a need to give some detail about the management of roads within the town.

The legal background to the maintenance of roads under local government

Though I am concerned with local authority control after 1854, there is a need to say just a little about road maintenance prior to that date. Essentially the parishes, even in the 'sprawling urban areas', were responsible for the highways. Though there were Turnpike Trusts, they were only responsible for 21,000 out of over 100,000 miles of highway (Smellie, 1957). In any case, by mid-19th century, the development of turnpikes was being killed off by the development of the railways. There were three turnpike roads running into Hexham (Carlisle and Newcastle, Hexham and Alston and Hexham and Alnmouth) but all the other roads appear to have been under the control of three Surveyors chosen annually (Rawlinson, 1853). It is not clear to whom they were responsible.

The term parish used here is not necessarily the ecclesiastical parish. There could be a highway parish with its Surveyor of Highways. After the Highways Acts of 1862 and 1864, highways districts were constituted consisting of a collection of parishes and administered by a Highways Board, the members of which were partly the resident justices and partly way wardens elected by the several parishes (Wright, Hobhouse & Fanshawe, 1894). In Hexham, the Local Board of Health seems from the outset to have taken over the responsibilities for the highways within the area of its jurisdiction, a fact enshrined in the Highways Act of 1862 setting up highways districts.

At common law, it was the duty of the inhabitants of each parish to maintain and repair all highways within it (Odgers & Naldrett, 1913). There was no escape from this liability and no contract would free the parishioners from it. Only *ratione tenurae* roads were an exception. These roads were formed as a result of enclosure. The owners of the land bordering such roads were responsible for their uptake. The roads were said to be repairable *ratione tenurae* (by reason of tenure). Further, until the Highway Act of 1835, a landowner was able to dedicate a highway to the public and from then on they would be responsible for its upkeep. However after 20 March 1836, this was no longer possible.

Having said that *ratione tenurae* roads were an exception, it should be understood that, after the Act of 1862, the owners of such roads were not exempt from the need to keep them in a reasonable state. The Act was quite explicit

> Where any highway which any body politic or corporate is liable to repair by reason of tenure of any land, or otherwise however, shall be adjudged in manner provided by the Act, to be in repair, the highway board of the district [which for our purposes is the Local Board of Health] in which such highway is situate may, if they see fit, direct their surveyor to repair the same, and the expenses to be incurred in such repair shall be paid by the party liable to repair as aforesaid (Foot, 1879).

As we shall see this gave the Board of Health (and later the Urban District Council) considerable power over those directly responsible for the *ratione tenurae* roads, since the local authority could hold over these persons the threat of carrying out repairs to the roads and then claiming back the cost. The Local Authority was under no obligation to do the job cheaply, it would be more important to have the road in a proper state of repair. The net result could be a large financial demand upon the owners. In Hexham, this situation never arose but there is no doubt that, because the Authority had this responsibility for overseeing the state of all the roads within its district, it was put in a position of moral ascendancy over the *ratione tenurae* owners.

Eventually the *ratione tenurae* roads were taken over by the Local Authority. In strict terms the roads were being dedicated to the authority, becoming 'repairable by the inhabitants at large'. Several steps that were necessary before a highway could be repairable at the expense of the authority (Odgers & Naldrett, 1913) but the most important from our point of view was that, before taking it over, the authority had to be satisfied that the road was in a proper state of repair had been properly made. The Local Authority in Hexham, whether Board of Health or Urban District, held completely firm to this principle for all roads which it took over.

Maintenance of the streets and roads within the town

When the Local Board of Health came into being in 1854 it assumed responsibility for the highways in the district, quickly producing bye-laws for the regulation of street cleaning and in June of that same year resolving unanimously 'that a Highway Rate of sixpence in the pound be immediately made out by the Clerk' (NRO/PHU/A1/1). In October, the Board received a notice from the Clerk of the Hexham [Carlisle and Newcastle] Turnpike Road of his intention 'to apply to the magistrates for an Order for the appropriation of a portion of the Highway Rate' levied by the Board towards the repair of the turnpike road. There is no indication in the Board minutes as to whether the matter was pursued. However, in July of the next year, it was resolved that the Clerk arrange with the Surveyor of the Hexham Turnpike Road 'to pay £40 or £45 as the Composition Money towards the repair of the above Turnpike Road.' In January 1857, it is noted in the minutes that a similar kind of payment was made to the Alston Turnpike Trust.

The Local Board must have felt that they wanted more control of maintenance of the turnpike road running through the town, because it was proposed on 14 February 1859 that the Board take 'into their hands the repair of such portion of their [the trustees] road as is within the Township of Hexham the trustees paying this Board £14.14s.3d towards such repair'. It was 28 September 1863 before the matter was resolved. The Local Board would take over from 31 December 1863 that portion of the road 'lying within the Township of Hexham, the same being first put into a good and sufficient state of repair', the trustees paying the above sum, namely the proportion of the tolls available for repairs. A similar arrangement appears to have been made earlier in July to take over that part of the Alemouth Turnpike Road from the top of Bull [Hallstile] Bank to Hunters House [census information suggests this to be the entrance to Tyne Mills Industrial Estate]'. The Board, 'having inspected the road', approved the taking over of the Hexham Turnpike Road on 1 February 1864.

For our purposes, from this last date until 1878, it can be taken that all the highways, within the district were under the control of the Local Authority. However, this did not prevent the Board from receiving complaints from to time from the Hexham Turnpike Trust about the state of its road through the town. In 1878, as a result of the Highways and Locomotives Amendment Act all roads disturnpiked after 31 December 1870 should be styled 'main roads' (Odgers & Naldrett, 1913). Prior to that date they became ordinary highways. The Act further enabled the county authority, at that time the justices in Quarter Sessions (who were already responsible for the bulk of the road bridges in the County), to declare any important highway as a main road. The Local Government Board in London also had the same capability. If the local authority was maintaining a main road within its district, it could make a claim towards meeting the cost of the maintenance. But a set procedure was involved in making a claim. In 1881, the Surveyor, George Dawson, failed to follow the procedure and caused the Town to lose between £100 and £200. When the County Council was formed in 1889, the main roads came under its jurisdiction.

At this stage, for the most part, we can leave the main roads as a separate issue. The rest of this section will be devoted to those highways that were under the jurisdiction of the Hexham Local Authority. From hereon what follows are essentially general remarks with some examples as to how these highways were managed and maintained.

I have already emphasised how the Hexham Local Board of Health, from its inception to the late 1880s was marked by an unwillingness to spend money if it could be avoided. Not surprisingly, as is often the case when budgets are tight, there were moves to have the work of maintaining the town's highways put out to external contract. The Board may have been stimulated also to move in this direction by the very critical report on the state of the roads produced by an external road surveyor James Marshall, who was scathing about the then maintenance procedures, particularly about the practice of the Board's workers to lay metal (stones) without cleaning off the mud already on the road (HLBH 18.3.1872). The job specification entailed much more than maintenance of the highways. The advert in the 16 March issue of the *Hexham Courant* requesting tenders said the contract was for 'Maintenance of the Highways of the Township, and for the Scavenging of the streets, Collecting of Refuse and the Sewage flowing into the Receiving Tanks [by the Railway Station]'.

The first contractor, Robert Story, was chosen because his tender was the lowest of the three received. He was appointed on 25 March 1872. The next year, Thomas Smith was appointed. He submitted marginally the lowest tender, though he had also been recommended by James Marshall. Smith was appointed on 17 March 1873; by 29 July, the Board were considering terminating his contract. Nevertheless he seems to have hung on. Whatever the cause, we know from a detailed report given to the Board of Health on 29 November 1873 that the highways and footpaths throughout the town were still in a dreadful state. One example from the report will suffice

> *East Turnpike* – This road is in a very bad state, the seughing [making channels at the side of the road] having been totally neglected up to this date, thus preventing the rainfall from escaping by its natural cause. In consequence of this neglect the water has stood on the roads, the constant traffic on which has broken up and nearly destroyed them. Deep ruts extend nearly the whole length of this road...... We also have to remark that very much to be regretted is the careless driving of Mr Dod's cartmen, who are constantly on the roads with heavy loads, and they invariably keep one track, thus cutting up this road very much in winter.

It would seem unlikely that the blame for this unsatisfactory picture of the state of the roads can be laid entirely at the feet of the contractor, even though there were concerns about his abilities. The problems appear to have a much more deep-rooted origin. One suspects that the state of the roads was the result of a lack of care and attention over a number of years. At any rate, William Robb did not feel that the situation was helped by having outside contractors and proposed they be no longer used (HLBH 21.2.1874). But the proposal was defeated, since it was felt to do the job properly it would be necessary to purchase additional plant. Those who were against the motion, Stainthorpe, Bulman, Robson, Smith and Taylor, were well-known for their antipathy to increasing Board expenditure. The next month, on 16 March, the Board demonstrated this antipathy further when it awarded the contract for repairing the highways and scavenging to John Jennison. Thomas Smith, knowing that it would now cost him more to do a proper job, tendered at a price of £446.4s.9d, Christopher Story at £400.0s.0d, while Jennison's tender price was £381.15s.0d. Not surprisingly, we learn that in March 1874, when the new contract was being decided Jennison 'had laid more whinstone than contracted for and overspent on the contract [agreed in 1874]' (HLBH 17.3.1874). In 1876, we learn that the then contractor, Wm. Oates, was unable 'to go down Hall Stile Bank or Loosey [Loosing] Hill with the water cart, until it is fitted with a break (*sic*)', suggesting that contractors might not have the appropriate equipment for the job for which they had been contracted.

The state of the streets was discussed at a Board meeting on 31 January 1876. The Surveyor, James Hay, reported that the scavenging was imperfectly carried out. Sometimes the ashes and sweepings were not removed before eleven or twelve in the morning. Gully grates were passed over, causing water to overflow. Board members were even more critical. Night soil, ashes and all sorts of rubbish were lying continuously during the day. Road scrapings could be left for a very long time.

Not surprisingly, on 22 March, 1877, it was quietly decided that the Surveyor 'engage men to do the other work of the Board and buy such articles implements and materials as he thinks necessary for carrying out such work.' As well as this a tender was accepted from Mr Wm. Oates for 'Horses Carts and Drivers for any work as may be required at 8/6 per day Horses Carts and Drivers at 1/- per hour Sand to Reservoir at 4/8 per square yard.'

From then on, the work on the roads was carried out by workmen in the employ of the Local Authority, under the control of the Surveyor, but making little difference to the quality of work that was being carried out. Thus, on a hot summer night in July with 'all the windows open' – and at a time when there was concern about the use of water keeping the dust down – the Surveyor had the horse sweeper out sweeping the streets, putting a great deal of dust into the air. At the Board meeting that discussed the matter, Joseph Catherall said 'it was not pleasant to be wakened at three o'clock by one man shouting at another some fifty yards off.' (HC 13.7.1878). Nevertheless, given the nature of the materials making up the roads and, it must be said, the quality of the persons appointed to the post of Surveyor, it would take time before the highways reached an acceptable standard. As has already been mentioned, the first Surveyor of quality was Robert Grieves, of South Shields. He provided wise leadership and the whole approach to the Board's construction projects and their running and maintenance became far more professional. But as well, materials were becoming available which reduced the need for highway maintenance. Thus, Fore Street was paved with granite sets at least as early as 1879 (HLBH 25.8.1879); they were replaced by wood blocks in 1894 to reduce the noise of passing traffic, made worse by the narrowness of the street (HLBH 17.9.1894).

However it was the use of concrete and of tar and chippings, because of the speed at which they could be laid, as well as their resistance to wear, that greatly facilitated the production of highways and footpaths as more permanent structures. The first record of the use of these materials comes in a report by the Surveyor to the Local Board on 2 February 1885 on materials that could be used for footpaths. His preference was for Caithness stone but he was willing to use 'cement concrete' and 'tar concrete', as he called them. He was concerned about the former material's tendency to crack and also 'turn slippery and greasy' and become hard to repair. On the other hand, he liked the latter because of 'its freedom from noise and [its] elasticity.' Beaumont Street was tar macadamised in 1901 and, according to the Courant, 'there couldn't be a more suitable street for such treatment' (*HC* 22.6.1901). Nevertheless, there was the downside of technological developments. The increasing use of heavier vehicles (traction engines particularly) and the carrying of heavier loads caused a greater amount of damage than previously. However, heavy vehicles in the form of steamrollers were of great benefit in compacting road surfaces. As early as 1888, the Surveyor was hiring one for road-mending (*HC* 29.9.1888).

Street building

The house-building which took place in the period 1890-1914 (Fig. 40) was not in small isolated patches, often along pre-existing roads, as hitherto, but in groups, frequently termed estates, on what we would now call 'green-field' sites (Fig. 41). In these situations, there was a need to provide services – water and sewage – but also streets (the term road was hardly ever used to describe these town highways). Frequently, there was a need for both 'back' as well as 'front' streets, the former being necessary for the delivery of coal and the removal of refuse. Streets were left unmade until at least one side had a completed row of dwellings (separate or terraced).

Though the streets were initially unmade (Fig. 42), their layout and their dimensions had to be approved by the Local Authority, working to its own bye-laws (NRO/LHU/B2/A1). In particular, the roads with footpaths had to be a prescribed width. When the housing along a street was finished, it could be made up. This was almost always by the Local Authority. But work would only commence when money for it was forthcoming. Either the money was raised first from the inhabitants ('frontagers'), or the Authority raised the money itself, usually as loan made after application to the Local Government Board in London to sanction one. Using this money, the street was made up, after which the Authority applied to the frontagers for their contribution towards the cost. This procedure was used extensively from 1894 onwards. A good example, picked because it indicates the spread of types of street, is the application that the Hexham Urban District Council decided upon on in 1904 with respect to the following private streets (*HC* 7.5.1904):

Kingsgate Terrace	£421
Commercial Place	145
Windsor Terrace back street	138
Orchard Terrace	125
St Wilfrid's Road back street	125
Maidens Walk back street	115
Burswell Avenue back street	110
Hudshaw House road	80
Richmond Terrace	63
Total	£1322

If the street had been made up by someone other than the Local Authority, the finished street had to inspected by the Surveyor to see if it matched his specifications. If it did, the street was approved as 'being repairable by the inhabitants at large' and thus taken over by the Local Authority. Thus, on 31 March 1879, the Works Committee of the Local Board reported

> It has been ascertained that the road in front of Leazes Terrace is an ordinary accommodation road. A considerable number of houses have been built beyond this terrace your Committee is of the opinion that the prayer of the memorial should be granted...... and if the road made and completed to the satisfaction of the Board's surveyor, it will be taken over and adopted by the Board......

However, as time went by, it became more and more customary for the road to be made up by the Local Authority. But, since payment for making up a street came out of the pockets of the house owners whatever the procedure used, the inhabitants of a row or terrace of houses could live for many years with an unmade street. A good example was Windmill Hill. In 1906, the Surveyor was trying to have the owners make up the road (*HC* 5.5.06); it was only after protracted negotiations with the owners that the road was finally made up in 1926 (HUDC 1.2.1926).

It is not appropriate to go into a great deal of detail about street development during the period 1890-1914. Here I instance three examples where there were problems, for the most part a consequence of differing interpretations of the bye-laws. My choices have been determined by the fact that, even today, there are visible consequences to the disputes that took place. First there was the long saga with respect to the property on the east side of Kiln Lane (Argyll Terrace) put up by Mr Anderson, a veterinary surgeon. On 25 May 1895, the Surveyor reported that Mr Anderson proposed placing railings on the street with a gate to each house. This was said to be in contravention of the Urban Districts bye-laws. Nevertheless, Mr Anderson put up the railings, which led to a very confused dispute between the two parties that went on for nearly three years, ending on 30 April 1898. The rather elegant railings can be seen today, having long outlasted all the disputants (Fig. 43).

In another dispute, the Urban Council opposed Mr Thomas Dorin, the builder of a large number of houses in Hexham (Higgins, 1995). He planned to build the row of houses, which are now at Monk's Terrace. The dispute revolved around the width of the road behind the houses. The Council required that the width be fixed by its bye-laws; Dorin stood by his opinion that the road was already in existence and had been so for some hundreds of years, thus pre-dating the bye-laws (*HC* 20.9.1909). Dorin went ahead with his houses. The Council tried to prevent him from having a supply of water. Undeterred, he took a firm line; his solicitor, in a letter to the Urban Council, indicated that he would take it to the High Court, since as the Water Authority it was obliged to supply him with water. His solicitor also said 'If your Council intend to take proceedings, it would seem only fair to Mr Dorin that they should do so at once.' (*HC* 17.7.1909). Eventually, the case went to the High Court. The Council lost its case; the Judge accepted the arguments put forward by Dorin. Thus Monk's Terrace is still a through road as well as a back street.

My third example concerns the west end of St George's Road, where the width of the road surface narrows from 23 feet (7.0 m) to a width of 12ft 6 inches (3.79 m) (my measurements). The latter portion of road there was laid down in the autumn of 1905, when only the terrace, which faces onto the narrow portion of the road, had been built. The bye–laws for the period stated that the carriage-way *be twenty-four feet at the least* (NRO/LHU/B2/A1). When the terrace was built, it was decided to build a carriage-way of half this width, anticipating that houses would eventually be built opposite. But that was not to be, even though houses were built, after 1912, on both sides of the road east of the terrace. The owner of the house (Idylwild) and land opposite, Councillor Pattinson, proved unwilling to give up land, not even for road widening. Nor could he be forced to do so, in spite of W. C. Rollingson (later to be a Councillor himself) of 3 St George's Road (now No. 5), bombarding the Urban District Council with letters about the problem. But the Chairman was quite clear 'that the Council had no opportunity and no power to deal with it', feeling there was no other way except through an Act of Parliament.

Ratione tenurae roads

As I have indicated, these roads were in the rural part of Hexham. The location of the roads that concern us are shown on the map in Fig. 44. When one sees their location, it should not surprise one that they were termed 'fell' roads by Rawlinson (1853), who also reported that these roads were rated separately from the town portion or 'ancient lands'.

When the Hexham Local Board of Health was formed, there was no longer any legal basis for separate rates. The situation became apparent to the Board itself by 1868, when we find the Clerk, Isaac Baty, writing to the Local Government Board about the matter. From an imperfectly preserved manuscript (NA MH13/91), we get confirmation that the 'Township or Town Division' has been rated separately from the 'Moor District'. Rates were raised from the inhabitants of the former for the maintenance of its roads. The owners and occupiers in the Moor Division maintained their own individual roads and were never called upon to contribute to the repair of the Town's roads. But, as Baty was to relate, the North Eastern Railway Company (seeking to reduce its rate payments to the town) had shown that a separate highway rate was untenable under the 1848 Public Health Act and that the cost of repair of highways should be defrayed from the General District Rate. The Hexham Board were clearly in a dilemma, for it meant that there was now to be a uniform rate across the whole district of Hexham, which of course meant that those in the rural (moor) parts would be making a contribution to the repair of the roads in the Town. Needless to say, the owners of the ratione tenurae from then on bore a grudge against the Board because they felt that they were being treated unfairly. John Lisle, speaking to a motion to take over the Houtley Road (see below) at a meeting of the Urban District Council on 9 July 1900 stated 'it was well known that this town offered to take these [ratione tenurae] roads over about 50 years ago but the parties said no, they would keep their own roads.' (HC 14.7.1900; the date of the actual decision by the Local Board was 11 May 1863). The owners must have come to regret their decision.

However, ratione tenurae roads did not present a problem to the Hexham Local Authority until the 1890s. It was then that the weight and amount of traffic started to have a serious effect on the state of these roads, which were not maintained to a very high standard. This is demonstrated graphically in a report the Surveyor made to the Local Board of Health at the end of 1898

> I have inquired into a complaint made at the last meeting against the road leading from Lane Dykes towards Dipton Mill. The worst portion that may be considered dangerous is from below Lane Dykes to the High Shield quarry. The lower length to Mr Fisher's Lodge [Loughbrow] has

a deep awkward channel which should be paved and the footway curbed; the soft places in the road should be drained, penned and coated to proper shape with hard metal not the limestone chippings which are used at present which just grinds into mud. The upper part wants cleaning, the heaps and large stones should be removed and the soft places penned and coated. Scattering loose metal on to a road is a poor attempt at repair, for most of it is either kicked off or worn too smooth and round to bed in. It is much better and more economical to coat properly and steam roll (*HC* 10.12.1898).

Though the problem of *ratione tenurae* roads first became apparent when the Local Board of Health was in operation, it was the Urban District Council that had to bring about a resolution of the problem. The extent of it is shown in Table 20A which is based on details provided in 1895 by the Surveyor, Robert Surtees, for the information of the Council (*HC* 2.11.1895) and up-dated by his successor, G.L. Murray, in 1905 (*HC* 21.10.1905).

As one can see, the length of road to be dealt with was considerable. In 1905, another road was added to the list, namely a short portion of the Elrington road from the Darden Burn to the Urban District boundary. On the other hand, the road involving Leazes Lane seems to have been incorrectly described. In 1905, the road is described as 'Shaws Lane commencing at Spital Cottage and finishing at Middle Leazes then to Leazes.' I have not dealt with these two roads further, concentrating attention on the five longest roads, each of which is greater than 1,500 yards (not too far short of a mile long). All of these roads are still important. Though racegoers might beg to disagree, that part of the Yarridge road running from just west of Rising Sun to the Alston Road is perhaps the least important highway; the other four, in their different ways, carry traffic between Hexham and Hexhamshire. The importance of that traffic was such that the condition of these roads was of increasing concern to the Rural District Council, which put pressure on the Urban District Council to take over the roads.

As the years progressed, the traffic on these roads increased. Most significant from the point of view of the state of the roads was the increase in timber haulage. John Story, Honorary Surveyor to the Dipton Road of Whitfield House, writing to the Urban District Council, speaks of the road taking traction engines (one weighed 13 tons) and timber wagons drawn by eight horses (*HC* 3.2.1913). Extraction of timber continued apace during the war and its transport out caused extensive damage. In the year after the First World War, it was predicted that the Rural District Council would be claiming (from the War Department) 'for the very large sum' of around £60,000 for damage to the roads in the Dilston and Slayley area (*HC* 13.12.1919).

Table 20B indicates the time-scale of the negotiations leading to the taking over of the major *ratione tenurae* roads by the Urban District Council and the final outcome, particularly as it affected the owners of the roads. As one can see, for some roads, it could take up to twenty years before there was transference of ownership. Nevertheless, by 1921, all these roads were in the hands of the Urban District Council. By then, road maintenance was not solely its concern; the County Council increasingly took a major role. However, that is another story, complicated, of course, by the rise in the increasing use of motor transport.

161

TABLE 20

A. *Information about ratione* tenurae roads *given by the Surveyor to the Hexham Urban District Council in 1895 (HC 2.11.1895), together with more precise descriptions of some of the roads provided by the Surveyor for the Board in 1905 (HC 21.10.1905).*

Road	Name used in rest of text	Distance (yards, unless stated)	More precise description given in 1905
A. *Thought to be* ratione tenurae *roads*			
1.Lane Dykes to Birks	Houtley Road	1,980	
2. Gallows Bank to Linnels	Fellside/Linnolds Road	2,640	Linnolds Bridge road commencing at the bottom of Gallows Bank
3. Oakerlands to Watch Currick (interrupted at West Quarter)	Yarridge Road	6,600	The road joining the Alston road and extending eastwards as far as the entrance to Blackhill farm, then from 230 yards from the Rising Sun to Linnolds Bridge road.
4. Low Shield to Dipton Mill	Dipton Mill Road	2,420	
5. Maiden's Cross to Rising Sun	Plover Hill Road	1,580	Causey Hill road extending from Highford road to Rising Sun
6. Leazes Lane to Summerrods		880	
7. Fellside to Delegate Hall		836	
Total		**16,936**	
Miles/kilometres		**9.6/15.5**	
B. *Doubtful* ratione tenurae *roads*			
Maiden's Cross to Highford		1,100	
East to West Causey Hill		990	
Cushat Lane to Fir Trees		1,540	
Total		**3,630**	
Miles/kilometres		**2.1/3.3**	

B. *Information concerning the taking over by the Hexham Urban District Council of the six most significant* ratione tenurae *roads in its District.*

Name of road	Apparent first mention	Taken over by the Council (date of report of meeting)	Means by which takeover was effected	Comments
Dipton	HC 10.12.1898			
a) Loughbrow Lodge to Black House		HC 2.5.1908	Council agree to take it over, provided owners pay £580 to put road into repair.	Owners fight off request to also give £1000 to be spent on future repair.
b) Black House to Dipton Mill		HC 5.12.1921	Long complicated saga from November 1919 (HC 3.11.1919) involving the owners, the War Department and the Guardians before the Council agrees to take over the road.	Owners provide £1,000, the War Department £550 and the Guardians £1 per week to around 40 men in receipt of relief to help with repair of the road.
Fellside (and Gallows Bank)	HC 28.2.1880	HC 2.7.1910	Council fail to make the owners make up the street, The Council applies to the Local Government Board for £450 to do the job. Money retrieved from owners.	
Houtley (Lane Dykes to Birks Gate)	HC 7.3.1896	HC 23.11.1916	Owners agree to pay £1,200.	
Linnolds	HC 19.5.1906	HC 6.12.1913	Owners agree to pay £500 and the County Council offer to pay £35 towards the repair of the road. It was taken over by the County Council in December 1891 (HLBH 14.12.1891)	The importance of this road for traffic to and from Hexhamshire seems to have underlane the relatively speedy resolution of the
Plover Hill	HC 13.8.1904	HC 22.8.1908	The Council take the owners to law to have	

163

| | | | the road repaired. The owners agree to pay £600 and the Council's costs in the case. | |
| Yarridge | HLBH 10.2.1890 | *HC* 18.2.1911 | Once discussions took place, there was speedy agreement with the owners agreeing to pay the required sum. | Said at one stage to be 'the finest promenade that Hexham has.' |

Chapter 17

Education

Introduction

Though the Grammar School might have had a higher profile in the town, in early part of the period covered by this book (*Hexham Historian* No. 9), it was the Subscription School that was by far the more significant in terms of the number of children it educated. There were other schools beside these two. Of the others, the Proprietary School (Fig. 45) was the most important. It was started in 1855 and owned by William Robb, John Ridley and William Temperley. The school was about the same size as the Grammar School and took girls as well as boys. Until its closure in 1889 it was a very effective competitor to the Grammar School (Jennings & Rossiter, 1999; Jennings, 1999). There were also many schools of very small size which tended to come and go. Thus in 1828, there were six such academies, two run by the Minister of the Scotch and Independent Churches, two teaching music run by the local musical instrument dealers, one for ladies and the sixth by a Thomas Morris of Priestpopple (Thomson, n.d.). The Post Office directory for 1879 show that as well as the Grammar and Proprietary Schools there was Miss Alexander's ladies' school in Battle Hill, the boarding and day school of Misses Hope in Market Street, the ladies' school run by Miss Rebecca Sewell in the Abbey house and St Mary's Catholic school in Battle Hill. Doubtless, a more intensive search would reveal other schools.

The Subscription School

On the 16 October 1812 there was a meeting in the Moot Hall of the principal inhabitants of the town to consider 'the propriety of establishing a school for the education of the children of the Poor'. The Lord of the Manor, T. W. Beaumont, was in the chair. It was believed that the strongest safeguard of the public and national welfare would be if the moral and religious conduct of the mass of the people were based on sound principles. It was also believed that the education of the poor was favourable to industry, sobriety, social and civil order and in short everything that constitutes either a good man or valuable citizen. The meeting resolved that the school should be maintained by annual subscriptions, each subscriber of a half a guinea or more being considered to be one of the Governors who were to choose a management committee and also visit the school on a weekly rota. A preliminary management committee was established which drew up regulations for the admission of children and the future government of the school and to produce a curriculum based on the systems of Dr Bell and Mr Lancaster (Thomson, n.d.; NRO/ZLK/SS/5).

The new School was built at the top of Eastgate at a cost of £347. The School could take 240 pupils, seemingly boys – surprisingly, though there is indirect evidence that only boys went to the School, I have not been able to establish this with certainty, nor I have found out the age group of the pupils. It is hard to believe that the building, that is still standing (Fig. 46), could cater for so many. On 29 September 1813, John Gouinlock of Sunderland was appointed the first Master at a salary of £80. The School probably opened before the year was out. Every scholar was required to pay a penny a week, except those from the old workhouse.

Gouinlock ran the school to the satisfaction of management committee till 1821, when he tendered his resignation. Henry Walton succeeded him and the school flourished. However, with the appointment of Thomas Maughan, the fortunes of the school, mainly due to his ill-health, took a turn for the worse and the numbers fell. Maughan resigned in 1851. On receiving the resignation, the management committee decided that Government aid should be requested and the school put under Government inspection, so that the school could meet the rules and standards of the Government scheme. The committee also, on the advice of Her Majesty's Inspector for Schools for the Northern District (the Rev. Mr Steward of Durham) appointed Mr James Reed as Master. He found the school building in a parlous state

> The benches and forms, during the juvenile industry of many years, had been cut and carved into the smallest dimensions: the props supporting them were nearly rotten: the walls were found denuded of plaster as far as either the kick of a clog, the hack of a knife, or the scratch of a nail could reach: the windows were neither wind or water tight: the flags were cracked and broken in many places; and last and not least, the only sources of heat and comfort for the poor Scholars, during the chilling frosts of winter, were from a diminitive (*sic*) fire-place in an obscure corner of the building, and an old rickety stove in the centre, which was often more prolific of smoke than heat...... (NRO/ZLK/SS/5).

All these considerable imperfections were quickly put right, in particular a large fire-place had been constructed 'on the best radiating principles', in the centre of the north gable of the building. The management committee then put great effort in raising extra money for the school and quickly brought in £100. The committee was also fortunate to obtain 'an excellent supply of books and maps from the Council of Education at 75% retail price'. But, in spite of considerable improvements, it was still felt that a better building for the school was required.

> The School-house, however, is found inconvenient and insufficient. It is close to, and unfenced from, the public road, and having no play-ground attached, the children necessarily cause considerable obstruction and annoyance to passengers. It is moreover much too small, so much so, that it will not accommodate even one-half of the children who seek the advantage it affords. Considering the increased desire for education, the requirements of an improved system, and higher class of teachers, it has become obvious that it would be disgraceful to this generation to rest satisfied with the present School-house, as it was creditable to that of 1812 to found it (NRO/ZLK/SS/5).

It so happened that two other events helped move the project forward. First, it became clear in 1851 that, in the likely event of the Lady Chapel of the Abbey being pulled down, following the removal of the houses in front of it, there would be a need for a new Sunday school (Jennings, 2003). This matter was raised by the committee set up in 1841 for the restoration of the Abbey with W. B. Beaumont who was concerned about the situation. Coincidentally, the management committee of the Subscription School had learnt that Beaumont was intending to erect a new girls' school. Although it was not to be built entirely at Beaumont's own cost, the committee felt that an approach to him could be of value, particularly as there might be an amalgamation of the boys' school of the committee with the school proposed by Beaumont. The latter was very much in favour of what was proposed. The upshot was that he was to offer a plot of land in the triangular portion in the northwest of the Seal and to the north of the track from Cowgarth to Cockshaw and £150 towards the cost of the project. There were objections to the school being built on the Seal but, in the end, it was decided by a vote in the Vestry that the new school should be built there (Jennings, 2003; Thomson, n.d.).

It was railway money, to the tune of £304.7.2, which helped to make the project feasible. This money came to the Parish Vestry as the result of it agreeing in 1836 to the Newcastle and Carlisle Railway Company purchasing land upon Tyne Green and Broken Braes for purposes of their railway (NRO/EP/184/171 & 172). Initially there were a variety of calls on the money – at first for a vicarage and garden, to which later were added 'an extension of the present burial ground, a convenience for the Dispensary, a soup kitchen and a stand for the fire engine.' As time went on there were other proposals for the use of the money – the improvement of Hall Orchard and the restoration of the Abbey, in reality probably the Lady Chapel (Jennings, 2003). In fact, though the money seems to have been received in 1841, it was only in 1853 that it was eventually decided to use it for 'the purpose of purchasing a site and building New Schools.'

The school building was originally planned for 500 pupils, together with houses for the master and the mistress and dormitories for the pupil teachers. Initially, the architect was a person called Gibson. However, he badly under-estimated the cost and had to be replaced by Thomas Austin. It was to his plans that the eventual buildings – two schools (boys and girls) in one block and the Master's house – were began in March 1855 and completed by Easter 1856 at a cost of £2,200 (*HC* 27.12.1873; Thomson, n.d.). They can still to be seen, facing the Sele (Fig. 47). The balance of the cost of the building programme (over and above that coming from Beaumont and the Railway) was met by public subscription and from the sale of the old school, which yielded something like £220 (NRO/ZLK/SS/5).

The buildings represented a great advance on the old building at the top of Eastgate. Each school was capable of taking 300 pupils. In 1856, the Girls' School had eight classes and was staffed by a Mistress, Under-Mistress and four pupil teachers, while the Boys' School had five classes, a Master and two pupil teachers. The difference in the number of classes in the two schools was probably the presence of an infants' classes in the Girls' School. The number of girls on the books was 236 with an average attendance of 166; for the Boys' School the figures were 170 and 148. Pupils paid on a graduated scale, i.e. one penny a week for those of poor parents, two pence for those of mechanics and labourers earning good wages and three pence for those of parents in good circumstances. The above figures indicate that many possible pupils were not attending school due either to pressure from parents to keep pupils away in order to assist in bringing in income into the household or simply due to a feeling that parents saw no need to have their children educated. Whatever the reason for non-attendance, there was concern in the town about children not receiving any education and even about the standard of education they might receive even if they were to attend school. A leading article in the *Hexham Courant* said

> Hexham is amply provided with school accommodation, such as it is, but one or two things we lack yet. Of these wants two are too conspicuous to need indication. We need the application of the compulsory clause, to compel attendance, in order to frustrate the selfishness of senseless and greedy parents, who are content to rob their children of every means of instruction that they may batten on their present earnings. And we need the dreaded presence

of Mr Inspector in all the schools, private seminaries and Royal Grammar School included (HC 24.5.1873).

Though the Subscription School was supported by a government grant via the Education Department (£211.12s in 1872) it was only equal to half the expenditure. That grant was determined by what, after 1861, was known as the Revised Code (so-called because it represented a revision of the authoritative statement of the Education Department as to grants and the conditions determining their application). The Revised Code resulted in each school receiving a single Grant paid direct to the managers, who were responsible for staff salaries. Grants could only be earned on pupils who were under 12 years of age, and were dependent on a certain number of attendances being made by the children and subject to the results of an individual examination by the Government Inspector of each child in reading, writing and arithmetic (the so-called 'payment by results'). The amount of grant was regulated also by reference to the income derived from school fees and subscriptions. Thus, entitlement to the grant was accompanied by the need to meet requirements of the Board, namely that the Schools should have competent teachers, this in turn meant the Managers had to be able to pay larger salaries to attract such persons. Further, there was a heavy expenditure for the books required by the Revised Code. Not surprisingly, with subscriptions and 'school pence' hardly rising, the Schools were in financial difficulties.

In fact, if one looked to the future, it was even bleaker, as the Local Board of Health had become concerned about 'the unsanitary state of the Seal Subscription Schools' (*HC* 25.10.1873). The stench from the privies was very bad and there was no water for drinking purposes. The *Hexham Courant* wondered why this state of affairs had been allowed to go on so long. It would have gone on longer had not William Robb, a manager of the Schools, raised the matter with the Board of Health. One suspects that Robb did this in a calculated way, because this forthcoming expense was added to those others listed above. A letter giving details of all the expenses was sent by the managers, after its meeting of 21 November 1873, to the Board of Education (set-up in 1870).

The School Board

Establishment of the Hexham Board

In the letter just referred to, the Management Committee were not only concerned about the increasing financial difficulties of the Schools but also about the fact that 'a large number of children of school age in the town do not appear at all on the books nor attend any school whatever and many of those who are scholars attend most irregularly'. The major element of the letter was the following

> The managers, after much reflection, see no means of escape from their unfortunate financial position, and have no other resource than to request your lordships, by issuing an order for the formation of a School Board, to relieve them from difficulties against which they can no longer contend (*HC* 22.11.1873).

It was at this same meeting that 'the managers hereby declare themselves unable and unwilling to continue the School under the present system of management.' Thus, the Management Committee made it clear to both the Board of Education and the local townsfolk that the situation could not continue as it had been.

School Boards were the result of the 1870 Elementary Education Act (33 & 34 Vict., c. 75) and were the vehicle by which elementary education was to be made available for all children resident within a school district. A new local rate was to be applied for Board Schools alone though they were also bound to charge fees. A Board was able to pass bye-laws to ensure compulsory attendance at school of the children within its district. Large conurbations quickly formed Boards; smaller places followed more slowly. Hexham was by no means the slowest to come forward with its request to form a Board.

The Board of Education decided that it could not act on the basis of what they had been told in the above letter. The Board suggested that an appeal should be made to the ratepayers (*HC* 13.12.1873) – a wise suggestion since, as we will see, they would be footing the major portion of the bill for running those schools managed by the Board. The Schools' managers on receiving the reply at its meeting of 5 December 1873 set in motion the necessary consultation with ratepayers. That took place over a fortnight later. Then about fifty ratepayers resolved 'that it is expedient that a School Board be formed for the township of Hexham', there being only three votes against. Though a relatively quiet meeting, concerns were expressed that the Board was only being formed because 'the managers of the Subscription Schools, who had no doubt done good work, were in difficulties, and could not pay their way' and as one might have anticipated there were murmurs about extra taxes.

The election for membership of the School Board took place 6 February 1874. Ruth Jennings (1996) has described in detail the run up to the election and the background of the eleven candidates who were standing for seven places. The election was notable for the first use of a secret ballot papers in a Hexham election. The successful candidates were the three managers of the Subscription Schools who were candidates – Revd. H. C. Barker, John Moffatt and William Robb – together with Robert Cook, John Hope Jr., John Lisle and George Robinson. The first meeting of the Board was held on 26 February; on 8 April, the Subscription Schools were formerly transferred to the Board (*HC* 11.4.1874). The information about the Board Schools that follows comes from the minutes of the Hexham School Board (NRO/ZLK/SB.1).

Staffing and income

One significant matter in the early meetings concerned the improvement of the toilet provision, which, as has been indicated, was required in the Subscription Schools by the Local Board of Health. However, in other early meetings, the Board had the important job of deciding upon salaries for the several staff in its three schools (henceforth to be known as departments) – Boys, Girls and Infants. Each department had a Head and an Assistant and a number of pupil teachers. The Head of the Boys' School was initially paid £120 a year, that of the Girls' £80 and that of the Infants £75, with salaries decreasing in the posts under them to those with the lowest pay, the two pupil teachers for the first year classes in the Girls' and Infants' Schools, each of whom received £6 a year. Initially the plans seemed to indicate that there would be an assistant for each school and the Boys' and Girls' Schools would each have five pupil teachers. The reality was that when the schools had be running for three years the total staff proved to be much less, there being only a temporary assistant for the Infants and only six pupil teachers for the three schools (Table 21). However by then a sewing mistress had been appointed. She was to spend one hour each week 'in teaching girls from nine to thirteen years of age the methods of household management applicable to working men's homes.'

As the years progressed the size of the staff increased very considerably, as can be seen from the Table 21

TABLE 21 *Staff in post in the three Hexham Board Schools in 1876 and in 1900.*

Staff post	Infants	Girls	Boys	Total
1876				
Head	1	1	1	3
Assistant	1 pro tem.	1	1	2
Pupil teacher	3	1	2	6
Sewing mistress	-	1	–	1
Monitor	-	1	1	2
Total				14
1900				
Head	1	1	1	3
Assistant	3	4	5	12
Pupil teacher	2	3	1	6
Monitor	1	1	–	2
Total				23

At the meeting that was responsible for fixing the salaries, it was established that a uniform fee of two pence per week be charged for every child attending the Schools. Where there were three or more children attending from the same family, the third and further children were charged at a penny per week (it should be noted that books, stationery were provided free). Fees from pupils were one of three sources of income coming to the Board for the running of its Schools.

TABLE 22. *Income of the School Board over the period 6 February 1874 to 31 December 1876.*

Source of income	£	s	d	% total
Rates	1440	0	0	71.1
Government Grant	278	3	11	13.7
School fees	308	10	4	15.2
Total income	2026	14	3	

Table 22 gives the breakdown of income during the period of the first Triennial Report of the Board, namely from 6 February 1874 to 31 December 1876. As one can see, though the bulk of the income came from the rates, there was a significant contribution from the fees, indeed more than from the Government (or more strictly 'Parliamentary') grant. However it needs to be said, in this particular instance, that there was no payment for 1874 and only a half-payment was made for 1876.

Subsequently, the Government Grant gradually increased until 1887, when it stayed at a relatively constant value of around £600 per year (Fig. 48), some of that increase being due to better attendance and examination results. Fees rose gradually in the period 1877-84, thereafter remaining relatively constant at around £200. Following the Elementary Education Act of 1891 (54 & 55 Vict. c. 56), it became possible for School Boards to offer free schooling, the fee element in their finances being replaced by a 'Fee Grant' from the Government. That grant came to ten shillings a year for each child between three and fifteen in average attendance. Not all School Boards availed themselves of this opportunity. However, on 12 August 1891, the Hexham Board agreed unanimously to abolish fees after 1 September 1891, the date when the new Act came into operation. The wisdom of this decision is seen in the dramatic increase after 1892 in the Board's income from coming from what was then the Fee Grant (Fig. 48). Throughout the whole period of the Board's existence, the money coming from the rates oscillated, often quite widely, the reason for this being not readily apparent. Some of that oscillation in a downward direction was due to good 'house-keeping' on the part of the Board, which kept it in good grace with the ratepayers of Hexham.

Clerk, Treasurer and Attendance Officer

Once the Board was established, it needed to make two appointments other than staff for its school. The first was that of Secretary to the Board; on 17 March 1874, Lewis Lockhart was elected post, after it had been advertised in the *Hexham Courant and Hexham Herald.* Later that year he was appointed Treasurer. He held the post of Secretary for duration of the lifetime of the School Board. He had to give up being Treasurer in August 1883. This was because the Education Department, following correspondence about combining the post of Attendance Officer (*see below*) with that of the Clerk, led to the admission about Lockhart being Clerk and Treasurer The Department made it clear that the same person should not hold both posts. Mr Hugh Fenwick of Lambton's Bank succeeded Lockhart.

The second post was that of Attendance Officer. The Board passed the required bye-laws with respect to attendance on 16 April 1874. Essentially, with certain exceptions, the parent of every child of not less than five years of age and not more than thirteen years residing in the district were to cause that child to attend school. The exceptions were straightforward, such as the child being efficiently instructed elsewhere, or that it was sick, or there was no satisfactory school within two miles. Children under thirteen who had reached the fifth standard were exempt, while children over ten who were beneficially at work were only obliged to attend for at least twelve hours. We need not go into further details, except to point out that when parents were unable to pay the fees, the Board were able to remit the whole or part of the payment. The need for the bye-law along these latter lines disappeared with free schooling.

Attendance

At the meeting on 18 June 1874, Robert Stainthorpe, a clerk at the Savings Bank, was appointed as Attendance Officer. His duties were detailed at the Board meeting of 2 July. His first task, decided at an earlier date by the Board, was to take a census of the children in the township between the ages of three and thirteen. This was carried out 'with due expedition' and a census ledger produced, added to with information from the Registrar of Births and Deaths and by systematic enquiry as to arrivals and departures from the town. In the great majority of cases regular attendance was obtained but in a number of cases a notice had to be served on the parent or parents. If the Board were not able to enforce attendance, the parents were summoned to appear before the magistrates.

If the parents were suitably contrite, a warning from the magistrates was sufficient. However, certain cases demanded action from the magistrates. In the first batch of prosecutions, there were two such cases (*HC* 9.1.1875)

> John Lynch was summoned for that he being the parent of a child named John Lynch, under thirteen years of age, did not cause such child to attend school. Mr Stainthorpe, the attendance officer, said the excuse in this case was that was that the child was a rather delicate one, but he put the question to the Sisters of Mercy, who conducted the Catholic Schools, who did not think that there was anything delicate about the child more than about any ordinary child – The Chairman told Mrs Lynch, who was present in Court, that the Bench would inflict a penalty of 5s including costs, if the child did not attend school.
> John Smith was also summoned for a similar offence. The attendance officer expressed the opinion that the boy, James Smith, was almost the master of his parents. He was eleven years of age – In this case, the bench imposed a fine of 5s and costs.

Robert Stainthorpe remained as Attendance Officer until the autumn of 1879. He was succeeded by Thomas Robson, who had been earlier in 1879 appointed to the post of Schoolkeeper. Robson retained this post as well as undertaking the duties of Attendance Officer, which post essentially became full-time. He was paid £60 a year and given free use of a garden. He did not stay long, resigning in September 1881. James Robson, the then Deputy Attendance Officer, filled the post until 1886; James Smith, James Robson's successor, was Attendance Officer until the demise of the School Board in 1902. Robert Stainthorpe, once he was no longer in post, was elected to the School Board in 1880, becoming its Chairman in 1898, following the resignation of Canon Barker.

The Boards were, by the 1870 Education Act, required to make reports to the Education Department. The Hexham Board decided that it should be done triennially on the expiration of the term of office of its members. The report was also written with the ratepayers in mind. These reports are a valuable source of statistical information. Here, it is appropriate to refer to the figures for attendance of school age given in the nine triennial reports covering almost all the years of the Board's existence (Table 23).

The increase in the total number of students on the books of the Board and Catholic Schools is to a great extent the result of the activities of the Attendance Officer. The children not accounted for are described as being in private schools, but this description is simplistic, since in later years of the Board's existence the shortfall could be subdivided (with numbers of children in each group in brackets) into:
    i)   at other schools in the district (Bagraw and Hardhaugh) (30);
    ii) [education] at homes (25);

iii) exempt and excused (due to having the requisite qualification and probably also education outside the district (74)

iv) not in attendance owing to barely reaching the school age (5 years) or illness (29).

Other matters of concern to the Board

From the very start of the Board's activities, its minute books details the many decisions that had to be made to ensure that the Board fulfilled its duties in a proper manner in keeping with the Education Act of 1870. Thus it had to arrange for the formal transfer of the Subscription Schools to the Board, establish standing orders and its bye-laws relating to attendance and fees and decide upon the scheme of education (which placed great emphasis on religious instruction) that should be followed. That said, the bulk of the minutes concern what might be called routine matters, such as the appointment of staff and the non-attendance of pupils. However, one disciplinary incident deserves a mention:

> On the forenoon of Tuesday the 28th January last [1879] Mr Peart the Assistant Master while in sole charge of the School had occasion to punish a lad called Taylor and slapped his hands with a cane. About a quarter of an hour afterwards the lad's mother came into the School and before the whole School abused Mr Peart with filthy language and struck him upon the face. A policeman was sent for upon whose coming Mrs Taylor left.

Mr Peart was upbraided; Mrs Taylor was written to warning against a repetition of her conduct; but most important the Board reaffirmed its rules about corporal punishment and also expulsion of pupils, which had lapsed in the present situation. The rules can be summarised:

1. That corporal punishment be only administered for heinous offences.
2. That it be administered by the headmaster and then only after due enquiry into the case.
3. That a record be kept of such punishments which will be presented to the School Committee every month.
4. No scholar be expelled until the case has been examined by the School Committee.

The above case apart, there was little mention of disciplinary matters in the Board's minutes. As far as pupils were concerned, the Board gave most attention to attendance. Of such cases coming before the Board, almost all were routine in nature. Nevertheless, in November 1884, the Board were seriously concerned that businesses in Hexham were illegally employing children. A circular letter was issued to the employers of such labour directing attention to the law on the matter.

There are a number of non-routine matters that stood out. The first stemmed from the failure of Mr John Hope, who was acting as temporary clerk until a permanent one was appointed, to give notice to members of the Board of an ordinary meeting that should have been held on the 13th March 1874. That notice was required by Schedule 3 (Proceedings of the School Board) of the 1873 Education Act (36 & 37 Vict., c. 86). Robert Cook took great exception to this failure to hold a meeting on that date. He raised the matter at the 16 April meeting with some ill-grace. He protested again at the following meeting on 7 May, at which meeting a letter from George

TABLE 23. *Information obtained by the Board's Attendance Officer, over the period 1874-1901, concerning the total number of children of school age, the numbers in each of the two elementary schools in Hexham and those who, for a number of reasons, were not attending either of the two schools. Except for 1874, when the figures are for that year only, the figures are for the last year of the triennium.*

	1874	1877	1880	1883	1886	1889	1892	1895	1898	1901
Total number of children of school age	722	889					1097	1056	1091	1243
Board School	380	455	666	762	838	898	837	745	764	784
Av. attendance				542	650	715	620	642	566	664
Catholic School	143	163	199	154	170	146	167	160	217	237
Av. attendance				123	120	129	120	146	158	176
Total on books of Board and Catholic schools	523	618	865	916	1008	1044	1004	905	859	945
Private Schools	199	281	-							
Exempt/sickness/private tuition/other schools						42	93	152	232	298

TABLE 24. *Details of those private schools and their head teachers the number of whose pupils had been determined by the Board's Attendance Officer. The other details are from the 1901 census. The number of assistants relates only to names of such who were living in the same house as the head of the school.*

Name	Age	Name and address	Number of pupils	Number of assistants
Miss Emma Hall[1]	46	St Hilda's College, Battle Hill	48	2
Miss Adeline Edwards[2]	34	Hallstyle Bank	19	
Miss Julia Edwards[2]	32			
Charles Rogerson[3]	45	19 Battle Hill	18	1
Miss Leah Scudamore	44	Birkdale House School for Girls, 19 Alexandra Terrace	11	
John A. Hyslop[4]	31	Battle Hill	8	
Wilson	other details not found		5	

[1] School founded by Susannah Hall, mother of Emma.

[2] Both are given as 'Principal of the School' in the census.

[3] Became first Headmaster of the Grammar School, when it opened at Fellside.

[4] Teaching carried out in the old Grammar School (R. Jennings, 1999).

Robinson was read supporting Cook. The next the Board knew about how deeply Cook felt was on 21 May when a communication from the Education Department was read enquiring as to the accusation of Cook and Robinson that the Board had condoned an illegal action. It appeared also that Cook had written a letter to the *Hexham Herald* that according to William Robb was a 'column of bitter and malicious falsehoods'. The response of the Board to the action of Robinson and Cook was for it to send a forceful letter to the Board of Education Department, particularly pointing out that, once the error had been discovered an extraordinary meeting was scheduled for 17 March when amongst other matters a clerk would be elected. The response of the Education Department, dated 6 August, was terse and to the point – 'My Lords see nothing in the statement made by Messrs Robinson and Cook, of a nature to require interference of this Department.'

George Robinson, a linen draper, had been amongst those first elected to the Local Board of Health in 1854, remaining a member until 1863. His outlook was characteristic of those first members who took a *laissez faire* attitude to the affairs of the town. The had not been in good health for some time; he was to die on 18 August 1874. However, apart from the one incident above, he had little effect on the running of the School Board. We know less about Cook. He was an accountant and, as a Roman Catholic, it was appropriate that he should be on the Board, because, though the Catholics had their own school, the Board was responsible for overseeing attendance there. But his relationship and approach to committee affairs indicates he was like-minded with Robinson. Following the second election for the Board in January, Cook was to be joined on it by another with the same outlook, namely Thomas Welford. Attention has been drawn before to his attitude to public affairs. Nevertheless, it is appropriate here to mention the views of the *Hexham Courant* as to Welford's capacity to co-operate for the common good:

> It was gossiped about that another very active and very legal candidate was nominated because of his lively and pugnacious disposition. Like an Irishman at Donnybrook Fair he wants somebody to tread upon his coat. For this pleasurable excitement he does not heed how much expense he puts the town. His performances as Don Orlando Furioso, upon several Hexham Boards have greatly added to the interest of their proceedings, although not much benefit may have accrued to the ratepayers from the grotesque and eccentric 'scenes' to which he has contributed (*HC* 3.2.1877).

During the period from 4 April 1878 to 17 May 1879, Cook and Welford did everything they could to stop money being spent on repairs and alterations to the school buildings. It is clear that the heating and ventilation of the school left much to be desired, the windows needed replacement and the interior of the boys' school needed renovation. Thomas Oliver of Newcastle was appointed to make the necessary plans that, in the event, were estimated to cost £1,500. The plans were approved by the Board and subsequently by the Education Department in London. The Public Works Loan Commissioners agreed to lend the money to the Board. Cook and Welford would have none of this, believing that the required repairs would cost no more than £15. The two of them did their damnedest to stop the work going ahead at all stages of the decision-making. Also they sent a memorial signed by 100 ratepayers against the scheme to the Education Department. But it was to no avail and the work went ahead. At the next election in February 1880, Welford was voted off the Board, though Cook was re-elected.

Cook continued to be troublesome but he met what was probably his match in January 1884 when Lockhart took him to court over slanders that he had made about Lockhart and over a libellous letter in the *Hexham Herald* (*HC* 19.1.1884). It all stemmed from the letter from the Education Department to the School Board pointing out that the same person should not be Clerk and Treasurer. It was written in what seemed to be strong terms, i.e., that the Department took 'grave objection' to the situation but it meant no more than it was concerned about a matter of principle and not a specific concern about Lockhart himself. Cook however interpreted the letter otherwise and accused Lockhart at a board meeting of gross irregularities and misconduct. Indeed, it appears that, also, he had been in contact with the auditor about the irregularities. Cook repeated his accusations in the letter to the *Hexham Herald* (9.5.1883). Essentially, Cook was concerned that Lockhart as Clerk was receiving orders from the teachers for stationery, etc. which he then passed on to the supplier; when Lockhart received the bill he paid it in his capacity as Treasurer. Cook complained that the Board's authority for these transactions was not obtained, though there is a minute to indicate that Lockhart was following procedures that had been agreed by the Board.

After Lockhart's counsel had presented his case there was, at the suggestion of the judge, a consultation with his counterpart for the defence. It resulted in Cook making a retraction and apology. The judge awarded Lockhart 40s and costs. The wind was probably taken out of Cook's sails for there is little evidence to suggest that he played a major part in the deliberations of the Board thereafter. In 1885, he seems not have attended Board meetings for several months before the Board elections in January 1886, for which he did not stand. From then on, the affairs of the Board became much more tranquil and remained so until the demise of the Board in 1902.

In the period from when the Board took over the Subscription Schools to 1883, as we have seen, the number of pupils doubled. Such an increase put tremendous pressure on the school buildings. Eventually it became clear that the problem of accommodation required resolution and on 5 March 1885 the Board set up a committee to look into the matter. As a first step, Oliver and Leeson were appointed architects. There were a number of problems, the most prominent of which were the amount of space available and compliance with the new rules of the Education Department with respect to buildings. In the end, it was decided that the best way forward was a separate building for the Infants' Department, additional land allowing erection of it being purchased from W. B. Beaumont for £300. The total cost was £2,800. Alterations were also carried out to the old buildings for the benefit of the Boy's and Girl's Departments. The new building was opened on 23 September 1887 (*HC* 24.9.1887).

The Schools come under the control of the County Council

With the Education Act of 1902 (2 Edw. 7, c. 42), the Board School came under the control of the County Council. Thus the School (which was now to known as the Hexham Council School) was no longer under truly local control. There was now a board of managers, not more than four representatives of the County and not more than two from the Urban District Council.

The Education Committee of the County Council must have realised relatively soon that its school in Hexham was overcrowded, because, in 1912, negotiations had begun with Lord Allendale to purchase a plot of land to the east of the old Board School buildings. The plot was purchased in

1912 for £925 (*HC* 2.3.1912). The extension was to be for boys; the building in which they were being taught was to be used by the infants and girls. The idea that boys and girls might be taught in mixed classes was turned down (*HC* 23. 11 1912). It was early 1915 before work on the new extension started; completion was sometime in late December/early in the New Year.

'The Education Act of 1918 (8 &9 Geo., 5 c. 39) is one of the most significant and far reaching of the war measures which necessity has imposed on the nation' (Thomas, 1919). The Act established a universal leaving-age of fourteen and abolished the system by which some pupils could attend part-time. It also allowed a local authority by a bye-law to raise the leaving age to fifteen. It is the raising of the leaving age that concerns us here.

That pupils were to stay in school until fourteen raised the problem of availability of places in the buildings that existed. Also it was questioned whether it was good for most pupils to spend their entire school career in one elementary school. These issues were addressed in the Hadow Report of 1926. It reiterated the need for the school-leaving age to be 15 and advocated the reorganisation of all-age schools into separate junior and senior schools and put forward the view that age of transfer be eleven. The thinking of the County Council on these and other matters in the inter-war period has been well documented by Taylor (1989). The County Council decided that, as from 1 April 1930 the school leaving age be raised from fourteen to fifteen.

As far as Hexham was concerned, there was not only the matter of providing additional space but the old space itself was inadequate in other ways. In 1928 H.M. Inspector reported that the work in the girls' school was greatly hampered by an inconvenient, ill-lighted and ill-ventilated building (*HC* 15.12.1928). The initial plan was for 'a new modern school' costing £14,500 and improvements to the old school buildings costing £4,675. Naturally, there was a concern about the burden on the rates. When the School Board was functioning, the 'education' rate was never more than 6d in the pound. In 1927-8 it had risen to 1/9¼ in the pound. Nevertheless, there was the feeling that the proposed new expenditure was necessary. By 1929, a site for the school had been found 'near Queen Elizabeth Grammar School'. The Senior School, built at a cost of £18,360, was opened on 1 February 1932. It was said to be modelled on the most modern designs and possesses all the latest improvements. The school was built to accommodate 440 pupils and was divided into girls' and boys' sections. The following was said about its location

> Perched on the slopes above Hexham, the school commands an unrivalled view of the Abbey Town, and having a south aspect, it will be in a position to catch all the health-giving rays of the sun (*HC* 30.1.1932).

The building of the Senior Council School was followed by remodelling of the buildings on the Seal at a cost of around £7,250. The school was divided into infants with standard one and mixed juniors (*HC* 6.2.1932).

Chapter 18

The 1914-18 War and its aftermath

The 1914-18 War marks a turning point in the history of Hexham. Previous wars had entered the conscience of its citizens. There was sufficient concern about the Franco-Prussian War for a public meeting to be held in the Moot Hall on 21 September 1870 'for the purpose of considering the best means for aiding the Sick and Wounded in the present Continental War' (*HC* 17.9.1870). Within a fortnight, there had been 136 donations over 1/-, totalling £83.19s.6d. The South African War had a more profound effect, as is evidenced by the two memorials, one, in the Abbey to those Hexham men of the 1st Northumberland Fusiliers who served in South Africa, including some who died as a result of the war, and the other, at the top of Beaumont Street, to Lt. Colonel Benson who was killed in action in 1901 (*HC* 5.3.1904 & 12.3.1904). Both the *Hexham Courant* and the *Hexham Herald* devoted a significant number of column inches to the South African war, yet that coverage was dwarfed by the coverage of the two papers to the 1914-18 War. According to the *Courant* of 1 November 1919, 218 men from the Hexham area were killed in the conflict. Given a population of around 8500, and taking the number of males as half that figure, it means that around 5% died. As there were many more wounded, few families are likely to have been untouched by the War. Nevertheless, in spite of the effect of the War on the town, I do not intend to delve into the town's history of Hexham during 1914-18; another publication is required for that. Here I focus on how the War specifically affected the way local Government operated.

Initially, almost nothing in the minutes of the Urban District Council indicated that the war was underway. Projects were initiated in September 1914, such as the provision of a better supply of water for Low Gate, while in October the new Seal entrance gates (commemorating Lord Allendale's gift of the Seal to the town) were completed. Nevertheless, by the end of the year, there are distinct signs that the war was beginning to impinge on the town. At the meeting of the Urban District Council on 7 December

> A letter was read from the Northumberland sub-Committee of the Northumberland Newcastle and Tyneside Belgian Refugees Committee enquiring whether the Council would be willing to forego the rates upon houses in their district occupied by the refugees.

The business of the Council at the start of 1915 was essentially similar to that in 1914, a particular item of concern being the possibility of taking over the Houtley and Dipton roads. The war intruded briefly into the business of the Council in February when there was a hope that captured German guns might come to Hexham for display (HUDC 1.2.1915). However as the year progressed, it became clear that Councillors would be dealing more and more with matters of national importance rather than the customary ones at local level. Thus the Urban District Council minutes highlight the following:

In 1915
30 March – The Council learnt that the Local Government Board would not sanction loans except for work of very pressing necessity.

5 July – Permission given to wounded soldiers to play football and other games on the Seal.

6 September – Two Circulars received from the Local Government Board:

The first suggested economies in the expenditure on parks, recreation grounds, street lighting and watering. The second postponed the election of District Councillors for a year. [In fact elections were not to be held until 1919. As will be seen later, the extended delay had a significant effect on the outlook of Councillors.]

In 1916

4 January – The Military Authorities plan to billet troops in the Town Hall building. It was suggested to the Council that earth latrines are constructed at the back of the building. As one might imagine there was considerable consternation about the latter proposal. There seems to be no information as to how the matter was resolved.

3 July – It was agreed by the Council that provision be made to store furniture of any married man in the district who might be called up for military service and who wished to 'break up his home' whilst on service. The Council agreed to defray the cost of removal and insurance against fire and enemy aircraft and that the storage would be free of charge.

2 October – The Council deal with applications under the War Charities Act; the following were registered:

> Belgian Soldiers Fund
> Hexham War Hospital Supply and Clothing Fund
> Hexham Branch of the British Red Cross Society.

One could go on but enough detail has been given to indicate how the business of the Council was being changed as a result of the exigencies of the War. It was to change even more. However, I want to highlight only, what seem to me, those major concerns of the Council in the last two and a half years of the War.

First, the Council were to lose staff for the war effort. At its meeting of 23 November 1916, Councillors learnt that the Government was to organise a Road Construction Force to work in France. It was to be composed of Surveyors and Council workmen. Also, the Government desired to take over such part of the Council's plant as could be spared. Mr Pooley, the Council's Surveyor, requested permission to offer his services and that permission was granted. It was also agreed that the following plant be released to the Construction Force: a road scraper, a road brush, a sludge cart and a tipping wagon (all horse-drawn). There is no information about how many of the rest of the work-force left for active service. In March, the following year, Mr Pooley received his commission in the Royal Engineers. He was to return to the service of the Council early in 1919 (HUDC 6.1.1919). During the period Mr Pooley was away, all his outdoor duties were taken over by a District County Surveyor, while Mrs Pooley undertook his office duties. Not surprisingly, in the absence of the expertise of the Council's Surveyor, only routine work seems to have been carried out.

The Clerk of the Council, Mr John A. Baty, had left for active service in February 1916 (HUDC 7.2.1916). In this case, replacement expertise was available, Mr W. Fisher a local solicitor, being appointed as Acting Clerk. John Baty was wounded in 1917 (HUDC 7.5.1917); he returned to Council duties shortly after Mr Pooley.

Second, the War brought a new outlook within the Council to the provision of allotments. The Allotments Act of 1887 (50 & 51 Vict., c. 48) allowed six registered Parliamentary electors or ratepayers to take proceedings against the local authority for the provision of allotments. If it approved the proposal, it might buy or hire suitable land and 'let it' in allotments to persons belonging to the labouring population. However, a petition, arising from a meeting in the Coach and Horses Inn, and sent to the Urban District Council in March 1895 met with little favour (*HC* 16.3.95). It was to be another thirteen years before the Council took advantage of the Act. Then, in July 1908, it received a memorial from occupiers of land adjoining Portland Cottages was being offered for sale and it was suggested the Council should acquire this or other suitable land for allotments (*HC* 25.7.1908). In fact, the owners intended the land for building (*HC* 22.8.1908). Over three years were to elapse before the Council had land that was available for cultivation when it signed the lease for the purchase of 1.96 acres land in the ownership of the Catholic Mission in Alexandra Terrace. The acreage allowed the establishment of seventeen allotments (*HC* 7.1.1911). There is little evidence that the 'labouring population' benefited from the allotments so established. The 17 plots were allocated as follows: in employment – three gardeners, two joiners, a poor rate collector, a railway gatekeeper, a signalman, a travelling draper, a clerk, a baker, an iron moulder and a labourer; retired – two farmers, the station master and an army pensioner.

TABLE 25. *Details of the Council's holdings of allotments at the end of the 1914-18 War. It has not been easy to interpret the Urban District Council minutes, so there is a degree of uncertainty about the information presented here.*

Location	Size	Number of tenants	Date (HUDC)	Additional information
Land near Quatre Bras	4.5 acres	78	3.1.1917	Offered by Mr J.J. Kirsopp.
Priors Flat		11	5.2.1917	
Rear of Croft Terrace			5.2.1917	Controversy with owner led to delayed use.
Slaughter House Field		19	5.2.1917	
Shipfield			5.3.1917	Unknown location – probably behind the east side of Elvaston Road
Rear of St Cuthbert's Terrace			5.3.1917	
Burswell and Osborne Avenues			5.3.1917	
Cuddy's Lane	1 acre		2.4.1917	Land belonging to Hexham Auction Mart Co.
Round Close			7.5.1917	Land purchased by HUDC
Land between Priors Flat and Park Avenue		45	4.3.1918	
Dene Park		19	2.4.1918	

However, the Council obtained unprecedented power in the establishment of through the Cultivation of Lands Order that came into force in 1916. When it was discussed in the Council at the end of the same year, a deputation led by Dr Duncan Stewart urged the Council to exercise the powers conferred on it. The Council were quick to act. By mid-1917, a considerable acreage of land had been converted to allotments with further land obtained in 1918 (Table 25). Some of the land, particularly that near Quatre Bras and between Park Row and Priors Flat, has remained as allotments. Shortly after the War, houses were built on the land at Burswell Avenue (HUDC 16.3.1920). The tiny parcel of land behind St Oswald's Road reverted to the owner at the end 1921 but has never been built upon (HUDC 6.6.1921). By 1925, the Council had 610 allotments laid out in twelve distinct areas of ground. We know that the Council leased Fairfield for allotments in 1921 (HUDC4.1.1921). If we take the information in Table 25 and knowing that there was loss of two areas of land by that date, the total above suggests that other areas of land were either purchased or leased.

However, during the War, not all the land upon which the Council had its eyes was readily obtained. Mr Rogerson and the governors of the Grammar School fought a fierce campaign against having their part of their playing fields at Dene Park being turned into allotments. However the Council, backed by those living at Woodside who were demanding them, won the battle. On the other hand, Canon Savage and the churchwardens prevented cultivation of the Cloister Garth by pointing out that during the restoration of the nave of the Abbey, human remains then discovered were re-interred there (HUDC 14.6.1917). Eventually, an independent Council committee was established to deal with the acquisition of land allotments and running them (previously the matter of allotments had been dealt with in a committee which dealt with pleasure grounds and markets).

With the increasing pressure on the resources of the nation, other duties fell upon Councillors. Thus, in 1917, the President of the Local Government Board and the Food Controller requested the Council to form a Local Food Control Committee to consist of twelve members to deal with the regulation and distribution of food supplies at the local level. There were six councillors, two 'lady' representatives, Miss Boyd and Miss Iveson (who was eventually to be Hexham's first woman councillor), John Sparke, a Grocer, R. J. Conkleton, representing 'labour', and, Mr J.W. Crozier representing the Co-operative Society (HUDC 8 & 22.8.1917). Not surprisingly, in view of the need to maximise resources for the war effort, in January the following year, the Council made a special effort to collect what we would now call recyclable material, namely wastepaper, scrap metal, woollen goods and bottles (HUDC 17.1.1918).

Later, the Household Fuel and Lighting Order resulted in the formation of a local committee, consisting of four councillors, together with representatives of the coal merchants and dealers, Hexham Gas Co. and Hexham and District Supply Co. (HUDC 22.7.1918). An overseer, Joseph Dodd of Kingsgate Terrace, was appointed to assess every house in the district with respect to the amount of coal, gas and electricity to which they were entitled on the basis of the number of rooms in each house.

Third, as the war progressed but in spite of an uncertain outcome, the thoughts of those in government and also others turned towards constructing peacetime Britain. Even as early as 1916, the Finance Committee was recommending to the Council that a letter should be sent to the Prime

Minister that the decimal system of coinage, weights and measures should be adopted after the War (HUDC 4.12.1916). Towards the end of 1917, the Government initiated thinking by local authorities about post-war issues, particularly the provision of better housing for the working population. This stimulated an impressive statement on Hexham's housing needs from the Medical Officer of Health, Dr John Jackson, strongly supported by numerical data (HUDC 1.10.1917). When, in April 1918, the Local Government Board requested to be informed as to any work likely to be undertaken on the conclusion of the war, the Council put forward three projects – housing, the widening of Haugh Lane and the extension of the Cemetery (Jennings & Jennings, 2003).

The feeling one obtains from reading the minutes of the Urban District Council was that, by the end of the War in 1918, it had a more purposeful view of its role. This was probably a consequence of the Councillors having worked together as an unchanged group for three years and as a result of having had thrust upon themselves responsibilities, not present in peace-time. Undoubtedly, the prevailing spirit, amongst those who had remained on the home front during the War, that every effort should be made towards making country 'fit for heroes' must have contributed to that more purposeful view. The post-war situation was helped also by a degree of continuity between the war-time Council and its successors, with eight of its members being re-elected in 1919 and five in 1920. It was this new-found confidence, as a decision-making body that led to the post-war Councils, particularly in the 1920s, displaying considerable energy over dealing with the major problem that faced Hexham, the provision of better housing for the less well-off.

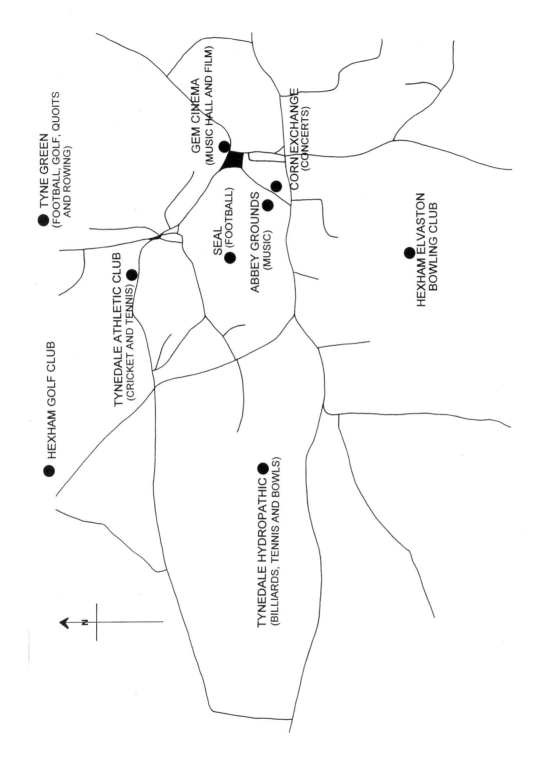

FIG. 49. The location of recreational facilities in Hexham prior to 1914. To those shown on the plan must be added Rugby Football played at Dene Park to the east of the centre of Hexham.

FIG. 50. The proposed open-air swimming bath located in the Abbey Grounds behind St Aidan's Church. Seemingly, the pool was fed by the Cowgarth Burn. The nearest the Hexham got to the swimming bath, that is shown above, was a paddling pool, close to where the Burn goes underground in the Grounds (*HC* 29.6.1935).

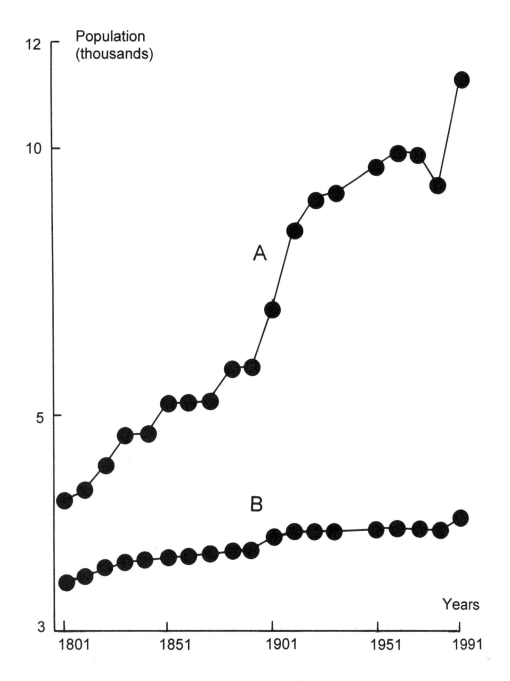

FIG. 51. The population growth of Hexham from 1801 to 1991, based on census figures. **A.** The graph of population figures for each decade. **B.** The same figures expressed as logarithms – this shows that the rate of growth of the population between 1831 and 1881 was virtually constant, with a marked increase between 1891 and 1911 (see the text for a discussion of the increased rate of growth). After the 1914-18 War, the rate fell to a value lower than that of the rate before the War.

FIG. 52. An aerial view, taken in May 1962, of that part of the east end closest the town centre showing the location of the housing estates built by the Urban District Council in the 1920s and 30s. A. Peth Head; B. White Cross; C. Wanless Close; D. Round Close; 1. Public slaughterhouses; 2. Workhouse schools; 3. Hexham Grammar School. The photograph also shows the Workhouse at the lower right-hand margin and in the centre the hospital as it was built 1939. Reproduced with permission of Simmons Aerofilms Ltd.

FIG. 53. Bungalow-type houses in Garden Terrace built during 1925 by the Urban District direct labour force to the design of the Surveyor, W. G. Landale. The houses are built completely of concrete but with brick flues.

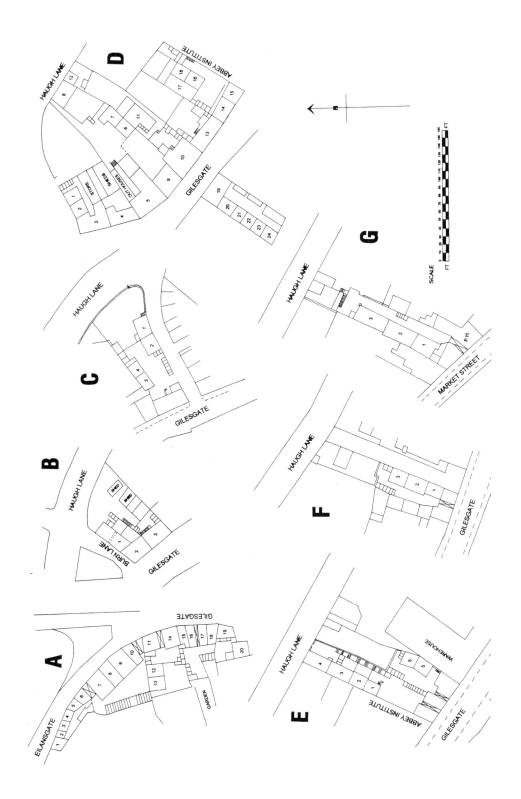

A

EILANSGATE
1 2 3 4 5 6 7 8 9 10 11 12 13 14 15 16 17 18 19 20
GARDEN
GILESGATE

B

HAUGH LANE
BURN LANE
SHED
1 2 3
GILESGATE

C

HAUGH LANE
1 2 3 4 5
GILESGATE

D

HAUGH LANE
1 2 3 4 5 6 7 8 9 10 11 12 13 14 15 16 17 18
SHEDS STORE OUT HOUSES
ABBEY INSTITUTE
GILESGATE
19 20 21 22 23 24

E

HAUGH LANE
1 2 3 4 5 6
ABBEY INSTITUTE
WAREHOUSE
GILESGATE

F

HAUGH LANE
1 2 3
GILESGATE

G

HAUGH LANE
1 2 3
MARKET STREET
P.H.

SCALE
FT 10 20 30 40 50 60 70 80 90 100 110 120 130 140 150 160 FT

N

FIG. 54. Plans of the individual slum clearance areas (redrawn from NRO/LHU/46/1), together with their official numbers and details of their location.

Part 1. (Across)
A. No. 1 – formerly known as the Mystery, now Alexander Place.
B. No. 2 – at the very bottom of Gilesgate, now Garland Place.
C. No. 3 – on the west side of Circle Place.
D. No. 4 – the south-west corner of Circle Place together with the car park on the west side of the Community Centre and the buildings opposite.
E. No. 5 – formerly Mills Yard, between the Community Centre and the Swimming Pool.
F. No. 6 – located on Gilesgate Bank; the area is now part of Gilesgate Court
G. No. 7 – located in Market Street; the pub was the Turks Head, now it is the Heart of All England, .

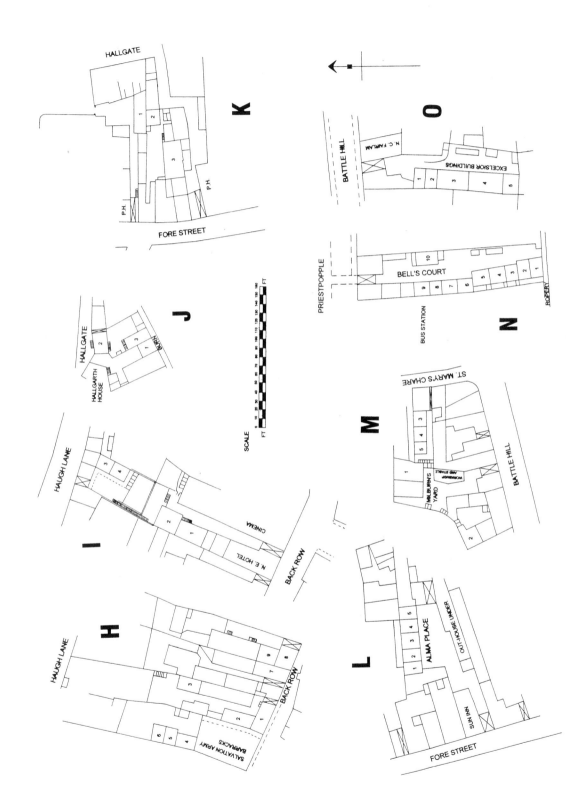

HALLGATE

K

FORE STREET

P.H.

P.H.

P.H.

1
2
3

BATTLE HILL

N.C. FARLAM

O

EXCELSIOR BUILDINGS

1 2 3 4 5

HALLGATE

J

HALLGARTH HOUSE

BURN

2
3
1

SCALE

FT
0 10 20 30 40 50 60 70 80 90 100 110 120 130 140 150 160 FT

PRIESTPOPPLE

BELL'S COURT

10

9 8 7 6 5 4 3 2 1

BUS STATION

ROPERY

N

HAUGH LANE

I

3
4

2

1

CINEMA

N.E. HOTEL

BACK ROW

ST. MARY'S CHARE

M

3
4
5

1

MILBURN'S YARD

WORKSHOP
AND STABLE

BATTLE HILL

2

HAUGH LANE

H

3

9

8

7

2

1

BACK ROW

SALVATION ARMY BARRACKS

6 5 4

L

1 2 3 4 5

ALMA PLACE

OUT-HOUSE UNDER

SUN INN

FORE STREET

FIG. 54 (Continued)

Part 2. (Across)
H. No. 8 – Salvation Army Yard; this together area together with No. 9 are occupied by Pudding Mews.
I. No. 9 – North Eastern Hotel Yard; see H.
J. No. 11 – now part of Robb's car park.
K. No. 10 – White Hart and Gibson's Yards. The area can be identified by passage still present from Fore Street to the Goose Market. The lower public house was the Blue Bell Inn, the upper the White Hart. Building No. 1 used to be the Police Station.
L. No. 15 – Alma Place in Fore Street, now the site of Robbs.
M. No. 12 – Milburn's Yard, now part of St Mary's Wynd
N. No. 13 – Bell's Court, on the east side of the bus station.
O. No. 14 – The yard of the Excelsior Building on Battle Hill.

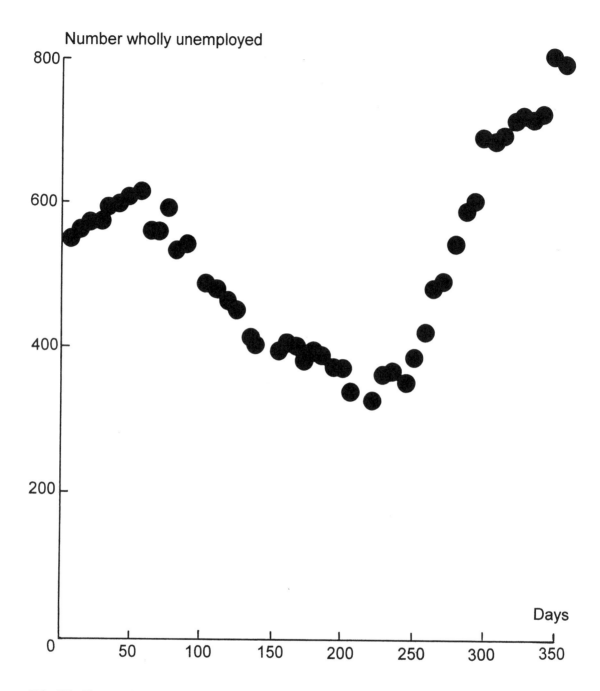

FIG. 55. The weekly number of wholly unemployed in the Hexham Unemployment Area during 1931.

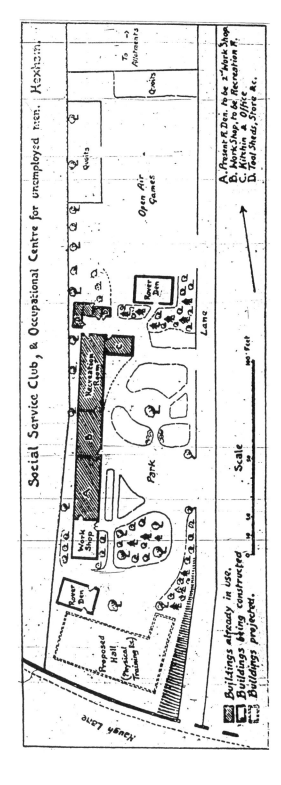

FIG. 56. A sketch plan from the 30 December 1933 issue of the *Hexham Courant* showing the constructional and other work that had been carried out at the Hexham Social Service Club and Occupational Centre at Haugh Lane.

Chapter 19

Support for recreation

Introduction

Organised sport and recreation began to develop significantly in the town in the latter part of the last century (Fig.49). As one would anticipate, those sports in which there is strong physical participation were the earliest to develop organisations and establish facilities of the kind similar to those we know today. William Robb (1882) in his memoir talks about football and cricket on the Seal. Tennis was also played in Hexham but 'seemingly only amongst the aristocrats'. Where those games of tennis took place was not divulged but, about 1887, tennis started to be played on a cement court in the Abbey Grounds (*HC*, suppl. 29.7.1939). The court was established by about 20 members, amongst whom were Jasper Gibson, Wilfrid Gibson, Daniel Jackson, John Nicholson, James Robb and Ralph Harry Robb. The next year, a public meeting led to the renting of the land at Priors Flat and its development for (cricket and tennis) by the Tynedale Athletic Association (Wood, 1988). Tynedale Rugby Club was first formed in 1876, establishing a base for home games at Halliwell Dene, followed by Dene Park in 1903 (*HC* 13.3.1926). The history of Association Football in Hexham is not clear but the author has come across sufficient references in the *Courant* to leave little doubt that the game was flourishing in an organised manner, with the presence of leagues, in the town at the turn of the century.

The more leisurely sports of golf and bowls developed more slowly, almost certainly because both sports require the acquisition and significant alteration of land to produce the requisite facilities. The history of the earliest days of golf in Hexham has been well documented (Barrett, n.d.). Here I focus on the development of bowls, specifically provision of bowling greens, not only because nothing has been written about the history of the sport in the town but also because it provides an insight into the role of the Urban District Council in financing recreational activity in the town in the 1920s and 30s. It is worth noting that during this period that the Council failed to establish a swimming pool and a library.

The start of bowls in Hexham

It is clear from a reference in the *Courant* (*HC* 18.6.1898) that, by the 1890s, the idea of a bowling green for the town was being openly mooted. Next to the tennis court in the Abbey Grounds and Priors Flat were suggested as possible sites. Nothing seems to have been done to proceed the matter, for three years later (*HC* 18.5.1901) we find the *Courant*, stimulated by the fact that Newcastle had opened its eleventh bowling green, lamenting there was still no green in Hexham. Councillor Shield, in what appears to be a somewhat diffident manner, raised the matter in the Urban District Council (*HC* 22. 6. 1901). It was then referred to the Pleasure Grounds Committee but never to re-emerge. Yet again, on the 27 September 1902, the *Courant* raised the issue, this time emphatically.

If Hexham is to become a residential town, this (the bowling green) should be one of its attractions. Keswick has several bowling greens, Tynemouth is equipped with bowling greens, while Newcastle has them in every part of the city

The Urban Council I hear now has the opportunity of providing a bowling green for the town. The three-cornered field between the Board School and the Seal can be purchased from Mr Beaumont and would furnish a capital site.

As will be seen later it is unlikely that the site just mentioned was for sale, certainly not for a bowling green. Nevertheless, the paper correctly assessed the value of a bowling green to the amenities of the town. As has been indicated before, census figures reveal the dramatic decline of leather-based industries in Hexham, there being only 9 glovers and 31 tanners and allied trades in 1891, compared with 125 and 102 respectively in 1851, yet no significant industry came as a replacement. Increasingly, Hexham came to see itself as a health resort and a residential town. The purity of the Ladle Wells water supply that opened in 1889 appears to have catalysed thinking about the town as a health resort. There are many references to this role both explicitly and implicitly in *Hexham Courant* in the first decade of this century. But easy access to Newcastle by rail and the building of houses with modern plumbing also made Hexham attractive residentially. Fig. 40 shows that, between 1896 and 1921, there was considerable house-building in the town, particularly in the south-western parts of Hexham and mostly for the more affluent members of the population. This is discussed further in Chapter 20. The house-building boom was associated with an increase in the rate of population growth of the town (Fig. 51).

It was a letter to the *Courant* (*HC* 27.5.1905) that eventually triggered action that led to the building of a bowling green and an associated club:

Sir - As an occasional visitor to your ancient town with its charming environment and many attractions and knowing how popular it is becoming as a residential and health resort would you kindly allow me to point out that it lags somewhat behind many less favoured rivals in certain particulars notably in the matter of outdoor sports. I do not specially allude to cricket and tennis...... all have not the robustness for these games and many have reached the age to which they no longer appeal, and it is the provision for these of which there seems to be a lack...... [golf] possesses potent attractions for many, yet does not altogether meet the want I have pointed. The game of bowls has a charm of its own and it is a quiet healthy exercise appealing more especially to those who have left youth behind or do not care for violent exercise necessary in other past times. In many of our northern towns bowling is very popular and there should not be a public green in a place like Hexham has often struck me as singular. The Urban Council could easily provide a splendid bowling green on the Seal...... my object in writing this letter is to see if some of the leading men of the town will not take the matter up alike in their own interests and that of visitors like myself...... I am sure if the council would lay the public green its popularity would prove that it had met a felt want and its cost would largely be met out of revenue. If the number of bowlers increased in the same proportion as they have done in other towns after the game has been introduced, a single green would not suffice. I hope the matter will be promptly taken and a good green speedily provided – I am &c., Visitor

There was an immediate response to this letter in the next issue of the *Courant* (*HC* 3.6.1905):

Sir - I...... quite agree with 'Visitor' that a bowling green on the Seal or some other central position would be a great attraction, not only to the residents but to many others who might be induced to spend their holidays in this town, if such a green existed, as there cannot be the slightest doubt as to the popularity of the game. The question is, how can such a green be established? 'Visitor' suggests the Urban Council might establish one. Yes, I thought so at one time and in order to try to rouse interest in the question I some years ago induced Councillor Shield to bring the matter forward at one of the meetings of the Council. Of course, as usual in such cases, the matter was referred to the Pleasure Grounds committee to consider and report. I don't know whether the question was ever considered but no report was rendered, and it is quite evident that if such a green is to be established it will have to be done by private enterprise. I may further state I have been trying for some time to get information as to the probable cost of laying a bowling green but so much depends on the nature of the site and the bower that would have to be erected that I have been unable to get what I consider reliable information. However, if those interested in the formation of a bowling green will kindly send me their names and addresses on or before June 10th I will undertake to arrange a meeting and advise all who reply as above of the date and place of the meeting – I am &c., John Anderson

We know from his obituary (*HC* 19.1.1920) that John Anderson came from Carlisle and was Head of the grocery department of the Co-operative Wholesale Society at West Blandford Street, Newcastle and thus one presumes that he had the required status to take successfully the necessary initiatives to get the bowling club started. There can be no doubt about his standing in the world of bowls. He became a vice-president of the English Bowling Association and, though he never became an international, in 1919 he captained the North against the South in a match at Leicester in 1919. Nor can there be any doubt as to his ability to drive the project forward. At the first meeting (*HC* 1.7.1905), presided over by Mr John Oubridge of Anick House and President of the Portland Bowling Club, Newcastle, in the Abbey (Beaumont) Hotel on 27 June, Anderson presented in very considerable detail the cost of laying down the green, building a bower, purchasing a lawn mower, roller, etc., together with running costs. At the same time he gave an idea as to how the project might be financed through share capital. Though the cost would depend on the nature of the site and the kind of bower they would erect, he thought that a green of ordinary character could be laid out at a cost of £250-320. Other costs, including interest on a loan for the total amount, would bring the total to £500. With fifty members, each buying one guinea shares (entrance fee in subsequent years) and the income from visitors and refreshments, he demonstrated that the annual expenditure could be readily covered. Following discussion about possible sites, a committee of eight was appointed, with John Anderson as secretary *pro tem.*, to take the matter forward.

Inevitably, the key to the success of the project was the purchase of a suitable site. At the next meeting on 1 August (*HC* 5.8.1905), eleven possible sites were identified. Two sites – 'Viewlands', on the Burswell estate and a plot of land situated in Tynedale Terrace – had insufficient area. Two sites in Hencotes belonging to the late Mr Temperley were too costly for purchase and, in any case there seemed little desire to sell. The field adjoining the tennis courts, at Prior's Flat, could be obtained at very favourable terms (£3 per annum for 40 years) and was desirable, being a flat site. But there was no approach to it, except via the cricket ground, and fencing was needed. Another site, for which the leasing situation was similar to the previous one, was located in the Spital Park, 60 yards west of Quatre Bras. There were three sites on the Haining Croft (Elvaston Road) estate, all in the same field, at different levels as one went up the hill. By the time the meeting took place, the middle site was withdrawn. Though the lower site had an area that was nearer the space required, the upper site was preferred for reasons not stated in the report. Finally, there were the Abbey Grounds and Fair Field (where the police station is now located), about which there was optimism at the first meeting. Both sites belonged to W. B. Beaumont, Lord of the Manor. On being approached about the matter, John Kaye, Beaumont's agent, said that both grounds were now ripe for building purposes – certainly in the case of the latter site, this was a real possibility, since Kaye had already been responsible for the Shaftoe Leazes estate across the road. He suggested Tyne Green as an alternative. This latter site was thought unsuitable.

Before I take the story on, it needs to be remembered that the Urban Council were only lessees of the Seal. Though certain activities were allowed to take place, such as the drilling of the Volunteers and pierrot shows, the Council were bound by the conditions of the lease, which as we shall see was a block to building on the Seal. It is almost certain for these reasons that the Seal never came into the deliberations of the bowling green committee.

Discussion indicated that the Haining Croft site and that at Priors Flat were the most preferred. The meeting concluded with it formally agreeing that a bowling club should be formed (with the suggested name of 'Hexham Bowling Club') and that the committee be empowered to secure a site and lay a green.

We hear next about progress of the Bowling Club in a report, in the *Courant* of 17 March, 1906, of the first statutory meeting of members. Then it is clear that the favoured Haining Croft site has not only been chosen but purchased. Dr Duncan Stewart, the Chairman, reported that the green had been completed and that tenders were being asked for the erection of the pavilion. There was a slight hiccup over this building, for the Works Committee of the Urban District Council (*HC* 10.3.1906) did not recommend for approval the first plans for the building submitted by Mr Maxwell. Apparently, the building was to be made of iron and wood. According to the bye-laws, since it was adjoining property, it should be of brick and stone. An amended plan of the building was approved at the next meeting of the Works Committee. Dr Stewart also reported that it was found necessary to build a retaining wall, 'to avoid shrinking of the made-up portion of the green'. Whether that wall is the retaining wall beneath the present north edge of the club's land is not clear. There is uncertainty about the surrounding buildings present when the green was built. 'Overstone' to the south was built in 1897. Of the others, there are indications that the houses, on St George's Road, on the north side of the green had not been built.

On the afternoon of Thursday, 21 June, 'in beautifully fine weather, the new bowling green in Elvaston Road was formally opened by the president of the Bowling Green Company, Dr Stewart, in the presence of a large assemblage of ladies and gentlemen' (*HC* 23.6.1906). The total cost of the green, pavilion, etc., was £1,070, twice that originally anticipated. The reasons for the dramatic increase in cost might have been due to the use of turf from Rockcliff Marsh, Dumfries and Galloway, which John Anderson, in his report to the first meeting (*HC* 1.7.1905), had pointed out was very costly. Indeed, initially he had counselled against using such turf. To meet the cost, £459 had been taken up in shares and £600 had been borrowed on a mortgage. There were between sixty and seventy members. The Club received the seal of approval of the Urban District Council via its Chairman, Mr W. Alexander JP, who presided over the opening, spoke of it being a valuable asset to the town. 'The Bowling Club had done good work for the town that was often done by the town itself' emphasised the realisation that the Urban District Council had a role to play in providing amenities for the town. After other formalities, there was a friendly match between teams chosen by the President and Secretary; that chosen by the former won by 43 shots.

Thereafter the Club, often referred to as the Hexham Elvaston Club, has prospered to this day.

A highlight in its history was the visit of the Australian team in 1912, seemingly through the influence of John Anderson (*HC* 29.6.1912) This visit is commemorated by a Sessile Oak tree planted at the southern end of Abbey Grounds, close to the eastern side of the main path.

But the Hexham Elvaston Club could only fulfil in part the bowling needs of the town. In October 1908, no doubt stimulated by the gift of the Seal to the town by Lord Allendale in the previous July a letter signed by 105 person was sent to the Urban District Council:

> We the undersigned ratepayers of Hexham beg respectfully to approach you with regard to the desirability of providing a bowling green in or near the town of Hexham. We believe it would be a boon to many people, both young and old, if you would see your way clear to grant this application, and we think it would be an attraction to visitors. The Sele [an unusual spelling for the time] would, in our opinion, be a suitable site for the proposed bowling green

The letter went to the Pleasure Grounds Committee, but before sending it there, the Chairman said that the Seal was not a suitable place, with the great amount of recreation going on. It would lead to considerable expense (in saying this he was probably mindful of the fact that earlier the meeting had received a memorial supported by 125 names asking for the re-opening of the golf course at Tyne Green, no longer used as a consequence of the opening of the Spital course). He was also concerned that it would be necessary to enclose the bowling green (HC 3.10.1908). A fortnight later (HC 17.10.1908), the Pleasure Grounds Committee, while approving of the re-opening of the golf course at Tyne Green, 'cannot see their way to advise the council to provide a bowling green on the Seal at present'. The Council approved this recommendation by 5 votes to 4, but it is not clear whether the recommendation was made on financial grounds or because Lord Allendale had placed conditions on his gift to the town. The air of mystery was compounded by a leader in the same issue reporting the Council decision which stated that 'The demand for a public green is so strong and sustained that we have little doubt the public authority will meet it, but, it is hardly fair to unduly drive them at a period of a somewhat perplexing interregnum'. Also the leader stressed that 'The suggestion that a bowling green on the Seal would meet general acceptance is open to some criticism.' In its November 7, 1908, issue, in 'Gossip and Comment' there is an indication of some ground swell of opinion against the Seal being used for bowls. Also, it is categorically stated that Tyne Green is too far away.

The establishment of the Council bowling green

After the War, pressure to have a bowling green in the centre of the town continued on into the 1920s. The purchase of the Abbey Grounds by the Council in 1910, meant that another possible site became available (*HC* 4.6.1910). Efforts were made when the Grounds were landscaped to have a bowling green included. However, the site chosen was an unsuitable one, because it was surrounded by trees that would not only affect the turf but also cut out the light. It seemed better to have the green on the Seal (*HC* 8.6.1910). At the next meeting of the Council (*HC* 6.7.1912), in a discussion of the issue (for which there were costings produced by the Surveyor), there were strong arguments against the idea. Prominent were expense and the desire not to have any part of the Seal partitioned off ('it should be open for the free use of all the ratepayers and not for any particular class'). It was implied that Lord Allendale desired that nothing should be erected on the Seal. The writer of 'Gossip and Comment' reporting on the debate said 'I am inclined to think that the project is indefinitely postponed'. But there were those who lived in hope. When a deputation from the Hexham War Memorial Committee, led by General Sir Loftus Bates, met the Council to finalise the position of the memorial cross, the argument raised by some councillors against the Committee's proposal to have the War Memorial positioned where it now is in the Abbey Grounds was that its presence interfered with the only possible (level) site for a bowling green (and tennis court). It was probably for this very reason that the Council had itself located the position of the memorial in the south-west corner. The public distinction of the deputation, supported by very strong public sentiment, gave the Council little option but to accept what the War Memorial Committee wanted (*HC* 6.11.1920).

Subsequent events in the history of proposals for the use of the Seal leave little doubt that any plans for making it a place for recreation requiring permanent facilities would meet considerable resistance. In 1924 and 1929, the District Council proposed putting tennis courts, plus in 1924 a bowling green on the top of the Seal (football and cricket being played at the bottom). On the first occasion, it seems to have been felt that the third Lord Allendale should be consulted, because of the conditions laid down by his father when giving the Seal to the town. Lord Allendale, even after meeting members of the Pleasure Grounds Committee of the Urban Council, was not in favour of the proposals. Amongst other concerns was his impression that the proposed green was an operation for making money out of visitors (*HC* 10.5.1924). In 1929, proposals came forward for laying six grass tennis courts at the top of the Seal (*HC* 10.8.1929). The Council were mindful of the fact that Lord Allendale had stated with respect to the earlier proposal that, while he was averse to any breaking up of the Seal for sectional interests, he would not object if he could be satisfied that there was a general desire among the inhabitants that the courts should be laid down. He suggested, to obtain an expression of opinion, a Town's meeting should be held (*HC* 21.9.1929). In spite of the fact that the *Courant* had supported the proposals and the Hexham Rotary Club gave well-publicised backing after hearing a spirited talk on 'Playing Fields' from Mr John Baty, clerk to the Council (*HC* 28.9.1929), the Town's Meeting rejected the scheme by 70 votes to 39. At that meeting, Mr Baty read out an extract from the Conveyance (of the Seal) from Lord Allendale to the Urban District Council. It should be noted that a clause, numbered 2 below, of the Conveyance had been made known publicly when the Council considered whether or not it should continue to allow 'sleighing' on the Seal. As far as I am aware, there is no earlier public mention of the clause 3 below.

> 2. The Seal shall be used as a public pleasure ground and recreation ground only and it shall be so used in a quiet and orderly manner, and so that no nuisance or annoyance may be caused in the neighbourhood.
>
> 3. No erection or building shall be made or set upon the Seal except such as shall be appropriate to and necessary for the purposes of a park or pleasure ground or recreation ground, and no such erection shall be made or set up except in such position as shall have been previously approved in writing by the donor or his heirs sequels in estate or assigns and in accordance with a plan and specification which shall have been previously submitted to them and approved in writing by him or them.

These extracts make clear why the Council had needed to be circumspect in making proposals for the use of the Seal. Knowledge of what Mr Baty had read out, plus the desire expressed forcibly, that children should have 'the free right to roam' contributed to the vote against the Council's proposals. However, the death blow was probably the view of Mr Walter Hetherton, the professional of Tynedale Cricket Club that 'the site suggested was one of the worst [for tennis] from a practical point of view' due to the cold east winds in the spring and in the back-end the strong westerly winds.

Fortunately for bowls, by this time, the problem of an additional green in the town had been resolved. The catalyst for change was the availability of land following the purchase of Hexham House and grounds by the District Council in 1926, after they had been offered to the Council for £3,500 by Mr J. E. Tully of Newton Hall, Stocksfield (*HC* 7.8.1926). The offer of Hexham House at a very attractive price was accompanied by a gift of £500 to the Town to be handled by a four leading citizens. The gentlemen concerned were John Baty, Clerk to the Council, Councillors George Ross (Chairman of the Council), J. W. Dent and R. F. Turner. The money was placed at disposal of these four 'for the good work of which they approve for the benefit of Hexham'. 'By good work I mean such as a free library and open space of benefit to all.' In October, the Council unanimously agreed that a bowling green be constructed in the Hexham House grounds, on the site shown by the Surveyor's plan' (*HC* 9.10.1926). By November, the Chairman, Councillor Ross, had turned against the idea (*HC* 6.11.1926) and gave notice that he would move 'that the motion to place a bowling green in the grounds of Hexham House be rescinded'. At the December meeting of the Council (*HC* 11.12.1926) he spoke at length of his antipathy to the whole idea. Essentially his argument was financial, centring on the probable cost of producing a green (£1,000) and a pavilion and the likelihood that fees would not cover running costs. Also 'he was not prepared to argue in favour of recreation for a small section of the community at the expense of the ratepayers generally'. His case was not helped by the fact that he gave a figure for the cost of producing a green, without waiting for estimates. Reading the text of the debate one has the feeling that there was antipathy for Councillor Ross's attempt 'to stop progress for the proposal [which] was carried unanimously by Council only two months ago'. The motion was defeated

A request for tenders to clear the land and build the green went out after the meeting. But in February, the Council considering the tenders 'in committee' decided that 'the proposal be in abeyance till the September meeting' (*HC* 12.2.1927). It was probably fortunate for the project, that of the five members of the Pleasure Grounds Committee, four (Councillors Ainsley, Dent, Emerson and Knight) were themselves bowlers, as was the Surveyor, W. G. Landale. Certainly these four councillors had shown themselves strongly behind the project at the December meeting. The other member, Councillor Thrower, could have been equally supportive but we have no clear information on that point. At any rate, the Committee had no compunction about bringing the proposal forward again for the September meeting of the Council. After considerable debate and two amendments attempting to stall progress, it was decided by 6 votes to 4 that 'the construction of a bowling green be proceeded with' (*HC* 8.10.1927).

A final attempt to prevent the bowling green being built was made by Councillor Ross at the next meeting of the Council, when the tender for building the green was to be accepted (*HC* 8.10.1927). But any argument that the project would be very expensive fell rather flat, when it became clear that the tender to be accepted, that of Messrs Welch and Darlington, was £625. Given that the project would probably get Mr Tully's £500, it would mean only an expenditure of £125. Indeed, Mr Tully approved of the idea that his money should be spent in this way (*HC* 12.11.1927). Building of the green took place in 1928; it was formally opened by Mr Tully on 3 May, 1929 (*HC* 11.5.1929). The opening was commemorated by a match between the Council and Hexham (Elvaston) Bowling Club, the former winning by 73 shots to 55, though the team was largely made up of Bowling Club members.

In the 15 June, 1929 issue of the *Courant*, there was a glowing account of the success of the green. Thus:

> The Hexham House green is so centrally situate that it was assured of a fair measure of support, but its popularity is such that there is rarely a vacant rink after shopping hours. This is all to the good, for the business man and the shop assistant can indulge in one of the least exhaustive and pleasantest recreations possible to imagine amid the most delightful surroundings.

At the end of the first season on 4 September, 'by kind permission of the Hexham Urban District Council, a largely attended meeting was held in the Council Chambers...... under the presidency of Councillor J. A. Smith, chairman *pro tem.*, when it was unanimously decided to form a bowling club...... to be known as the Hexham House Bowling Club' (*HC* 7.9.1929). Most persons who played on the green were members of the Club, however the green was open to the general public and visitors frequently play there.

Swimming pool

Certainly in recent centuries, both the Tyne and the fleam that ran from it to the mill on the eastern side of the bridge across the Tyne have been attractive to bathers (*see* Chapter 14). A measure of the enthusiasm for swimming in the River was the formation in 1878 of the Hexham Rowing and Swimming Club (*HC* 26.11.1878). However, though I have come across plenty of evidence that rowing was a successful activity, I have not been successful in finding out further about the swimming side of the Club's activities. Nevertheless, in the 1920s, a town guide spoke about 'Excellent facilities [for bathing] are provided at the Green.' At around this time, toddlers could use the paddling pool carved out of the Cowgarth Burn, which gave them physical safety but now one does wonder about the purity of the water if any were to be ingested (*HC* 14.3.1936). A correspondent to the 27 May 1933 issue of the Hexham Courant expressed a similar view about the quality of the Tyne water, believing it should be labelled 'poison'. He also said that, while one cannot bathe from the north bank of the river; it was 'embarrassing to strip on the south bank'. The Tyne was probably safer than it is today, since photographic evidence shows that the banks shelved more gradually towards the centre of the river (*HC* 14.3.1936). Gravel extraction from the riverbed in the 1950s and 60s is probably responsible for the disappearance of anything like a distinct shoreline to be replaced by steep banks (Archer, 1992).

Today, no one would think of bathing in the Tyne, feeling it to be dangerous. Nevertheless, scattered references indicate there has always been a concern for safety for those entering or trying to cross the river, be it in the warmer months or during winter when the river might freeze. Thus we learn from the following minute of the meeting of the Local Board of Health on 27 December 1870:

> In consequence of the Frozen state of the River a considerable number of persons skate daily upon it and the danger of Accident is thereby increased Mr Ellis kindly offered the loan of Planks and ropes which were gratefully accepted by the Board. The Board to make good any damage which may occur to these implements That the Blacksmith at the Brewery [almost certainly Bridge End] be requested to take charge of them.

There is evidence that, in the 1920s and probably the 30s, life saving equipment was installed on Tyne Green (HUDC 7.7.1924).

Throughout the first part of the 20th century, there was continuing concern about people learning to swim. Indeed, in 1916 and 17, a Mrs Hutchinson gave swimming lessons on Tyne Green. It appears that a cabin, to be used as a 'dressing room', was erected there (HUDC 8.8.1917). The concern about learning to swim was expressed in the several requests for the building of a swimming pool. The first move came from within the Council, when Councillor Young proposed that 'The Council take into consideration the advisability of [amongst other matters] providing a Public Open Air Swimming Bath on Tyne Green.' In spite of this proposal and external pressure, it was 1930 before the Council instructed the Surveyor to prepare plans, specifications and estimates for an Open Air Swimming Bath on Tyne Green' (HUDC 3.11.1930). On 6 July 1931, the Surveyor submitted a sketch plan; consideration of it was deferred. Then the Pleasure Grounds Committee recommended the plan in principle but recommended that it be sited in the north-east corner of the Seal, only to have the matter deferred by the Council for one month so that an estimate of costs be made (HUDC 4.8.1931; *HC* 8.1931). As one might have anticipated from our knowledge of the failure of a bowling green on the Seal in 1924 due to the antipathy of Lord Allendale (see Chapter 14), there were concerns that he would in similar manner not sanction the proposal. However, it was financial considerations that led to the proposal being further deferred (*HC* 12.9.1931).

Similar attempts to get a swimming bath built continued in the early 1930s. Tyne Green remained a favoured site but there was a proposal to build the bath in the Abbey Grounds behind St Aidan's Presbyterian Church (Fig. 50). The site was preferred to Tyne Green because the latter was too far away and because a bath in the centre of town could be used for skating in winter. At the same time, it was suggested that the bath could be sited on the Common Bank, presumably on the flat land by the Cockshaw Burn (*HC* 18.8.1934). In the end, financial considerations killed off all attempts. Thus in 1936, the Council having resolved by seven votes to one 'that this Council consider a Swimming Bath desirable' instructed the Surveyor to bring forward plans for a bath to be built on either Tyne Green or the Common Bank (HUDC 6.7.1936). The scheme was realistic in that it included plant for water purification and took in the need for upkeep and maintenance; it was to cost £4,000. The Council baulked at the sum and agreed not proceed further with the matter. It was to be another 38 years before Hexham got its swimming pool in the converted wool warehouse of Henry Bell in Gilesgate.

A public library

We are fortunate in that the library provision in Hexham in the 19th century has been well documented by Day (1987; NRO/4607). Two libraries standout – that of the Mechanics' Institute (1828-1892) and Pruddah's Circulating Library (1826-1868), the former provided more substantial literature, while the latter provided somewhat lighter fare. Our knowledge of the Mechanics' Institute Library has been subsequently enhanced by the diligent research of Jenkins (2002). The Hexham Mechanics' Literary and Scientific Institution (the full name), which was founded on 15 July 1825, together with its library, had several locations, commencing with the Blue Bell Yard and finally in the upper floors above the present 'Sewing Box' at the top of Hall Stile Bank. Table 26 presents an analysis of the 1849 catalogue of the Institute's library holdings. As one can see there is a good cross-section of volumes devoted to serious topics. When the Institute closed for good on 9 February 1892, because of lack of support, the library contained over 2000 volumes that were sold off by auction later that year. The closure was a loss to the Hexham community. William Robb cannot have been the only person to have felt that the presence of the Mechanics Institute with its library had a beneficial effect on the town (Robb,1882).

TABLE 26. *A breakdown of the holdings in 1849 of the library of the Hexham Mechanics' and Scientific Institution (Davis, 1987).*

Subject	No. of volumes	% total
Mathematics and engineering	40	2.5
Chemistry, electricity and natural history	151	9.5
Architecture and antiquities	14	0.9
Geography; voyages and travel	164	10.3
History and biography	370	23.2
Philosophy; Education and miscellaneous	315	19.7
Poetry and drama	91	5.7
Encyclopedias and dictionaries	51	3.2
Magazines and reviews	340	21.3
Novels	60	3.7
Total	1596	100

There were other libraries in Hexham, apart from the two mentioned above. Almost all were run by booksellers but few lasted more than a decade. Such small privately run libraries continued to function well into the 20ᵗʰ century. Two stand out – those of Pegg in Priestpopple (started in 1910) and Denton in Battle Hill (started in 1924 in a stationers) lasted until after the 1939-45 War. They were joined in 1931 by Boots the chemist with its national chain of subscription libraries with two categories of readers, those who paid a higher subscription and got first choice of new books and those who paid less and had to wait. Privately run libraries almost certainly charged their borrowers.

Since 1850, as a result of the Public Libraries Act (13 & 14 Vict., c. 65) borough councils could spend money on building and furnishing a library (but not on books). The Act was restricted to boroughs with a population of more 10,000 and any decision of a council had to be ratified by a referendum of two-thirds of the burgesses, thus did not apply to Hexham. Nevertheless, the Act was significant in that it established the principle of a local authority being responsible for library provision. It is only in the 20ᵗʰ century that we learn of moves towards a public lending library. The first glimmerings come in 1902, when it appears that Alderman Robert Stainthorpe was in communication with Andrew Carnegie about library provision in Hexham. Presumably, Carnegie was willing to provide some of the funding but it seems never to have come to anything. More specifically, at the instigation of Councillor Green, it was decided to establish a free library (HUDC 2.8.1918). The proposal in all probability resulted from the possibility that the Urban District Council might purchase what was called the 'Town Hall buildings', now the Queen's Hall, where presumably the library could be housed. However the idea came to naught, as the Hexham Entertainments Co. purchased the building (Johnson & Jennings, 2000).

Though from time to time there were letters in the *Courant* containing arguments for free library provision, they fell on deaf ears. The situation was to change as the County Council started to take a lead. The 1919 Public Libraries Act (9 & 10 Geo. 5, c. 93) gave County Councils the power to establish public libraries and, at the same time, removed the limitation imposed on borough councils to a penny rate of the amount that could be spent on libraries. The Northumberland Library Service developed first in the rural areas, stimulated by financial support in 1923 from the Carnegie United Kingdom Trust (Taylor, 1989). A major development was the mobile library scheme. In 1928, it was decided to expand library provision to the urban districts. On 3 November, the Clerk to the Council reported a communication from the Director of Education to the effect that

> The Carnegie Trustees had announced that for the period 1931-35 they propose to set aside a considerable sum for the assistance of Authorities who decide a systematic forward policy in regard to the establishment of library facilities in their industrial and residential centres. It was impracticable to deal with certain Urban Districts on the same footing as Rural areas of the County and the proposals of the Carnegie trustees appeared to afford a solution to some of the difficulties. The Trust indicated that the only satisfactory method of dealing with urban areas was to set up a branch library with 'full-time' paid staffs, substantial collections of both non-fiction and fiction, a selection for children, table and chairs for readers and a modern issuing counter. The Trustees were prepared to assist with initial capita; expenditure...... (*HC*

8.11.1930)

In order to carry the scheme forward, the County Council would levy a 1½d rate.

The proposal was received by the Urban District Council in a jaundiced manner. Councillor Emerson moved that the proposal 'lie on the table', i.e., that it not be considered. He did not think the town could afford the proposed rate. The majority of councillors were of like mind. Councillor Knight speaking about an amendment (that representatives should meet the Trustees) said that

> He failed to see any enthusiasm of the youth of today to grab any further education. They were building new schools and training certain scholars in certain special trades but he wondered if the finished product was worth all the money being spent.

The *Courant* was scathing about the attitude of the Council, complaining that it had showed a lack of judgement and indicated it had 'shown a singular lack of the progressive instinct'. The paper felt that a library was one of those amenities of a town like Hexham whose cost should not be the primary consideration. Interestingly, Haltwhistle almost immediately took advantage of the scheme, probably because of the availability of space for the library in the building of the Mechanics Institute.

The council remained of like mind until 1939. In years from 1936, the issue of a public library for Hexham re-surfaced from time to time. The Council debated the matter with full consideration in December 1936 but, in perceived need for financial probity, deferred the matter until March the following year (*HC* 12.12.1936). When the time came to consider the estimates in 1937, any chance of funding the development of a library disappeared beneath the perceived greater need to fund such items as road repairs and the provision of additional street lighting. Even the housing budget was under fire. According to Councillor Cullen

> I think Hexham has spent sufficient on housing. I don't see where in the name of saints in heaven the money is coming from for overcrowding or anything else.

There were further financial difficulties in 1938, when concern about the outstanding loan debt of £251,743 surfaced – equal to £28 per head of population (*HC* 13.2.1938). In July 1939, the Director of Education for Northumberland enquired as to whether or not the Council wished to change its mind about library provision (*HC* 8.7.1939). There are indications that the Council might have done so but war intervened and other more pressing matters surfaced.

Hexham got its County Library in 1945 when it opened in the north wing of the Queen's Hall. In 1946, Mr and Mrs J. W. Brough of Thornley Gate, Allendale, presented a library of 12,000 books to the townspeople of Hexham to commemorate the Allied Victory in the 1939-45 War. The library was housed in the Moot Hall and the formal presentation in the presence of Lord Allendale took place Tuesday, 2 November 1948 (*HC* 29.10.1948). The Library was opened to subscribers on Monday, 8 November. The Library was absorbed into the stock of the County Library when it moved in 1948 into its present position in the Queen's Hall, with the local collection being renamed the Brough Local Studies Collection.

Chapter 20

Housing

Introduction

Over the period under consideration, the population of Hexham grew gradually (Fig. 51), at a much slower rate than that of the United Kingdom. If we consider the rate of growth from 1801 to 1931, it declines after 1831, the slower rate of growth continuing until 1891. After that date, the rate increases until the start of the 1914-18 War. Following the war, the rate of population growth dropped to the lowest value for the whole period. The increase in population between 1891 and 1914 was matched by a boom in house-building, very considerably helped in 1889 by the new supply of water from Ladle Wells. As one can see from Table 27, between 1891 and 1901, the amount of house building is four times that of the previous decade. Between 1901 and 1911, the number of houses doubles yet again. The rate of building drops between 1911 and 1921, no doubt due to the 1914-18 War. From 1921 to 1931, the increase in the number of houses in the town is due to the building in both public and private sectors, predominantly the former.

TABLE 27. *Figures from censuses for the number of houses in Hexham allowing estimates of the amount of house-building in each decade from 1841 until 1931 and in the twenty years from 1931 to 1951 (Jennings, 2000).*

Year	Inhabited	Uninhabited	Total	Built in the preceding decade
1841	693	29	722	
1851	667	22	689	-33*
1861	740	45	785	96
1871	840	57	897	112
1881	914	66	980	83
1891	984	52	1036	56
1901	1298	–	1298	262
1911	1652	82	1734	436
1921	1896	81	1977	243
1931	2101	86	2187	210
1951	2705	70	2775	588

*At least part of this decline in the number of houses can be accounted for by the removal of property round the Abbey (Jennings, 2003).

A map of the census areas (Fig. G) for Hexham shows clearly that the areas where there was most overcrowding incorporated Gilesgate, Market Street, St Mary's Chare and Fore Street. Overcrowding was associated with buildings that were mostly poorly maintained and without proper sanitation. Examples of the horrors of such housing, which extended into the 1930s, have been given by

Jennings (1998). The Medical Officer's concern about the poor quality of much of the housing has already been referred to in Chapter 15. However, we must turn to census data for a quantitative picture. Table 28 shows that as much as 55% of the population could be living in four rooms or less, many in overcrowded conditions. In both 1891 and 1921, an average of nearly three persons could be living in one room.

TABLE 28. *The number of tenements containing 1,2,3 or 4 rooms and the number of individuals living in such sets of rooms in Hexham in 1891 and 1921, as given in the published summary information relating to the two censuses. The average number of individuals found in each set of rooms has been calculated from the census figures. It needs to be noted that, for the 1891 census, the Registrar-General established the criterion of overcrowding as more than two persons to a room (Jennings, 2000).*

Number of rooms forming habitation	Number of tenements with this number of rooms		Total number of individuals in this number of rooms		Average (and maximum) number of individuals found in this number of rooms	
	1891	1921	1891	1921	1891	1921
1	179	164	490	435	2.74 (9)	2.65
2	328	348	1454	1386	4.43 (10)	3.98
3	283	397	853	1721	4.66 (11)	4.33
4	250	311	683	1339	4.55 (16)	4.31
Total	840	1220	3480	4881		
%			58.7	55.2		
(population)			(5932)	(8843)		

The situation for those living in these terrible properties was exacerbated by the lack of alternative accommodation. For those at the very bottom of the pecking order, i.e., those in unskilled jobs, movement out of Hexham was probably the only way to obtain better living conditions. The cheaper end of the new housing built between 1891 and 1914 went to those with jobs providing sufficient money to pay for the rent and to support a standard of living appropriate to the better living conditions. Table 29 gives information from the 1901 census about the employment of the head of household in the recently built four roomed (Tyneside) flats in Kingsgate (Higgins,1995). Finances were almost certainly helped by the small number of children in the great majority of families in these flats and by the presence of more than one person bringing money into the household. There could be up to eight persons in the household. Though a large number in a flat by today's standards, it does not constitute overcrowding in the official sense.

The 19ᵗʰ Century and prior to the 1914-18 War

There were fairly frequent inspections by the Medical Officer of Health and the Inspector of Nuisances of the more insanitary properties within the town. They reported to the Local Board of Health/Urban District Council and details can be obtained from the minutes or reports to the *Hexham Courant.* However, the best quantitative picture of the housing conditions

TABLE 29. *Information from the 2001 Census about the occupation of the heads of the household living in the flats in Kingsgate. Occupants refers to those in the household other then the head (and his wife, if present). A, refers to adults who may or may not be the offspring of the head; B, boarder; C, children under 18 years of age; * indicates that the person is in employment.*

Number	Occupation	Occupants	Number	Occupation	Occupants
1	Platelayer N.E.R.	No C +1 B	17	Tanner	2C*
2	Draper's peddler	2C + 2A (1*)	18	Draper's assistant	2C
3	Dressmaker	No C + 1*	19	No employment[2]	2C*
4	Postman	1C + 2A (1*)	20	No employment[3]	1C*
5	Joiner	No C + 2A	21	Dyer and cleaner	1A* + 1C
6	Garment dyer	1C + 1A	22	Seedsman	1C
7	Fellmonger	4C	23	Mason	3C
8	Locomotive fireman N.E.R.	4C	24	Grocer's assistant	1C
9	No occupation[1]	4C* + 2C	25	House painter	4C
10	Glazer	2C	26	Platelayer	1C +1B
11	General carter	1C	27	Sanitary labourer	1C + 1B
12	Domestic gardener	2C* + 5C	28	Railway clerk	4C + 1A* +IB
13	Stonemason	3C	28	Compositor	No C
14	Painter	2C	30	Undermanager coal mine	2C
15	Corn miller	2C* + 4C	31	General labourer[4]	1C + 4A* + 1A
16	General house painter	3C	32	Assistant schoolmaster	1C

[1]Four children in employment – three working in a laundry, one a groom.
[2]Two children in employment – assistant schoolmaster and baker's apprentice.
[3]Son a compositor.
[4]Four children also in employment.

is to be found in a detailed report by 'Inspector' (as the report has it, otherwise Nurse Spurr) in 1911. The report, although covering much of the town, focuses on properties in the valley below the town and in the Cockshaw area. It indicates that the great majority of properties were seemingly in reasonable condition. In the centre of the town, e.g., in Back Street, houses are without through circulation of air, due to being back to back or because of the proximity of other buildings. Surprisingly, only a few were considered damp and only one property (31 Gilesgate Bank) was thought to be in poor condition, the roof letting in water. This particular property, a tenement, was inadequate in other ways. Of the seven flats, five consisted of only one room, the remaining two having two rooms. Of the one-room flats, one contained four persons and another three persons. There were two toilets for the property – one toilet for four families. A number of properties were considered to be unclean. However, it is the inadequate toilet facilities particularly in the older properties that is most striking (Table 30). It is only in the newest properties, e.g., Argyl, Cecil, Diamond, Garden, Prior, Spittle (*sic*) and Vine terraces, that families have their own toilet. The flats comprising Eilansgate Terrace come into the same category in terms of age but here one toilet had to be shared by two families, presumably the upper flat and the one below.

TABLE 30. *The number of families sharing one toilet in the older areas of the Hexham as found in the 1911 sanitary report of Nurse Spurr (NRO/LHU/BI & B2). Because of the difficulty of extracting information from the data, the figures below must be considered somewhat approximate.*

Families per toilets	2	3	4	5	6	7	8	9
No. of families	51	21	15	9	9	0	2	1

It has to be said that the toilet facilities for some of the older properties might often have been even worse had not, at a much earlier date, the Urban District Council stepped in to ameliorate an unsatisfactory sanitary situation. This is demonstrated by two minutes of the Health Committee of the Urban District Council, that followed a report of Dr John Jackson on the presence in 'The Mystery' of metal trough closets ('engraved in filth') and which needed to be replaced:

> Council to procure one of Day's Patent Waste Closets and place it in the Mystery yard and that the owner of these premises be required to procure another closet and have it placed there (HUDC 24.6.1895)

> It is recommended that water closets in accordance with the plans of the Surveyor be constructed in the 'Mystery' and adjoining yard at an estimated cost of £36 and that the cost of such works be declared private improvement expenses and be repayable with interest at 4% by the owner over a period of eight years (HUDC 5.8.1895)

Following the formation of the Hexham Local Board of Health, inspection of the town with respect to its sanitary condition became routine. Inspections when carried out might be by the Surveyor, the Inspector of Nuisances or even by Board members. Later, the Medical Officer of Health took an active role. However, while overall the information gives a snap-shot of the sanitary conditions in the poorer parts of the town, there is no quantitative information to help us properly assess the magnitude of the sanitary problems. We are fortunate that someone, it is not clear who, between

1913 and 1915, carried out what seems to have been a methodical inspection of properties within the Hexham Urban District such that one obtains a quantitative picture with reference to the state of housing in the District (Table 31).

TABLE 31. *Figures for problems concerned with housing in the older parts of Hexham obtained from the three year's data in the Inspector's Report Book. (NRO/LHU/H3/B3). The identity of 'inspector' is not known.*

Year	Housing		
	Structural defects	Unfit for Habitation	
1913	19	9	
1914	17	8	
1915	11	3	
	Water supply		
	Insufficient	Burst pipes	Defective taps
1913	6	59	58
1914	8	34	30
1915	–	41	20
	Conveniences (w.c.s)		
	Structural defects	Insufficient	Foul
1913	114	4	26
1914	88	8	33
1915	84	12	55

The above figures presented above, together with the figures for overcrowding within Hexham (Table 28), leave one in no doubt that many dwellings deserved demolition and the occupants housed in more sanitary conditions. Without going into detailed comparisons, the housing conditions in Hexham throughout the 19th century, and at the start of 20th, were as bad in Hexham as anywhere in the North-East (Jennings, 2000). Something needed to be done. With the passing of the Public Health Act (38 & 39 Vict., c. 55) in 1875, it became possible to get an unsanitary property closed under. The closure order was made through the Petty Sessional Court that, if agreed, prohibited the use of the house for human habitation. Closure orders were used in a small number of cases. Further they could be cancelled, if the court was satisfied that it had been rendered fit for habitation. Demolition of a property given a closure order required a resolution from the Council, the owner could object and he might be allowed a further opportunity to put the property into a fit state (Housing of the Working Classes Act 1890; 53 & 54 Vict., c. 70). A major difficulty facing the Urban District Council was the provision of accommodation for those displaced by demolition. As I have indicated, the persons so displaced were unlikely to be able to afford the accommodation provided by the private sector. John Ainsley opposed closure orders for this reason, even though only a few orders were proposed.

In the second half of the 19th century, legislation was passed by Parliament to allow local authorities to build housing. The Acts are as follows (Pooley, 1996):

1. Labouring Classes Lodging Houses Act (Shaftesbury Act), 1851 (14 & 15 Vict., c. 34) This permitted local authorities to purchase land and erect lodging houses.
2. Labouring Classes' Dwelling Houses Act, 1866 (29 & 30 Vict., c. 28) This permitted local authorities to borrow money for the purchase of sites.
3. Artizans' and Labourers' Dwellings Act (Torrens Act), 1868 (31 & 32 Vict., c. 130) This encouraged clearance of insanitary property but there was no provision for rebuilding by the local authority.
4. Artizans' and Labourers' Dwellings Improvements Act (Cross Act), 1875 (38 & 39 Vict., c. 36) This permitted local authorities to clear insanitary areas and build labourers' dwellings for later resale.
5. Housing of the Working Classes Act (1890) This amended and consolidated the various Acts passed previously by Parliament. In particular, Part III of the Act allowed local authorities to build lodging houses for the working classes, including separate houses or cottages, whether containing one or more tenements. Cottages might include gardens of no more than half an acre, provided the value of the gardens shall not exceed £3 of an annual rental.

The 1851 Act was largely a dead-letter from the beginning, being before the creation of sanitary authorities in 1872. Thereafter, clearance of insanitary properties was be-devilled by the matter of compensation. Not only could the property be valued at a generous level for its purchase from the owners but there could also be liberal compensation to them for the forced deprivation of their rights. Not surprisingly, local authorities baulked at paying large sums to owners, particularly as the people dispossessed had to be housed near the clearance site. The 1890 Act remedied this problem by explicitly directing arbitrators to base their estimates on 'fair market value' and to allow for defective sanitation and dilapidation. Nor were owners to receive their customary allowance for compulsory purchase (Bruce, 1961).

Hexham was late on the scene with respect to slum clearance; seemingly the 1890 Act initially did not seem to enter the collective consciousness of the Local Board of Health. However, in November 1899, the Council adopted the Small Dwellings Acquisition Act (62 & 63 Vict., c. 44) and in April 1900 Part 3 of the Housing for the Working Classes Act. The former Act empowered the local authority to advance money to a resident occupier of any house (not exceeding £400 in value) in the area for the purpose of enabling him to acquire the ownership of the house. What the latter Act allowed is given in 5 above. The adoption of these Acts seemed to trigger action by the Urban District Council. In the 24 November 1900 issue of the *Hexham Courant,* the leading article indicated that the Council intended to erect some sixteen workmen's houses in a field in Wanless Lane being purchased from the representatives of Dr Thomas Stainthorpe, who had died the previous year. It was also stated that 'as public bodies move slowly it will probably be into next year before these cottages are erected.' Indeed these houses were never erected as planned. The matter of the Council providing houses using the above Acts was debated nearly ten years later (*HC* 19. 2.1910). The matter was deferred for three months but there is no indication that it surfaced again in the business of the Council. Doubtless, financial considerations were responsible. At the very time when the matter could have been brought forward for debate, the Council was deciding not to purchase the Abbey Grounds because of expense.

However, the Council could not avoid censure from the Local Government Board as is seen from this extract from Assistant Secretary, Nathan T. Jerrard, writing about the annual report for 1911 of the Medical Officer of Health, so far as it related to the housing conditions in the district:

> The Board directs me refer to the statements in the report as to the difficulty in dealing with unsanitary property owing to the lack of other suitable dwellings for persons who would be displaced and to state that these statements are borne out by the report of the Board's medical inspector, Dr Farrar, after his visit to the urban district on September [in fact on 4 October] 1911. I am to enquire what steps the District Council propose to take in the matter and in particular whether they have considered the advisability of taking action under Part III of the Housing Of the Working Classes Act, 1890, as amended by the Housing, Town Planning, etc. Act of 1909 (*HC* 3.11.1912).

The Chairman's response was that 'there were many places in their district which were not very creditable to Hexham...... the Council would endeavour to go into these matters'. However, little was done, in spite of a number of letters from the Local Government Board enquiring about progress on the housing front. Nevertheless, the first faltering steps towards solving the housing problems of Hexham were taken in 1914 when the Housing Committee proposed a scheme for the purchase of the field to the east of the Workhouse, with draft plans for the layout of houses on the field, produced by the Surveyor. Though the Council did not wish to proceed with the scheme, it was taken up after the war, when conditions for house-building had changed very much for the better.

Post-1914-18 War

The history of urban housing in the inter-war years is complicated (Daunton, 1984) but there can be little doubt about the great expansion of local authority housing in the U.K. in general and Hexham in particular. As will be seen, Hexham Urban District Council was able to forge ahead with new house building, essentially because of financial aid from central government. Nevertheless, the very positive motivation of the Council to achieve a solution to the town's housing problems also played its part in the process.

With the commencement of peace, there was little doubt in the minds of many in Hexham that something significant must done to solve the housing problems. The Medical Officer of Health, Dr John Jackson in a report to the Urban District Council set the scene as to what would have to be done and the problems facing the Local Authority:

> The question of housing is more acute than ever and I sincerely hope that if you do not voluntarily move quickly in this matter the permissive 'may' which I fear is frequently read 'may not' by local authorities, will, by the legislation now in progress be replaced by the compulsory 'must'. I am aware that many difficulties have to be overcome, the awakening of the public has come at an embarrassing moment in the history of the nation, with its future wealth mortgaged by the past war, and a shortage of all necessary materials but we must make still heavier drafts on our credit in order to cut out what has been described as a cancer which menaces our national existence. Unless we master the housing question there can be no real improvement, material and spiritual, in the people of this country. The slums cannot be reformed; they must be removed. Bad houses herd disease and appreciably shorter life; cramped tenements

occupied by 4, 5, or 6 and more human beings create festering sores, which are not only perilous to the community generally but a source of economic loss to put the matter on no higher plane (*HC* 10.5.1919).

The *Hexham Courant* pointed out that, as well as the need to get rid of slum property there were also problems for private housing, quoting from a letter:

> The housing problem is one that is engaging the minds of many people at the present time. In the vicinity of Hexham houses are not to be had for love or money, and a number of tenants have been put to no end of trouble and annoyance by finding that their houses have been sold by their landlord without having the option of purchase. There is also overcrowding and the death-rate per thousand is far from satisfactory. Hexham is not the only town that is faced with this important problem. The land adjacent to towns is mostly in the hands of owners who ask a prohibitive price for the carrying out of a housing scheme. Yet in looking round the town of Hexham I find there are some 20-30 acres of land lying to the west of Loughbrow and running parallel to the main road from Hexham to Dipton (*HC* 19.5.1919)

Hexham initiated its housing programme underpinned by two Parliamentary Acts:
1. Housing, Town Planning &c. Act (Addison Act), 1919 (9 Geo. V, c. 35)
This Act made it a duty of local authorities to conduct, within three months, a survey of their housing needs and submit plans to remedy any shortage. The work was to be supervised by the Ministry of health through a Housing Commissioner in each of eleven regions.
The financial liability of Local Authorities was limited to the product of one penny in the pound on the rates; the residual cost was to be borne by the Exchequer.
2. Housing (Additional Powers) Act, 1919 (9 & 10 Geo. V, c. 99)
Under this Act, houses built by private enterprise in compliance with certain building conditions were eligible for a lump-sum subsidy (in practice £130-£260).

Before plans with respect for housing needs had been drawn up, indeed, even before the war ended, the Council was in pursuit of land to purchase for house building. The unsuccessful attempts of the Council to gain the necessary land can be easily summarised:

i) The land adjoining the Workhouse that had been put before the Council before the war (HUDC 2.9.1918 & 2.12.1918). The proposal was turned down by the Local Government Board because there was uncertainty about the cost of acquiring the land (HUDC 8.4.1919).
ii) Land at Craneshaugh (the location of which is uncertain) was turned down by the Housing Commissioner, as being unsuitable, e.g., dealing with sewage would be difficult. Further, numerous ratepayers petitioned against the development, not apparently against local authority housing per se, but because of the distance from the centre of the town and railway station and the steepness of site for building purposes (HUDC 2.2.1920 & *HC* 7.2.1920).
iii) Land owned by the North-East Railway Company in Maiden's Walk, originally purchased by it in 1899 to build 41 houses for its employees. The Council planned to buy the land for housing on 16 March 1920, the eventual purchase not being completed until 7 August 1923. It was not used immediately for housing; no indication was given as to why.
iv) A request to Lord Allendale to use Fairfield (then being used for allotments as a result of the war) for housing was met with the response from his lawyers that he would take steps

to repossess the land and sell it for (private) building purposes (HUDC 16.3.1920).

Finally, it was reported at the Council meeting of 6 April 1920 that 'negotiations for the purchase of Land at Peth Head had been placed in the hands of the District Valuer.' On 3 May it was agreed to purchase the land for £2550. Thereafter, events moved quickly. The Housing Commissioner gave provisional approval, the Ministry of Health approved a loan of £2700 to purchase the land and the architects, J. R. & L. E. Hetherington drew up plans for the site. At the 16 November meeting it was reported that the Housing Commissioner had agreed to the erection of 68 houses being built at Peth Head by Mr J. E. Hamilton. Nevertheless, there were still delays due to the loan not coming through and the difficulty in obtaining an adequate supply of bricks. Indeed with respect to the latter, Councillors visited Seghill and Gateshead to look at the 'cement system of construction' of houses. Seemingly, they were not impressed as they indicated that the Council should stick with brick. In spite of these problems, the Chairman of the Council, Robert Richardson, cut the first sod on 1 January 1921 (*HC* 15.1.1921). The estate seems to have been completed towards the end of 1922; the loan required for the completion was £8,000. Houses were allotted to tenants in three batches as houses were completed. Ex-service men with families were to be given preference in the allocation procedure (HUDC 26.9.1920). This could well account for the fact that when addresses of those applying were given, and that was the case in the third batch, they indicate that a number of the new tenants came from properties that were of respectable quality, e.g, Burswell Avenue, Kingsgate Terrace, Millfield Terrace, Spital Terrace. It is not clear the extent to which tenants came from dwellings considered to be insanitary but addresses like Back Row and Milburn's Yard suggest that some might have done. Even so, it is unlikely that there were many, if any, tenants from these latter properties in view of the weekly cost of renting a house on the estate (9s rent + rates of c 5s.9d) (*HC* 12.11.1921). At a later date, there was talk of selling some of the houses (*HC* 11.3.1922) and, indeed in 1925, the Ministry of Health agreed to sales, but only to the then present occupiers and then provided that the price had been approved by the District Valuer (HUDC 2.2.1925).

The houses at Peth Head today still form a significant part of Hexham's housing stock, eighty years after they were built. An aerial view shows the location of the Peth Head estate and the other Council housing estates subsequently built in the same area (Fig. 52). However, at the time of their erection, the houses at Peth Head were compared unfavourably with much older houses in the town which had stone walls (0.5 m thick), the walls of Peth Head houses being 'hollow' and 0.27 m thick (*HC* 9.12.1922). Details of the extent of the Peth Head estate and others established by the Council in the interwar years are given in Table 32.

As the Council moved towards getting the Peth Head scheme off the ground, it finalised its housing survey. It calculated that 225 houses were required. However, the Housing Commission put the figure very much higher, namely 418. On the basis of the evidence of the Commission, the Council revised its survey to 350 houses and resolved to acquire land to complete the scheme (HUDC 3.5.1920). A number of councillors did not readily acquiesce to that figure. Essentially they were worried that, although the Council were only liable for a rate of a penny in the pound, a change of government might leave the Council saddled with the whole cost. On the other hand, 350 houses meant the Council had to generate and maintain a significant momentum if the number was to be achieved over not too long a time scale.

Scheme	Number of houses	Net weekly rent
Peth Head (3 bedroom)	68	7s.6d
Round Close*	24	6s.6d
Round Close* (3 bedroom)	24	6s.6d
Round Close* (3 bedroom)	70	5s.6d
Garden Terrace	6	5s.0d
White Cross (2 bedroom)	64	5s.0d
Chareway (2 bedroom)	14	5s.0d
Round Close* (2 bedroom)	66	5s.0d
Round Close* (2 bedroom)	128	5s.0d
Chareway (flats)	40	5s.0d
Total	504	

*It seems that here Round Close encompasses both Round Close in the strict sense and Wanless Close (*see* Fig. 52).

Before the Council entered the next stage of its housing programme there was another Act of Parliament concerned with housing, namely the Housing Act (Chamberlain Act), 1923 (13 & 14 Geo. V, c. 24). Houses built either by private enterprise or by the local authority could qualify for a subsidy if they complied with certain standards. The first houses that were so subsidised, were six erected during 1924 by the Council in Garden Terrace (*HC* 17.1.1925). The District Surveyor, W. G. Landale, designed these semi-detached bungalows, which are constructed almost wholly of concrete, and have stood the test of time well (Fig. 53)

However the process towards fulfilling the major part of the housing programme did not go entirely smoothly. Thus while the next stages were being considered, the Council learnt from the Government that only a further 50 houses could be erected in Hexham at that time. Nevertheless, the Council, on 13 January 1924, agreed to purchase land at Chairway Lane. Then there was a considerable delay, for it was only on 6 July 1925 that it decided to build 33 houses there. The whole process from then on went at a snail's pace such that, as late as the 2 November 1925 meeting, the Council were producing an alternative plan for 14 houses to be built in three blocks of four together with one block of two. One and a half years were to pass for the formulation of a still further plan, in this case for 40 tenements of the flat type, for the remaining land (HUDC 5.4.1927). The minutes of the Council appear to provide no explanation for the delays.

The estate at White Cross went through an even longer gestation, in spite of the field, when its purchase was proposed in October 1923, being considered 'the mainstay of the Council's scheme' (*HC* 6.10.1923). There were difficulties over purchase of the land; it was eventually compulsorily purchased almost a year later (HUDC 8.9.1924). At the start of 1925 tenders were requested for the erection of 54 houses (*HC* 31.1.1925). They were designed by N. E. Leeson (of Knowles, Oliver and Leeson) and consisted of a living room, scullery, two bedrooms, bathroom, &c., lit by electricity with gas cooking and heating (HUDC 1.12.1924 & 6.7.1925). In May, some additional land adjoining the site was acquired, a proposal to use it for building additional larger houses for sale being defeated (HUDC 4.5.1925). This was a minor complication compared with the Council being informed by the County Council that the line of the proposed new road from Monks Meadow to Priestpopple would run through the site, thus necessitating a revision of the layout.

Hexham's next estate, that built at Round Close seemed to have gone without any seeming hitch from its inception at the Council meeting of 4 November 1929 until its completion of Round Close early in 1932, when the architect reported that all the keys had been handed over (HUDC 21.3.1932). This was far from the case for the next proposed development at Hudshaw, where it was agreed to purchase 8.5 acres of land, lying between Hudshaw House and White Cross, for additional houses (HUDC 7.3.1932). Two meetings later, the Council were informed by Mr C. J. Rogerson that a petition about the proposed development had been submitted to the Ministry of Health. The Council made its application to purchase the land, and by doing so, learnt that the minister did not feel justified in approving the proposal in view of the petition and suggested that the Council explore the purchase of land near to Round Close. The Council demanded a Public Enquiry; the Ministry thought full consideration had been already given to the matter. Even at that stage, the whole Council was not behind the proposals. Councillor Ridley Robb believed that the number of houses (110) that the Council proposed to build on the site was not justified. The town could not afford the repayment of the debt that would have to be financed; it meant that the debt per head of population would be £22 (*HC* 5.3.1932).

The publication, on 2 April 1932, of the petition to the Ministry of Health in the *Hexham Courant* indicated why there was disapproval of the development:

> Your memorialists are owners or occupiers of the houses respectively, the address of which is set opposite their names. As such, they humbly pray that the Ministry of Health shall take into consideration the objection they hold to the above mentioned scheme and their reasons for such objection.

> It must be borne that Hexham is a shopping town, noted for its beautiful old Abbey and other ancient and interesting buildings situated at the junction of the North and South Tyne, surrounded by most beautiful scenery and in close proximity to the Roman Wall. This being so, it is important that the 'lay out' of the Town shall be and remain, as far as possible, of an attractive nature. There are no industries of any moment.

> The approach to the Town from the East has already been much marred by the erection of working men's houses of an ugly and common appearance.

> The present scheme of the Urban District Council is to purchase 8 acres or thereabouts of land adjoining your Memorialists properties and erect thereon further Workmen's houses which of necessity must be of a totally different nature to those occupied by your Memorialists and which naturally not only alter the character of the neighbourhood, but will cause your Memorialists serious financial loss.

> It is not within the province of your Memorialists to enter into a discussion as to the need or otherwise of additional houses, that is a matter for Members of the Hexham Urban District Council to decide, but it must be remembered that the population off Hexham was shewn to have increased by 47 only at the last Census. The total amount expended on housing by

Hexham U.D.C. is to date £195,000 0s 0d, and should this scheme be carried through this amount will be increased to £250,000 0s 0d. This is more than Hexham ratepayers can or should afford.

The unfavourable view by those living in the private housing at the east end of the town of the local authority houses already built was probably held by others living elsewhere in the town, as is evidenced by the naming by 'Hexham Born' of the Round Close estate as 'the African Village' in a letter to the *Hexham Courant*, earlier in the year (*HC* 20.2.1932). Further, the last paragraph of the petition was somewhat disingenuous. The housing was not needed for an increase in the population but to provide better conditions for those living in those parts of the town, particularly in the Gilesgate Ward, where overcrowding and insanitary conditions still prevailed. Testimony for this is given by the need for slum clearance (to be described later) and the description of some of those slums by S. P. B. Mais in 1935 (Jennings, 1998). Nevertheless, the financial case of the memorialists demands attention. We are fortunate that, at the time when the petition was discussed by the Council, the Council auditor, A. H. Crawford, provided a full picture of the then present financial position of the housing programme from which it was clear that the above claims about the expenditure on housing were exaggerated (*HC* 9.4.1932)

Summarising, the key points of his statement were:
Present position
i) There were now 282 houses that were a charge on the rates.
ii) Those at Peth Head were a fixed charge of 1d.
iii) Contrary to belief (because they had been built with subsidies) there was a charge on the rates for those houses built at other sites, because an economic rent could not be charged. Therefore there was a rate of $2^3/_4$ d in the pound on the 282 houses.
iv) In total the present housing debt was £146,254.
The figures for the proposed (Hudshaw) estate
i) Cost of land, £1650, roads and sewers, £3,500, 110 houses at £335 each   giving a total of £42,000.
ii) If the houses were let at 6s 11 each, there would be no charge.
iii) If £42,000 was exceeded, there would be for every additional £1,000 excess an annual charge of approximately £50. If the new scheme did not cost more than £42,000, the total housing debt would be £188,254 (£146,254 + £42,000).
iv) Adding the general debt of the Council (£48,114), the net debt was approaching a quarter of a million, namely £236,368.
It should noted that, except for Peth Head, where the method of financing was different, the building of each house had been or would be subsidised.

There were quite a few column inches in the *Hexham Courant* about the impending building of the Hudshaw estate. It came out that there was concern about the adjoining fields being played on by the children from the White Cross and that 'yards and yards of wood fence were gradually disappearing' (*HC* 16.4.1932). It was suggested by a businessman that others would be driven from settling in Hexham if the estate was to be built. The *Courant* took up the refrain and came out strongly against building the estate (*HC* 23.4 1932). Indeed, it made out a numerical case against it, not believing the final figure of 1,800 persons or a fifth of the population would eventually be housed in Council (rate-subsidised) dwellings (*HC* 30.4.1932).

The Council, at its 5 April meeting, confirmed its decision to go ahead with the scheme. However, in September the scheme was terminated by a letter from the Ministry of Health informing them that the Minister did not approve the acquisition of land at Hudshaw. Nevertheless, he did not draw the line at building more houses; he recommended acquiring other land adjoining or nearer to Round Close. At the Council meeting following the receipt of the letter, it was revealed that 300 applications had been received for the 100 houses to be built at Hudshaw (*HC* 10.9.1932). Thus there was little doubt about the continuing need for local authority housing. Not surprisingly therefore, the Council at its 7 November meeting, set in motion the compulsory purchase of land between Wanless Lane and Maiden's Walk (Round Close) for which the owners refused to accept offers. Eventually, just over five acres in the area just indicated was obtained by this procedure (*HC* 11.2.1933). The final acreage used for housing appears to have been 8.26, probably some of the additional acreage (2.2 acres) was that land already owned by the Council in Maiden's Walk that it had purchased from the NE Railway. Hetherington and Wilson were appointed architects of the houses to be built on the site (HUDC 3.7.1932). However, while the scheme started to get underway, it became clear that the Council's housing policy had to adapt to a major new factor – slum clearance.

Slum clearance

The idea of ridding the town of undesirable property had been in the minds of the Council since the turn of the century. Then the means for achieving this riddance was via closure orders, which as we have seen, were not very effective. However, the Housing Act 1925 (15 Geo. V, c. 14) seemed to offer a way forward:

> Where an official representation [by the medical officer of health] is made to the local authority that within a certain area either (i) any houses, courts, or alleys are unfit for human habitation, or (ii) the narrowness, closeness, and bad arrangement of the streets and houses or groups of houses within the area of the want of light, air, ventilation, or proper conveniences, or any other sanitary defects, are dangerous or injurious to health of the inhabitants...... the local authority, if satisfied of the truth of such representation and of the sufficiency of the resources shall make a scheme for the for the improvement of such an area (sec. 35 of the Act).

The Council petitioned the Ministry of Health to issue an Order for an area at the lower end of Gilesgate including Holy Island. A Public Inquiry was held (*HC* 8.5.1926) which resulted in a large measure of agreement between the Council and the owners as to what properties should be pulled down. Thereafter, it was a long struggle to achieve some concrete results. The problem lay with the nature of closing orders. The Medical Officer of Health, Dr John Jackson made clear what the problems were. He said

> It is very evident that unless we take some special steps and place a time-limit on these Closing [Closure] Orders, nothing will be done. A Closing Order existing on a property is an excuse for the landlord to spend as little as possible even in temporary repairs or improvements and it is not to his advantage to make any effort to get his tenants out of the property. The tenants themselves, so long as no pressure is brought upon them, equally make no effort to find fresh

quarters. The one-room dilapidated property, which is mainly that condemned, is occupied at a rent at which it would be quite impossible for the Council to find adequate alternative accommodation. So we are at a standstill (*HC* 5.4.1927).

Probably because of the difficulty of obtaining closure orders, original scheme had to be ditched and a smaller one put in its place. It was reluctantly agreed by the Ministry of Health after another public enquiry (HUDC 3.10.1927). But the situation did not seem to improve. On 5 March 1928, the Council decided the owners of four properties should demolish the them within fourteen days, yet nothing had happened by 4 June 1928. The scheme appeared to peter out in 1930. One cannot make out what properties were eventually demolished because i) there are no lists of demolished properties and ii) it is difficult to follow the fate of a property as the numbering over the period of the scheme changes from a ledger number to a street number. But the number of properties that were demolished seems small. This scheme made very little impact on the amount of slum property in the town (*HC* 28.5.1933).

The Housing Act 1930 (20 & 21 Geo. 5, c. 39) offered a way out. This Act gave local authorities the power to acquire 'clearance areas' of slum property (requiring total demolition). However, before clearance began, local authorities had to provide accommodation for the persons displaced. The subsidy from the Government Was to be £2.5s per annum for 40 years for each person rehoused. The Local Authority contribution was in most cases £3 15s per annum per house.

Hexham delayed action over slum clearance. However, the Ministry of Health had been reviewing the town's progress in the matter and were dissatisfied with it. The Ministry therefore requested an immediate survey of individual houses in the town with respect to their condition in relation to slum clearance and this should be completed not later than 31 January (HUDC 2.1.1934). The survey was made by the Medical Officer and the Inspector, whose report to the Council (HUDC 22.1.1934).can be summarised as follows:
>i) There were fifteen areas needing clearance, comprising 107 houses, displacing 580 persons, totalling 165 families.
>ii) There were 35 houses for demolition displacing 308 persons, made up of 79 families.
>iii) To re-house this population 212 houses will be required.
>iv) It is proposed that 80 houses should be built in 1934 and 132 in 1935.

The proposal in iv) was submitted to and speedily agreed by the Ministry of Health (HUDC 3.4.1934).

The fifteen slum clearance areas were officially declared (Fig. 54). There were two public enquiries. The first took place on 31 June 1934, when the first instalment of the scheme (eight clearance areas) was considered; the second (the final seven areas) took place on 8 January 1936. The first enquiry was a relatively quiet affair. At the second, according to the *Hexham Courant*, 'property owners took strong exception' but some of the complaints were the result of the Council having not been purposeful in the past, allowing notices for improvements to lapse with out any follow up. On the other hand, in the report of the enquiry in *Courant*, there is a description of a clear case where the owner, a Mr Mills, had failed to make the necessary improvements to his property. He excused himself as follows

As regards this property the council are to blame for I have never got any satisfaction as to what to do with the place. I have never been given a fair crack of the whip' alleged Mr Mills. Discussing the ventilation of one of the houses, he caused laughter when he said that one of the upstairs tenants had stated that she had got too much d—— ventilation (*HC* 11.1.1936).

Though both enquiries had formal sessions for owners or their legal representatives to put their cases, the Inspector from the Ministry of Health, who ran the inquiry, also inspected the actual properties in the clearance areas. One imagines that it was the inspection, as much as anything that was said in the formal sessions, which governed his conclusions. The Clearance Orders considered at the first inquiry seem to have been approved by the Ministry of Health with minimum modification (HUDC 5.11.1934). After the second inquiry a number of Orders were modified (HUDC 6.4.1936). Thus for Area 11 it was stated 'Order [was] not to be confirmed on the offer of the owners to use the property for business purposes only'. Four properties were removed from the Orders.

From mid-1936 onwards, the transference of families from the clearance areas to council properties was underway. The emptying of condemned properties was followed by Orders for their demolition. Interestingly, there were still some owners holding out against fulfilling their undertakings to improve or alter property following one or other public inquiry. A particular example was property in White Hart and Gibson's Yards that the owners undertook not to use to house tenants once they had been found alternative housing by the Council (HUDC 2.6.1936). It has not been possible to find out when the slum clearance programme finished, nor when the final council houses were completed. We do know that just before the start of the 1939-45 War, one final block of property, 24 houses for aged persons, was planned and built at Wanless Close (*HC* 10.6.1939).

TABLE 33. *The housing of Hexham Urban District as capital assets, presented in terms of the various housing schemes in the financial records for 1940 (NRO/LHU/C1/14).*

Housing scheme	£
Peth Head	58515
Chairway No. 1	7853
Chairway No. 2	11551
White Cross	31379
Garden Terrace	3447
Round Close*	34892
Seal View	600
Bog Acres No. 1*	28164
Bog Acres No. 2*	40689
Holmdale	6817
Total	223907

* The names used here are confusing. Round Close as used above, is probably correct, while, Bog Acres is almost certainly Round Close (*see* Fig. 52).

Table 32 shows the number of houses built by the Council by the start of 1936. The total figure falls somewhat short of the total finally built, since the Council were still building houses well into

1936 and, of course, the 24 houses just mentioned are not included. Nevertheless the figure in Table 32 is a pretty good measure of the impressive effort that the Urban District had been putting into providing better housing for its less well-off citizens. Further the rents charged were at a level commensurate with the majority of those for the slum properties in the clearance areas. Only the rents for one-room flats were much lower (NRO/LH1/B1 & B2). While there is some uncertainty about the final total of houses built, there is no uncertainty about the magnitude of the financial cost to the District Council and the Government since we have all the Council house-building in the inter-war years presented as their value as capital assets. The figures are presented in Table 33.

It is not clear when private house building got under way after the war. What evidence there is indicates that the first such houses in any number were erected on the so-called Elvaston Park Estate. This formed the continuation to Elvaston Road, which on the 1920 Ordnance Survey map of the town finished at Overstone House. The road was extended at the end of 1922 (HUDC 4.12.1922). A variety of houses were being built there in 1923 (HUDC 4.6.1923). Some of the houses built on the estate merited a government subsidy. From then on private house were built throughout the town. However, with the arrival of the 1930s there was a step-change in the rate of such building. That decade saw the erection of houses in Beech Hill, Kingsgate, Langley Avenue, Millfield Gardens, Park Avenue and Southlands.

FIG. 57. Buses in Beaumont Street In the 1920s. Reproduced with the permission of Newcastle Libraries and Information Service.

FIG. 58. The turntable at Hexham Bus station. The photograph is a little difficult to date but the car registration plate suggests c1970. Reproduced with the permission of Beamish.

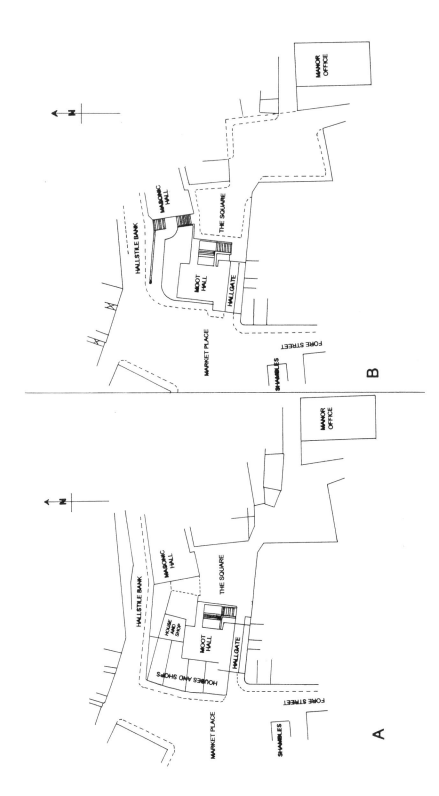

FIG. 59. The area around the Moot Hall A. As it was in February 1926 and B. the alterations that were proposed at that time. As described in the text, all the alterations to the area were eventually carried out, together with a road from the square to the Market Place running round the north side of the Moot Hall (HC 13.2.1926).

FIG. 60. The view from the square shown in Fig. 59 A, showing the back of the Moot Hall sometime in the first decades of the last century and prior to alterations to the Hall's external appearance. Reproduced with the permission of Newcastle Libraries and Information Service.

FIG. 61. Sketch published in the 25 May 1935 issue of the *Hexham Courant* to illustrate the proposal to break through the archway from Old Church and St Mary's Chare into the Market Place.

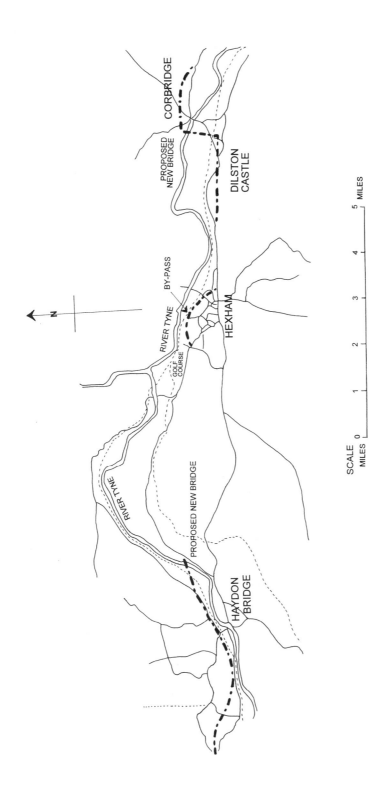

FIG. 62. Ministry of Transport proposals for the line of the Sunderland to Carlisle trunk road (as it was then termed) from Howden Dean in the east to Barden Mill in the west. The thick black dashes indicate the proposed new line of the route of the trunk road; the small dashes the line of the railways Redrawn from the original published in the *Hexham Courant* (25.3.1939).

Chapter 21

Unemployment

Introduction

Prior to 1922, when proper statistics became available, the information about unemployment in Hexham is only fragmentary. However, a century earlier, in 1826, conditions were such that there was serious unemployment amongst the glovers, leading to a situation that has a modern ring to it. Our knowledge comes from a handbill, dated 26 April 1826 (*HC* 17.1.1931), that starts as follows

> We manufacturers, being aware of your distress occasioned by being out of employ, and feeling anxious to render all the assistance in our power towards your relief, do hereby engage to employ as many of you as possible, providing you will work on the following terms, which although we acknowledge are not a sufficient remuneration for your labour, yet we do assure you that even with this sacrifice on your part we shall not be able to effect sales without suffering considerable loss.

The scale of wage reduction was at least 20% and affected all stages in the production of gloves known as the 'Hexham tans'. The signatories to the handbill were John Ramsey, William Potts, John Cooke, Nevison Loraine and John Ridley. William Noddal and Joseph Ridley added to the notice that that they had so much stock that they had decided not to continue with the manufacture of gloves. However they were prepared to give a subscription towards the relief of the unemployed.

The reason for the downturn in the sale of gloves was explained in the handbill as being due to an

> Article [French kid gloves] which is already introduced into the London market which, in our opinion, is cheaper than ours even at the unprecedented low price at which we are selling them

The unemployment of glovers, as described here, was an example of structural employment and presaged the eventual downfall of the gloving industry in Hexham later on in the 19th century.

As far as I know, there are no other incidents of like widespread unemployment in particular sections of Hexham's workforce. One imagines that what unemployment there was a result of particular persons losing their job for one reason or another or due to their being in casual or seasonal employment. As we will see there is good evidence for the latter being the case in the nineteen twenties and thirties.

Prior to the 1914-18 War, the unemployed were given assistance through the Board of Guardians, either through becoming inmates in the workhouse (indoor relief) or as a result of receiving outdoor relief. Nevertheless, there was concern that something more was required than the provision of assistance; the unemployed should be given some kind of work. This was particularly so for those on outdoor relief, who tended to be the more able-bodied. In Hexham, those on indoor relief were able to work on the Workhouse farm. The problems came when a workhouse became full, which could be the case in winter months. By 1893, one senses this was becoming a problem in Hexham. That year the Urban District Council received a circular from the Local Government Board about increased unemployment in the winter months and the need to provide employment for those who 'as a class do not ordinarily have recourse to Boards of Guardians for relief'. The Urban District Council viewed the suggestion favourably (HUDC 16.10.1893). However, as far as one can gather, no action seems to have been taken until 1895. Then, at the start of the year, the Surveyor was ordering several loads of whinstone, in 50-100 ton batches, to broken by the unemployed in order to provide a suitable road surface, at that time, Fleamsides being one of the roads being made up (HC 9.2.1895 & 32.2.1895). Stone-breaking seems to have continued intermittently until at least 1914. Sometimes the work was not carried out very well – the large amounts of the end-product being unsuitable for roadwork (HC 10.6.1911)

After the reasonable conditions during the late 1890s and during the years of the South African War, the economic situation deteriorated rapidly during 1902 and 1903 and by 1904 was causing anxiety. Unemployment was rising rapidly and with it the amount of pauperism, which until 1901-2 had been falling steadily for years. It was during this period that concern arose about the provision of more meaningful work than afforded by the Poor Law (Bruce, 1961). Walter Long exemplified the changing view of the old system, in a speech in the House of Commons:

> Many a man has told me that when he entered on his career of destitution the fact that he had been put to polish the same brass knob or clean the same window which half a dozen had cleaned before degraded him (Bruce, 1961).

By 1908, Hexham Urban District Council had been exposed to this new thinking. In that particular year, it received a circular letter from Tottenham Urban Council concerning the national problem of unemployment, highlighting the need for works of national necessity, such as afforestation, reclamation of foreshores and waste lands (HC 21.11.1908). Though stone breaking was still the major means of occupying the unemployed, other work had been found. Thus, in December 1908, the Surveyor reported that 'good progress has been made with the altering the contour of Causey Hill road near Benson's Fell where a considerable number of unemployed are being found work.' Three hundred cu. feet (8.5 m3) of clay had been removed. One hundred men, sixty of whom were unemployed (the majority good workmen), took part in the operation (HC 12.12.1908 & 26.12.1908). Employing those out of work was not an easy operation. The surveyor tried to employ those with dependents and, where possible, give three days work. There were problems of dealing with applications from those who had not worked during the summer (the Surveyor was speaking about the matter in January 1909) and others who were physically unfit (HC 23.1.1909).

1919-1939 period

There are few who are not aware of the economic slump or *The Great Crash 1929* (Galbraith, 1955) of the 1930s and the disastrous effect that it had on employment. During the period

TABLE 34. *Employment figures for Great Britain and Northern Ireland, 1922-1939 and for Hexham and the North Eastern Region, 1922-1935 (Ministry of Labour Statistical Returns; NA LAB/85/7-22).*

| Year | GB & NI % | Hexham | | | | | | North Eastern Region | | | |
| | | Highest | | | Lowest | | | Highest | | Lowest | |
		Date	No.	%	Date	No.	%	Date	No. ,000	Date	No. ,000
1922	14.3	19.6.22	334	3.8	2.10.22	167	1.9				
1923	11.7	29.1.23	306	3.5	6.8.23	151	1.7	January	248	April	205
1924	10.3	28.1.24	308	3.5	14.7.24	137	1.5	October	241	May	168
1925	11.3	7.12.25	512	5.8	22.6.25	196	2.2	August	345	January	253
1926	12.5	11.1.26	428	4.8	2.8.26	225	2.5	June	396	April	231
1927	9.7	31.1.27	436	4.9	22.8.27	256	2.9	January	329	May	243
1928	10.8	2.1.28	520	5.9	30.7.28	288	3.3	December	378	March	245
1929	10.4	21.1.29	601	6.8	15.7.29	176	2.0	December	327	June	254
1930	16.1	6.1.30	632	7.1	11.8.30	326	3.7	December	555	January	324
1931	21.3	14.12.31	802	9.1	10.12.31	336	3.8	July	623	December	514
1932	22.1	December	994	11.8	July	612	6.9	August	652	March	541
1933	19.9	February	951	10.7	July	610	6.9	January	622	December	462
1934	16.7	March	975	11.0	August	503	5.7	July & August	502	December	446
1935	15.5	January	850	9.6	July	560	6.3	February	499	December	393
1936	13.1							In 1936, the North Eastern and			
1937	10.8							North Western Regions were			
1938	12.9							dissolved and new structures put in			
1939	10.9							their place.			

214

unemployment in Great Britain and Northern Ireland doubled, the largest increase being in the period 1929-31 (Table 34). In that period, unemployment nationally rose from 10.4% to 21.3%, the bulk of those unemployed being men.

Table 34 also gives figures unemployment figures for both Hexham and the North Eastern Region. In the foregoing description of how unemployment developed in Hexham, the emphasis is on male unemployment because the number of women unemployed rarely rose to a value that was more than 10% of the number of men unemployed. Apart from a relatively large increase in 1925, unemployment in Hexham area rose gradually from 1923 onwards, the rise increasing in rate after 1930, with maximum unemployment being seen in 1932. Thereafter, the numbers of those unemployed start to show a decline.

I have not been able to obtain figures for the Hexham area after 1935 and, because, after that date, the North Eastern region was sub-divided, neither do I have a regional figures post 1935. However, the figures for Great Britain and Northern Ireland would suggest that unemployment continued to fall in the period up to 1940 in both Hexham and the surrounding region.

Unemployment figures for Hexham showed a trend similar to those nationally (Table 34). It is not possible to properly compare the Hexham figures (actual numbers unemployed) with the National figures (numbers of unemployed as percent of those insured) because we do not have figures for the number of insured workers in the Hexham unemployment area. It should be noted that the Hexham unemployment area was much larger than the area of the Urban District Council, since it stretched from Kielder to Shotley and included the whole of the North Tyne area and Allendale. On the east, it bounded on the Prudhoe area, while to the west it bounded on the Haltwhistle area (*HC* 15.8.1932). The population of Hexham Urban District in the period 1921-1939 was around 8,850. We do not have a population figure for the unemployment area but guesstimate would put it at 12,850. Approximately half would be men and, at a guess, two thirds might be insured, giving approximately 4000 such persons (ignoring the relatively small number of women unemployed). In December 1932, the number of unemployed in Hexham reached its highest level of 994 persons, giving a percentage unemployment of 16.5% – not as high as nationally but still bad enough.

Unemployment in the North East fluctuated throughout the year. However, the lowest figure was achieved at different times of the year during the period 1923-1935. In Hexham, over the whole period (except for 1931), unemployment was always cyclical with the lowest level achieved sometime in the months of June, July and August and the highest level around Christmas and the New Year (Table & Fig. 55). Given the highly rural nature of the unemployment area, the strong seasonality of employment is not altogether surprising, though one would like more factual evidence for this assumption and, indeed, what was the actual basis of the seasonality.

The indications are that the effect of the economic downturn of the slump on Hexham was very much less than the overall effect on the country. Nevertheless, from 1920 onwards, there was a continuing concern about unemployment, even at the relatively low level for much of the period, by those in positions of responsibility in the town. One reason is likely to have been the more sympathetic attitude, as a consequence of the 1914-18 War, to (predominantly male) unemployment, though, as far as Hexham was concerned, I have not been able to find out how

215

many of the unemployed had fought in the War. Another reason might lie in the fact that, being a small town, members of the Urban District Council would have a reasonable knowledge of the workings of the Guardians and vice versa. Not only that, members of the general public could readily keep up to date with what was happening in both institutions from the detailed reports of the proceedings of both bodies published in each issue of the *Hexham Courant* following the meeting.

Be that as it may, as early as December 1921, the Urban District Council received a letter from J. H. Nicholson, Clerk to the Board of Guardians saying that the Relieving Officer had 41 able-bodied men on his books in receipt of relief. The Guardians believed 'that it be much better if these men, or some of them, were given work instead of relief from the rates from which no return was received'. He was therefore asking the Council to employ as many as possible. They would, subject to the sanction of the Ministry of Health, be prepared to make a contribution of £1 a week to the Council to each of the men when so employed Alongside the ongoing discussions amongst the Guardians, the local M.P., Major Clifton Brown had been in contact with the Ministry of Labour about the scheme outlined in Nicholson's letter only to find that the scheme only applied to the local authority, as opposed to the unemployment area, having at least 300 unemployed men in its area. The Hexham Urban District had nowhere near this number of unemployed. Nevertheless, following discussions with a deputation of Guardians, it appeared possible for the Urban District Council to apply to the Ministry of Health for loans for public works on which the unemployed could be involved. It appeared that, as a result of the meeting, the Council decided to apply for loans to accomplish the widening of Haugh Lane and improving the road up Gallows Bank (HUDC 5.12.1921 & *HC* 10.12.1921).

In January of 1922, it learnt that the Ministry of Health had sanctioned two loans of £10,000 in respect of Haugh Lane and £1,000 in respect to Gallows Bank schemes (HUDC 4.1.1922). The former scheme quickly got under way. Nevertheless, the Guardians soon became concerned that only eleven, out of 50 able bodied men whose names were on its books, were employed as planned. In actual fact, 22 were so employed (on the widening of Haugh Lane), half on the Workhouse books and the other half who would have been on the books had the Council not employed them (HUDC 6.6.1922).

Although the above scheme hardly touched the underlying problem of unemployment in the Hexham area, *vide* the unemployment figures in Table 34, nevertheless the moves by the Board of Guardians were a step in the right direction, namely the provision of relatively meaningful employment for those on the Board's books. The scheme was to develop further. In February 1923, the Rev. J. E. McVitie, the Chairman of the Guardians, and Mr C. Robson, a member, informed the Urban District Council of the following proposals that the Guardians had made to the Ministry of Health:
1. A man receiving £1 relief should perform 20 hours of work (1/- per hour).
2. The local authority should make use of his services in the interests of the community.
3. If the arrangement were to be agreed, there was to be no reduction in the permanent workers of the Council, or in any way compete with local men who would otherwise have been employed had such an arrangement not operated.

The Ministry desired to know whether the Urban District Council would agree to employ the men put forward by the Guardians on the terms proposed and the nature of the work on which the men would be employed. The Urban District Council agreed to the scheme (*HC* 24.2.1923).

This arrangement seems to have continued until well into the 1920s. Nevertheless, in July 1929, the Urban District Council at the instigation of Councillors Rollingson, Smith and Ainsley decided to discuss unemployment (HUDC 22.7.1929). It is not clear what stimulated the discussion, the unemployment figures, both locally and regionally, had changed little. The debate brought forward a number of interesting ideas about schemes that would help to alleviate unemployment

1. Make up the old road from Duke's House to Dilston,
2. Cover Tanner's Row Burn,
3. Widen Eilansgate (connect properly with Haugh Lane?),
4. Persuade the County to go ahead with the road from Woodlands to Priestpopple.

Surprisingly, it was suggested that the scheme, in the process of being carried forward, to put in another water main from Ladle Wells should be scrapped. An editorial in the *Hexham Courant* did not think much of the idea (*HC* 27.7.1929). The *Courant,* in another editorial published the following January, pursued the matter of generating projects to give work for the unemployed. It didn't think that covering Tanner's Row Burn would employ many people. On the other hand it gave support for new buildings behind Burn Brae for the St Mary's Roman Catholic School, plans for which had just been approved by the Council. The provision of proper school facilities 'has been a long and uphill fight for the Catholic community in Hexham'. Again, the *Courant* gave strong backing to the new water main and the new road from Woodlands to Priestpopple. Eventually, these last two schemes came to fruition (*see* Chapters 13 and 22), that for the new main from Ladle Wells receiving a grant to relieve unemployment from the Ministry of Labour, under the conditions laid down by the Unemployment Grants Committee (*HC* 3.1.1931). Contacts for the work were advertised almost immediately after the letter informing the Council that this grant had been received. The new Catholic School was opened by Archbishop Downey of Liverpool on 28 September 1930, attended by a great crowd of parishioners and townsfolk (Nicholson, 1980) It is not known whether either the building of the Catholic School or indeed of the new road involved taking on unemployed men.

So far, the attitude to unemployment in Hexham can be considered to be relatively passive, it being assumed that help for the unemployed would come through institutional channels. However, in August 1932, the *Hexham Courant* drew attention to the fact the weekly number of unemployed stood at 644 with the number on short time being 288. The total of 932 was the highest figure reached since the Employment Exchange was located in the Drill Hall (*HC* 15.8.1932). Though date for this taking place is not known, the figure was without doubt the highest since the keeping of unemployment figures had commenced in 1922. It may be coincidental that, shortly after the publication of the figures above, the clergy and ministers of all the religious organisations held a meeting, chaired by the Rev. J. V. C. Farquhar, Rector of Hexham, to discuss 'the urgent and pressing problems of unemployment amongst our people.' They appealed to the local authorities to take immediate action in the provision of the following works

1. Slum clearance; the provision of better and cheaper houses.
2. Improvement and repair of roads.
3. Extension of the County Council's scheme of allotments and smallholdings.

4. The possible establishment of a training school for workers on the land.
The meeting urged members of the community to put in hand immediately necessary repairs and improvements to their property wherever possible and called on them to spend a larger proportion of their income on commodities likely to provide a maximum of employment (*HC* 17.11.1932).

More tangible help came in February 1933, when the Hexham Aid Association decided to provide dinners for the unemployed and their families for three-pence per head (*HC* 4.2.1933). The scheme was inaugurated the following week at the Abbey Institute under the auspices of the Aid Society and members of the Hexham Branch of the British Legion, 1st Hexham United Rover Scouts. The unemployed themselves helped in the preparation and serving of the dinner, which seemingly was taken by unemployed men. At the same time G. N. Henson, chairman of the Social Services Committee of Hexham Branch of the British Legion, set up a free library for the unemployed in the Drill Hall and successfully appealed for books for it (*HC* 18.2.1931). Hot on the heels of these initiatives was the proposal to set up a voluntary assistance scheme that was based on contributions of 1/- per week, or multiples of this sum, being paid by persons anxious to assist. Every man employed would work a full 41-hour week for £1.18s.5d after insurance had been paid. It was proposed that ninety men would be given work over a three-week period, with 30 men working each week. The voluntary scheme was recommended as it did without the need to obtain loans that would be cost on the rates through the interest that had to be paid (*HC* 25.2.1933). The Works Committee of the Council suggested the widening of Maiden's Walk and Eilansgate, the improvement of the Common Bank on the Seal and the weiring of Tyne Green as possible projects.

However, though the scheme was a virtuous one, it failed to capture the imagination of many people with in Hexham. £298.5s.11d was collected, the bulk (£225.15s.10d) coming from private donations, the remainder coming from employers, church collections and collecting boxes at various locations. At the time of this information only ten men were being employed. Both the Surveyor and the manager of Hexham Employment Exchange made pleas for further help, the former pointing out that a number of men had been unemployed since 1926, while the latter emphasised that the scheme allowed men to compete anew in the labour market (*HC* 13.5.1933). In actual fact, the scheme never really got off the ground, only a few being given employment.

Yet, alongside the report in the *Hexham Courant* of the problems facing the voluntary assistance scheme was the description of a project that augured a development of great help to the unemployed. The scheme promoted by Neville Hadcock among Rover Scouts and seemingly involving unemployed young people, was involved in converting land at Haugh Lane into facilities for sport and recreation. At the time of the report a hut, obtained from the Wooley Settlement, had been erected on the site. By June, the *Courant* were speaking about the site as being the Social Services Centre. Another hut had been erected involving unemployed men, who were now numbering 70, each paying 1d per week towards the scheme. One hut was for the Rover Scouts, 30 in number; the other indoor recreational activities. Plans were afoot for other buildings but in the meantime the men were clearing the site, chopping dismembered trunks of trees presented by Mr Allgood and involving themselves in various sporting activities of which one was in an open-air boxing ring (*HC* 3.6.1933).

Viscount Allendale opened the Centre in the middle of August (*HC* 12.8.1933). At the time, there was a membership of 138 but the centre was overcrowded with a long waiting list of those wanting to join. Viscount Allendale must have been impressed with what he saw because he wrote a letter to the *Hexham Courant* from which I quote:

> I write this letter to draw attention to the activities which are being carried out to face the ever-present problem of unemployed in Hexham through the means of the Social Service Club.
>
> Here is a centre where the man out of work, and the youth who has never known what a day's work means, may go and may take his part in a communal club life with facilities for occupational, physical and recreational training during his hours of enforced leisure.
>
> The Club provides for these men, at a subscription of 1d a week, a carpenter's shop with free use of tools and the services of an expert carpenter, boot repairing, gardens and allotments, and a club room, where billiards and other games, newspapers and a wireless set provide some cheer during the winter evenings. For the younger men, a Rover Scout Crew is organised, and there are ample facilities for athletic training and Association and Rugby Football (*HC* 4.11.1933).

The remainder of the letter was an appeal for funds for the centre. The response to Viscount Allendale's appeal was, according to the *Courant*, 'gratifying', £202.14s.1d being raised (*HC* 23.12.1933). By the time this information was available, several new buildings were in the course of erection and the grounds had been laid out. It was proposed to erect a larger hall for physical training. The plan of the site of what became known as the Hexham Social Services Club and Occupational Centre is shown in Fig. 56. There is little further information about the centre, though we do know that it was flourishing in 1935 (Jennings, 1998).

Chapter 22

Road traffic

Early problems

Apart from the occasional runaway horse or a cow becoming enraged and charging off, road traffic caused few problems in Hexham prior to the 1914-18 War. Moving livestock to market and horse-drawn vehicles could leave a trail of excrement, while heavy wagons and coaches could cause ruts in the road surface (see Chapter 16). The latter could be as much a result of the relatively low resistance of the road surface to wear as it could result from the weight of the vehicle travelling over it. Nevertheless, there was a major exception, namely steam (heavy) locomotives, which because of their weight and bulk had to be kept off roads unfitted for their use according to the Locomotive Act of 1898. A locomotive was defined, as a vehicle propelled by steam or by other than animal power (Foot, 1879) and, in Hexham, the County Council, in 1908, scheduled following roads as being unfitted: Fore Street, St Mary's Chare, Cockshaw Lane, Pearsons Terrace, Portland Terrace, Leazes Terrace, Leazes Lane, Eilansgate Road, Burn Lane, Fleamside Road to Kingshaw Green from Hexham (County Council Bridges and Roads Committee Minute Book No.10). Essentially, locomotives were kept out of the residential areas to the west and the two narrow streets in the centre – Fore Street and St Mary's Chare. That said, such locomotives were probably not very frequent users of the roads.

Advent of the motor vehicles

Following the War, the motor traffic made itself felt and issues relating to such traffic soon enter the deliberations of the Council. Some, seemingly important at the time, quickly disappear. Thus, early on, the Council became concerned about the speed of motor traffic, requesting the County Council to impose a speed limit of 10 miles per hour from Quatre Bras to Woodlands, from the Boundary on the Tyne Bridge and from the Fox and Hounds to the Hydro (HUDC 4.1.1922). However, there is no sign of the proposal being implemented.

On the other hand some matters relating to motor vehicles became part of the routine business. Thus, approval of garages/motor-houses became a regular feature of the minutes of the Works Committee of the Council. This was so for petroleum storage. Since 1871, with the passing of the Petroleum Act (34 & 35 Vict. c. 105), the storage of petrol, except in securely stopped containers holding no more than a pint, required a licence from the local authority (prior to that Act, in Hexham, it would have required the permission of the justices). Though I have not searched diligently, I have only come across one request for such a licence before the War, namely that from Thomas Johnson to store 300 gallons of petroleum spirit and 1 cwt (50.8 kg) of calcium carbide (presumably for acetylene lamps) at No. 46 Priestpopple (*HC* 17.11.06). After the war, the nature of the requests changes – they are for storage facilities associated with pumps and large-scale storage of petrol. Thus, at its meeting of 4 April 1922, the Council approved a petrol store for

British Petroleum Co. Ltd. at the railway station and a petrol pump for outside the premises of George and Jobling in Priestpopple at a rental of £25 per year.

However, the matter of 'standage' (a term also used with respect to fairground equipment and stages for outdoor entertainment), as parking of motor vehicles was to be called, has been, as we all know well, a continuing problem almost from the outset of the appearance of such vehicles. Already, in 1921 car parking couldn't be ignored and on 6 June the Council appointed a man to collect standage charges. Speaking in support of the proposal, Councillor Young expressed concern about a char-a-banc standing outside a house with a low window for as long as ten hours. Nevertheless Hexham seemed to live relatively amicably with parked cars until around 1928. Then there was little doubt that action needed to be taken. The situation had been gradually exacerbated by the steady increase of buses running in and out of Hexham (*HC* 14.4.1928). A particular concern of the police was the parking of buses in Beaumont Street (Fig. 57). They viewed it as illegal as the buses were interfering with the full use of the thoroughfare by the public. By April 1928, police had already conveyed a verbal intimation to the bus authorities that parking could not be indefinitely prolonged and that the Police would be compelled to take action in the near future.

On 22 May 1928, the Council set up a sub-committee that reported on 4 June as follows:
It had met Superintendent Taylor of the police to discuss bus standage and he informed the sub-committee that he would not allow motor omnibuses to stand for any length of time in Beaumont Street and, more significantly, he would not allow cars at any time in Beaumont Street. The sub-committee did not believe it could support such draconian measures. They proposed
1 That for the relieving or preventing congestion of traffic, it appears necessary to provide suitable parking places.
2. In accordance with the provisions of the Public Health Act 1925 (15 & 16 Geo. V, c. 71), that the Council by order authorise the use as a parking place of the following parts of streets within their area
   a) A portion of the western side of Beaumont Street to the south of the Robb (War Memorial) Gateway,
   b) A portion north of the Gateway,
   c) A portion to the north of the entrance to the police station,
   d) A portion of the Market Place lying to the east of the Abbey.

These proposals were fine-tuned by the Council, which decided that there should be two parking places for buses immediately north and south of the Robb gateway. Parking was to be from 7.0 a.m. to midnight with a maximum period for buses of 30 minutes and cars two hours. Cars were to park in Beaumont Street in single file with their off wheels next to the kerb, in the Market Place with the bonnet facing east. Char-a-bancs were to park on Tyne Green.

These proposals drew forth a long letter of complaint by the lawyer George Dixon, representing the ratepayers (*HC* 7.7.1928). They were against bus parking in Beaumont Street because it would destroy the street's beauty and affect the amenities of the Abbey Grounds. Also the sites chosen for bus parking close to the Robb Gate would destroy the possibility for quiet contemplation for those visiting the War Memorial Cross. They were also concerned that bus traffic on Sunday evenings was disturbing to the churches in the street. Finally, they felt that the congestion of the traffic in the evenings would deprive pedestrians of the proper use of the footpath on the west side of the street. There was also considerable concern that the Council, by providing such parking places, was subsidising a form of transport carried on by private individuals for personal profit that makes no contribution to the rates of the town. It was felt that the proposal is virtually an attempt to establish at public expense a bus station with all the obstruction, congestion, smells, dirt, grease and litter that are necessarily associated with such a use. There was also a formal letter of complaint about the proposals from Hexham Parochial Church Council. The Urban District Council were stony-faced about these complaints, John Ainsley speaking of the 'sloppy sentimentality' of Dixon's letter. Rightly, the Council saw the proposals as a short-tem measure but, as we will see, it took some time before an alternative to the use of Beaumont Street by buses could be found. When the notice for the arrangements was finally published, the time buses were allowed to stand was reduced to fifteen minutes.

TABLE 35. *Bus companies serving Hexham in the period 1910-1931 – based on information in Warn (1978).*

Newcastle Corporation – Began operating electric trams in 1901 and motor buses in 1912. By 1930, there were bus services to most parts of the city and outside the boundaries. The Hexham service via the north side of the river was started in 1925 (HLBH 7.9.1925) but an appeal was made to the Minister of Transport who vetoed the service.

United Automobiles Services – Formed in Lowestoft in 1912, expanded into Northumberland after 1918. In 1929, the LNER acquired a major financial interest in the company. The Hexham service started sometime after 1926.

T. Armstrong, Ovington – Ran Ovington-Hexham until 1926.

Blaydon Omnibus Proprietors Association – A loose consortium of over 30 small operators running Newcastle-Hexham via Branch End and other routes.

J. Charlton ('Hexhamshire'), Steel – Ran between Hexham and Broadwell. Finally sold to C. R. Robson in 1948.

M. S. Charlton & Sons, Newbrough – Began in 1919 to run between Hexham and Haydon Bridge. Later routes extended to the Roman Wall. Taken over by Mid Tyne Transport 1961.

T. Charlton, Wark – Ran between Hexham and Wark on both sides of the River North Tyne. The company lasted until 1962 as W. A. Charlton.

J. Dickinson, Gunnerton – Began in 1921 running between Hexham and Gunnerton and continued until 1966.

R. Emmerson & Sons, Walbottle – Began with a 14-seater in 1923 and developed the Newcastle-Carlisle route.

Joseph Foster & Sons, Otterburn.

E. Marshall & Sons, Gt. Wittingham – Started as a coal merchant and bought a wagonette in 1918. Developed routes to Hexham from Ingoe and Hallington, as well as his base, plus the Morpeth-Hexham route.

G. G. Ridley, Haltwhistle – Ran between Hexham and Haltwhistle and between Newcastle and Keswick until a serious depot fire in 1928.

C. R. Robson, Smelting Syke, Hexhamshire – Active in 1927 running between Hexham and Hexhamshire.

W. Wharton, Fourstones – Ran Hexham-Haydon Bridge via Newbrough in opposition to M.

Charlton until 1931.

Operators with less than 5 vehicles – R. W. Ord, W. C. Rollingson, F. Sutcliffe.

Bus services

Between the wars bus services were for Hexham the most important form of public transport. Trains were well used but buses were able to serve a wider area. A list of such services is given in Table 35. As can be seen the list is extensive and the area round Hexham was well catered for by bus services. Significantly, Tom Scott, managing director of the company running Hexham's two cinemas, the Gem and the Queen's Hall, indicated to the *Courant* that 'suitable buses' were running that allowed patrons from as far away as Alston, Nenthead, Wearhead and Prudhoe to attend one or other of the cinemas in Hexham (*HC* 5.7.1930). As more services came to Hexham, the system demanded a degree of regulation. As from 1 July 1928, all buses plying for hire in the Hexham Urban District were to be inspected and also be licensed, as were the drivers and conductors (HUDC 4.6.1928). On 2 July, Harold Perceval was appointed as Inspector. Nevertheless, his appointment did little to answer the complaints as to the service provided by the companies. Importantly, the parking arrangements in Beaumont Street were not being so rigorously observed as they once were. There was also a problem of congestion at the top of Beaumont Street caused by the through buses (*HC* 18.1.1930) as well as a difficulty that was rarely mentioned, yet must have caused considerable inconvenience, and that was the need for buses to turn in the Market Place. According to the Council, buses were required to turn round the Market Cross and Fountain and come past the Shambles. One is left with the impression, that on Tuesdays and Thursday when stalls were in place drivers were left to their own devices. In a sense, the Council itself did not help, since it tended to feel that buses were so great an asset to Hexham they should be given every encouragement. It was becoming clear that the arrangements for buses to take on and let off passengers within the town needed an overhaul.

The situation was discussed at a meeting of the Council on 8 April 1930. Surprisingly, even though it was earlier indicated that parking of Buses in Beaumont Street was a temporary measure, two years later, the Council had no plans for moving parking to another part of the town. The only suggestion brought forward at the meeting was to use Fairfield, then not built on, now the police station is located there. Nevertheless the Council felt it must get its teeth into the problem. Following the meeting of the Council on 2 February 1931 there is the terse minute 'Recommended that the Council approve the proposal for the provision of a Bus Station in Hexham.' Either there were already moves afoot or the resolution stimulated activity, because on 15 June 1931, the Priestpopple Bus Standage Sub-Committee reported a series of negotiations for the purchase of the property in the area. An advertisement in 25 July 1931 issue of the *Hexham Courant* brought clarity to the situation. It stated that the Council were proposing to acquire land in Priestpopple for the purpose of a bus station. The land was on the east side of Commercial Place. There must have been minimum opposition to the purchase, since just before the end of the year, the Council advertised for tenders for the demolition of property and concreting the site (*HC* 26.12.1931). The bus station was completed in November 1932 (*HC* 5.11.1932). It had a waiting room and parcels office and, unusually, a turntable (Fig. 58). The latter was not automatic but it was so well balanced 'that very little effort is necessary to enable a bus to be turned.'

Many of the Councillors viewed the bus station with disfavour, looking longingly back at the use of Beaumont Street. But the United Automobile Services, who were to be a major user, seemed to like it (*HC* 4.6.1932). Nevertheless, the following year, all the bus companies must have wanted to return to Beaumont Street for they seemed to have complained to the Traffic Commissioner. John Baty, as Clerk to the Council, reiterated the arguments in favour of the move; the Traffic Commissioner concurred (*HC* 18.3.1933). The bus companies fell into line and the *Hexham Courant* in its 8 July 1933 issue reported that the bus station was working satisfactorily. In the meantime, arrangements had been made for the major user of the bus station, United Automobile Co., to use it for £310 per year for all services running into and through Hexham. They were to rent the offices for £100 per year. Other operators of bus services were to make similar arrangements with the Council. By the end of 1931, the United Co. had built a garage with an inspection chamber for its buses at the bottom of Gilesgate, now Tyne Green Road.

The one-way system

Though the opening of the bus station solved the problem of buses waiting in Beaumont Street, there was still concern about parking in the street and in the Market Place. In order to minimise the problems, an arrangement was made with the British Legion to appoint two men to act (without a salary) as supervisors of parking in the two places. They were allowed to receive and keep gratuities from those parking their cars (HUDC 6.6.1932).

However, the major problems were not associated with parking but with the traffic flow in the narrow streets of the centre, St Mary's Chare, Meal Market and Fore Street. The idea of a one-way system surfaced in the Works Committee of the Council in October 1932, coupled with the recommendation that it be discussed with the Superintendent of Police (*HC* 1.10.1932). He fully approved provided that all traffic enter the system from Priestpopple or Battle Hill ends of the streets (6.6.1933). The Council therefore decided to make an application to the Ministry of Transport for an Order under the Road Traffic Act 1930 (20 & 21 Geo. V., c. 43) for such a system. In July the Roads and Bridges Committee of the County Council gave its approval; in September the Council advertised the proposals indicating objections should be made to the Clerk of the Council (*HC* 9.9.1933).

Both before and at the enquiry itself the shopkeepers made themselves felt. The Hexham Courant has them 'up in arms.' Here is a selection of reasons for not having the system made before the enquiry – some are simplification of quotes, two are direct quotes:

> A vehicle coming up Bull [Hallstile] Bank and having to make a call in Fore Street will have to go round by Beaumont Street.
> Vehicles which have calls at the south end of Fore Street will be unable to turn round the Midland [HSBC] Bank but will have to continue down Fore Street.
> The proposal will not solve the problem of congestion due to stopping and unloading goods in Fore Street.
> 'The more restrictions you have in a small town like Hexham the fewer motorists will come to do their shopping.'
> 'One way traffic would inevitably mean that traffic would be faster and this would be a source of great danger to pedestrians, as accidents might easily occur through people stepping off the pavement in front of on-coming vehicles.' (*HC* 18.11.1933).

The enquiry chaired by Mr F. Knight of the Ministry of Transport was held on 23 November 1933. Mr Harvey of the County Council presented the case for the application. He pointed out that Fore Street was one of the main shopping streets, containing many of the principal shops as well as three licensed premises, for which there were hardly any back entrances. Even in the widest part of Fore Street large lorries were unable to pass and in none of the streets was it possible to turn round. The vehicles had on occasion to mount the pavement to pass and inconvenience was caused to pedestrians by this procedure. The Urban District Council could have applied for an Order prohibiting heavy vehicles from entering Fore Street but this would create great hardship on shop-owners.

TABLE 36. *Figures for the traffic in Fore Street over a six-hour period during a day in August and October 1933 (HC 25.11.1933).*

Type of vehicle	Number of vehicles passing down Fore Street between 9.0 a.m. and 3.0 p.m. on a selected day in the following two months of 1933	
	August	**October**
Heavy motor	123	102
Motor cars	228	355
Motor cycles	45	37
Pedal Cycles	330	302
Horse-drawn	43	41
Total	769	837
Total per hour	128	139

Then, figures were presented for the amount of traffic going along Fore Street on two different days, showing that the street was quite a busy thoroughfare, with a significant number of heavy vehicles and horse-drawn vehicles, many, if not all, probably involved in deliveries (Table 36). The figures in this table were provided by Police Superintendent T. J. Shell, who pointed out that, in three years, there had been eleven motor accidents in Fore Street, though not serious, they had had to be reported. Further, in answer to a question as to whether business would be affected by the one-way system, he thought

> Order would come out of Chaos and the new regulation would be more likely to attract customers than to drive them away.

J. Ridley Robb, spokesman for the Chamber of Trade put the case for the 34 'tradesmen' in Fore Street. The arguments were more restrained than what one might have anticipated from the statements presented the previous week. Indeed, there was a very sensible suggestion that restrictions on unloading should be made to apply between 10.30 a.m. and 3.0 p.m. However what came out of the enquiry was much of the concern related to the fact that 'lady shoppers in particular liked to do their shopping from cars' and there was concern that 'if they happened to be in the Market Place and wanted to shop in Fore Street they would be compelled to travel up Beaumont Street and down Battle Hill'.

In April of 1934, the Ministry of Transport informed the Urban District Council that the Minister had made an Order with respect to the one-way, system. Details were given about the required traffic signs and the Ministry was to be informed as to their location. Importantly, the Order was considered experimental and a report might be forwarded to the Minister after six months had elapsed (HUDC 3.4.1934). The system came into operation on 29 October (HUDC 5.11.1934).

The early months of 1935 saw businesses very dissatisfied with the new traffic arrangements. In March, 69 out of 71 petitioned the Ministry of Transport that the Order as to the scheme be removed but they also requested again that a regulation be imposed restricting the hours for delivery of goods by heavy vans or other vehicles (HUDC 2.4.1935). This time, the hours suggested when delivery was not to take place were between 10.30 a.m. and 4.30 p.m. (HUDC 7.5.1935). The Council remained firmly convinced of the need for a one-way system but, on the other hand, were attracted to the idea of restricting the hours for deliveries. Discussions took place with the County and the Ministry of Transport, in particular with the latter over how to define 'heavy'. Somewhere along the way it was decided that an Order also be applied for unilateral parking in Fore Street. The requisite enquiry about the Orders and concern about the one-way system took place on 5 February 1936, and, as in 1934, a representative of the County Council put the case for the Orders and the maintenance of the one-way status quo. In essence, the arguments about the latter revolved around one fact, namely that the number of motor cars had been reduced – said by the representative of the tradesmen, J. Ridley Robb to be from 632 to 276 (one should note that the former number seems to bear no relation to those in Table 36). Those in favour of the one-way system, saw this reduction as beneficial to pedestrians; those against felt this indicated a drop in shoppers. It was also a conflict between two Robsons, who both had petitions signed by 300 persons – that of Charles Robson of the 'Corner Shop' being in favour, while that of Mr G. I. Robson, Meal Market was against. Interestingly, no proper evidence was brought forward about a loss of earnings by a shopkeeper. In April, the Ministry confirmed the Order about the one-way system and the two new Orders, namely that for unilateral parking and the other for a restriction of the hours at which deliveries could be made (*HC* 11.4.1936).

New roads

Most of the road building in the 1920s was associated with the erection of Council houses. Also, during that period, there was a small highway's project that had a very significant effect on the townscape of central Hexham, namely the removal of buildings at the north side of the Moot Hall and locally in the street to the east, all the properties having been acquired by the Lockharts. The driving force behind the project was Mr J. F. K. Lockhart, who broached the idea with the Urban District Council in 1924 (HUDC 1.9.1924). But it was 1926 before there was any movement to progress the project. It was death of Mr Lockhart's brother, Lewis Lockhart, in June the previous year that triggered action, as it meant that dealing with the properties concerned could no longer 'remain in suspense' (HUDC 1.2.1926; *HC* 6.1.1926). Two weeks later, the plans for what was proposed were published in the *Courant* (Fig. 59). Fig. 60 shows a view of the rear of the Moot Hall before the changes were made. The plans were greeted warmly in a leader in the *Courant* (*HC* 13.2.1926). All of what was proposed – the widening of entrance to Hall Gate and the demolition of the building abutting the north wall of the Moot Hall – was carried out, albeit rather slowly. The properties at the entrance to Hall Gate earmarked for demolition quickly disappeared. It was to be

1930 before the house on the north side of the Moot Hall was demolished (HUDC 6.10.1930) and 1951 when the houses in front of the building were removed (*HC* 13.7.1951).

The largest new road project in Hexham between the two Wars was that to Corbridge. It had reached the planning stage in 1926 (*HC* 6.4.1926). It was built in two sections. The first was from the end of Priestpopple to the top of Dean Street and the second from the latter to Park Well. The first stage was not completed until around the beginning of August 1933, even then trees had not been planted along the pavements. It is not clear why it took so long, though the delay was probably due to the legal complexities of buying the land and the properties at the end of Priestpopple. Of the buildings that were demolished, were the house attached to the dye works, the house of W. Potts when he was Headmaster of the Seal Schools and the old sale ring and accessories of the Tynedale Auction Mart (*HC* 2.7.1932). Suggested names for this new road were: Tyne Avenue, Hexham Approach, Carlisle Street, Newcastle Avenue and Cherry Tree Lonnen. The latter was on the basis that the County Council, who built the road, had planned to plant wild cherries along the road (*HC* 2.12.1933). As we know, they never materialised, lime trees being planted in their stead.

The second stage was built much more quickly, seemingly finished sometime in 1937 (*HC* 14.5.1937). The land in front of Woodlands had to be excavated to maintain the same level as the first section. Hence the two sets of steps in front of each house in the terrace – one set at the front door and the other set close to the pavement. According to the *Hexham Courant* the property now had 'a more spacious and commanding aspect.'

Almost all of the other road building was associated with building estates. However there were two other roads built during the period under consideration that can be considered as providing additional through routes for traffic within the town. They were Kingsgate Terrace to Cockshaw (Kingsgate) and Allendale Road to Alexandra Terrace (Whetstone Bridge Road). Both built in the years 1931-3.

For a while, in the 1930s, it seemed as if the car was becoming king. Two proposals, both believed to enhance traffic flow, that came forward during that period and illustrated in the *Courant*, would be considered now to be totally mis-conceived. The first was the proposal to extend St Mary's Chare into the Market Place (Fig. 61); it got no further than the illustration in the *Courant* The second was the plan made by the Ministry of Transport for what was termed a bypass for Corbridge, Hexham and Haydon Bridge – in reality it was not a proper bypass, more a rerouting of parts of the A69 trunk road from Howden Dean in the east to Bardon Mill in the west (Fig. 62). This was considered at a Public Enquiry but received little in the way of public support (*HC* 18.3.1939). The plan was almost certainly killed off by the Second World War.

CHAPTER 23

Overview

If one were to doubt the importance of the date of 1854 for the history of Hexham, one need only to turn to William Robb for his thoughts on the matter. Looking back in 1881, he wrote

> What is par excellence called "Society" was in my young days [in the 1830s] quite as exclusive, if not more so, than it is now. The Upper Ten drew the line around themselves so tightly that no tradesman, however opulent or intelligent, could get within the magic circle. They were a select community among themselves and expected to be approached with deference and subservience which their high position seemed to entitle them to demand. With the exception of here and there a sturdy democrat who refused to take off his hat reverentially to the neighbouring squire or lording, there was fear and awe of them enough in the town to have satisfied the most exacting of aristocrats. If the Lord of the Manor happened to visit the town, the bells rang a welcome peal, and men spoke of him with "bated breath and whispering humbleness." To resist their will, to vote against their candidate, to assert in any way the independent spirit which makes the lowliest a man, was a crime unpardonable to be visited with a loss of custom and all the terrors of the great man's frown. Now this slavish fear would be universally laughed at. Hexham today has a will of its own to-day, which even she would never have had, had there been either a Duke or a Bishop in our midst (*HC* 17.9.1881).

'Hexham's will of its own' formally arrived with the establishment of the Local Board of Health in 1854. Initially, the Board hardly knew what to do with the power it had assumed. But that was to change nine years later, when Robb and other like-minded men realised that the poor health of many in the town demanded sanitary improvement. That sanitary improvement took place but the democratic underpinning of the process of improvement was only partial in that the franchise was based on property. Not surprisingly, the restricted electorate felt it should safeguard its interests. Consequently, expenditure by the Board was continually under scrutiny so that it remained at an acceptable level. Hexham had become an example of what Prest (1990) has called a 'ratepayers' democracy', a valuable way of emphasising where the power lay in the early decades of the government of Hexham.

The view of the ratepayers in Hexham was that they were overtaxed. It is very difficult to argue for or against that view. The facts are not there. To pursue this matter further, at a very minimum, it would be very helpful to compare the rates in Hexham with those of towns of similar size and economic activity. But we also need to know about the ability of the electorate to pay higher rates if they were to be increased. It is not easy to find out about the wealth of individual ratepayers.

However, it may not be a very profitable line of enquiry. I have pointed out that, irrespective of whether or not the rates were considered to be too high, the town has been able to pay from its own revenues only for a few capital projects of any magnitude. The two schemes in 1864 and 1888 for improving the water supply stand out. But the former required a large loan, the size of it and the length of time to pay it off, provided valuable ammunition for stymieing the financing of other capital projects. Indeed, Hexham could only make any large-scale investment in infrastructure through an injection of capital from outside, as was the case in the 1920s and 30s, when Government grants allowed the Urban District Council to undertake its very considerable housing programme. Otherwise, during the period under consideration, the town has been dependent on the private sector or outside agencies to finance capital projects. Thus the formation of a private company was the means by which gas lighting, the town hall, the auction marts, and even bowls, made their appearance in the town.

Had there been industry and large businesses in Hexham, the rates that they would have paid would have given both the Board of Health and the Urban District Council much greater financial flexibility. As far as I am aware, there was only one attempt to attract an industry to Hexham in the 19th century and that was in 1864 when shareholders were recruited for the purpose of manufacturing woollen goods (*HC* 5 & 12.10.1864) in a mill on Tyne Green. It came to nothing. Thereafter, the town stated to think of itself as a health resort. As it was, the increase in wealth of the town was generated by it being a commercial centre for the local region, well served in the late 19th century and afterwards initially by railways and latterly also by buses, bringing people to buy and sell. Service activity became by far and the way the largest employer (Jennings, 2000).

Though the Board of Health and the Urban District Council were the most important determinants of the direction of Hexham's development, there were significant outside influences. A developing print culture, of which newspapers were a crucial component helped in the 18th century to shape and define the public domain of urban England (Eastwood, 1997) By the mid-19th century that culture was flourishing. In Hexham by 1866, it was also to be the case, for by then there were two newspapers, the Liberal *Hexham Courant* (founded 1864) and the Tory *Hexham Herald* (founded 1866). Ruth Jennings (1998) has described the role of the two papers in publicising the activities of the Local Board of Health in its early days. We know, in considerable detail from the columns of both papers, what individual members of the Local Board and (at least up to the 1914-18 War) the Urban District Council were thinking as they strove to decide about the key issues before them. Sadly, we no almost nothing about the other networks to which Board members and Councillors might have belonged whether as members of church or chapel, or of various clubs and (prior to the 1914-18 War) the Volunteers. Certainly, there are indications throughout the history of Board of Health deliberations that some decisions were arrived at outside the council chamber.

After the 1914-18 War, the *Courant* started to compare from time to time Hexham with other towns (see particularly the series of articles titled 'As others see us' in 1932, starting on 5 March). Doubtless, those who travelled around the UK would inject into any discussions how they saw Hexham in relation to other places. But the biggest external influence (if one can call it such) on the affairs of Hexham in the 20th century was the County Council. It was to play an increasingly important role in the governance of the town, through its control of roads, education and (following the demise of the Board of Guardians) heavy involvement in public assistance. By 1939, when this story finishes, Hexham was less an independent entity and much more part of the larger administrative area, Northumberland. Hexham was to become even less so after the Second World War. The Urban District Council was to lose its water undertaking and a local concern no longer supplied gas. Local Government reorganisation in 1974 meant the disappearance of the Council and Hexham became a part of the administrative area of Tynedale District.

Thus, many changes have taken place in the governance of Hexham since 1854 when the Hexham Board of Health was formed to better the sanitary condition of the town, following the Public Health Act of 1848. Along with these many changes, there has been inexorable improvement of the sanitary state of Hexham. Now, not only do we take good health for granted but also, for the betterment of it, a state-of-the-art hospital opened in Hexham in 2003 – all of which is a striking contrast to the state of affairs 150 years ago, as described in the early chapters of this book.

References

Aitken, T. (1900) *Road Making and Maintenance.* Charles Griffin: London.

Archer, D. (1992) *Land of Singing Waters.* Spreddon Press: Stocksfield.

Barrett, L. (n.d.) *From Tyne Green to the Spital: A Centenary of Hexham Golf Club.* Published privately.

Bruce, M. (1961) *The Coming of the Welfare State.* B. T. Batsford: London.

Cadman, G. A. (1976) *The Administration of the Poor Law Amendment Act, 1834, in the Hexham Poor Law Union, 1836-1930.* Master of Letters Thesis, University of Newcastle upon Tyne.

Checkland, S. G. & Checkland, E. O. A. (1974) (eds.) *The Poor Law Report of 1834.* Penguin Books: Harmondsworth..

Chief Medical Officer (1939) *On the State of Public Health: Annual Report of the Chief Medical Officer of the Ministry of Health for the Year 1938.* His Majesty's Stationery Office: London.

Crew, A. (1926) *Rates and Rating.* Sir Isaac Pitman & Sons: London.

Daunton, M. J. (1984) *Councillors and Tenants: Local Authority Housing in English Cities, 1919-1939.* Leicester University Press: Leicester.

Davidoff, L. & Hall C. (1987) *Family Fortunes: Men and Women of the English Middle Class 1780-1850.* Routledge: London.

Day, J. C. (1987) *Library Provision in Nineteenth Century Northumberland.* Typescript in the Northumberland Record Office (NRO/4607).

Dormandy, T. (1991) *The White Death: A History of Tuberculosis.* The Hambleton Press: London.

Dubos, R. J. (1951) *Louis Pasteur: Free Lance of Science.* Victor Gollancz: London.

Dumsday, W. H. (1906) *Hadden's Overseers' Handbook* (3rd Edition). Hadden, Best & Co.: London.

Eastwood, D. (1997) *Government and Community in the English Provinces, 1700-1870.* Macmillan Press: Basingstoke.

Foot, J. A. (1879) *Consolidated Abstracts of the Highway Acts, 1862, 1864; The Locomotive Acts, 1861, 1865, and the Highways and Locomotives (Amendment) Act, 1878.* Shaw & Sons: London.

Galbraith, G. K. (1955) *The Great Crash.* Penguin: Harmondsworth.

Greenwell, A. & Curry, W.T. (1896) *Rural Water Supply.* Crosby Lockwood: London.

HC Hexham Courant.

Hexham Medical Officer of Health (1874-1930) Annual reports, usually in the *Hexham Courant.*

Higgins, R. (1995) The growth of Hexham in the 1900s. *Hexham Historian* **5**, 39-45.

Higgins, R. & Jennings, D. (2004) Two militia lists (1762 and 1803) for Hexham. *Hexham Historian* **13**, 23-29.

Hinds, A. B. (1896) *A History of Northumberland.* Vol. III *Hexhamshire*. Part I Andrew Reid: Newcastle.

HLBH Minutes, Hexham Local Board of Health (NRO/PHU/A1).

Hodgkinson, R. G. (1967) *The Origins of the National Health Service: The Medical Services of the New Poor Law, 1834-1871.* The Welcome Historical Medical Library: London.

HUDC *Minutes, Hexham Urban District Council* (NRO/LHU/A1).

James, M.R. (1978) *The British Revolution: British Politics 1880-1939.* Methuen: London.

Jenkins, B. (2002) Hexham Mechanics' Literary and Scientific Institution. *Hexham Historian* **12** 15-33.

Jennings, D. (1998) Two (1872 and 1935) contemporary accounts of poor housing in Hexham. *Hexham Historian* **8**, 63-68.

Jennings, D. (2000) Economic and social indicators for Hexham: an analysis of the 1851 and 1891 censuses. *Hexham Historian* **10**, 53-76.

Jennings, D. (2002) The 1853 cholera outbreak in Hexham. *Hexham Historian* **12**, 45-50.

Jennings, D. (2003) 1841 and a revolution in Hexham's townscape. *Hexham Historian* **13**, 66-86.

Jennings, D., Corfe, T., Rossiter, A. & Sobell, L. (2005) *The Heart of All England: Hexham's Story in Original Documents.* Hexham Local History Society: Hexham.

Jennings, D. & Jennings, R. (2002) *Hexham Cemetery: A Place of Charm and Historic Interest.* Hexham Town Council: Hexham.

Jennings, D. & Rossiter, A. (1999) Queen Elizabeth's Grammar School from the foundation to the mid-19th century. *Hexham Historian* **9**, 3-27.

Jennings, R. (1996) A school board for Hexham. *Hexham Historian* **6**, 45-52.

Jennings, R. (1998) Joseph Catherall of the *Hexham Courant*, 1839-1881. *Hexham Historian* **8**, 33-62.

Jennings, R. (1999) A new school for a new century. *Hexham Historian* **9**, 28-44.

Keith-Lucas, B. (1952) *The English Local Government Franchise.* Basil Blackwell: Oxford.

Latham, B. (1873) *Sanitary Engineering; a Guide to the Construction of Works of Sewerage and House Drainage.* E. F. Spon: London.

Mandl, G. T. (1985) *Three Hundred Years in Paper.* Published privately.

Marshall, (1992) *Tyne Waters: A River and its Salmon.* Witherby: London.

Morrison, K. (1999) *The Workhouse.* English Heritage: Swindon.

Muthesius, S. *The English Terraced House.* Yale University Press: New Haven.

NA The National Archives.

NRO Northumberland Record Office.

Odgers, W. B. & Naldrett, E. J. (1913) *Local Government.* Macmillan: London.

Parson, W. & White, W. (1827) *History, Directory and Gazeteer of the Counties of Durham and Northumberland.* Vol.I White & Co.: Newcastle.

Payne, E. (2002) The Rev. John G. Bowran and the building of Hexham Primitive Methodist Church. *Hexham Historian* **12**, 34-42.

Prest, J. (1990) *Liberty and Locality: Parliament, Permissive Legislation, and Ratepayers' Democracies in the Nineteenth Century.* Clarendon Press: Oxford.

Rawlinson, R. (1853) *Report to the General Board of Health on a preliminary Inquiry into the Sewerage, Drainage and Supply of Water, and the Sanitary Condition of the Inhabitants of the Town and Township of Hexham in the County of Northumberland.* Her Majesty's Stationary Office: London.

Redlich, J. & Hirst, F. W. (1958) (ed. B. Keith-Lucas) *The History of Local Government in England.* Macmillan: London.

Registrar-General (1856) *Nineteenth Annual Report of the Registrar-General of Births, Deaths and Marriages in England and Wales.* Her Majesty's Stationery Office: London.

Registrar-General (1919) *Eightieth Annual Report of the Registrar-General of Births, Deaths and Marriages in England and Wales.* His Majesty's Stationery Office: London.

Reid, G. (1892) *Practical Sanitation: A Hand-Book for Sanitary Inspectors and Others Interested in Sanitation.* Charles Griffin: London.

Riddell, S. J. (1894) *A Manual of Ambulance.* Charles Griffin: London.

Robb, W. (1882) *Hexham Fifty Years Ago, and Sketches of Members of Parliament and Local Celebrities Whom I have met with.* J. Catherall & Co.: Hexham.

Rossiter, A. (1996) The government of Hexham in the 17th century. *Hexham Historian* **6**, 17-44.

Russell, C. A. (1996) *Edward Frankland: Chemistry, Controversy and Conspiracy in Victorian England.* Cambridge University Press: Cambridge.

Saul, B. (1972) *The Myth of the Great Depression 1873-1896.* MacMillan: London.

Smellie, K. B. (1957) *A History of Local Government.* George Allen & Unwin: London.

Taylor, J. M. (1989) *England's Border Country: A History of Northumberland County Council 1889-1989.* Northumberland County Council: Morpeth.

Teale, T.P. (1881) *Dangers to Health: A Pictorial Guide to Domestic Sanitary Defects.* J. & A. Churchill: London.

Thomas, A. A. (1919) *The Education Act 1918.* P. S. King & Son: London.

Thomson, S. D. (n.d.) *Education in Hexham.* Northumberland Record Office: Gosforth.

Ward Lock (n.d.) *Gossiping and Practical Guide to Hexham, Gilsland and the Borderland.* Ward Lock & Co.: London.

Warn, C. R. (1978) *Buses in Northumberland and Durham.* Part I. 1900-1930. Frank Graham: Newcastle.

Webb, S. & Webb, B. (1908) *English Local Government, The Manor and the Borough.* Longman: London.

Webb S. & Webb, B. (1963) *English Poor Law History* (2 Vols.). Frank Cass: London.

Whitaker, H. (1949) *A Descriptive List of the Maps of Northumberland, 1576-1900.* Society of Antiquaries and Public Libraries Committee: Newcastle.

Wood, R. E. (1988) *A Tynedale Centenary 1888-1988.* Published privately.

Woods, R. & Shelton, N. (1997) *An Atlas of Victorian Mortality.* Liverpool University: Liverpool

Wright, A. B. (1823) *An Essay towards the Study of Hexham.* W. Davison: Alnwick.

Wright, D. G. (1970) *Democracy and Reform 1815-1885.* Longman: London.

Wright, R. S., Hobhouse, H. & Fanshawe, E. L. (1894) *An Outline of Local Government and Taxation.* Sweet & Maxwell Lund: London.

APPENDIX

FIG A. Local Authority Time Chart (Constructed by Ruth Jennings)

1100 1200 1300 1400 1500 1600 1700 1800 10 20 30 40 50 60 70 80 90 1900

LIBERTY, REGALITY AND MANOR of Hexham under the administration of the Archbishop of York

1572 Hexhamshire absorbed into the County of Northumberland

1623 MANOR COURT under lay administration

------ MANOR COURT and other bodies ------ Some minor functions of the Lord of the Manor continue
(law & order, town environment, poor relief, control of trade, repair of roads & bridges, etc.)

------ 1857

------constables under the Manor Court enforce law and order------
Northumberland Police Force

From 1572?
MAGISTRATES with county jurisdiction in Petty and Quarter Sessions
(law & order, asylums and some administration of the highways)

Act 1888
County Council takes over administrative roles of magistrates

Poor Law Acts of 1597 & 1601
Church-wardens and overseers of the poor

From the 1780s
Poor Law administered by the PARISH VESTRY
(poor rate set, collected and dispensed; lighting, watch and minor roads)

Act 1836
Parishes combined to form HEXHAM UNION

Act 1872
RURAL SANITARY AUTHORITY
(as LBH for Hexham Township)

Act 1894
RURAL DISTRICT COUNCIL
(until 1974)

Union Workhouse administration continues until 1930 ------

Manor Court had some public health powers

Public Health Act 1848
LOCAL BOARD of HEALTH for Hexham Township from 1853
(drainage, street cleaning, water supply, etc.)

Act 1872
URBAN SANITARY AUTHORITY
(as LBH)

Act 1894
URBAN DISTRICT COUNCIL
(until 1974)

from 1839
some schools inspected and aided by government grants

Education Act 1870
HEXHAM SCHOOL BOARD formed 1874
(elementary education)

Act 1902
elementary and secondary education under COUNTY COUNCIL

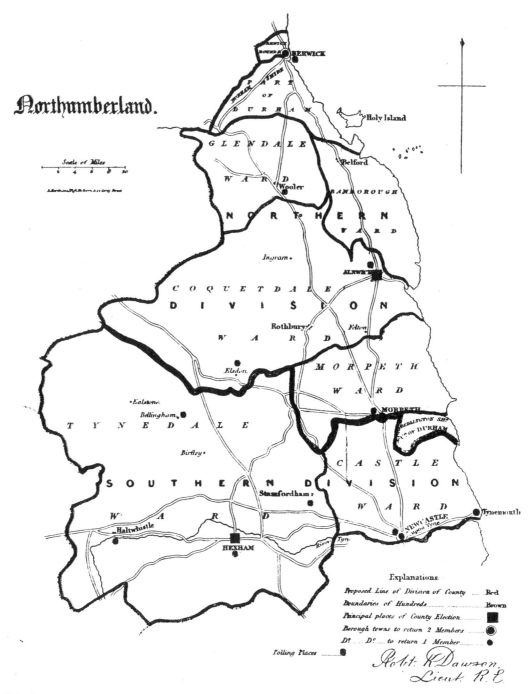

FIG. B. Map of Northumberland, drawn by Lieut. R. K. Dawson, showing the two Parliamentary Divisions (North and South; the thick black line being the boundary) formed with passing of the Reform Bill of 1832. Each Division returned two members (Whitaker, 1949).

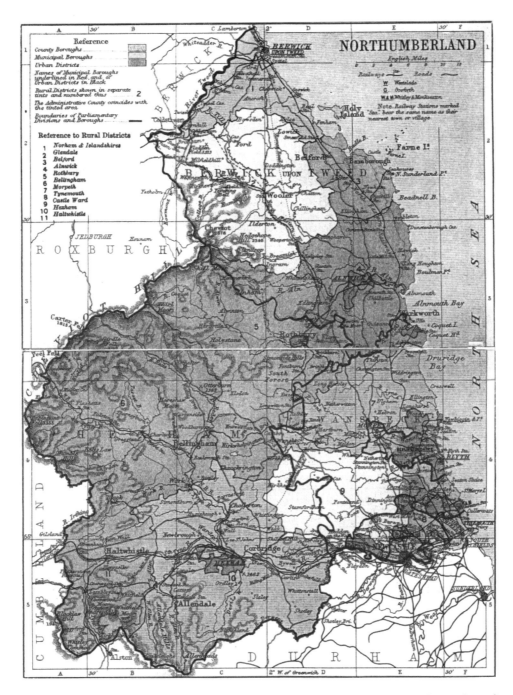

FIG. C. Map showing the Northumberland Parliamentary Divisions and Boroughs after the Redistribution Act of 1885 – as was the case for all the Divisions, Hexham returned one member. The map also shows the boundaries of the Rural Districts (Philip's Handy County Atlas of England and Wales, n.d.).

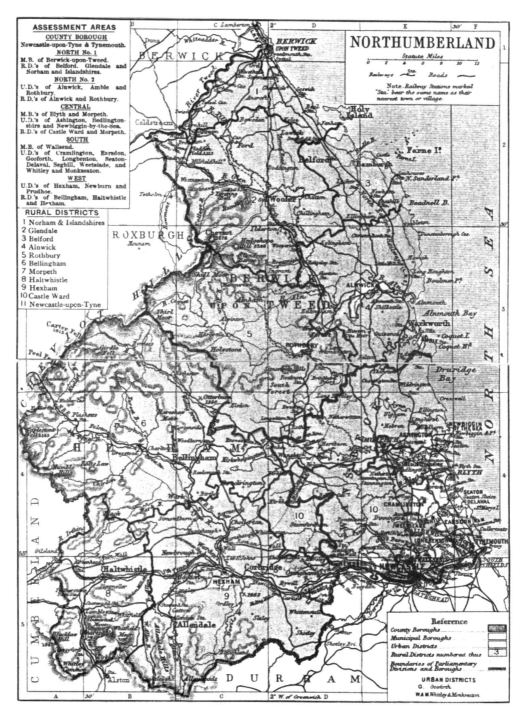

FIG. D. Map showing the Hexham and other Parliamentary Division after the Representation of the People Act of 1918 (Philip's Handy Administrative Atlas of England and Wales, 1928).

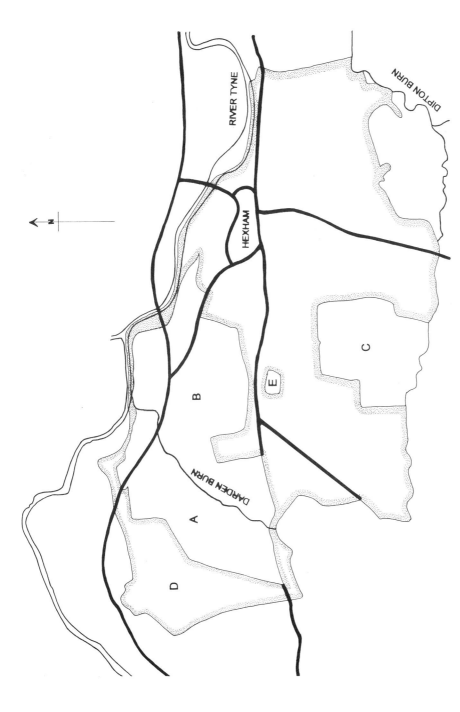

FIG. E (across). Map showing the boundary (line +stippling) of Hexham Local Board of Health at the date of its establishment in 1854. The boundaries were that of Hexham common land (Rawlinson, 1853). Areas A, B, C, and E represent parts of Hexham West Quarter. Area E (15 acres of land at Summerrods) became part of Hexham Urban District Council in 1894 (*HC* 23.6 & 14.7.1894). As part of the Parliamentary review of County Districts, in 1934 the following changes came into being (NRO/O/CM/P/9 & CC/CM/P5): 1) Areas B and C (bounded on the south by the Dipton Burn) became part of the Urban District Council. 2) Both that part of the West Quarter (D) and that part of the Urban District Council (A) west of the Darden Burn became part of Hexham Rural District Council.

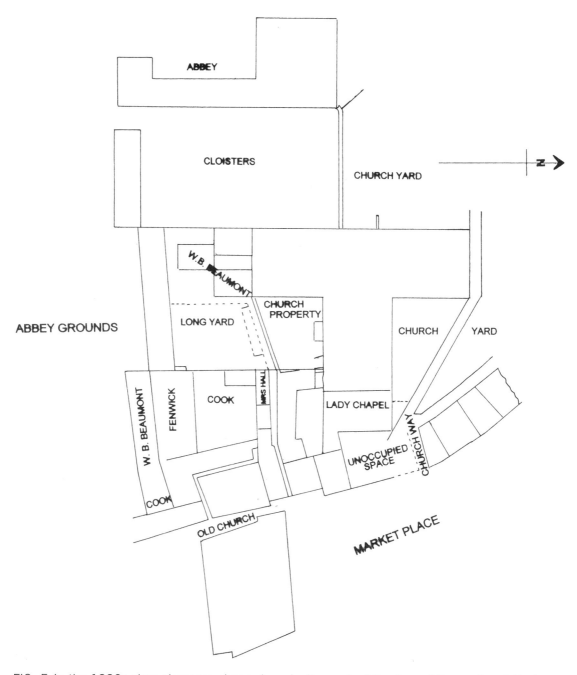

FIG. F. In the 1930s slum clearance changed markedly much of the face of the centre of Hexham. In the period 1841-1866 the centre of Hexham was also changed in dramatic fashion when the buildings at the east end of the Abbey were removed and Beaumont Street was built. The plan above shows what the area was like before clearance got properly underway. Redrawn from NRO/672/A/36/1.

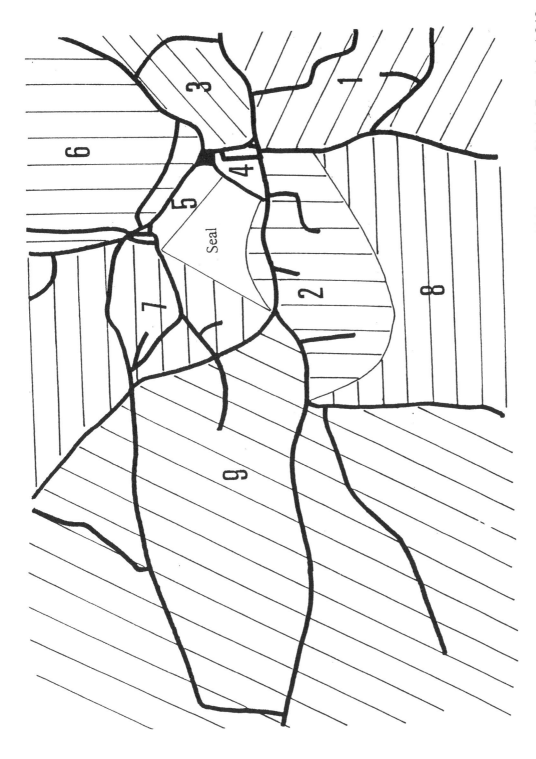

FIG. G. Plan of the town of Hexham showing the disposition of the nine districts of the 1891 census. District 7 contained 943 inhabitants, district 1,2,3 and 6 contained between 400-500. The plan shows dramatically the crowded nature of the central area (districts 4 & 5) of the town (Jennings, 2000).

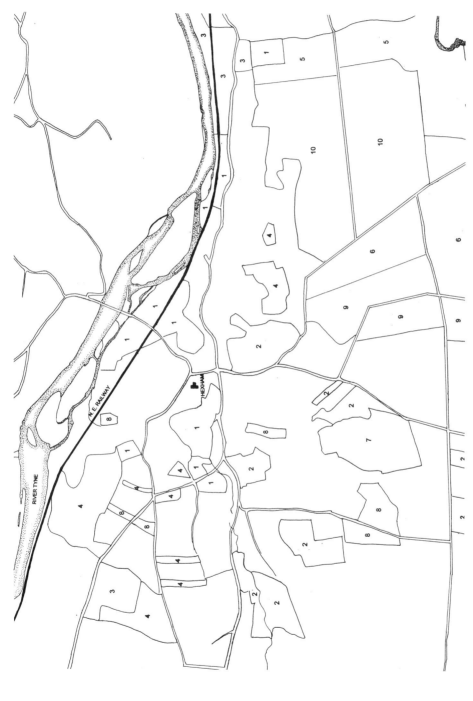

FIG. H (across). A map based on the Tithe map of 1844 and the accompanying schedule (NRO/EP/184/243 & 244) providing some examples of land ownership in Hexham and the surrounding area. The owners represented are (the numbers in the list and on the map indicate the owner of the block of land): 1, T. W. Beaumont (Lord of the Manor); 2, William Bell (farmer, High Shield); 3, Thomas Dodd (gentleman, The Riding, St John Lee); 4, James Kirsopp (Magistrate, The Spital); 5, Ralph Ramsey (?); 6, John Ruddock (attorney, Oakerland) ; 7, Matthew Smith (farmer, Loughbrow); 8, Smith Stobbart (tanner, The Abbey); 9, William Waddilove (clergyman, Beacon Grange); 10, Heirs of Nicholas Walton Esq.

INDEX

235